Lamar Underwood's
BASS
ALMANAC

Lamar Underwood's
BASS
ALMANAC

NICK LYONS BOOKS
DOUBLEDAY & COMPANY, GARDEN CITY, NEW YORK 1979

For
TED KESTING
Who, during his 25-year editorship
of Sports Afield *magazine,*
did more to promote bass awareness, bass fun, and bass conservation
than anyone in the nation.
And besides all that—
I've never raised a rod or a glass with a better man

Contents

Foreword

LAMAR UNDERWOOD

I've been wanting to throw this party for a long time.

Welcome, friend, to a bankside gathering of bass fishermen I think you'll enjoy. Some of your old friends are here, and the strangers will soon be buddies. I've invited the best bass fishermen I know to spend some time with us and talk about their favorite theories, observations, experiences, and bassing tales. If I've put this thing together without any backlashes, you'll feel like you're right there in the boat with men like Roland Martin, Bill Dance, Homer Circle, Tom Mann, Jerry Gibbs, Glen Lau, Grits Gresham, Charlie Elliott, Dave Whitlock, Byron Dalrymple, and many, many others.

I got them together because it has seemed to me over the years I have worked as editor of two major outdoor magazines, *Sports Afield* and *Outdoor Life*, that this kind of book on bass was missing from my fishing-library shelves.

The excellent bass books I've enjoyed over the years have each been one-author efforts. From them, I've gained new insights into the habits of my favorite fish, and even felt that I was sharing days on the water with a wide cut of bassing men who really know their stuff. But wouldn't the fish fry be even better, I thought, if between the pages of one great big mamu of a bassing book we could enjoy the company of many anglers whose individual skills and experiences touch on every detail of modern bass fishing? And wouldn't it be fun to come away from that book with more than mere knowledge that might improve my own catches, but with a sense of sharing moments, sights, sounds, places and bass action?

Now I've gone and done it: stressed the phrase *modern* bass fishing. What's it mean? Fishing with lots of new gear? Well, yes, that's partly it. Its origins have also been fixed on such varied happenings as Buck Perry's introduction of the bottom-digging Spoonplug that caught bass in the middle of the lake, Ray Scott's arrival with the tournament concept, the introduction of depth-flashers and recorders, concepts like "structure," new theories on feeding lanes and movement patterns, the creation of the bass boat, the development of the plastic worm.

All of these events did indeed bring new stars into bassing's galaxy. And when considered together they form a picture of *modern* bass fishing: good bass fishermen begin to see their waters as a three-dimensional, total environment. Bass had to be located before they could be caught. And locating them might mean turning one's back on traditional shoreline haunts. The skillful cast that drops the lure alongside a stump; the tantalizing crawl of a topwater retrieve; the delicate touch of a jig bounced on the bottom—these things are still the keystones of our fishing. But the bassing talk of today reveals modern dimensions Grandpa never thought about: structure, scatterpoint, thermocline, hard bottom, soft bottom.

In the pages ahead, you'll get to know Mr. Bass a lot better. We'll focus on the fish itself, with all his amazing characteristics and contradictions. Then, lures and techniques, equipment, conservation, and plain old bassing sense will be covered. Our contributors will not only help you catch more fish, but they will be sharing with you the kind of information you need to make every hour on the water richer.

Finally, we have a section we've called "Fireside Bassing." We've filled it with some of the greatest bassing stories ever published. I hope you'll agree that it's a grand dessert to the kind of book trout fishermen often got but never us bassing men. Our time has come. The bass has arrived in all his glory.

Well, that's not true.

He's always been here, and the sport has been here—maybe we only needed a fat, basslike book to put it all together.

Ole Iron Jaw

PAT SMITH

In the musty theater of American angling, the black bass has always occupied a balcony seat. Had he ever been evaluated on his combat talents, he would certainly have been placed front row center, but in the opinion of those who make such appraisals there were other things to consider. One was his family name. To the tweedy followers of *Salmo salar* and *Salvelinus fontinalis,* such words as "black bass" soured on the tongue like domestic caviar. For another thing, his appearance: thick-lipped and big-bellied, the bass was strictly low life. But his greatest disadvantage is that he was born in Middle America, an origin simply unacceptable to that anglophiliac set that rules the sacred waters of American angling. In short, the black bass has been culturally deprived.

But if the salmon and trout must be classified as elite in this mythical social structure then let the black bass be given permanent status as the working class of American gamefish. He's tough and he knows it. He's what Burt Reynolds is to Laurence Olivier, Ethel Merman to Vivien Leigh, Tom Jones to Mel Torme. He's a mural by Diego Rivera, a novel by Hemingway, and a movie by John Ford. He's a thick slab of sirloin instead of filet mignon; a belt of rye whisky rather than a chilled daiquiri; he's *vin ordinaire,* not haute brion. He's a bass sax grumbling get-down blues in the bayou. He's a factory worker, truck driver, wild catter, lumberjack, barroom bouncer, dock walloper, migrant farmhand, and bear wrassler. And if it's a fight you're looking for, he'll oblige anytime, anywhere. Whether it's a backwater at noon, a swamp at midnight, or dockside at dawn, he'll be there waiting. He's a fierce-eyed, foul-mouthed, tobacco-chewing redneck who has traveled to every corner of the nation, paying his way and giving no quarter. He's the working class all right, the brawny base upon which everything rests; take him away and American angling would crumble like a child's sand castle before the flooding tide.

With all his machismo, this underwater pug with the two-sized mouth is also our most pervasive and enduring symbol of all that is still wild across a national landscape that grows a little tamer, a little more predictable with each passing season. As his more delicate brethren shrink before the crunch of time, the black bass, God bless him, stays to slug it out with dams, bridges, highways, irrigation canals, too many second homes, and too many people. No matter how we batter, shackle, and poison his world, he somehow survives and in so doing invests that world with a whisper of wilderness. The black bass is the ultimate holdover—our past living in the present. He's the guts and soul of American angling.

Today the black bass is finally receiving recognition as our most sought gamefish—and with this recognition has emerged a new fishing culture more atuned to the times than the one drawn from the yellowed parchments of Sir Izaak Walton and Dame Juliana. While the traditionalists lounge in their clubs amid burnished memorabilia recalling better days, a thousand lakeside taverns across the land are ringing with a lusty new language peppered with terms like "hawg stick," "blooper," "limper," and "lunker-lugger." It's the argot of the bass-buster—an unpretentious sport who views his fishing not as a genteel pastime but a fierce avocation. He loves his wife, his children, his dog, and his flag. But if time and money are any measure of this man's interests, then he is taken most with ole iron jaw.

"Inch for inch and pound for pound," wrote Dr. James A. Henshall in 1881, "the black bass is the gamest fish that swims." Back then in the days of Calcutta cane, cat-gut leaders and horse-hair tippets, the good doctor's evaluation was no doubt diagnosed by his colleagues as a sure sign of dementia praecox. But today when the Atlantic salmon and brook trout are more objects of memory than quest there are perhaps 20 million Americans who would agree that Henshall was one of the

"Inch for inch and pound for pound, the black bass is the gamest fish that swims."　　　Glen Lau

more level-wound anglers of his time. Henshall—who must go down as the first guru of bassdom—further shocked his contemporaries by predicting that the black bass would one day be the most popular gamefish in America. Well, as anyone reading this book knows, Henshall was dead right.

But one wonders if Henshall knew just how right he was back in 1881. Could he, for example, have foreseen the range of the bass extending from Middle America to every state except Alaska? Could he have envisioned the fifteen-pound largemouths that are taken regularly from Florida waters? Or how about the huge manmade lakes that have flooded the South and Far West since World War II? Could he have predicted that such lakes would prove to be bass fishing bonanzas? Not likely. But even in his most vivid dreams, Henshall could not have pictured the modern bass tournament in all its technological glory and competitive heat. Sparkling, shallow-draft boats, piloted by men in florescent jumpsuits, scampering across the surface at speeds exceeding the fleetest thoroughbred. Boats laden with depth-finders, sonar, live wells, air pumps, electric motors, swivel seats, refrigerators, speedometers, tachometers, and drink holders. Men who cast

perfumed, plastic worms with rods spun from glass, men who catch more bass in a day than were once caught in a season—and, above all, men who fish for money, more money than Doc Henshall made in a year.

But if Henshall would have popped his pince nez at such a sight, he would surely have swooned at the vision of Ray Scott, president of the Bass Anglers Sportsman Society (B.A.S.S.), leading a thousand or so of the faithful in the Bassin' Man's Prayer—invoking the big fisherman in the sky to calm the waters and provide good weather—before signaling the thunderous start of one of his pro tournaments. No, Henshall never had such a nightmare.

But not too long after the good doctor entered the big sleep, we plunged into an era that would change us forever. If we weren't fighting a war, we were battling each other in the streets or climbing out of a depression. None too slowly, we changed from an agrarian society that moved easily to the rhythms of the seasons into an aggressive, urban, buck-hungry rabble that some say is rattling on into future shock. Today the keynote is no longer how you played the game, but whether you won or lost, and the ultimate reward is money. Indeed, to a generation weaned on such commercial pap the

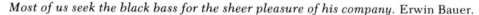

Most of us seek the black bass for the sheer pleasure of his company. Erwin Bauer.

notion of going fishing with the promise of winning a year's salary is no nightmare. It's the American dream.

But most of us seek the black bass for the sheer pleasure of his company. Whether the corner of his mouth ends even with his eye or extends beyond it, the bass is a creature of extraordinary power and beauty. In much the same way that an eagle fulfills the thin, crisp heights of the Rockies, the black bass makes whole each secluded pond, lake, and river in which he lives. He is primative elegance, swimming free and clean in the bright shallows of a northern lake or lurking in the blackwater of a southern flowage. He is my fish and yours, ever-present, easily approachable, and a model for all gamefish in the world—strong, fast, and capable of extended fight.

To compare the fighting talents of the largemouth with those of the smallmouth seems to me as invalid as arguing the merits of a great middleweight with a heavyweight. I've been in the ring with both fish more times in more places than I could remember. I've caught them every conceivable way under all conditions. There are differences, certainly, as distinct as the styles of Sugar Ray Robinson and Joe Louis. The smallmouth is more compact, flashier, faster, and quicker inside. But if the largemouth is slower, he moves with greater power and seems always to act with firmer purpose. Both fish go to the air readily. But the largemouth is more likely to throw your plug back in your face. After thirty-five years of sparring with both of them, I say they are separate but equal, each a king in his own realm.

Nevertheless, there isn't a bass fisherman who doesn't have his favorite. Though he tries to justify his choice on the basis of superiority, the roots of favoritism run deep into his background. My love of the smallmouth began on the limestone ledges of Sturgeon Bay in northern Wisconsin, where each summer I would go to fish the waters and walk the woods of my father's boyhood. I was a city kid, raised in the streets of the east Bronx, which is a wilderness all its own. I was no better or worse than most of the kids, some of whom died in those streets. I was just luckier, because each summer I had Wisconsin to go home to. Don't misunderstand. I look back on the east Bronx with warm, misty eyes. Those streets were as colorful and rich as any in the world and no kid from the suburbs or Small Town U.S.A. would not be better for having visited them and heard the wisdom that lives in every Jewish candy store, Italian butcher shop, and Irish saloon. But even then in those sunshine years of the forties and fifties I knew that Sturgeon Bay was a far, far better place to be when the hot months arrived and the ice was off the water and the smallmouth was on the move.

As I think back now it seemed I did most of my growing up in Wisconsin fishing for bass. I know that can't be totally true, for the confusions of adolescence were very real back in the Bronx. But when I was out on Sturgeon Bay in that plywood boat, catching bass with my father and grandfather, the world was a clearer place; and while my problems didn't go away, it seemed I could see them better. Out in that plywood boat I had the benefit of two generations, quite different from each other, to guide me, to correct me, rebuke me and compliment me. Those summers were undeniably the happiest times of my life, and now whenever I catch a smallmouth I remember that plywood boat with my father, my grandfather, and me. I suspect my reasons for favoring the smallmouth are not unique. For I have a theory that bass fishing, largemouth or smallmouth, is not just a pastime for most of us, like golf or tennis. It's a connection to a better time and a better place—a gift of perennial childhood.

So, ladies and gentlemen, I give you Sir Bass, the green knight of the working class. In the following chapters you'll learn all that is known about him, much of the best how-to and where-to ever accumulated in a single volume. My task was to provide the why-to. Although I can think of nothing else to add, it seems I haven't said enough. But then how could I? Bass fishing is deeply personal, as private a matter as any form of true love.

Perhaps it can only be felt.

Bass fishing is deeply personal, as private a matter as any form of true love. Erwin Bauer

PART ONE

WHO HE IS
AND
WHERE
HE LIVES

It first happens when a stranger's boat slides in alongside yours while you're taking a break. Then it occurs again amid the ohs *and* aahs *of the dockside gathering, then above the juke-box din of some smoky bar, then later perhaps beside some service station island. The questions will always be the same threesome.*

"How'd you do?"

"Where'd you go?"

"What'd you get 'em on?"

Tell me those things, *thinks the friendly admirer,* and my only problem will be getting the day off. I either have, or can buy, the baits you used. Just give me a chance to fish your lucky place. Be truthful with me, and tomorrow evening I shall be smiling and cracking the jokes and answering the questions instead of asking them.

Tomorrow's stringer never happens, of course. For even if our friend manages his day's escape, and even if a storm front doesn't clamp down during the night, he will probably find the hours passing fruitlessly as he pounds the water with Old Sure Thing and curses his luck for not being there twenty-four hours earlier. The meager fund of information provided by "Where'd you go? What'd you get 'em on?" will be the dead battery of his hopes.

No, friend, to catch bass on anything like a regular basis the first trick is to know something—no, it is to know a great deal—*about this marvelous critter that swims and leaps through our dreams. Your three questions should have been, "Where are they right now?" "What are they doing there?" "What do I have to fish with that relates to what they're doing?"*

Yesterday's winners cannot answer those questions for you. Square One in the fishing puzzle is your knowledge of the bass's habits, movements, prejudices, weaknesses, and indulgences. And since you usually cannot see him in the water, you will have to discover what he's up to at a particular moment by training yourself to translate obvious water characteristics into a mental three-dimensional picture of the place you're fishing.

And that's Square One of our BASS ALMANAC. *The gentlemen who did the chapters assembled here have experiences and observations on bass characteristics that would take one person a lifetime to obtain.*

When things work well, they have always asked, "Why?"

1

The Basses

GRITS GRESHAM

The Largemouth Bass

The largemouth bass, *Micropterus salmoides*, varies widely in color depending largely upon the water in which he lives. Generally, however, the fish is dark green on the back and almost white on the belly, with the coloration gradually becoming lighter from back to belly. Along each side is a dark band, less conspicuous in older fish, which is made up of a series of irregular patches. Bass from many lakes—some in Florida are good examples—are almost black. Those from ponds or lakes that are turbid much of the time are almost white by comparison.

The largemouth is a spiny-rayed fish with a dorsal fin that is almost divided. The principal species of bass—largemouth, smallmouth, and spotted—have three anal spines and usually ten dorsal spines, occasionally nine or eleven.

Since all three species have similar fins and spines, these features are of little help to the angler who wants to identify his catch. Here are the best ways for you to identify a bass you have just taken from the water:

Smallmouth—A series of dark *vertical* bars or stripes along each side, and usually three dark streaks on each side of the head, which radiate backward from snout and eye. The entire fish is a uniform brownish-green.

Spotted Bass—A series of *horizontal* stripes on the lower side of the body on each side. These are the result of dark spots on the scales, which are arranged in rows, giving the appearance of stripes.

Largemouth—If neither the vertical bars of the smallmouth nor the horizontal stripes of the spotted bass are present, it is a largemouth bass. The dark lateral band on each side of the largemouth, from which it gets the name "old linesides," is absent in the smallmouth and much less well defined in the spotted bass.

The length of the upper jaw with respect to the eye is significant. In the largemouth the upper jaw extends beyond the eye. In the smallmouth and spotted bass it does not.

The following overall coloration pattern may be helpful in identifying a bass. As mentioned before, the general coloration of a largemouth is dark olive-green on the back, grading progressively to a pale greenish-white on the belly. Spotted bass, in contrast, have a general appearance of being green on the top half of the body and whitish on the bottom half. It is in this whitish bottom half

9-11 dorsal spines

dark-green back

dark irregular band

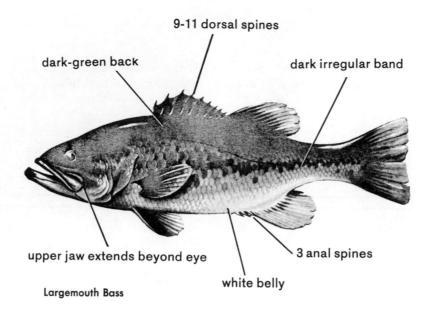

upper jaw extends beyond eye

3 anal spines

white belly

Largemouth Bass

brownish-green back and sides

9-11 dorsal spines

3 dark streaks

dark vertical bars

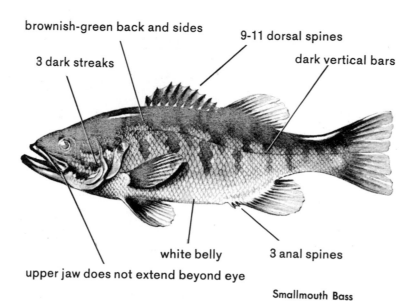

white belly

3 anal spines

upper jaw does not extend beyond eye

Smallmouth Bass

Spotted Bass

9-11 dorsal spines

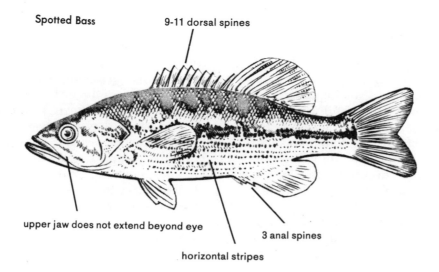

upper jaw does not extend beyond eye

3 anal spines

horizontal stripes

that the horizontal "stripes" show so conspicuously. Smallmouth bass are called "brownies" in some localities because the fish is an overall greenish-brown with the whitish belly area being very narrow. Again, remember, the sides are usually marked with the vertical bars, which may fade and reappear.

RANGE

The largemouth bass was originally at home only over the eastern half of the United States, but because of its adaptability and popularity the fish has been introduced into many other areas. The largemouth is now found in all of the forty-eight contiguous states, plus Hawaii. It is at home in southern Canada and in Mexico, in Cuba, Puerto Rico, and other islands of that area.

HABITAT

Lakes, rivers, creeks, ponds, reservoirs, canals, drainage ditches, irrigation ditches, bayous and marshes.

Fresh water or brackish water; clear water or turbid water; still water or running water; weedy water or weed-free water.

That about covers the subject of the largemouth's habitat. The fish is extremely adaptable and is tolerant of a wide variety of aquatic situations. It originally flourished in slow-moving rivers, bayous, oxbow lakes and marsh ponds. It found a home in the hundreds of manmade lakes that have been built throughout the nation for water supply, flood control, hydro-electric production, and irrigation. As a near perfect stocking fish, it is now firmly established in millions of farm ponds. It has been introduced into natural lakes and streams far out of its original range and has prospered.

Largemouth tend to favor still water and slowly moving streams, but there are times and places where the reverse is true. One such situation occurs in the overflow terrain of the Gulf South when water levels are changing, particularly when flood waters are receding. At these times the greatest concentrations of largemouth bass are found where the current is swiftest—at constrictions as water pours through narrows, cuts back into the streams, and on points around which the flow is greatest. However, in a stream that offers a variety of water situations ranging from swift to still, most of the largemouth will be found in the calm pools and eddies.

As for temperatures, largemouth prefer water in the 65- to 75-degree bracket and will seek that strata if it is available. They consume more food in water of this temperature, a fact that has implications for fishermen. They will, on the other hand, tolerate water temperatures higher than 75 degrees, which makes them particularly adapted to life in the shallow lakes and sloughs of the South.

One of the interesting things about the largemouth is its ability to do well in brackish water. This offers the angler a unique opportunity for a mixed creel in some areas, particularly along the coasts of Virginia, North Carolina, and Louisiana. In those spots it's not rare for a fisherman to take a bass on one cast and a spotted weakfish or channel bass on the next.

SPAWNING

Largemouth bass spawn once each spring when water temperature reaches a certain level. Some fisheries men say this is about 65 degrees; others put it as high as 74 degrees. There is probably basis in fact for both assertions, but most fish will lay their eggs at 65 to 70 degrees. One Minnesota study revealed spawning two to five days after daily mean water temperature reached and remained above 60 degrees.

The reproductive process of bass is similar to that of all the sunfish. The male largemouth moves into the shallows, from 1½ to five feet of water, when water temperatures are still a bit cold for spawning, and begins to build a "nest." This is a circular area in the lake or stream bottom which the bass fans clean of debris and silt. It may be from twelve inches to three feet in diameter, and may actually be a small depression.

When water temperature has reached a point suitable for spawning and has remained there for four to six days, the female largemouth moves to the nest and lays her eggs. As they are laid they are fertilized by milt from the male fish. More than one female will sometimes lay eggs in one nest. The eggs are enveloped in a glutinous mass when they are laid, and sink to the bottom where they become glued to rocks, sticks, and other debris.

The male bass remains over the nest, guarding the eggs from the many creatures that might eat them. He fans the nest with his tail almost constantly to keep silt from settling on the eggs.

The eggs hatch in from six to twelve days, depending upon the temperature of the water. If the water temperature continues to rise daily during the period, they hatch quickly. If a cold snap occurs the process is slowed.

The number of eggs laid by the female varies widely; as few as 2,000 by a small fish and as many as 35,000 or more by a large one.

Once the eggs have hatched, the swarm of bass fry remains around the nest for a week or so, and the male bass stays there to protect them. After that it's every little bass for himself, since the male turns cannibal and begins to feed on his own offspring.

FEEDING

Bass fry begin to feed on minute animal life in the water almost as soon as they are hatched. As they grow, the size of their prey increases, from small insects and small fishes to larger insects, larger fishes, and crawfish.

Once a bass has reached a length of six or eight inches, he will eat almost anything that he can swallow. Anything that runs, swims, crawls, or flies is in danger within striking range of a bass.

Bass fry are themselves food for bluegills soon after being hatched, but when they grow a bit the tables are reversed. Then bass become the hunter and the bluegill the quarry.

Crawfish and small fishes of many kinds are the favored foods of an adult bass, but the variety of creatures that have found their way into a largemouth's stomach is astonishing. Included are snakes, frogs, ducklings, turtles, crabs, muskrats, mice, and birds of several species.

Bass don't feed constantly—a fact fishermen should consider. All of the factors that influence their feeding habits aren't known, and probably never will be, but we do know some of them.

The erratic feeding behavior of bass has been observed in aquariums time and again. For hours, the largemouth will lounge contentedly in his niche in the glass bowl, paying no attention to the small bluegills and food minnows swimming around within easy reach. Then, as if on signal, the bass will devour the nearest unsuspecting fish. A quick charge—and there is one less bluegill in the aquarium. He will repeat the process several times and then, apparently satisfied, return to his docile role.

Bass usually feed at dawn and at dusk. They frequently go on a feeding bender just before the approach of a storm front. In some situations, with schooling bass, a feeding spree is triggered by the presence of schools of shad near the surface of the lake.

All other factors being normal, bass feed at some time during the day, usually twice, in accordance with the moon phase.

Bass need not be feeding for you to catch them; instincts other than hunger will cause them to strike.

REACTIONS TO TEMPERATURE

The largemouth bass is apparently most comfortable at a water temperature of about 70 degrees, and therefore will move to find that temperature if it is possible. In general this movement is vertical, from deeper to shallower water, or vice versa. This search for the preferred temperature tends to explain several actions of bass, particularly when we realize that it is not only the temperature of the water itself that affects the bass. The penetrating rays of the sun, for instance, can cause a fish to be uncomfortably hot even when the water temperature is acceptable.

Remember the many times you have been uncomfortably hot while riding in an automobile if the sun shone directly on a part of your body. The temperature of the air inside the car wasn't high, but the direct rays of the sun on your arm or shoulder heated that part beyond comfort. To escape these direct rays of the sun a bass finds cover. He will lie in the shadow of a log, stump, boat dock, lily pad, or anything else that casts a shadow. Or he goes deeper. How deep depends upon the clarity of the water, the strength of the sun's rays and their angle to the surface, and the temperature of the water itself.

Keep in mind here that, from spring until fall, the water in most lakes graduates in temperature downward from the surface, which is warmest. Thus a bass may search for the right temperature for his body for two reasons: either to move away from the penetrating rays of the sun, or simply to get into a strata of water that is of a different temperature. The reverse is also true. Bass will move toward the direct rays of the sun, or upward to a water strata that has a higher temperature if that's to their liking.

Fix these principles firmly in mind, for they greatly affect where you will find the fish. By

To the largemouth bass, cover means avoidance of light, and concealment for the perfect ambush. Glen Lau

applying a bit of reasoning you can understand the interplay of various factors on bass behavior: cloudy days versus bright days; early morning versus midday; dingy water versus clear water; warming water trends in spring; cooling water trends in the fall; night versus day.

REACTIONS TO LIGHT

It is difficult, if not impossible, to separate the reaction of bass to light from their reaction to temperature. The two are closely connected.

Extreme light intensity seems to have an adverse effect on the feeding behavior of the fish. They don't bite as well on bright days as on dull days. Like most rules about bass fishing, this one is not inflexible. I have caught bass when the sun was bright, and you have too, but that's not generally the case.

The new federal reservoir research program has turned up a rather interesting fact about bass at night. All the fish they have observed thus far seem to be "sleeping." The bass can be approached very closely, then appear startled and confused as if roused from a snooze. Carl Lowrance, inventor and manufacturer of the Fish Lo-K-Tor, doesn't believe the bass are sleeping under these circumstances. He has made extensive scuba observations in connection with the development of the Lo-K-Tor, much of it at night with lights, and Lowrance believes the bass are just blinded by the light.

SIGHT

Bass have keen eyesight. They will frequently move considerable distances while a lure is in the air, meeting it when it hits the water. They will frequently react to the slightest quiver of a topwater lure.

Nobody knows whether or not bass "see" things as we see them, particularly in the matter of colors. Maybe they see a blue as we do, or maybe that blue looks like a red to them. Perhaps they see both as mere shades of black or white. Such a discussion is really academic, for it is true that bass can *distinguish* between various colors as we know them.

REACTIONS TO SOUND

Bass can "hear" if the noise is in the water. Along the entire lateral line of the fish is a series of nerve endings which act as sensors to pick up the slightest vibrations. This ability of bass to detect and locate objects by their vibrations, quickly and accurately, is of great importance to fishermen. It determines many of the things they should do to catch bass, and quite a few they shouldn't.

SCENT

As most fish have a rather keen sense of smell, it is reasonable to assume that bass are fairly well gifted in this quarter. Despite this, I doubt that bass seek their food by scent to any great degree. I think it is significant that bass seldom take dead bait that is just hung in the water. They will take dead bait if it is fished in a lifelike manner, but here sight plays the major role.

Work done in recent years indicates that trout and salmon may react adversely to the scent of humans. A hand dipped into the water upstream has, in some of these studies, caused agitation among the trout downstream. But nothing in my experience indicates that bass react to human odor at all.

Some artificial lures such as soft plastic worms have been impregnated with an artificial odor which the manufacturers claim makes them more palatable to bass. If scent does play a part in making bass artificials more attractive, it would work well with worms, for in taking them a bass does so deliberately, chewing on them until he is hooked or lost.

EFFECTS OF WATER FLUCTUATION

Changing water levels affect bass, but their pattern of behavior when the fluctuation occurs is inconsistent and unpredictable. Here are some general observations about how bass react to water fluctuations:

Sudden lowering of a lake after the level has been constant is apt to be followed by poor bass fishing. A classic example of this was provided one fall by Center Hill Lake in Tennessee. Bob Witt, Outdoor Editor of the Nashville *Banner*, and I arrived there to fish with A. J. Hayes, who owns and operates Cove Hollow Resort. Hayes is an extremely good bass fisherman anywhere. On Center Hill, which he knows like a glove, he is deadly. The day we arrived, the lake had dropped some eight inches, and before we left thirty hours later it was down twenty inches. Before we got

Bass do not feed constantly, a fact concealed by the viciousness of their strikes. Glen Lau

into the boat, Hayes said we'd catch no bass, although good strings had been taken the day before. Hayes was right. Three of us caught five bass in two days, most of them too young to know better.

But when floodwaters are receding from overflow areas, the reverse can be true. At such times bass may gather in numbers in some spots and savagely hit a passing lure.

Rising water levels are just as unpredictable. If a torrential rainstorm causes the level of a lake to rise suddenly, bass usually stop hitting. When the rise is gradual, however, fishing is frequently good, as bass move into the new territory made available by the enlarged lake.

BASS AS PREDATORS

Largemouth bass, in their predatory habits, resemble members of the cat family, despite the presence of scales on one and fur on the other. Remember the house cat playfully stalking a sparrow on your lawn? He moved slowly and casually until he had a bush between himself and the bird; then he began a stalk which was a study in concentration, advancing paw by paw with agonizing slowness until he was within striking range.

I've seen bass follow an almost identical procedure before smashing an insect—or a popping bug—lying on the surface. As the ripples caused by the lure hitting the water disappear, the bass eases nearer, sidling in a circular path until he has the protection of a stick, log, stump, or clump of weeds. Next the fish moves directly toward the quarry, pauses briefly once he is in range, then strikes.

Consider, too, a cougar lying on the broad, low limb of a tree, watching a deer approach up a game trail that passes directly beneath. The big cat does not move so much as an eyelash until the buck is in exactly the right position, then he launches himself through the air and has venison for supper. I have watched bass, on many occasions, lie in wait in just such fashion, using for concealment a

"The lip that swims," the late Joe Brooks described the largemouth bass. Elgin Ciampi

stump, a weed bed, the piling of a boat dock, a rock or ledge. If the deer passing beneath the cougar is too far away, the cat will usually wait for the next one. But if the deer happens to stop, the cat may make his leap, apparently counting upon the inertness of the standing deer to compensate for the distance being greater than the cougar would prefer. Conversely, sudden movement, a quickening of pace, even flight, will often trigger a cougar's strike.

Bass react in a similar fashion while lying in wait for prey. Factors that trigger a bass to strike are nearness of the prey, pauses, or sudden flight. The angler's awareness of this aspect of bass behavior is fundamental to fishing success.

Often bass will strike and kill for sheer pleasure. Observe a school of bass feeding on shad. They slash viciously into the school time and again, bouncing them from the water and leaving dead and crippled shad scattered across the surface. It is common to catch a largemouth after such a foray with his stomach full of shad, with shad in his gullet, and with shad in his mouth.

Smallmouth and Spotted Bass

There are more similarities than differences between the smallmouth, the spotted bass, and the largemouth. Many of their characteristics and habits are virtually identical—for example, their catlike tendencies when stalking prey. This is natural, for the three are close relatives. Even their habitats overlap to a substantial extent.

RANGE

The original range of the smallmouth bass was generally the Great Lakes and the river systems of the St. Lawrence, Upper Mississippi, Tennessee, and Ohio. It has been widely introduced now and may be found just about anywhere.

The current range of the smallmouth can be considered to be east of the Rockies, north of the Gulf Coast states, and the southern part of Canada. There are no smallmouth in Louisiana or in Florida. There is some excellent smallmouth fishing in the streams of northern Arkansas and in and below Wilson Lake in northern Alabama. Maine is a state where introduced smallmouth have prospered spectacularly.

Manmade reservoirs have provided excellent habitat for this species, with two of the most noteworthy being Center Hill Lake in Tennessee and Dale Hollow Lake, which straddles the Tennessee-Kentucky border.

Lake Erie, in the nineteenth century, quite possibly had the greatest smallmouth population of all time. According to Trautman's excellent book, *The Fishes of Ohio,* bass were commercially important in Erie from about 1830 until commercial fishing for them was made unlawful in 1902. One report gave the 1885 commercial catch for both black basses, taken from Erie and landed at Ohio ports, at 599,000 pounds. Western Lake Erie still provides excellent smallmouth fishing. Northern Minnesota and southern Ontario are great smallmouth areas.

The range of the spotted bass, also known as Kentucky bass, is more restricted than that of either the largemouth or smallmouth. It extends to central Texas, Oklahoma, and Kansas on the west; about midway up into Kansas, Missouri, Illinois, Indiana, and Ohio to the north; to western North Carolina, Georgia, and Florida on the east; and to the Gulf of Mexico on the south.

Although the spotted bass is best known as a stream fish, it is found in most of the manmade reservoirs within its range, and in many of the natural lakes. Allatoona Lake, in Northwestern Georgia, is a rarity in that 90 percent of the bass taken there are spotted bass.

The world-record spotted bass, an eight pounder, was taken from Alabama's Lewis Smith Lake in 1966.

In Louisiana, Mississippi, and Alabama, particularly, many small, fast creeks are magnificent spotted-bass streams. Floating most of these bears only passing resemblance to the comfortable floats of the Current River in Missouri, or the White or Buffalo rivers in Arkansas. There are no facilities on most of these little creeks—no boats, boat landings, or guides. Fishing them requires frequent pauses to maneuver past a log or fallen tree. These streams offer only solitude and fish.

As a leaper and fighter, the smallmouth bass knows no peer. Erwin Bauer

HABITAT

The spotted bass prefers and can tolerate cooler and swifter water than can the largemouth; the smallmouth prefers and can tolerate colder and swifter water than can the spotted bass.

Stream gradient determines where the three species will most frequently be found in flowing waters. Smallmouth prefer a gradient of four to twenty-five feet per mile, while spotted bass like a gradient of less than three feet per mile. In streams the largemouth stick to sluggish pools or connected coves. Strangely enough, the spotted bass is more tolerant of turbid water conditions than are the other two basses.

Smallmouth like a sandy, gravel, rocky bottom in a stream or lake with clear, moving water. They tend to shun weedbeds whereas largemouth bass gravitate to them, but they do like brush.

In reservoirs where all three species are found, the spotted bass will be at the deepest levels— frequently over 100 feet; the largemouth will be in the next layer above; and the smallmouth will be in still shallower water.

SPAWNING

Smallmouth begin spawning when water temperatures move from the 50s into the 60s. Although these fish apparently prefer water depths for spawning similar to those favored by largemouths, Trautman reported that he observed smallmouth bass eggs hatching at a depth of twenty-two feet in Whitmore Lake, Michigan. Despite this extreme, all three species of bass normally utilize much shallower water for their spawning. Most spotted-bass nests in Bull Shoals were about twelve feet deep.

In streams, both smallmouth and spotted bass tend to move downstream in the fall, wintering in the deeper pools. As the waters warm up in the spring, they move back upstream and spawn.

The most important cause for failure of smallmouth spawning attempts is abandonment of the nest by the guarding male. When that happens the eggs are quickly eaten by predators. In turn, the most important cause for the male leaving the nest is low temperature. It frequently happens that the water will warm up into the 60s, nesting activities and spawning takes place, and then a cold snap drives temperatures back down into the 50s. When that happens the male will invariably leave the nest and it will fail.

The average smallmouth nest will contain from 2,000 to 10,000 eggs, resulting from one or more than one female spawning in the same nest.

The feeding habits of smallmouth and spotted bass are similar to those of the largemouth, as are their reactions to light, vibration, sound, and water fluctuation.

Friendly Invader
The Striped Bass in Fresh Water

BYRON W. DALRYMPLE

When we heard the two fishermen in the distant boat yell, we thought they were in trouble. We started for them, then cut the motor fifty yards off. It was obvious their kind of trouble should happen to everybody. One was fighting a big fish.

"I can't hold it! I can't stop it!" we heard him shout. Line was pouring through the guides of his light bass rod. We saw a tremendous bulge of water as the fish swirled on the surface away off.

"What have you hung, Don?" I heard the excited partner of the busy one ask.

The other shook his head and worked on the fish, now deep and running. Then he said, "You'll have to start up and follow. I gotta get back some line."

Tom Hennessey and I were fishing for largemouth at Lake Spence, an impoundment on the Colorado River in west-central Texas, a short drive north of San Angelo. We eased our boat along, following the action but staying wide of where we figured the fish was. The fisherman named Don finally cranked the fish close enough to the boat for his partner to net it. When they had it in the boat the netter grabbed a motor wrench and whacked the fish on the head.

The fishernan's eyes were glassy, his hands were shaking. He had had the lightning strike him, sure enough. Mesmerized, he kept stroking the dark-striped side of the silvery brute and he said, "You oughta *feel* that devil. It even *feels* rough. Why we fooling with black bass anyway?!"

It was a landlocked striped bass that, we found out later, weighed a little more than fifteen pounds.

That same kind of lightning has been striking more and more regularly, and in more and more places across the nation over the past few years. Fifteen pounds, measured against the saltwater world record of over seventy, might not seem so large. But when you are tied up to a striper's special brand of roughnecking with an ordinary light bass casting outfit, your viewpoint swiftly changes. An authentic "hawg" black bass becomes a piglet by comparison.

Not long ago few people believed fishermen in the middle of Texas would be catching striped bass. Not so today. Texans are sharing, with fishermen from coast to coast, the benefits of the widespread introduction of the saltwater striper to freshwater as a landlocked fish. From Virginia, the Carolinas, Florida, and the Deep South all the way to California, and even up into the plains in Nebraska and Kansas, the striper invasion is booming. A whole new category of fishing specialists, dedicated to outwitting this brash newcomer, has emerged.

A striped bass that was bred, born, and raised in the fresh waters of a southern impoundment provides top action. Pete Elkins

It is a curious paradox that while this landlocked striper explosion has been in progress, fishing for stripers in their original marine domain has been declining. It is not unusual nowadays for avid striper addicts along the Atlantic and Pacific coasts to travel inland to find better fishing for their favorite in its freshwater environment.

Although that fifteen-pounder I saw caught in Lake Spence was a good fish in anybody's book, landlocked striped bass in that weight class are fairly common. In Virginia, where citations have been given in past years to anyone catching a landlocked striper weighing ten pounds or more, the minimum had to be boosted in 1975 to fifteen pounds. Too many ten-pounders were being caught.

State after state has logged twenty and thirty-pounders, and quite a few forty-pounders have been caught. In two widely separated states—South Carolina and Arizona—fish weighing more than fifty pounds have ended up in taxidermy shops.

The striped bass, or rockfish as it is known along the middle-Atlantic coast and as far inland as Tennessee, has possibly the most-traveled history of any North American gamefish. Since colonial times it has been an important commercial and game species in its native marine range along the Atlantic. In 1879 stripers taken from New Jersey's Navesink River were hauled by train to California and stocked in the Carquinez Straits. In 1882 another stocking was made in Suisun Bay. From those areas the fish have spread along the coast to San Diego and central Washington.

Perhaps the striper would have retained its status as a strictly marine gamefish had it not been for an occurrence in 1941 that accidentally landlocked some stripers in South Carolina. At that time a huge damming project was completed on the Santee and Cooper rivers near Charleston. Two enormous lakes were formed—Moultrie and Marion. Not long after the lakes had filled stripers were found in them, presumably trapped there during a spawning run.

The striped bass lives natively in saltwater but makes spring runs up tributary freshwater streams to spawn. The big "bulls," as the outsize specimens are called, are not males but females. Far up a spawning river a group of males swarms around a ripe female as she rolls near the surface. As she releases her eggs the males, splashing furiously, fertilize them.

To survive, the eggs must be released in a cool stream that has enough turbulence and flow to keep them floating. They are heavier than water, and if they sink to the bottom they smother and die. Depending on water temperature, the eggs hatch in from thirty to seventy or more hours. This requires that the length of float must be somewhere between forty and one hundred or more miles. That's why only certain streams are suitable for successful striper reproduction.

Some fisheries people suspect that the stripers trapped in the Santee-Cooper lakes were fish that

The white bass (top) and yellow bass (bottom) are both freshwater purists. The striped bass (center) was successfully introduced to fresh water from the briny. Tennessee Game and Fish Commission

had adjusted to year-round life in freshwater. Regardless, with the dams thwarting movement down to the coast, they were landlocked. Soon different age classes began turning up, some of them too young to have been trapped behind the dams. It was obvious that natural reproduction was occurring. Meanwhile, a tremendous sportfishery had developed. Estimates based on a creel census taken in 1957 showed that close to 300,000 landlocked fish had been caught.

Hampton Williams, a fisheries biologist with the South Carolina Wildlife and Marine Resources Department, told me, "Our state had only one fisheries biologist then. He was extremely enthusiastic about the stripers. He had visions of getting them into a lot of lakes in the state."

The first brood fish were caught by hook and line, eggs taken and cultured, and fry placed in several lakes. The fame of the Santee-Cooper stripers swiftly spread.

Soon other states were clamoring to get eggs or fry or fingerlings to experiment with in the many new lakes being impounded across the Midsouth and South. Eventually a hatchery for striped bass was built at Monck's Corner on South Carolina's Cooper River. Here fish running up from saltwater in spring are shocked and taken for brood stock.

Today South Carolina has landlocked stripers in numerous lakes, and also provides millions of eggs and fry, as do North Carolina and Virginia, to states farther west.

The limited availability of eggs and fry has been troublesome nationwide. Other states must depend on one of the Atlantic states—chiefly the two Carolinas and Virginia—to supply them until they can get fisheries established. Then they must catch their own brood fish and learn how to hatch eggs and raise fry and fingerlings themselves, a difficult, costly, and highly specialized process.

"The Santee situation," Hampton Williams explained, "is virtually perfect. The landlocked population sustains itself by successful reproduction. But it's the only South Carolina stream where this appears to be consistently possible. They try in the Congaree and Wateree. We've found eggs there within possibly eight hours of hatching. But when the eggs drift and get into backwater areas they sink and smother. Our other rivers just don't have long enough flows."

Arkansas has authenticated natural reproduction in the Arkansas River system, and many large fish are caught in this river all across the state. Some have also been caught in the Missouri River

in Missouri, and in the Mississippi, though Missouri fisheries people say that so far there is no indication of reproduction in those streams. The Arkansas River, however, is a bright spot. Fingerlings of age classes never stocked have turned up in Lake Dardanelle. Young of the year were found as early as 1972 below both Dardanelle and Ozark dams.

Oklahoma has confirmed natural reproduction from the Arkansas River above Keystone Reservoir every year since 1970. Keystone got the original stocking in Oklahoma (along with Lake Texoma) in 1965, and the fish have been successful there. It is likely that the Arkansas River and the lakes along it may develop one of the most important fisheries in the country for self-sustaining striper populations.

There has been successful spawning in the Washita River arm of Lake Texoma, the huge impoundment shared by Oklahoma and Texas. Bob Kemp, Texas fisheries chief, says it is at least possible that reproduction can occur in the Red River in years when there is enough flow to allow it. He also hopes for reproduction in the Brazos, the river Texas biologists feel offers the best chance the state has.

All across the nation, however, fisheries people are skeptical about the landlocked striper finding many opportunities for consistent natural reproduction, with the striking exception of Arizona and probably, in the future, Utah.

Arizona and California have a success situation for self-sustaining striper populations in the Colorado River and its lakes. Striped bass were introduced into the Colorado River in the late 1950s. The last stocking was done in 1970–1971. Davis Dam, which forms Lake Mohave, is the upstream barrier to spawning, and the backwater of Lake Havasu about sixty-five miles downstream is the lower barrier so far as floating eggs are concerned. This distance apparently is enough to make successful spawns possible.

The Colorado, primarily in the stretch based at Bullhead City, Arizona, has become famous for its big stripers. Anglers have swarmed to the Colorado during recent years as weight records toppled there one after the other. In late June of 1976, Robert Stahl, a fisherman who lives in the Los Angeles area but has a place on the Arizona side of the Colorado River, set a new state record with a fish that weighed 52 pounds 8 ounces.

I visited Stahl and he told me about his experience. He was fishing about twenty miles below

Bullhead City at what is called the Sand Bar near the Boy Scout Camp. He started about 6:00 A.M.

"Toward morning," he said, "water is let down to lower the river. This cuts down the amount of evaporation during the day. Early morning is a fine time to fish for stripers. With low water, the fish have less depth and less area to move around in."

His custom is to troll upriver some distance on one side, then drift back on the other. He was using a husky spinning rod, open-face reel, and 20-pound-test line. For bait he used an anchovy, a Pacific saltwater baitfish that is packed, fresh-frozen, and sold along the Colorado for striper fishing.

"I had caught a good many of these fish," he told me, "but until then my largest was twenty-six pounds. The big one picked up the bait on a downstream drift. After it had been on a few minutes I knew it was nothing like what I'd caught before. It just took charge."

When the water is down, he explained, the fish will try to get into the deepest places available, and will move downstream to enlist the help of current. During the next half hour the fight was dogged. But after a forty-minute fight, he had it beside the boat. He was astonished as he stared down at roughly 4½ feet of fish.

"I have to tell you that it scared me," he said. "Some of the fisheries people thought later it might be an all-tackle landlocked world record. But during low-water periods I have seen larger ones, fish that would weigh sixty or seventy pounds."

Stahl's fish is the Arizona state record—as this was written. Scale samples showed it to be nine years old. Striped bass grow faster in freshwater than they do in salt. A biologist who checked Stahl's fish figured that a comparable fish taken from saltwater would be nearly twenty-five years old.

As large as Stahl's fish was, South Carolina apparently is still out in front with a fish caught in Lake Moultrie that weighed fifty-five pounds. Hampton Williams said he knew of at least one fifty-pounder caught there last year. It is just a matter of growing-time, many people believe, before a landlocked fish will be caught exceeding the saltwater all-tackle weight record of seventy-two pounds.

Barry Freeman, fisheries chief in Mississippi, told me his state launched its striper-stocking pro-

Jigs and jigging spoons work with baitcasting tackle on freshwater stripers. Pete Elkins

gram in 1966, had its first success in 1969, and is now into it heavily, stocking fingerlings instead of fry whenever possible. Ross Barnett Reservoir is its best lake so far, and Sardis is probably second.

Roy Schoonover, chief of fisheries in Kansas, told me that some of the best catches of stripers there had been made by ice fishermen. At Wilson Reservoir several stripers were caught last winter, many of them on white and yellow jigs. They weighed from nine to twenty-eight pounds.

Interest in establishing landlocked striped bass was sparked primarily by three interdependent concepts of fish management. The prospect of having a slam-bang gamefish of trophy size was obviously appealing. Beyond that, however, was the basic need for an aggressive species large enough to feed voraciously on gizzard shad.

Scores of large lakes, particularly across the southern half of the United States, are loaded with exceedingly prolific gizzard shad. Black bass can handle young shoreline shad, but they are not big enough or aggressive enough to go after adult shad.

The striper was envisioned as a predator that would mop up shad by the ton. It was known to be a roamer and to be predominantly a pelagic, or open-water, fish. Hundreds of thousands of acres of offshore waters in the nation's large impoundments are little used by native species—except shad. Thus the striper would in effect add much fishable water to the big lakes, while assisting in rough-fish control.

Whether or not the striper has proved to be important in controlling rough fish is questiona-

Surface-breaking stripers can be conned with poppers by fly-rod addicts who can throw a long line.
Pete Elkins

ble. There is little documented evidence that shad populations are actually declining because of striper presence. Nonetheless, stripers feed heavily on them.

Not all fish managers see the striper only as a shad killer. Chuck Purkett, fisheries chief in Missouri, told me the state needs shad for native gamefish forage and is not thinking of the striper just as a shad killer. It's a trophy. In Utah, where there is substantial emphasis on trying to establish the fish in Lake Powell, fisheries chief Don Adriano indicated that the state's main interest is in the open-water trait of the striper. Vast areas of Powell see hardly any fisheries use. The same is true of Lake Mead, shared by Arizona and Nevada, where stocked stripers are doing well. They are forcing Nevada to scatter-plant trout because the schools of stripers decimate compact trout plants.

In surveying attitudes of fishermen across the nation, I asked two questions. Did the fisheries people get any flack about striper stocking? Did fishermen like the fish?

I was told that here and there black-bass fishermen have been uneasy for fear striped bass would gobble up young blacks. That hasn't happened, and biologists are certain it won't.

I was also told that fishermen have accepted the striper with tremendous enthusiasm. In Tennessee, fisheries chief Hudson Nichols spoke glowingly of the fish. "When there are runs of fish on our rivers here, the banks are lined solidly with fishermen," he said. "At lakes such as Cherokee and Percy Priest our fishermen really catch them. Many have become dedicated." In Mississippi, Barry Freeman agreed. "During our best fishing, which usually begins during the February–March period, many of our fishermen simply live with them," he said. "A lot of our true-gospel black-bass fishermen have become born-again striper converts." Such were the comments all across the nation.

There is so great a demand for stripers in Oklahoma that the fisheries people have outfitted some fish with "beepers"—location transmitters. It is believed the beeping fish will join schools. Maps of their routes are being made by monitors and given to fishermen to help them find the concentrations.

Finding the fish and learning when and how to catch them have been prime puzzles for many anglers. A cross-country check shows, in broad terms, that spring and fall are prime times in most areas. Exact timing varies by latitude, and also

from water to water. At Nebraska's Lake McConaughy October turns up the most fish. Winter is great in Texas, fall-winter in Arkansas, March on into summer in South Carolina. Most spring movements everywhere begin in March or April. But summer can also be good. The July–August fishing on the Colorado River in Arizona is fast, though movement upstream in the Colorado begins in March.

Summer brings "jump fishing" to impoundments everywhere. Shad schools surface toward late afternoon and evening. Stripers slash into them. An angler watching for "jumps" races to within casting distance. He casts a heavy spoon or a popping surface plug longrange so not to disturb the fish and put them down. All agree that this is the most dramatic approach to landlocked striper fishing.

Answers to my queries coast-to-coast revealed that the following lures are most productive: deep-diving plugs such as the Hellbender when the fish lie deep; fairly heavy silver, gold, and white spoons, such as Mr. Champ and Kastmaster; floating-diving plugs for times when the bass are up, with Rapala, Rebel, Redfin examples noted, and even poppers such as the Lucky 13 for the surface; jigs, in yellow, white and, in Mississippi, green; jigging spoons just off bottom is paying off in Arizona; Mississippi addicts have developed a home-made metal attractor called the Spillway Lure for tailrace fishing below dams.

Bait is highly productive all across the country. In Tennessee and Texas live bluegills have proved to be the best bait going. In other states shad, herring, or live shiners take as high as 80 percent of the catch, with drift fishing the high-catch method.

Most productive times of day to fish are dawn and just after, late afternoon and early evening, and night. In many states night fishing, especially spring and summer, produces the most fish.

Rocky areas, the water off points, over submerged islands, tailraces, and places where there are strong currents get many votes as hotspots. In summer the deep main channels of lakes, in spring the rivers above the lakes, and in fall often surprisingly shallow shoreside waters all attract the fish.

What is the future of landlocked-striper fishing? In the final analysis, it depends upon the fisheries management people. They have the decisions to make. To do so, they must assess how enthusiastically their fishermen accept an introduced species and if the return in "catchability" is worth the cost. They must consider what if any harm an introduction may do. They must consider whether an introduced species does the job they envisioned, and, if not, if its acceptance is such that it should stay anyway.

In Florida, for example, return of stripers to fishermen has been discouragingly low. That state does not intend to continue its striper programs except in water systems in which they were originally native. But the state will push its program with hybrid white-striped bass. Texas does not want a continuous-stocking striper situation; it sees the hybrid it is stocking as a better bet. Unless there is successful reproduction (in the Brazos, for example), Texas may be out of the landlocked striper picture and totally shifted to hybrids within four years.

Coast to coast, the feeling is that not many rivers tributary to large impoundments offer water quality or length of proper-velocity flow conducive to reproduction. But for the most part management people will be happy with continuous stocking.

"We don't really want reproduction," Tennessee's Hudson Nichols told me. "Undoubtedly this fish can do no harm. But it is big, and prolific, and I prefer absolute population control." Tennessee was among the first to develop hybrids, but is deemphasizing them. Nichols considers the striper a fish far superior to the hybrid, and last March Tennessee dedicated a new $2 million rockfish hatchery on the Clinch River near Norris Reservoir.

State after state is learning to culture its own striper eggs, and to depend on its own waters to supply brood fish. This is slowly cutting down the dependency on eastern hatcheries, and it will also mean vastly greater numbers of fish stocked. Stocked fry do poorly, but fingerlings have a good survival rate.

No one knows how many big reservoirs contain stripers, but there must be two hundred now. Comments from state fisheries chiefs about their striper programs run from "substantial," to "intensive," to "major." Sheer momentum of the program nationally would be difficult to stop, and no one wants to stop it anyway.

The landlocked striped bass boom, though impressive today, is unquestionably just getting started.

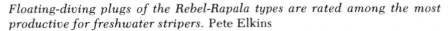

Floating-diving plugs of the Rebel-Rapala types are rated among the most productive for freshwater stripers. Pete Elkins

3

The World Record Bass
History and Perspective

VIC DUNAWAY

On the morning of June 2, 1932 an avid but meagerly equipped young bass fisherman named George W. Perry flipped a cast into the dark waters of Montgomery Lake, Georgia. His topwater plug bobbed on a surface pelted by driving rain and rippled by strong winds.

Perry thought at the time, and he never changed his mind over the years, that it was the worst fishing weather any angler could face. Nevertheless, he and companion Jack Page had arisen before daylight and labored mightily to reach their fishing hole, so in a half-hearted attempt to convince himself that it was all worth while, Perry gave the big plug a couple of twitches.

"I don't remember many details," Perry told me shortly before his accidental death in the mid-seventies, "but all at once the water splashed everywhere. I remember striking and then hauling back and trying to reel. But nothing budged. I thought sure I'd lost the fish—that he'd dived and hung me up. I knew it was a pretty big fish, but what really worried me was the thought of losing the lure. It was the only one we had between us."

To Perry's great relief, the "snag" soon began to move. The rest of the tussle, he recalled, was suspenseful enough, though not spectacular. Using all muscle and no finesse, the fish bulled his way

around until exhausted. Even though Perry was by then excited at the prospect of catching a bass of extraordinary size, he wasn't prepared for the monstrosity he hoisted into the boat.

Later that day more than forty-six years ago in the town of Helena, the bass was weighed in at twenty-two pounds, four ounces. It has stood ever since as the world record for largemouth black bass.

And today the catch ranks, by all odds, as the most impressive angling record ever set—and the roughest to challenge. There are older records in the books, and larger ones, but none has stood so firm against such massive assault.

America is a nation of bass fishermen, and it would take a battery of computers to calculate the number of bass caught since Perry's record, to say nothing of the number of man-hours expended in pursuit of everybody's favorite fish.

The most recent figures show that in 1975, sixteen million Americans spent 250 million fishing days angling for bass.

Records are made to be broken, it's said, but George Perry's bass record seems made to be frustrating.

So what are the chances that a heavier largemouth bass will ever be caught?

Many veteran anglers say the chance is there,

despite more than four decades of fruitless flailing. They point to any number of *reported* catches of twenty-five, and even thirty-pound, bass allegedly made over the years but, for one alibi or another, not officially recorded. Almost every sector of Florida, and a few other states too, has its local legends of monster bass caught sometime in the dim past.

Where might a basser turn in a calculated assault on the record bass? Logically, he would explore every detail available on George Perry's catch in search of any little clue. The location of the lake would be an obvious starting point.

It happens that there are several Montgomery lakes in Georgia, and the residents near each lay stout claim to the record—not really in an attempt to fraudulently promote home waters, but merely because they simply assume *their* Montgomery Lake is *the* Montgomery Lake.

George Perry clarified this point: "Montgomery Lake where I caught the fish," he said, "is sort of a big horseshoe bend in the Ocmulgee River in Telfair County between Jacksonville, Georgia, and Lumber City."

But in the same breath he discounted the possibility that Montgomery Lake might harbor another record fish. "It's filled up since then. Too shallow and weedy."

No encouragement there, so let's listen to the rest of Perry's story:

"I was nineteen years old that year, and I'd just become my own man. My father died the year before. I had my mother, two sisters and two brothers. We lived three creeks farther back in the woods than anybody else, and in those days it was a good deal of a problem just making a living.

"I took money we should have eaten with and bought myself a cheap rod and reel and one plug. I've never regretted it, either.

"I used to fish every chance I'd get, usually with my brother, Jim, or with Jack Page. We never had more than one lure at a time because money for a bait was a long time coming. Once when I was out with Jim, we were taking turns rowing and casting with our only bait. One of us—I don't remember which one—had a strike and lost the lure. Well, we just sort of sat around in the boat looking at each other and wondering what to do. We'd come a good distance and had hardly started fishing.

"Must have been at least fifteen or twenty minutes later when a big jackfish [chain pickerel] came up, thrashed his head, and left our plug floating right alongside the boat. We tied it on and started fishing again.

"I fished for fun all right, but the fish I brought home were awful welcome. When I caught that twenty-two-pounder, the first thing I thought of was 'what a nice chunk of meat to take home to the family.' It was almost an accident that I had it weighed and recorded. It created a lot of attention in the little town of Helena—just think what kind of excitement it would create today. The old fellow who ran the general store weighed it, and he was also a notary public and made the whole thing official.

"No, I never even thought of mounting it, or even taking a picture. I just hauled the fish home and we ate it."

Perry never received much tangible reward for posting the top angling record of all time—and only much later, after bass fishing reached boom proportions in the sixties, did he and his record gain wide recognition and respect.

"I suppose if I caught the same fish today," he

The late George W. Perry's largemouth bass record of twenty-two pounds, four ounces, set in 1932, has never been equaled despite the greatest assault in angling history. Caples Studio

mused, "I could really profit from it. But that thought doesn't bother me."

Just what sort of riches might accrue to anyone lucky enough to set a new largemouth bass record is, of course, conjectural, but many a fanatic basser feels he would live on easy street for life if he managed to do it.

And perhaps there's good reason to think so. The total value of bass fishing is figured by the government at no less than $3 trillion, counting indirect spending for all kinds of contributory items. And actual expenditures by bass fishermen each year exceed $7 billion.

Obviously, bass fishing supports an industry with enough financial resources to douse a new national bass hero with big money from endorsements of tackle, boats, motors, and other gear—plus lectures, tournament activities, personal appearances, store promotions, books, and magazine articles.

Perry said, finally, "I'm afraid there's not much in my story that could help anyone catch a new record. It seems to me there just aren't as many big fish as there used to be. Over the years I caught only two other really big bass, both around fifteen pounds."

While he enjoyed bass fishing to the last, Perry turned to saltwater fishing eventually, and was rewarded with heavier catches. His top fish was a fifty-six-pounder, a black drum, taken on the Georgia coast. He was a pilot and owner of an aircraft service and especially liked flying to the Bahamas to fish for husky grouper.

One mass attack on Perry's record already has been waged in Cuba, and another is ongoing in southern California, where Florida-bred bass fingerlings were introduced in 1960 into San Diego's city reservoir system, and have since grown—some of them, at least—to prodigious size. Officially, Perry's record was subjected to its only close call on June 23, 1973, when Dave Zimmerlee of Claremonte, California, pulled in a bass weighing twenty pounds, fifteen ounces. A number of other San Diego bass have topped fifteen pounds, and a couple have pushed twenty.

In 1958 and 1959, a stream of American bassers trekked steadily to Cuba's Treasure Lake and invariably came home with wild stories of record-size fish there. Typical of them is this remembrance by the late Charlie Ebbetts, a well-known Miami outdoors photographer. "Frankly," Ebbets said, "we went down there with the idea of breaking the record, but those bass made monkeys out of us. Three of us had fish on that might have topped twenty-five pounds, but we lost them. In my case, it was a simple matter of getting too excited. Anyway, we must have caught fifty bass that weighed over ten pounds apiece."

Veteran fishing writer Lefty Kreh of Baltimore was another who visited Treasure Lake in its pre-Castro heyday. "I've still never seen anything like it," says Kreh. "Every few casts you'd have a bass, and the majority of them weighed between four and ten pounds. On each of our two days, the party must have caught a dozen in the ten to fifteen-pound range. And both days I saw much bigger fish than any we caught. My guide showed me a photo of what he said was a thirty-three-pound bass speared by a native fisherman."

With tales like that floating around, it's no wonder that so many bass anglers dreamed for nearly twenty years of getting back to Cuba, and what they considered a sure record. But ichthyologist Luis Rivas, who stocked those bass in Treasure Lake originally, never shared the dream.

"Record-size bass were probably there when Castro closed the door," Rivas told me a few years after travel to Cuba was halted, "but after so long a time the chance dwindles."

Why? Because when bass are introduced to new waters—or when a new impoundment is created—the population explodes in both size and number. It is mainly because there is such an abundance of food for the number of bass. After a few years, the bass catch up with the food supply.

"Then," said Rivas, "one of two things probably will happen: the lake will settle down to produce good, but no longer fantastic, fishing, or—and this has happened in some other Latin American introductions—the bass may actually wipe out the food supply and consequently begin to die out themselves."

In 1977, American anglers again began going to Treasure Lake, and their disappointed reports seemed ominously to bear out Rivas' observations. Action was good, and some of the fish weighed eight or ten pounds. But even the big ones showed obvious signs of malnourishment—the large head and thin body typical of stunted fish.

San Diego's reservoir, like Treasure Lake, may already have produced its very biggest bass during the early years following introduction of the Florida-bred stock. But maybe not. The species has become solidly entrenched there, and the conditions and food are ample to assure growth of

California angler Dave Zimmerlee holds the second biggest bass ever taken, a twenty-pound, fifteen-ounce monster taken in 1973. The fish was a Florida-bred transplant. Chuck Garrison

some of the bass to extraordinary size.

Still, Florida is the state where bass have the best chance of growing to record weight, and in various waters. Far more fifteen to eighteen-pound largemouths are caught in Florida than in all other bass areas combined. And let's face it—a bass of twenty pounds or more is simply a rare freak, like an eight-foot human being. A bass heavier than twenty-two pounds would be a sedentary, lazy matriarch, staked out in some good spot where she wouldn't have to chase around much after food.

Just where this fabled spot might be is still anybody's guess. Many lakes and larger rivers might harbor the old lady—and when it comes to catching her, no amount of bass-fishing expertise, no amount of expensive gear, will matter as much as sheer, starstruck luck.

Florida fishermen have always been rankled that Georgia holds the world record. Should a new mark be set in the Sunshine State there would be great rejoicing.

But if George Perry's record *is* ever broken—whether in Florida or California or some new impoundment elsewhere—don't bet against another half-century passing before angling's roughest record is challenged again.

When anglers returned to Cuba's Treasure Lake in the fall of 1977, they found plenty of hefty bass but not the world records they expected. Erwin Bauer

4

How Light and Color Affect Bass

JERRY GIBBS

The light blue-and-silver balsa plug sailed through the sunlight and landed with a gentle spat. It was off target, possibly five feet out from the peak of a rocky spire formation that barely broke the still water surface. It didn't matter that the cast was short. Before the lure could be moved, really almost before it hit the water, the slender plug was socked from below. The bass came up and went over in one splashy movement. The line tightened, the hooks went in and the fish boomed for deep water—just for an instant. Then he came up all the way. He cleared the water, gills splayed, head shaking, mouth open wide. The next run was toward shore and the knot of weed growth that filled a little cove. It was a good fight, and when it was finally over and the largemouth was slipped gently back to swim away, I wished I had been taking motion pictures from beneath the surface instead of still shots from the boat.

Largemouth bass have the ability to see the approach of potential food or danger from beneath the water surface. If it is a probable meal sailing through the air, a bass can easily move into position to intercept it. Consider this. I know of a man who keeps a pond stocked with largemouths that he has conditioned to expect food at the sight of a human on the pond banks. The bass jump vertically clear of the water to snap food from an out-stretched hand. Beyond that, if a morsel of food is tossed high into the air, the bass will see it dropping toward the surface and rush to grab it when it hits, sometimes before it lands. They are able to do this only on calm days when the water surface is not disturbed by wind or rain, but the ability is indicative of the excellent vision possessed by bass.

The underwater vision of bass is marked by special features that adapt it for life as an ambush predator. The curved shape of the bass's eye lens allows five times more light to enter the fish's eye than enters a human's eye. This lens shape also gives more peripheral vision. Conflicting reports have insisted the bass is farsighted and nearsighted. The latter is closer to being correct, but does not give the total picture. In the relaxed position, a bass's eye is focused for near objects, but the fish does have the ability to focus on distant objects, too. Extreme distance-focusing ability is not important to the fish because even in the clearest water, visibility is limited compared to air visibility.

The human eye focuses by flattening the lens. A bass's eye focuses on distant objects when the retractor lentis muscles pull the lens back toward the rear of the eye. When the lens is pulled back like this, less light falls upon it. The effect is much the same as a person squinting to see a distant object clearly. The subject of light entering the bass's eye has been one of debate. Because a bass's eye is not equipped with a pupil that contracts in the presence of light, and because a bass's eye has no lid, it has been assumed that the fish cannot stand bright light. Not true. Even on bright days, light from the sun is subdued under water. Also, the eye of a bass controls the amount of light affecting it through the type receptor cells in use at the time. And despite all scientific reasons, station-holding as well as moving bass can often be found in the brighter underwater areas rather than shade.

Receptors deserve discussion because the way they work applies directly to your fishing. The receptors in the retina of a bass's eye are in the form of rods and cones. Each is used alternately depending on the light level. The cone cells go into use when the light level rises in the morning. They are also the color receptors. Toward evening or when the light level is reduced because of weather or depth, the rods come into use. They are about thirty times more sensitive than the cones but they are not color receptors. When they are in use a bass sees in shades of gray, black, or white.

When not in use the rod cells move back into dark pigments in the retina of the bass's eye. Here there is protection for them from bright light. As light decreases, the rods move forward and the cone receptors back where the rods had been. This changeover from rod to cone receptors is not instantaneous. It begins near sunset. A predator like the bass adjusts more quickly than many of the forage fish on which it feeds. The same holds true near dawn. A bass begins switching over from night to day vision just before dawn. If you've been fishing all night and experience a lull when the first grayness of false dawn appears, wait. Because of its excellent light-adjustment abilities, a bass will be ready to attack its prey by daybreak, a time when the forage fish have not quite finished their switch to daylight vision.

When they have their night vision, fish in shallow water can be shocked by bright light suddenly flashed in their face. The bass is no exception. Fish develop a sensitive biorhythmic "clock," and if it is upset they will cease feeding. Such clocks can, however, develop a cycle around artificial stimuli. Bass can time themselves to take advantage of dock or boathouse lights. They lurk on the dark side of the shadow line while forage fish swim into the light to feed on plankton or insects.

A bass begins switching from night to day vision just before dawn and will accomplish the switch more quickly than the forage fish on which it feeds.
Erwin Bauer

When the forage fish stray over the line of shadow, bass nab them. If such lights are on in the evening, bass will adjust themselves to the pattern. Turn these lights on irregularly, however, and you will most likely spook any bass present.

Because of these physical visual capabilities, it seems safe to say that we can do away with another long-held belief. Light does not bother bass just because they don't have eyelids or contracting pupils as do humans. This is not to say that light does not affect bass behavior. We've already discussed how artificial light can affect largemouths. We've seen how bass take advantage of the changeover period, from day to night vision and vice versa, to ambush prey. Now consider other reasons why light affects largemouths.

As fingerlings pursued by many different kinds of larger predators, bass quickly learned the relationship between heavy cover and safety. Thick cover also screens out light. Surely a connection must become imprinted upon the young bass: dim light means safety. As I observed more and more schools of fingerlings underwater, I became convinced that the assumption is correct. Out of heavy cover the young bass consistently hover in the shadows made by natural and manmade structure. The abutments of bridges, piers, a single boulder or large fallen tree trunk are good examples. What about adult bass?

As they grow older, largemouths learn to use the cover of reduced light for ambushing purposes during other than the rod-cone vision turnover periods. They take advantage of reduced light both in the shallows and in deeper water where they frequently lurk below forage species in the dimness. Older bass do not forget the lessons of youth, however. Though they have far fewer enemies as adults, bass still display their attraction for reduced light when frightened.

I performed a series of experiments that proved this behavior to my satisfaction. I worked on groups of bass that were located out of heavy cover in the shallows, others that were near various forms of shallow to mid-depth structure such as pilings or rock outcroppings and those fish that were holding off-cover near some structure in open water. I made these tests in very clear water so that I could get some distance from the fish and still see without disturbing them. Still, as in all of my observations, I waited until the only movement was from my bubbles, which I tried to reduce by slow gentle breathing.

Above, a friend in a boat would wait the allotted time we had agreed upon, then move in on the fish that I had pinpointed for him. He would alert the fish by various means, coming directly over them with the boat and stopping, then scraping a tackle box or knocking on the boat with a hard object, churning a paddle in the water, or causing a shadow to hover over the bass.

Depending upon how badly they were spooked, the fish had a variety of reactions. Severely frightened bass would scoot for deep water. Nervous fish would inevitably move to the shadowy side of any structure or cover that existed in the area. Open-water fish would drop deeper or toward the darker side of any hump or sunken island nearby. Fish that were a little more frightened would try to get as close to the cover or structure as possible, but always on the shady side or section.

Clearly low light-levels mean security to bass of all ages, and good ambush country for adult largemouths. Light level is, of course, directly dependent upon the nature of the water, and the prevailing weather.

The weather-water correlation is why bass anglers fish by the following gameplan: colored water, work the shallows; clear water, fish deep unless it's raining, foggy, or overcast. The formula is successful to a large degree, but you can also find bass deep in colored water or shallow in clear water even in fair weather. The largest bass can be reluctant to bite in the shallows during bright weather, however. Medium-size bass or yearlings still provide excellent sport under such conditions.

Though the sun is never as bright underwater as above, in the clearest of lakes on a crystal day, light penetration at mid day in the shallows is high. Using an underwater photo exposure meter I watched the rapid drop of light that occurred as the sun's angle to the earth decreased. Water acts as an excellent reflecting medium, greatly cutting down the penetration of the sun's rays except at high noon.

If you keep these factors in mind, watching the movement of shadows as they relate to other known cover, you should increase your bass fishing success. Just don't fall into the trap of thinking that largemouths are always stuck in the shade. There is usually cover near if bass are in the shallows, but that cover is often quite sparse and unable to reduce light levels effectively. I've frequently located groups of bass tight to bare tree branches right next to shore, or in branches of standing timber on humps away from shore. The sun was out and the bass were not in shadow. Deeper water was close at hand, providing a handy route to the safety of dimness and depth, but the bass were holding shallow out of shade in bright weather.

In addition, roaming bass pay little attention to bright light and are as likely to be moving near the surface inshore as they are in open water. Bass following schools of forage fish will do so in open water away from any shade-making cover. If they choose to remain out of sight they do so by descending, and that is the only way such bass can lower the existing light level in which they are operating.

When Vision Counts Less

Though bass are able to focus on distant objects they are primarily concerned with what is happening within that magic fifteen-foot circle of awareness surrounding them. But bass cannot always see even as short a distance as fifteen feet. Visibility in many lakes is limited to a few feet—in some cases a few inches. Still, the fish are aware of what is taking place nearby. At night or in dingy water, bass rely on other sensory abilities. They are fully able to detect odors in the water. They can sense vibrations as a combination of sound and touch.

Bass, like other biologically successful animals, have the ability within certain extremes, to adapt to their environment. If you take a bass from extremely clear water and put him in dingy water, he will have trouble at first. The trouble will arise because he has developed his visual abilities while his other sensory capabilities have not had to do much work. He will not be able to catch his food as well as the bass who has always lived in murky water.

Documentary film producer Glen Lau discovered just how great an impairment such environmental switching can be to largemouths.

Lau keeps various fish species in huge aquariums for study. He generally keeps these tanks dark to retard the growth of algae. In one aquarium Glen had a group of largemouths that had originally come from a murky lake. At one point he added some additional bass that had come from a clear-water environment. The tank also held shiners and other forage fish. The next time Glen looked into the tank after adding the clear-water bass, he was amazed. The original largemouths were fat and healthy. The newcomers had battered and bloody noses and were slimmer. Used to feeding by sight, the clear-water bass had butted their front ends into the glass tank trying to capture the shiners. The dingy-water bass had never had such a problem for they homed in on their prey using other than visual senses.

Doesn't this suggest something that has direct application to your fishing? It did to me. If clear-water bass rely that heavily on their visual acuity you'd better be prepared to spend some time making sure your tackle is as close to perfect as possible. Such critical bass call for light lines, small lures, and precise presentation with lures rigged to run properly.

Other Senses

It is difficult to separate the bass's ability to taste, detect odors, and discriminate through feel of an object taken into its mouth. These sensory capabilities probably work together. Some anglers, hoping to demonstrate the unimportance of odors when bass fishing, soaked their lures in one obnoxious solution or other. The bass still attacked the lures. However, the lures were fast moving. Spoiling the odor of a slow-moving natural bait will frequently destroy its fish-catching ability. In the case of the lures that were exposed to repellent substances, the bass were responding to attractive vibrations plus what they saw, and did not stop long enough to get a good whiff of what they were biting.

The truth is that bass are able to detect the odor

of extremely small quantities of various substances in water. One is of great interest to anglers. It has been called the alarm substance. No studies by qualified biologists have been performed to show the workings of this substance on bass, but such work has been done on minnows (*Cyprinidae* family); but several amateur naturalists have done such work and proven to their satisfaction that bass do emit the substance when injured. Here's what has been discovered.

If a school bass is fairly hooked, carefully taken from the water, dehooked and released, he will return to the school with no reaction on their part save for closing ranks around him. Take that same bass and break its skin and the school's reaction

seems to be quite different. Those who have performed the experiment report that as the injured fish heads for the school, the other fish will move away, opening a path in their ranks. They want no part of this injured comrade who will usually give up trying to rejoin them after a few minutes and head for cover.

The feeling is that some sort of substance exists just beneath the skin of bass. A bass need not bleed to give it off. A small break in the skin seems to release the danger odor; a natural lesion on the bass's skin does not seem to trigger the release of the scent. I have not tried this experiment, but fishermen should be aware that such a warning odor could exist.

Night Fishing

The sun had set and it was rapidly growing too dark for me to see much even in the clear water of the big sink hole. I swam somewhat wearily back toward shore, making a point to pass a bankside jungle of fallen trees that formed the cover for a group of extremely large bass.

I tried to check on these fish periodically during the day, because they never seemed to move from this shallow water sanctuary, regardless of the weather. Only once, at the start of a heavy rainstorm, did they break their school and begin roaming. I liked to watch these bass because they represented the real survivors among their species, and because they were just so big and impressive.

In the growing dusk, I rounded the point where their log maze thrust out from shore. I stopped, then let myself sink slowly. Something was happening. Several of the patriarchs of the group had turned from their usual positions. Their bodies rocked tail to nose. They flared their gills, opened and closed their jaws, and finned actively. It was the same "wakeup" movements that I had observed smaller bass performing prior to a feeding session. I waited.

Several more of the big bass repeated the movements, then swam from the sanctuary and headed down and out toward open water. Soon another bass followed. Shortly only two of the original group of twelve were left.

It was now far too dark and I headed in with my thoughts on the breakup of the big bass group. On several other evenings I observed the same thing.

I attempted to follow the fish but they seemed bent on moving and I could not keep pace with them. Once on a night dive, I thought I might have located one of the group of big bass holding near the bottom over the weeds where a long point projected from shore. My light was an unnatural element, however, so with the exception of the spawning season, night observation underwater never showed natural behavior. Still, I did learn several important facts before continuing my observations above water.

First was a matter of vision. Without a light I was virtually blind underwater at night. If it was a bright night or if I was swimming at dusk I could keep track of the silhouette of the dive boat that followed me. It was a white-hulled boat but the bottom looked dark in the dim light. Soon I began to relate the sight to angling for bass. Why else would surface lures scorned by bass at midday in clear water become so effective at night? Why else the choice of dark lure colors at night by long-time fishermen? Here was old-time bass lore that was accurate. The clearly visible silhouette of a surface plug on a bright night must be the reason that every fleeting glimpse I had of a bass at dusk showed the fish to be near the bottom in relatively shallow water. It was obviously the place for them to be in order to gain a better visual picture of potential forage swimming by.

This wasn't the whole story, of course. Bass obviously make use of sensory abilities during night feeding. Despite their ability to see better than humans under low light levels, I am certain

Experienced night fishermen know that night-feeding bass make erratic strikes. Before setting the hook, they wait for a solid tug on the line, not just a noisy splash. Erwin Bauer

that without the use of their other sensory equipment they would not be able to locate and attack a plastic worm swimming low in the water, or a subsurface plug or spoon that's skimming the deep edge of a weedbed after dark.

Bass are not constantly active at night, as any night fisherman knows. While diving without a light at dusk I came upon bass that appeared to be sleeping. Perhaps that is not scientifically correct, but if they were not actually asleep in the way we think of sleep, they were certainly at rest. I found fish in this condition in several lakes and quarries in different parts of the country. They were on ledges or the bottom near various forms of weed growth. They rested in a normal swimming attitude but their tails were slightly elevated. They seemed to be balancing on their fins, which were erect. I found fish both on a horizontal bottom and on steeply sloping banks or cliff walls in an inclined position. I also found "sleeping" bass at various times of night using a light, but in those cases it was most likely the shock of light on their night-vision that held the fish immobile, as though they were asleep. When I consciously began looking, I also observed this sleeping behavior by day. The bass rested on their fins on the bottom and were quiet except for very slight gill movement.

From all this I decided it would be tough to predict when bass would feed at night. They could sleep or rest at any given time. There was some correlation with bad weather; fish began to feed much later at night, if at all, following a lengthy storm. I was left with the conviction that

to be successful a bass fisherman had better plan to stick with it all night. I also decided that the color or finish of a plug did not matter much at night, but found myself favoring darker colors. Line size, too, seemed to make little difference after dark, unless it affected the action of a delicately tuned plug.

Night fishing also provided a chance to reach the largest bass in a clear-water lake. Time after time I saw the biggest bass leaving their holes or disbanding their stackup formations at dusk. Besides the safety that came with darkness, the smaller lakes cooled off a little on some summer nights, though this was most noticeable just before dawn.

Because larger fish were on the prowl at night I chose to use big plugs. But I found myself missing far too many surface-feeding bass at night by striking at a splash. I learned how to wait before striking and to keep out slack that you can't see building up after dark. I also learned the value of a consistent retrieve.

When there is no moon bass have a tough time seeing the silhouette of a surface lure even with their better-than-human night vision. To a large degree, they home in on a lure using their other senses. Whether you execute a stop-and-go retrieve or a steady swim, you should maintain the pace.

Bass fix on the rhythm of a retrieve. If it becomes erratic they can over- or undershoot their mark. This may explain the heavy swirls around my surface lures that did not result in solid strikes even after I had learned to control my reflexes and hit only when I felt a fish solidly.

Moon Phases

I tried to establish some patterns between fishing success and phases of the moon. The only thing that seemed fairly consistent was that spawning activity frequently intensified with the approach of a full moon. Not always. Localized weather conditions punched holes in many of my flowering theories.

If weather was stable and the bass were ready, prespawning activity intensified during the four-day period prior to the night of the full moon. During this period the fish would bite. If a rising temperature coincided with this four-day period, you could expect fantastic fishing. Ideally the water temperature should be in the 50s and rising.

With the actual full moon the bass would normally spawn and fishing would drop off drastically for a few days.

If severe cold weather occurred just prior to the full moon, the bass would hold off spawning until the full moon of the following month. When conditions finally permit a spawn to bass that have held off for a month or two, the period before the actual full moon can provide truly wild angling.

Fishermen differ on when the better night angling occurs. Some like a moonless night—even with a little rain. Others swear by a bright full or nearly full moon. Brackish-water bass are affected by the moon which, of course, plays with the tides.

Many devoted night fishermen take their largest bass in the dark of the moon. Other bass seem to become disturbed with the commotion of a surface-fighting brother largemouth during periods without a moon; once I catch a fish that puts up a good surface fight during a dark night, I am not usually able to take another fish from the immediate area for some time. During full-moon periods this does not seem to hold true. But maybe it's just that I'm more effective with a moon.

I prefer to fish during a moonlit night because I can see better and fish better. If you become familiar with a lake (which you *should* to be an effective night fisherman) you will have little trouble on a dark night finding the areas that produce the better fishing. You may even find you'll take bigger fish then. But you won't get to see the silhouette of a mighty bigmouth jumping at the edge of the weedbed in the silvery light from a buttermilk moon. And that, to me, is what really makes night fishing.

Color Preference

The largemouth bass may see color better than any fresh water fish. Of course we do not know if bass see colors as we do, but there is enough evidence now that shows bass do distinguish between various hues, and actually prefer some colors to others. "Prefer" may not be exactly correct. It's possible the bass are just more sensitive to different colors, or that some shades make them excited. Experimental psychologist Dr. Donald F. McCoy, of the University of Kentucky, is one of the pioneers in studying bass behavior. His choice of subject is no doubt influenced by the fact that Don is an avid bass fisherman.

McCoy established that bass distinguish between various colors. He found that they can distinguish between shades of green that are not always discernible to the human eye. In his experiments, using a complex filter system, McCoy eliminated the possibility that the bass were responding merely to brightness or to intensity of color. McCoy's bass were trained to attack a colored target to receive a food reward. One interesting sidelight was that once the fish learned that a particular color would result in food, they could not *unlearn* the fact. It follows then that if a bass learns something at any stage of its life, it may continue the behavior resulting from that learning indefinitely.

Don observed some fascinating behavior based on color preference. He conditioned some bass to expect a food reward for hitting a red, yellow, or green target. The bass responded equally to these colors. Next Don stopped rewarding the fish when they hit the target. The bass reacted by slowing their attack response. They still continued to respond well to the green target, somewhat slower to red, and slowest to yellow. McCoy began to believe that a preference for green existed.

Then it struck Don that his studies had not been done in an influence-free environment. The walls and ceilings of his laboratory were green; thus the tank-held fish were subjected to the greenish overtones of the environment. McCoy then took some other bass and carried out the same experiment (with blue added) in a colorless environment. The results were entirely different. The bass continued to respond best to red, then yellow, next green, and finally blue after the food reward was taken away.

Did the new experiments invalidate the results of the first? "No," says McCoy. "What we are beginning to suspect is that color preference can be modified by the bass's environment."

This is a breakthrough for fishermen. If it continues to prove accurate it may take the guesswork out of line-lure color selection. But there are factors to consider first. Though bass in a colorless environment seem to prefer the longer light wave-lengths (reds, orange, yellows) no bass lake I know boasts a colorless environment. Even what we refer to as clear water is tinted slightly. It is either blue-green or bluish or reddish or the color of weak tea. Dark or dirty water can be plain muddy yellow or dark brownish.

In highly colored water the color choice should be easy if you want to match the environment as Dr. McCoy's research indicates you should. Dark opaque worms in dark water, yellowish or chartreuse lures in lighter muddy water. Clear water is trickier. The overall tint of clear water may not be discernible except underwater. Often, though, the surrounding lakeside vegetation or the underwater vegetation can give you a clue. Weather, too—such as a bright blue sky—will affect the tint. Experimenting, I found the formula of matching lure finish to the tint of the water was proving pretty reliable. Then I hit a snag.

The problem sprang up in Utah's Lake Powell. As elsewhere, bass would take lures of various colors but they were quite consistent on red worms. At first I couldn't understand why. The water was extremely clear. The sky was a bright blue dome. It took time, but then I felt I had the answer. We were catching bass with plastic worms on crumbly rock ledges and rubble points. These structures were formed of a color rock that had come from the surrounding steep canyon walls. The walls of the canyon loomed up stark and red. Naturally that reddish overtone would permeate the clear water, even overpowering the effect of the sky close to the cliffs.

In the end we must wonder whether or not bass may be sensitive to wave-lengths (colors) not even visible to man. The time will no doubt come when we will be able to learn such things. For now it is good that we are at least getting an inkling of the largemouth's preference for colors we can see.

Every bass fisherman knows that in different places on different days, various colors are more successful than others. If you haven't proven that to yourself, you can do so by trying the same lure in a variety of finishes when fish are feeding steadily. Even during a schooling period when the fish are madly tearing into bait fish near the surface, one or two colors or finishes will usually prove more successful than others. Underwater the results are even more startling.

My underwater observations proved that bass respond in a variety of ways to your lure colors, ways that you have no way of knowing about in a boat on the surface. For instance, there are negative responses to a lure—a bass can simply ignore the artificial or actually flee from its presence. And there are a variety of positive responses. Some fish turn toward a passing lure and watch it. They follow it for a ways, inquisitively. They chase a lure for some distance before breaking off the pursuit quite close to your boat. Or, they can strike. When I first told the anglers with whom I was working how many fish chased their plugs or spinners while I watched below, they wouldn't believe me. When they did, they became terribly frustrated. Now I try not to mention it any more. Instead I just handle a color experiment like this.

I ask two anglers to fish from the same boat. They use lures identical except for finish. I can only make good observations performing this experiment in clear water. I station myself inconspicuously while the anglers cast, switching rods or alternating lures cast to a prime spot. The results have been fascinating.

The experiment has proven that different groups of fish definitely have particular color preferences on given days. Not all bass groups in the same lake will have the same preference on the same day, though that sometimes occurs. Color preference is far less exacting the deeper the bass are.

There is a high degree of color discrimination with surface lures. There is also a high degree of color preference with slower moving lures. Bass seem to strike fast-moving lures more as a reflexive reaction. There is none of the leisurely examination of the lure that I mentioned earlier as one of the positive bass responses. Largemouths respond quickly. They have to. Though lure color or finish may sometimes be responsible for bass turning away at the last moment, with quickly moved lures it is action and general overall impression that triggers a strike response.

How Color Reacts

When considering a finish for slow-moving or surface lures keep in mind something scientists call positive or negative contrast. Will your lure appear brighter than the surrounding background? How will light affect that lure? Anything that causes the lure to lose brightness or appear dark against a darkish background will cause it to be less visible. A negative contrast lure will appear dark against a light background: a dark lure on the surface at evening, or a lure viewed horizontally in front of the light source.

After you've considered the backdrop against which your lure will be worked, you must consider what water does to color. Bass showing color preference at one depth will not necessarily prefer that color at other depths.

As you go deeper, colors lose their characteristics in varying degrees. Red loses its characteristic first, turning brownish and finally black. Depending on the nature of the water this can happen in from ten to thirty feet. Orange is next, followed by yellow, then green and finally blue, which maintains itself to considerable depth. Of course you needn't be concerned over how quickly red becomes something else if you use that color while fishing for bass in relatively shallow water. Fluorescent dyes in paints and finishes react to daylight and the ultra-violet rays that bombard the earth. Such fluorescent brighteners help colors to retain their characteristics far deeper underwater than normal colors. I have seen a fluorescently brightened red maintain its characteristics to twenty-seven feet, and other observers report fluorescent reds and orange maintain their characteristics to over forty-five feet.

Opaque colors seem to hold together solidly under most dim light conditions. Translucent colors do something else. They tend to pick up light and emit a glow when struck by sun rays. Depending on how the light hits them, they can develop a mottled appearance or remain fuzzy yet extremely visible.

Lures

We have considered the tint of the water, the background against which your lures will work, and how water itself changes nonfluorescent colors. How does the information apply to choice of lure finish?

I haven't noticed any increase in success using fluorescent-finish lures in deeper water. Though the brightened colors maintain their characteristics to greater depth than normal colors, isn't it unnatural for bass to see these colors deeper? If so, the sight of a hot orange plug scooting along at thirty feet or so may spook them. Other fish, like salmon and lake trout, seem pleased with the bright colors in deep water, but such finishes have not produced better deep-water bass catches or responses for me. In shallow water, however, especially if conditions are somewhat dingy, the fluorescents have been good. I especially like combinations of fluorescent colors arranged in patterns that simulate fish—yellow and green, for example.

Aside from fluorescents, in water with poor visibility I use solid or opaque plastic worms— usually purple and black. For plugs and other lures I like a metallic silver or gold finish—also white, lime green, chartreuse, or a combination of red and white.

In clearer water I'll use translucent plastic worms. If the water has a brownish or reddish tint I'll usually use red worms. With a clear sky and clear water with limited vegetation, I'll usually use blue worms. I like to use this color for fishing around pilings, old cribbing, and rocks. For plugs, I'll use white or bone, and the metallic finishes such as black back with silver, gold, blue, or green body and white belly. The crayfish finishes are also good.

Underwater I've noticed that bass sometimes show negative reactions to the metallic finishes. This usually occurs in clear water on very bright days. If everything else seems right and I've been fishing a flashy finish without catching fish, I'll suspect that it's just one of those days when they don't want such glitter. I'll change to a natural forage-fish-scale finish or a red and white combination.

Line

There's a popular belief that as long as you can see it well, the color line you use is not important. This may be true with many fish. Not with bass. On some days it's not so important, on others, the choice of line color and type is critical. We fuss over the lures we use, their action and finish, but many fishermen choose lines based on advertising claims, what the local "pro" is using, or just on how pretty the line looks. No matter what we do, a line extending from a lure is still an unnatural looking thing. By careful consideration of the water we're fishing and the background against which our lures with line will be presented, we can make some decisions. Water, depth, and background considered, the choice of line must be made on the basis of whether you want to disguise your line as much as possible, use it as an additional attractor, or incorporate it as a visual aid in your fishing.

Today we can choose clear, light-colored, dark-colored, and brightened lines. Your choice of line color must also be tempered with choice of line weight. The broadest statement I can make concerning line weight is that in clear water where your fishing will not be in the very thickest kind of timber or weeds, it is wise to use extremely light line. Do not, however, choose a line so light that you cannot cast a chosen lure with it.

I made a series of tests on line weight in clear water. I used line testing from twenty pounds down to six. In every test, as the line test decreased the number of hooked fish increased and the number of follows I saw from an underwater vantage point, increased, too. If the sun were shining, the success of light over heavy line increased even more. Besides the visual aspects, line that's quite heavy can affect the action of some sensitive or very light lures. The choice of light line must, of course, be weighed against the number of fish you may lose on the lighter line. As previously mentioned, if you do not need to fish in the heaviest timber, you should not have much of a breakage problem. You must check a lighter line more frequently for fraying and you cannot horse bass around rocks and pilings without the heavier stuff; otherwise there is no reason to fear using the light line. My choice is eight, sometimes even six-pound test when I can use it. I do not like to use line heavier than ten-pound test if at all possible. In dingy water the visual impact of line weight is considerably less important. Line color is the next consideration.

One would think that the overall best choice would be a clear line because it is less visible to the fish. But it is not always less visible. If we had a line that adjusted automatically, to match the water clarity, we would have a nearly invisible line. We don't. Because of that, clear lines can appear darker against a lighter background, or lighter against a dark background. Still they have low visibility characteristics underwater and are good choices for much all around fishing. Dark lines, especially brownish, are barely discernible when fished in front of mottled vegetation or brush. They are excellent for such subsurface fishing, but they show up in silhouette when used on surface lures or against light backgrounds. Lines brightened with various fluorescent dyes are another interesting matter. After spending many

hours observing this line from fish level and seeing how bass react to it, I am left with some definite impressions.

First, such brightened lines do not magically disappear from view underwater, especially in clear water. If you fish a slow-moving lure like a plastic worm in the shallows in very clear water using a brightened line you will frequently catch fewer fish. Ultrabright lines look bigger underwater; this optical illusion is caused by the bright glowing appearance of the line. In clear water such glowing lines show up very well. This is not to say that bass will refuse all lures presented on bright lines in ultraclear water.

In clear water the splashy entry of a lure will not necessarily disguise a brightened line. Depending on the angle of the sun such lines can show up immediately. If you are fishing shallow water and the fish are spooky this extreme line visibility can inhibit a strike. Depending on the background against which these lines are viewed, they will show up well or break up visually. Brightened lines that are more opaque break up less than those that are more translucent. In general, blue or blue-green brightened lines give the appearance of breaking up against a light bottom or multicolored vegetation (though they are still more visible than brown or clear lines). They also give this affect when viewed against the surface from below. Yellow-brightened lines are less visible against light or yellowish weeds.

The angle of the sun does interesting things to the brightened lines. For instance, when viewed from underwater in clear to marginally clear water if the lines are frontlighted they show up extremely well; if they are backlighted they show up well, but not quite as brightly. If these lines are sidelighted they will appear far less bright, and some such lines break up in appearance.

You do not need brightened lines when using crankbaits or for straight retrieves with surface lures or spinnerbaits. Where, then, do such lines fit in the angling picture? Experienced bass fishermen have learned that the best line is not always the most "invisible." This is true especially in colored or moderately dingy waters where most anglers fish for bass. The ability to descern a slight twitch or "kick" of the line often makes the difference between catching or not catching bass. As plastic-worm specialist Bob Martin says, "I watch that line all the time. I keep my eyes just glued on it. I concentrate so hard on the line I often get a headache."

Line-watching is where the brightened lines prove their worth. They are at their best in dingy water where the bass rely quite a bit on senses other than sight until the moment before they hit a lure. A plastic-worm fisherman or an angler who tightlines (keeps slack from developing in the line while the lure sinks) leadhead jigs or flutters a tailspin or spinnerbait lure down to the bottom ought to try the bright lines. Anglers who use natural bait and have their best results when they let a fish run a little way before striking, find bright lines of help. Their trick is to watch the line carefully and open their spinning-reel bails or snap their casting reels into free spool the moment the line starts marching off.

Bright lines let you see the slightest twitch or line motion much easier. If the water is especially clear, you can always employ a technique used by generations of bass fishermen who never knew the benefit of monofilament. You can tie on a low visibility leader that will be best suited to the conditions you must fish. Use a monofilament leader of from five to fifteen feet. If you use a conventional casting reel you may have some trouble with the line-leader knot passing through the level-wind bracket. If so, use a leader short enough to keep the knot outside this control. There will be no such problem using a spinning reel. Normally a small neat knot like the Double Duncan loop or a blood knot will pass through the level wind and rod guides. If your rod guides are excessively small I'd recommend replacing them with larger guides.

A long leader of up to fifteen feet would prevent the bright section of line from entering into that circle within which bass are extremely aware of what's going on around them. Using such a rig you will gain the benefit of a high-visibility line where you need it, plus the concealment of indistinct line close to the lure.

We still have much to discover about color as it applies to bass angling. One question that still intrigues me concerns a bass's ability to learn and inability to unlearn. Given enough time, you would think that the bad effects of a learned situation must wear off. Maybe not. McCoy has yet to prove that. It makes you wonder if bass caught a number of times on a particular color lure will learn to avoid that color on all lures. Maybe the fish will avoid the color only on a type of artificial with the specific action that caused the traumatic experience of being hooked.

You've no doubt been aware of the success of a new lure lasting for a season of two, after which the artificial seems to produce fewer fish. Is it only that the lure's popularity has declined so fewer anglers are fishing it, or have the bass been stuck by the lure so many times they've learned that it's bad medicine? If that's true, how do you explain the consistency of purple plastic worms or chartreuse spinnerbaits over the years? No one is ready to give all those answers yet, but one thing's for sure. To gain a more complete understanding of the behavior of largemouths we'll have to explore areas other than vision.

5

How Bass Lakes Differ
Characteristics that Affect Angling

DAVID E. MORRIS

The 100-degree July heat didn't lessen our enthusiasm as my dad and I pulled up to a small camp on the south shore of Lake Talquin. We had heard a lot about the excellent bass fishing on this north Florida impoundment, but this was the first time we had ever had a chance to sample its wares.

Stepping from the air-conditioned car was like opening the door of a blast furnace. Even the trees on the far shore were distorted by the heat mirages arising from the mirrored waters of the lake. But visions of big bass spurred me on.

Realizing my dad had a tendency to forget about bass in the presence of overwhelming heat, I tried to get him back on track.

"Look at that!" I said, pointing to an area of the lake strewn with logs and standing timber. "There ought to be a bass behind every stump."

His reply was quick. "Now wait a minute, David. Let's don't get in too big a hurry. We don't know a thing about this lake, and besides that, it's the middle of the day and I feel a little nap coming on."

"I'll walk over to the bait house and see what the fish have been doing."

Before I reached the store, a teenage boy met me and offered to help launch the boat. He looked like a native and a veteran of the lake, so I decided to quiz him about the fishing.

"Anybody catching any fish?" I asked.

"Nope, pretty slow," he answered as we walked toward the boat ramp. "Might catch a few brim if ya got any crickets."

"We're after bass," I snapped, a little insulted that he thought we looked like anything but cracker-jack bassmen.

He gave me a quick glance and just nodded his head. Then he volunteered, "Ya need to talk to Jim. He's a bass guide. Was up at the store a minute ago."

After we launched the boat, my dad and I headed to the bait house to talk to Jim. Jim wasn't the talkative sort, but we got a little information from him.

"Bass doing anything?" I asked.

"Yep, caught three this morning. One about four pounds. As soon as it cools off this evenin', I'm going out for a few more."

"What are you catching them on and where?" I asked.

"Catchin' most of 'um on Rapalas and rubber worms," he answered reluctantly. "They seem to be around the grassy banks. Might be a few on that point over there," he said, pointing to a distinctive point across the lake.

With that, my reluctant dad and I took off to catch a load of Talquin bass. First we tried the point Jim had suggested; two hours and one year-ling bass later we headed for the grassy banks. After an hour of fruitless casting, we had enjoyed about all of that we could stand. Already a steady stream of comments about the heat was coming my way, and I knew Dad was about ready to find a cool, shade tree.

"Let's examine this situation and try to figure out where these bass are," I suggested.

"They're deep, where it's cool," my dad answered, obviously still thinking about the heat.

"That's probably right. This reservoir looks a lot like our home-lake, Eufaula. If I were fishing it right now, I'd try the downstream side of outside creek channels near the main river."

"Well, let's see if we can find anything like that," he said.

Since the only map we had was a small, single-sheet outline of the lake, we had to rely on our depthfinder and the shoreline topography to find the structure we wanted. Our search centered around Rocky Comfort Creek on the north shore.

Within minutes, we found a thirty-foot channel that ran through fifteen-foot flats. Our depthfinder lit up almost from top to bottom, indicating plenty of brush. This area looked like any of a dozen places I had fished on Lake Eufaula. We dropped anchor and started casting.

"There he is," came a familiar cry from my dad.

He set the hook and soon had a struggling five-pounder beside the boat. Before he had unhooked the bass, I had a three-pounder stretching my line. During the next hour, we landed four more nice bass.

When the action slowed in this spot, we pulled up the anchor and eased down the creek channel toward the river. Another outside bend in the creek ledge flashed on the dial of the depthfinder, so we dropped anchor. Suddenly, gizzard shad skipped across the water in front of us, and big swirls appeared under them. That could only mean one thing—big bass!

We grabbed our Little George rigs and flipped the tailspins into the panicked shad. The lures had

Contour and characteristics of reservoir banks are good clues to the type of terrain and structure that will occur under the water for some distance into the lake.

not dropped a foot before we were both fast into good bass. This action started two- and one-half days of some of the best bass fishing we have ever enjoyed. When our first trip to Lake Talquin ended, my dad and I had taken seventy-eight bass from that creek channel that averaged better than four pounds each!

That happened July 4th weekend in 1971. Since that time I have had an opportunity to fish many new lakes and to develop an organized approach to some of the mysteries of strange lakes.

Because of the vast number of lakes and rivers available in the United States, fishermen commonly face this question. To help fish a new lake effectively, I rely on a system that involves studying the habits and habitat of bass, relating past experiences to present circumstances, and lastly, classifying lakes into different types based on physical characteristics. These factors all combine to help form an image of a new lake and determine the patterns followed by its bass populations at a given time of the year under a certain set of conditions.

If a fisherman is to fish for bass successfully on any lake, either familiar or unfamiliar, he must first understand the basics of bass behavior and habitat. This can be accomplished by reading, by studying the bass itself whenever and wherever possible, and by first-hand experience, for which there is no substitute. He must learn about the trends of seasonal movement, the bass's need for cover, its affinity to structure, the high points of its life cycle, its biological requirements, and its preference in baits and lures. Only after this information is combined with countless hours of experience can it be put into its proper perspective and be called upon to solve current fishing problems accurately. Even the most insignificant fact may become the key to understanding a complex fishing situation.

As more information is gathered and stored in a fisherman's memory, the ability to recall that data and apply it to a specific fishing situation becomes critical. Every experience and every bit of knowledge an angler has must be at his disposal to solve the often complex problems of where bass are located and how to catch them, especially on strange lakes. Without this ability, each fishing challenge must stand alone, without the benefit of past experiences and lessons learned.

What Kind of Lake Is It?

Before an angler can challenge a strange lake, he must know something about the many types of lakes and reservoirs and how to locate and catch bass in each of them.

The general classification I have found most useful first divides lakes into the natural and the manmade (impoundments). Natural lakes are then further classified as either lowland or highland. The natural lakes of the coastal areas of the South, such as those in Florida and Louisiana, and the flat country of the North, most notably Wisconsin and Minnesota, are typical of lowland natural lakes. Highland natural lakes are exemplified by the deeper and often rocky lakes of the Northeast and West, such as the smallmouth waters of Maine and the Great Lakes region.

Impoundments include lowland, midland, and highland reservoirs. Some impoundments will have characteristics of more than one type of reservoir. In this case, a fisherman should base his search for bass and his fishing techniques on the physical characteristics, as they relate to the classification system, of the different areas of the impoundment. Let's take a look at the features and characteristics of each type of lake and explore the tactics that will help put pounds on your stringer when you meet one for the first time.

Lowland Natural Lakes: Fish the Cover

When I was a boy growing up in a small town in south Alabama, much of my time was spent fishing shallow lakes filled with lily pads, mossbeds, and grass. I didn't need a boat because I could cover most of the lakes by wading—that is, if I kept a close eye out for gators and cottonmouths. I'd read stories about fishing points and underwater islands, but as far as I was concerned, these stories were about some mystical faraway place since I had never seen anything like that.

My fishing consisted of tossing Mepps spinners, Hawaiian Wigglers, Creek Chub Cripple Minnows, and plastic worms at anything that showed above the water. Even though I had always secretly dreamed of catching fish from points and underwater islands, I would later realize that fishing the shallow waters of lowland natural lakes is one of the most exciting ways to catch bass.

Lowland natural lakes are typically shallow, bowl-shaped bodies of water with an abundance of vegetation, usually lily pads, grassbeds, moss, cyprus trees, or brushes. There is a distinct lack of bottom structure in most cases. Few, if any, channels or dropoffs can be found. These lakes usually have a rounded shape with little irregularity in the shoreline when compared to reservoirs. In other words, the shoreline distance of the lake is small when compared to the acreage.

Cover is most often found around the edges or in the shallower areas but can be distributed throughout the entire lake. This is especially true of the clearer lakes like Lake Jackson and Orange Lake in Florida. Since sunlight penetrates deeper into the clear water, vegetation is able to grow at a greater depth.

When fishing lowland natural lakes, the depth in which the fish are located is seldom of concern. Since the lakes are usually shallow enough that any shallow or medium-running lure will be noticed by nearby bass, the problem of finding fish becomes one of searching the horizontal plane (surface area) rather than the vertical plane (depth). This is an important advantage.

The key to catching bass in natural lowland lakes is cover. Since these lakes are shallow and without bottom structure, the fish stay near the vegetation (often visible above the surface). The question becomes, What type of vegetation are the fish holding in? Once that problem is solved, the angler must find areas with concentrations of bass and an effective method of taking them from the cover.

Although the basic principles behind catching fish in lowland natural lakes are simple, putting them to practice can be difficult. For instance, bass may be found only around a certain type of weed, at a particular depth, and in an area where the wind has stained the water. I once found a pattern very much like this on Lake Kissimmee in Florida. I could only catch bass from points of small bullrush patches on the windward side of the outside edge of the grassline. In addition to this, they would only hit eight-inch, raspberry worms, of which I was in short supply.

Lowland natural lakes require that a fisherman be keenly observant. He should be ever watchful of minnows jumping, grass or pads shaking, birds studying something in the water, signs of feeding fish, or currents created by the wind. While fish can usually be caught from visible cover, the fisherman must still find the key to the pattern of the day. The surest way to insure success is to fish the various types of cover systematically with many kinds of lures and try to eliminate the unproductive. This process can be greatly shortened when a fisherman has a wealth of past fishing experiences to draw from.

Even though bass in lowland natural lakes are found near visible cover most of the time, the extremes of winter and summer can drive them to the deeper parts of a lake and away from cover, even though the depth variance is only a few feet. When this happens, a depth-finder is valuable in pinpointing the areas likely to be productive. But, the problem still remains one of locating the fish on the horizontal rather than the vertical plane due to the shallowness.

Lure selections for lowland natural lakes are

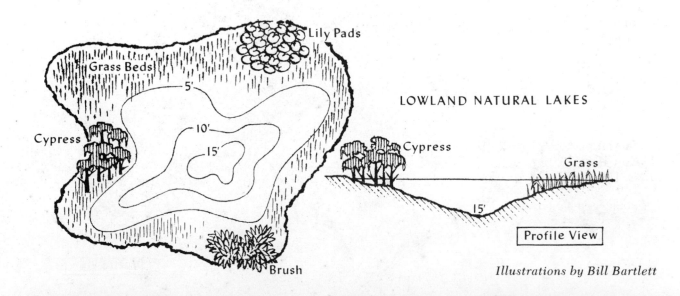

Lily Pads
Grass Beds
5'
Cypress
10'
15'
Brush

LOWLAND NATURAL LAKES

Cypress
Grass
15'
Profile View

Illustrations by Bill Bartlett

somewhat limited by the cover that must be fished. Plastic worms with and without weights are favorites. Topwater lures of all types are very effective. Weedless spoons like the Johnson Silver Minnow, shallow-running plugs such as the

Rapala, and spinnerbaits account for many fish. Some anglers find live bait, especially shiners, to be ideal for big bass in these shallow, weedy lakes.

Highland Natural Lakes: Look for Structure

Highland natural lakes are best exemplified by the rocky smallmouth lakes of southeastern Canada and the northeastern United States. Unlike their lowland counterparts, they often have ragged shorelines with an abundance of rocky or gravel points. Some above-water vegetation is present in the shallow regions, but much of the vegetative cover is found below the surface. In most instances, vegetation is much less common than in the lowland lakes.

Most of these lakes were formed when the massive glaciers of the Ice Age plowed across North America, scraping off the surface soil and exposing the underlying rocks. When the glaciers subsided, the gouged-out basins filled with water and became the lakes we know today. Rock and gravel bottoms are common.

There is a surprising amount of structure in many of these lakes. Rock points, submerged islands, bluff banks, gravel bars, and underwater

HIGHLAND NATURAL LAKES

Rock Shelf

Emergent Vegetation

Gravel Bay

Rock Island

Island

Rocky Point

Submerged Vegetation

Fallen Tree

Rocks

Emergent Vegetation

Island

Submerged Vegetation

Rock Shelf

40'

Profile View

ledges are prime fish-holding areas. The water is often clear, and an angler can see much of the structure under the water. By careful observation of the shoreline topography and underwater structure, a fisherman can quite easily and accurately visualize the layout of the lake, or at least the area of immediate interest.

Bass tend to stay on or near this structure all year. Of course, during the spring spawning season, they venture into the gravel flats for a short time; but most bass will be taken near the structure, whether it is along the shoreline or in the middle of the lake. The fisherman must search both the horizontal plane and the vertical plane. The depth in which the bass are located becomes important. The fisherman must work each type of structure with a variety of lures that allow him to test the various depths thoroughly. It is necessary to have an organized and careful approach to finding the fish so that no possibilities are overlooked.

A wide range of lures and baits will take fish from highland natural lakes. Crankbaits are very popular, especially those with natural colors resembling crayfish or native bait fish. Small spinners are good, and topwater plugs are effective if the bass are shallow. The deadliest artificial may well be the jig-and-eel combination. This rig is equally effective in either shallow or deep water. Anglers also experience good success with small worms, flies, streamers, and pork-rind lures. Preferred natural baits include minnows, spring lizards, crawfish, hellgrammites, and nightcrawlers.

Lowland Impoundments: Classic Bassing Water

Lowland impoundments, as the name implies, are located in flat country. They are found primarily in the coastal plains region of the South, but the North and Midwest also have representative lowland impoundments. Lake Seminole, Santee-Cooper, Toledo Bend, Lake Talquin, Rodman Pool, and Lake Eufaula (both Georgia's and Oklahoma's) are examples of well-known lowland reservoirs.

They are typically characterized by broad expanses of shallow water cut by distinctive channels, ditches, and gullies. There is usually an abundance of standing timber, brush, logs, grass, weeds, or stumps. In most cases, the shoreline is not especially long in relation to the surface area. The points and shoreline features are rather nondescript in comparison with other types of reservoirs. The water usually has good color, although lakes with a great deal of vegetation are sometimes quite clear.

Most of the bass will be found close to cover or structure, and usually both. Their location seldom has anything to do with the proximity of the bank, even though they may be found near the shore if cover or structure is present. A creek ledge with brush, an old hedgerow along a ditch, trees on a flooded pond dam, or stickups on a long, sandy point are all places frequented by bass in lowland reservoirs. Daily movement and seasonal migration tend to be along the channels and ledges. When bass are dispersed in the broad flats, they will usually hold near some type of cover.

The search for bass in these impoundments should be focused mainly on the horizontal plane. Of course, fish are sometimes found in rather deep water, say fifteen to twenty-five feet, but then they are usually on or near the bottom. In fact, when bass are in water deeper than ten feet in lowland impoundments, they are probably on the bottom near brush or structure. If they aren't, the chances of catching them are low, and these exceptional fish should be of little concern to the angler unless they are schooling on the surface.

During the spring and fall, bass move to the shallower channels, ledges, and ditches and into the flats. Spinnerbaits and shallow-running plugs are hard to beat at this time. Plastic worms and topwater lures are good bets during the warmer periods. Deep-diving crankbaits are deadly when fished along the ledges around cover. It is important to keep the lure in contact with the bottom or brush. Bass will sometimes strike a bottom-bouncing lure out of an involuntary reflex. Natural baits such as shiners, shad, spring lizards, and frogs are also dependable.

In the extremes of winter and summer, an angler is forced to go to the deeper ledges and channels. Tailspins, plastic worms, deep-diving crankbaits, and leadhead grubs are good choices. They work best when cast into shallow water and

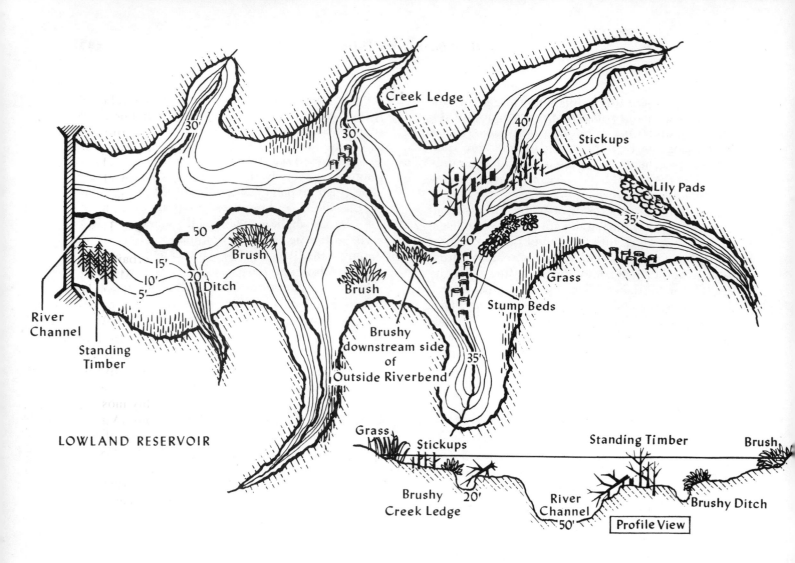

Creek Ledge

30'

30'

40'

Stickups

Lily Pads

50

15'

Brush

35'

10'

20'

5'

Ditch

Brush

40'

Grass

River
Channel

Brushy
downstream side
of
Outside Riverbend

Stump Beds

Standing
Timber

35'

LOWLAND RESERVOIR

Grass

Stickups

Standing Timber

Brush

Brushy
Creek Ledge

20'

River
Channel

50'

Brushy Ditch

Profile View

retrieved back to deep water. Bass tend to congregate on the downstream side of outside channel bends. This is the area swept by current when water is released at the dam. Large concentrations are sometimes encountered by lucky anglers on these types of ledges.

One of my favorite ledges on Lake Eufaula is such a place. The old Chatahoochee River channel makes a huge bend that extends from the Georgia bank to the Alabama bank in a mile-wide section of the lake. This is known as Alexander's Bend or Buoy 52 and has produced many heavy stringers of bass when the Corps of Engineers "pulled" water at the dam. The depth of this area ranges from fifteen to twenty feet on top of the ledge for about a quarter of a mile. The channel is close to sixty feet deep. I can depend on any one of about five brushy spots along the channel to produce bass—big bass—anytime the turbines are working. My best catch from Buoy 52 came late one July day when my companion and I boated thirteen bass from five to nine and one-half pounds. Eight topped seven pounds, and four bass bettered eight pounds.

Midland Impoundments: Cover Is Scarce

If a fisherman pulled out a map of a reservoir and the outline of the lake gave the appearance of a centipede, it's a pretty sure bet that he'd be looking at a midland lake. On these impoundments, the shoreline is interrupted with a multitude of points and coves. The most significant features of midland reservoirs are the abundance of distinctive points and, subsequently, the great length of the shoreline compared to the surface area. The water can be fairly clear, but most often it has good color due to plankton blooms. Clark Hill Reservoir and Lake Sinclair in Georgia, Lake Greenwood in South Carolina, and Lake Murvall in Texas are typical midland lakes.

Unlike lowland lakes, large portions of midland impoundments are too deep for bass; they cannot make contact with the bottom. Even when bass occupy this deeper water in pelagic schools, they are difficult to locate and catch.

Points are by far the most important feature of midland lakes to the fisherman. Most bass will be in some type of association with points during all times of the year. Channels, ledges, and ditches are present but usually indistinct and often adjacent to points. Submerged islands may be important fish-attracting structure in midland lakes when found at proper depths. Shoreline substrate can range from sand to gravel and clay to rock. Bank cover such as fallen trees, brushes, boatdocks, and stumps will hold bass during all but the hottest and coldest times of the year. Midland lakes are usually short on cover, and the bass are, therefore, a little cover starved. This can be used to the fisherman's advantage if he can find cover on the points or along productive shorelines.

Crankbaits are made to order for midland lakes. An assortment of sizes and types that can be used to comb the entire length of a point is required. Plastic worms are an excellent choice. Many prefer to use the Carolina rig on the points, which involves floating a buoyant plastic worm about eighteen inches above a barrel swivel and slip sinker. This is particularly effective on a clean, cover-free bottom. Tailspins like the Little George fool a lot of midland bass.

When fish are on the banks, spinnerbaits and crankbaits will account for good catches. Midland lakes offer some of the most consistent shoreline fishing to be found. The reason is simple: banks offer cover and structure that are generally lacking in the lake. The most productive banks are near deep water and have cover of some sort. Overhanging brushes provide shade that holds fish.

Many good catches are given up by the underwater islands of midland lakes. Probably most island fish are taken on worms and tailspins. A good topographic map will show the location of the submerged islands and is invaluable when taking on a midland lake for the first time.

Points, the most important type of structure, differ. During the summer and winter, bass stay

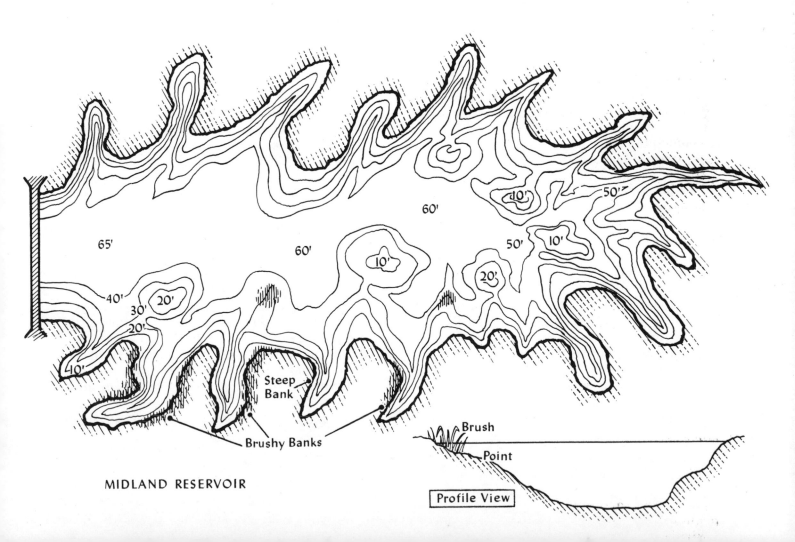

MIDLAND RESERVOIR

on points that are near creek or river channels in the "big water." Spring, early summer, and fall will find many bass on the smaller points and those in coves and creeks. These points serve as travel lanes to the bank as well as feeding and holding areas.

Highland Impoundments: The Toughest to Fish

Highland reservoirs may well be the most difficult lakes to fish since an angler must concern himself equally with the vertical and horizontal plane. These lakes are deep, and fish can be found at great depths, because the lakes are usually oxygenated. Steep, bluff banks that plummet to considerable depths are normal. The ratio of shoreline to acreage falls between that of lowland and midland lakes. Points are fairly abundant but drop into deep water quickly. Underwater islands exist but are not as common as in midland lakes. The shore and bottom substrate usually consists of rock, gravel, and sometimes clay. Highland impoundments are often clear with little color. Dale Hollow Reservoir, home of the world-record smallmouth, and Lake Mead, are well-known examples.

Fishing these impoundments is a deep-water proposition. Even when fish are tight on the banks, they can be holding in twenty to thirty feet of water. One definite advantage of highland impoundments is that most fish are usually in association with the shore. The shoreline structure will provide much information about what is underwater—thus aiding in the location of bass. It is safe to assume that whatever is above the water will be below the water. Rock slides, rock bluffs, steep clay banks, blowdowns, and changes in bank type often signal bass beneath the surface. The problem is getting the lure to the depth at which bass are holding.

Bass are often so deep in highland impoundments that it is difficult to fish for them with conventional methods. This is when vertical jigging comes into its own. Spoons, worms, grubs, Little Georges, and jigs dangled in front of a deep bass will entice strikes. Even though it is difficult to find the right combination of vertical and horizontal planes, the rewards can be great since highland bass often congregate in large schools. One benefit of the bass being so deep is that the boat can be positioned right on top of the fish without spooking them. This allows a fisherman to take full advantage of finding a school, which is especially important in light of the difficulty in pin-pointing individual bass.

Vertical jigging can yield good catches along the bluff banks, around deep boat docks, in submerged standing timber, over underwater islands, or around any significant structure at a productive depth, which may be as great as sixty-five feet.

Of course, as with all lakes, there are times when bass are in shallow water, even though this can mean fifteen feet on some highland reservoirs. Crankbaits, midwater lures, worms, and even topwater plugs will draw strikes then. Shallow coves, ledges, points, and flats would be likely places to look for "thin"-water bass. Because of the extremely clear water normal in these impoundments, light tackle is required unless fishing in very deep water. In addition, more bass will be boated using small lures. During the warm months, night fishing can result in good catches in these clear lakes. Spring lizards, nightcrawlers, small shiners, and crawfish are proven natural baits.

A good topographic map is handy but not absolutely necessary when fishing highland impoundments. A pretty good indication of where the bass are located can be gained by observing shoreline features. The odds are excellent that an angler can find bank-related bass easier than those in open water. He must be very observant and able to translate what he sees above the water into information that will help locate fish.

Fishing strange lakes can be an exciting challenge or a disheartening experience. The outcome depends on an angler's basic knowledge of bass, his ability to recall his knowledge and draw from his past experiences, and, lastly, his general understanding of the different types of lakes and how to locate and catch bass in them. If an angler can accomplish all of this, it's a sure bet that his next trip to a strange lake will be a happy one.

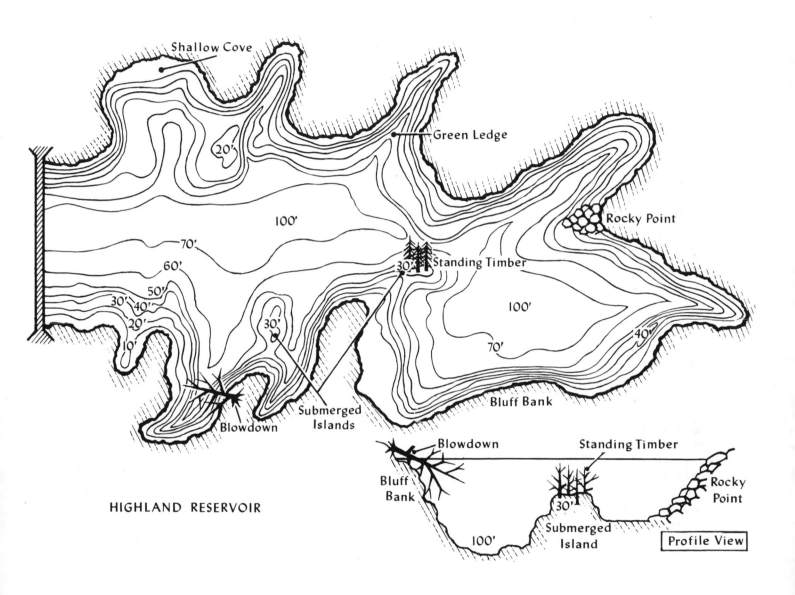

Shallow Cove

Green Ledge

Rocky Point

100'

70'

60'

50'

30' 40'

30'

20'

10'

Standing Timber

30'

100'

70'

40'

Bluff Bank

Submerged
Islands

Blowdown

HIGHLAND RESERVOIR

Blowdown

Standing Timber

Bluff
Bank

Rocky
Point

30'

Submerged
Island

100'

Profile View

6

Reading the Water

Bass Fishing's Most Important Art

MARK SOSIN and BILL DANCE
Drawings by Dave Whitlock

It is impossible to tell when the first bass fisherman turned his back on the shoreline and decided that most bass spend the major portion of their adult lives in deeper water. Possibly the early beginnings of fishing for bass in deeper water happened more by accident than by design, yet in the past quarter century this technique has gained momentum.

Today, structure fishing is the modern bass angler's cornerstone of success. With the ability to locate structure comes a working knowledge of the black bass, its habits, and its habitat. Consider that many of the large reservoirs across our country offer hundreds of miles of shoreline and thousands of acres of open water. That's a lot different from the tiny farm pond or tank out behind the barn where you can cast the shoreline a couple of times each evening, covering every foot of it.

If you're going to find fish on big water, you have to know where they are most likely to appear and then concentrate your efforts on only those spots that offer the greatest promise. You won't be right every time you launch your boat, but the law of averages is tipped heavily in your favor. Over the course of a year, you will do much better fishing structure than limiting your efforts to the shoreline.

WHAT IS STRUCTURE?

Consider structure to be the floor of the lake extending from the shallows to the deeper water. More precisely, it is unusual or irregular features on the lake bottom that are different from the surrounding bottom areas. A stump tipped on its side in a foot or two of water along the shoreline would be structure, and a creek bed meandering along the bottom of the lake at a depth of twenty-five feet is also structure.

Structure comes in all sizes and shapes. It can be straight or crooked, contain dents and depressions, or be flat. Some structure is long while other is short. Some is steep, sloping, barren, brushy, grassy, stumpy, rocky, mossy, or stepped. It can be shallow or deep—on the shoreline or offshore in open water.

One of the best ways to grasp the concept of structure is to use your imagination when you're driving along a highway. Look at the surrounding countryside and picture what it would look like if the entire area were suddenly inundated with water. Start trying to pick the places where bass would be most likely to hang out. You might start with the drainage ditch alongside the road you're driving on and around the culvert you just crossed.

As you go through these mental gyrations, you will start to associate stands of trees along the field perimeters as a specific type of structure. Some fields will slope and others will be flat with perhaps a drop-off on one side. The idea is to be able to visualize what your favorite lake might look like if the water was suddenly drawn down. Most anglers find it difficult to picture the physical features of a lake bottom once it is covered with water. You know that there's a roadbed or ditch down below the surface, but unless you train yourself, you don't always visualize it when you are fishing.

A map and depth sounder can help you to gain the necessary mental picture, but if you also associate features with those you can see above the ground, it becomes a lot easier. Then, the next time you fish a creek bed shouldering into a point, you might be able to compare it to one you've seen on the way to the lake.

THE GOLDEN RULE

For any type of structure to be productive, it must have immediate access to deeper water. This rule applies regardless of whether the structure sticks up out of three feet of water near the shoreline or happens to be a stand of trees in thirty-five feet of water in the center of the lake.

Bass consider the quick passage to deep water as an escape route from predators or any type of danger. Call it instinct or habit, but bass definitely won't wander very far from that escape route. Like submarines, the bass want the option of crash diving when they feel it necessary.

The same largemouths and smallmouths need a route to travel from their home in deep water to shallower areas for feeding. We believe that creek or river channels moving under a lake are in reality highways for bass and that bass move up and down the creek channels just as a car moves along a road. There are other routes, to be sure, but creek channels are one of the best.

Another theory says that bass don't simply swim from deep water to shallow water without pausing along the way. Usually the fish will hesitate at natural breaks, which might be the edge of the drop-off or some kind of object at that junction. Some anglers believe that they may rest in these areas for periods of from a few minutes to a few hours. At any rate, keep in mind that all bass don't move into the shallows at the same time, so there are always some fish along the deeper structure.

Structure fishing is most popular throughout the southern half of the United States, but it is equally valid as a technique in northern lakes. Bassing authority Bing McClellan points out that northern lakes are not as productive per acre and most of them are naturally formed instead of being man-made; but structure still exists, and that is where the bass will be.

CREEK BED POINTS

If you were to limit an experienced structure fisherman to one type of underwater terrain, his first choice would undoubtedly be a creek channel. Channels wind their way across and around the lake floor in every man-made reservoir or impoundment and they are present in a number of natural lakes. As we mentioned earlier, bass use these creek channels as highways, and there are times when they will use the channels for shade and cover.

Anytime a creek channel runs in close to the bank or a point, it has to be a good place for bass. You may not always find the bass in residence, but sooner or later they should be there. These creek bed points, however, are always worthy of your attention, and if you're going to fish points, pick the ones where a creek is nearby.

In Illustration 1, we show a typical shoreline that might occur in any type of lake—lowland, midland, or highland. This classification is primarily based on elevation, and each type of lake exhibits certain typical characteristics. Highland lakes are in hilly country and are usually deep and clear. Lowland lakes are shallow, flat lakes at low elevations that have a minimum of structure because the surrounding terrain is relatively flat. Midland lakes are found at intermediate elevations and exhibit characteristics of the other two.

All three points in the illustration (#1, #2, and #3) look as if they would hold fish, and they very well might, but Point #2 would obviously be the most productive. The reason is that #2 is a creek bed point—that is, the creek coming out of the cove moves right alongside this point of land.

The creek bed point is an excellent place to find and catch bass. Let's assume you have located a school of largemouths at daybreak one morning on the inside cove end of Point #2 (marked Spot A). It's a great beginning and you pick up a few fish, or perhaps you take your limit right there.

The next morning you can't wait for the alarm

clock to ring; you rush through breakfast and hurry right back to Spot A. You're using the same lure and technique you employed yesterday, but this morning you draw a blank. That's when you start analyzing the situation. There could be several reasons and it's your job to find the right one.

Your first two impressions would be that the fish have either moved or for some unknown reason aren't hitting. These mental exercises may pacify the mind, but they are not going to catch fish for you until you begin to experiment. They may not prefer yesterday's lure, so you had better get busy trying a variety of other offerings. Possibly it's the retrieve that is bothering them. Yesterday they wanted the lure slow and today they want it fast or they want it with a stop and start motion. Maybe they are a little deeper than yesterday, so you try that, too.

When you have gone through the routine and still haven't produced results, you must assume that the fish aren't there. That's a far better option than throwing in the sponge and convincing yourself that they are there but won't hit. This is where a good contour map pays dividends. If you know the area well, your options are apparent.

You then assume that the fish have moved from Spot A to Spot B (Illustration 1). They could very easily be at Spot B hitting exactly the way they were yesterday on the same lure and same retrieve. If that doesn't work, you go through the routine a second time before you conclude that they may not have moved into the point but are hanging around the creek bend at Spot C. By knowing an area, you always stand a much better chance of catching fish.

It is equally important to remember that the bass might not be feeding, but remain schooled at Spot C because the water temperature is more to their liking or they just don't want to move into shallower water to feed. There's no reason you can't catch fish at Spot C if they are there, even though the water is much deeper.

Another way to think about this hypothetical case is to consider that you caught fish early in the morning at Spot A or B. The fish were along the drop-off, but suddenly the action stopped. That's when you might want to give Spot C a try. The fish could have moved down the creek channel and right back to the U bend in the creek.

On other days, they may not be at Spot A or B at all, but you know that, when they do move into shallower water, the odds are that they'll follow their own underwater highway down the creek channel.

Finally, if you find fish at a certain depth in Spot A, B, or C, you can assume that fish will also be in similar places around the lake. Check your contour map, select similar spots, and give them a thorough workout.

CREEK CHANNEL POINTS IN COVES

You already know that creek channel points are among the best places to fish and you know that coves can also be productive. Take a close look at Illustration 2 and study it for a few moments. The first thing you should notice on this drawing of a typical cove in a lowland- or midland-type lake is that this particular cove has six points in it. The

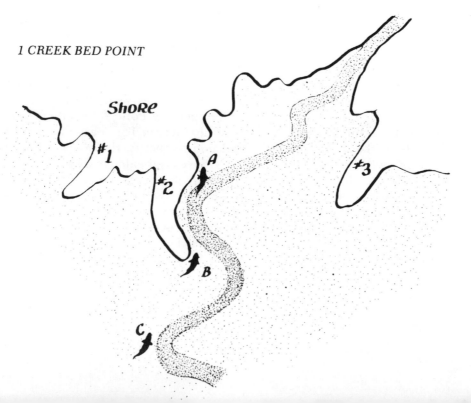

1 CREEK BED POINT

thrashing. It is entirely possible that the fish settled to the bottom of the creek channel at a depth that is suitable. This is especially true during the colder winter months.

It's a common mistake to think that bass won't bunch up in cold water. Not only do they bunch, but they can pack in so tightly that if you're not extremely careful, you might miss them completely. A large school of bass can occupy an area no larger than your boat.

BLUFF POINTS

Anytime you can locate a bluff point with a ledge moving out into the cove along a creek channel, you've found a hot spot that should produce fish for you over the course of time (see Illustration 3, Bluff AB). We have enlarged the bluff area (Illustration 4) and added some imaginary depths to help you visualize a bluff point.

When you find one, study the shoreline carefully and you'll get an idea of how it will look underwater. The land contour above water doesn't normally change very much after it disappears beneath the surface—at least for a reasonable distance. In our example, the bluff point forms a continuous ledge underwater, moving deeper and deeper as it parallels the creek channel.

Notice how the creek gets deeper as it follows

the bluff, giving you a variety of depths to fish in the immediate area. Refer to Illustration 3 again and you'll see that there is another shoal area below the bluff point which means that the bluff will slope and shoal to the left as you follow it out from the shoreline.

The bluff on the other side of the cove can also be very good if fished at the edge of the shoal, but the prime area in this cove is the bluff point. As we said earlier, we have shown a creek channel that moves from side to side for purposes of illustration. On the water, this is not always the case. There are many instances when a creek channel touches a bluff or two, forms a couple of shoals, and then moves out right through the middle of the cove (Illustration 5). It would be fished the same way as we have described, only there will be fewer places to fish.

Finally, at certain periods of the year the water level or the pool stage of a particular lake is at its low point or exceptionally low when compared to other years. This might not be a good time to fish, but you'll never have a better opportunity to explore. Get your boat as far back as you can in many of these coves and sketch the structure. Much of it could be exposed. If you have an interest in photography, you may even want photograph it. When the lake fills up again, you'll have a firsthand idea of what the coves look like under water.

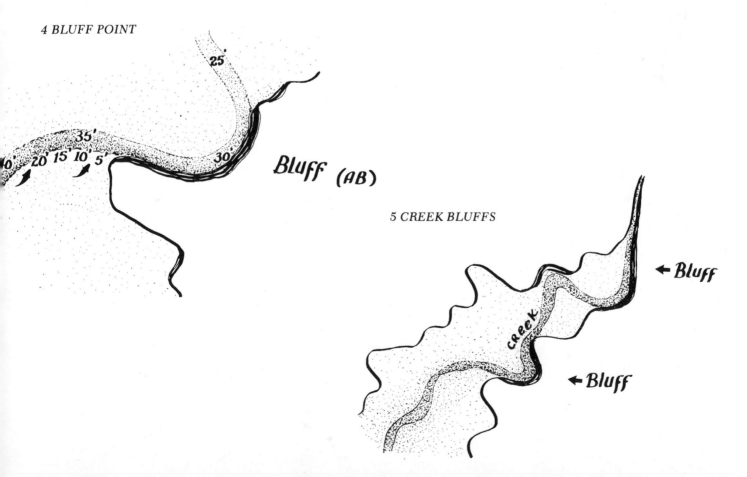

4 BLUFF POINT

25'
35'
20' 15' 10' 5'
30'

Bluff (AB)

5 CREEK BLUFFS

← *Bluff*

CREEK

← *Bluff*

CREEK OR RIVER CHANNELS

Locate a submerged creek and you know that somewhere along its length you are going to find bass. In fact, bass will probably be at a number of locations. Remember that you should have an idea of the preferred depth for bass on that specific day and then look for structure along the creek channel within the depth zone.

When compared to the main impoundment, the creek itself is structure, but there is also additional structure along the creek channel. It might take the form of a bend or saddle and it would certainly be amplified by the presence of some type of cover such as weeds or brush.

Fish could be stretched along a straightaway in a creek channel, but you know that they will be concentrated along the bends, so that's the place to begin. You can locate these on a map and then pick them out easily with a depth sounder. Marker buoys will help you get the picture in a hurry.

Whether you select a U bend or S bend, the first thing to remember is that the fish will normally be on the outside bends. That's where the channel

cut through, and this is part of a fish's behavior pattern if the channel weren't impounded (see Illustrations 6 and 7). If there is any cover, such as brush, on these outside bends, you can bet the fish will stay right there. If the banks are seemingly barren but there is cover a short distance away, the bass may trade back and forth from the cover to the channel.

The tighter the U or the S bend, the better the fishing should be. An ox bow can also be an effective place, but remember that the fish are seldom in the middle of the bend, but rather on either side of the middle. The more you know about a lake, the easier it is to find these places. If there is no cover nearby, the bass could be in the creek channel, using the submerged banks or bluffs as protection against the sun. These banks create the shadow for them, and the fish remain in the darker portion.

Another excellent place is a creek saddle, which is similar to a U bend except that the middle of the sides turn inward. They are really two outside bends that almost touch and the fish should be between the two. Saddles are difficult to find, but they are extremely productive and worth the effort to locate. You should fish the area between the two channel segments thoroughly (see Illustration 8).

When you are fortunate enough to find a saddle formed by two creeks running close together, you can start the victory celebration, because you've uncovered the greatest of all bass hangouts. When we look at a map for the first time, this is the object of our initial scanning. If the lake has two creeks that run parallel or seem to angle toward each other, we try to pinpoint this spot. It is productive nearly all the time and it is worth any effort involved to find it (see Illustration 9).

You'll benefit from the flow of two separate bass populations—those that use one creek and those that use the other as a highway to move back and

6 CREEK U BENDS

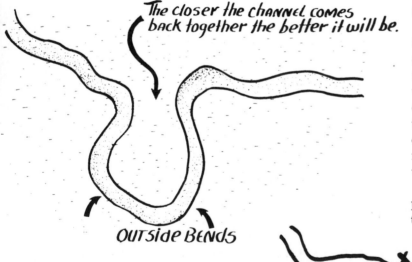

The closer the channel comes back together the better it will be.

OutSide BENdS

7 CREEK S BENDS

8 CREEK SADDLE

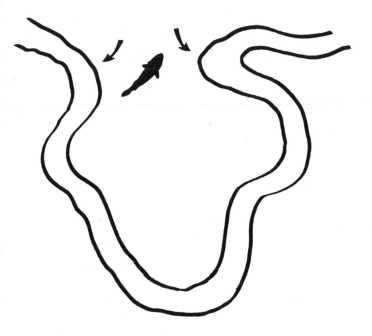

forth. From a fishing standpoint, you would work the area between the two creeks first; then, if for some reason that didn't produce, you might try the creek channels on the outside bends. When you find this type of structure, mark it well in your mind and notebook because you're going to want to come back to it time and time again.

Another place to find schooling bass is near the junction of two creeks (Illustration 10). Usually the outside bends (marked A and B) are best. They will probably run along bluffs, while the shoal

(marked C) is sometimes good if the depth is correct. In most cases, the shoal will be the deepest part and may hold fish if there is a drop-off on it or if the outside bends near the bluffs are too shallow or the temperature is not suitable.

Before the lake was impounded, the flow of current in the creek cut into the outside banks when the creek turned, forming a shoal opposite the bluff. The bluff should have a sharper drop-off from the surface, but the bluff will also be shallower than the shoal.

When both banks of a creek channel are about the same and you don't have a bluff and shoal arrangement, the fish could be on either side. Your clue in this case is the amount of cover and secondary structure. Whichever side has more to offer the fish is the one the fish will be on—so study it carefully and you should come up with the answer.

If a slough, creek, or river channel runs through flat country such as under a lowland-type lake, long, flat points extending out will hold the fish.

We talked earlier about creek mouths and running springs, but it is worth alerting you again to their productivity, especially during certain times of the year. The key is to recognize that a flowing creek or spring will have a different water temperature from the water in the lake it enters. This means that the water near it will be warmer in winter and early spring, but cooler in late summer and early fall. Running water also produces oxygen, and this can sometimes draw fish into the area. Remember that running water indicates a temperature difference and an oxygen difference.

9 A TWO-CREEK SADDLE

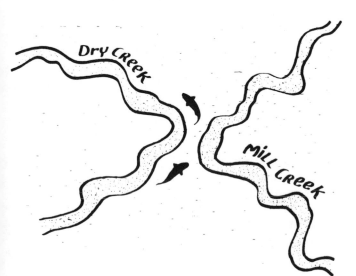

10 CREEK JUNCTIONS

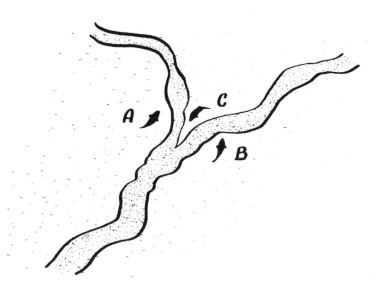

STANDING TIMBER

Standing timber is inviting structure, and it can keep the average angler busy all day just casting at the base of every tree or between the trees. To fish it properly, however, and make the most of the time available, you should have some type of plan based on experience. The most productive areas of standing timber would be near a creek channel. This channel may be along the edge of the timber or right in the thick of it, but you know you've found a highway, and if bass are moving that's the route they are going to take—and that's probably the route they'll use to leave the timber, so you can bet they'll be close by.

Look at Illustration 11 and refer to it as we point out some of our favorite spots when fishing timber. We would probably make our first stop right where the channel enters the timber (Spot A) if the depth is correct. Otherwise, we would pass it up and move down to the first bend inside the timber (Spot B). Spot B would be good if the bass were feeding along the timber edges. If the first bend is too far into the timber, you may want to pass it up.

11 KEY SPOTS IN STANDING TIMBER

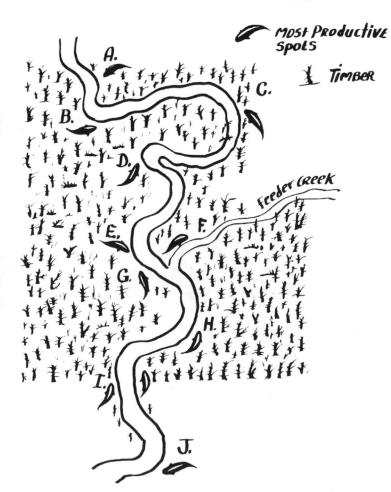

Spot C is very similar to Spot B, except that you have a U bend very close to the edge of the timber. Bass working this sector would most likely be right on the edge of the timber. If you don't find fish at Spot C, move on to Spot D, which is a very sharp U bend. We know from our experience with creek channels that a sharp U bend is usually a prime spot, and it would be worth checking out this part of the timber. Remember that bass would follow their normal pattern and probably stay on the outside of the U bend.

As we move down the creek channel, we find Spot E, which is an open U bend. Bass may use this as a holding place for a short time as they move back and forth between the creek junction at Spot F and the sharp U bend at Spot D. It's always worth a cast or two at the junction of two creeks, and Spot F would get that type of treatment before we moved down to Spot H. Spot G, of course, is the other side of the U bend that contains Spot E.

If you've followed us so far, you may want to make a stop at Spot H and fish the outside of that bend in the creek channel. This could be a holding point for bass, but it depends on depth and other factors. It won't take long to find out if the bass are using it.

Finally, the point where the channel comes out of the timber can also be excellent (Spot I), particularly if there is a good bend close by in open water (Spot J). Early in the morning and late in the afternoon the bass could be at Spot I, en route to the outside bend at Spot J providing Spot J is only fifty or one hundred yards away from the timber. We've seen bass follow this pattern time and time again.

Another very productive type of terrain in timber is the hump (see Illustration 13). Bass will move in on top of it and take up station on this rise above the lake floor. If the hump has a sharp drop-off, you can expect to find fish very close to that drop-off, but if it is just a high sloping area, the bass could be anywhere. Of course, they will seek the correct depth, and a good place to fish is near the heaviest cover on the hump.

The quickest way to find humps in the timber line is to look at the standing timber. If the growth is relatively the same age, simply look for trees that are standing higher than the others; chances are they appear higher because the lake bottom is higher—and that means a hump. It's not always true, but it can save a lot of time.

In young timber, it may be hard to notice a difference in height among the trees, yet your map

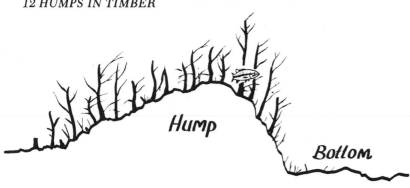

Hump

Bottom

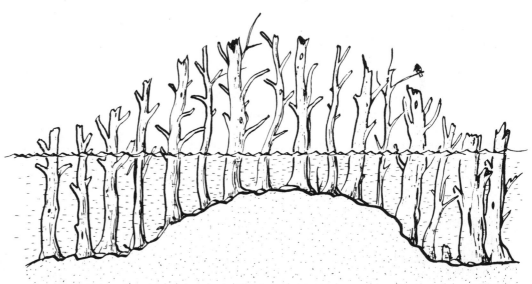

13 HIGHER TREETOPS MAY INDICATE HUMPS

could show a high spot in that area. That means that you're going to have to check the area out with your depth sounder and find the hump. Don't forget to mark it with buoys at least the first time and you can get an idea of the physical layout of the hump.

When you're fishing timber, you should be alert to the fact that bass often show a preference for one type of tree or bush over the others. We've seen it happen time and again. With all the different species of trees in a block, the bass will hang out at the base of cedars, pines, ironwood, sycamores, fruit trees, or something else. We can only speculate that the tree type they select grows in certain soil or gives them some favorable type of cover. The important consideration, however, is to be aware that this happens and identify the tree the moment you catch a fish. If the next fish comes from the same species of tree, then concentrate on that species right away and pass up the other trees.

ROADS, CULVERTS, AND OTHER FEATURES

Anytime man has a hand in creating an impoundment or reservoir, it is generally in an area that was formerly inhabited and that means that there will be roads, foundations of houses, old cemeteries, and other forms of unusual structure. All these places can hold fish and they are usually worth investigating.

Before the landscape was flooded, for example, the cemetery was moved to another location, but no one took the time to fill in the open graves. The cemetery might have been on a hillside and the open holes provide a sanctuary for bass, giving them plenty of cover and a lot of shade. Need we suggest more?

Roadbeds seem to fascinate bass and, for a reason that we can't truly explain, bass will move over the roadbed and feed. In fishing a roadbed, it

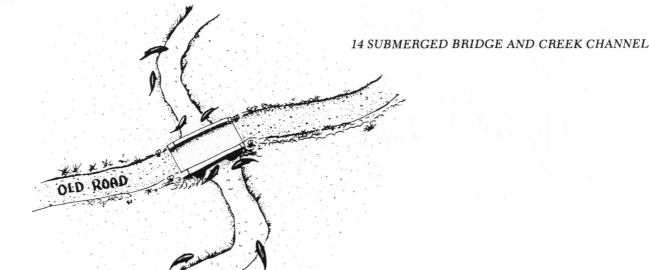

OLD ROAD

▲ MOSt PRODUCtIVE SPOtS

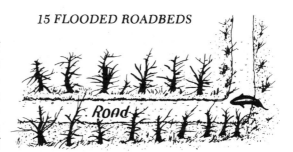

15 FLOODED ROADBEDS

Road

Ditch

Road

is always best to look for an unusual feature: if there's a dip in the road, the bass might be right there; or they could be along a curve. When the road crosses a creek channel, there's a culvert under the road and this can be a key area. If the cover is the same on either side, you'll have to scout both sides for fish; but if there is a patch of brush on one side and nothing on the other, figure that the bass are in the cover and work that area first.

If the creek channel is wide enough, you know that the road would span it with a bridge rather than a culvert. The bridge may or may not be left standing, but the supports certainly will be there and this is good structure to fish. Work the four corners where road and bridge supports meet (Illustration 14) and check nearby bends in the creek channel both upstream and downstream. The fish could move into the bridge area at times and spend part of the day at the bends.

Drive along most country roads and there is a drainage ditch on at least one side and probably on both sides. These ditches can be great bass habitat, especially if they are filled with brush. The place to explore the roadbed and the ditches is wherever the road varies from its straight path. As we suggested a moment ago, look for dips or depressions or any spot where the road curves, and check that out first (Illustration 15).

By this time, you should be well aware that you must search for the unusual aspects of structure. Stay alert to differences from the norm and then concentrate on these areas. It is impossible to out-

line every type of structure in detail, but we do hope that the examples we have provided will show you the things we look for when we are on the water. It won't be long before you start to develop your own patterns and theories. Just remember to record your spots and your ideas so that you have a constant source of reference for review.

SUSPENDED BASS

Unless there is a current, it takes no more physical effort for a bass to sit a few inches off the bottom in twenty feet of water than it does for the same fish

FLOOR OF LAKE

to suspend in treetops at the twenty-foot level over perhaps sixty feet of water. Finding suspended bass is another matter. There's no other way to describe it except to note that it is an extremely difficult task.

In many cases, suspended bass are located by accident and that is probably as good a way as any. However, there are some clues that can be gleaned and we would like to direct your attention to them. We also reemphasize the need to hone your powers of observation and think through the problem. You must be alert to any eventuality in bass fishing and recognize it as soon as it happens.

If you've fished objects along the shoreline and structure in deeper water without catching any fish, you might suspect that some of the bass in that lake may be suspended at an intermediate level. If you're lucky, you may pick some fish up on your depth sounder, but don't count on it. When this happens, we may still fish those creek bed points, but we'll vary the technique somewhat to check for suspended bass. Instead of fishing at or near the bottom, we'll employ the countdown method and try different levels. We'll also try several lures that work in more places than just on the bottom.

Trollers can provide an excellent clue to suspended bass. If they start taking fish, you can surmise that the fish are out in the main part of the lake and that they are suspended. Work the creek bed points from both angles. Hold the boat off the point and cast in toward it, using fan casts to cover the area. Try to get the lure at various depths. Then try moving in close to shore and working out, fishing deeper and deeper. The mouths of coves are another good spot when you have an idea bass are suspending. Don't forget to try baits

that will sink, such as a tailspin, spinnerbait, spoon, and swimming bait. Count down on each cast so you know where the lure was if you should get a strike.

Bass love to suspend in timber, and show a marked preference for cedars and sometimes pines. Cedars and pines usually hold most of their limbs and provide more cover for fish than other species of trees. The bass can stay in the treetops and still enjoy the protective cover they seek (see Illustration 16).

Largemouths are particularly prone to suspend during the winter months when the water is cold. They'll pack tightly in the schools and will often go very, very deep in winter, but they can still be caught. As a rule, they will bunch together on the bottom and also suspend at the same depth (see Illustration 17).

Bass are likekly to suspend more in clear water than in murky or dingy water, and in some lakes may be in treetops at forty-five or fifty feet during the chilly months. One cloudy day in the winter, we were busily fishing Toledo Bend, which has always been a good lake for suspended bass. The area we selected had a ledge or high spot in twenty-five feet of water, and we were catching bass in the three- to five-pound class using structure spoons and jig-and-eels. The drop-off was pronounced and the depth plummeted sharply from twenty-five to forty-five feet. Using our depth finder as a guide, we hung over the drop-off, but very close to it. There were trees along this edge in forty-five feet of water, and we finally started to ease up to a tree and drop either the structure spoon or the jig alongside the base of the tree.

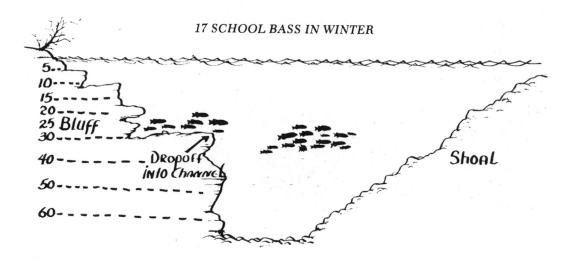

When the lure hit bottom, we would jig it up a foot or two and let it fall right back to the lake floor. Using this method, we happened on a good school of fish. Sometimes they would hit the lure on the first lift and other times on the fourth or fifth lift. Those fish had the trees surrounded at the bottom of the lake in forty-five feet of water on a cloudy day.

You can bet we went right back there the next day and worked the base of each tree. Nothing happened. Maybe the bass were along the ledge, so we worked the entire length of that structure without a hit. Something was different today and we had to find the secret. Then we remembered that bass will often move close to the surface in timber on a winter day when the sun is bright. They're seeking a little added warmth from the sunlight. The sun was shining brightly.

After turning the boat around and repositioning ourselves over the same spot, we quickly dropped the lure to the bottom and jigged it a few times. No

fish. We then took five turns on the reel and jigged again. Still no fish. We continued doing a countdown in reverse by lifting the lure about five feet each time. Finally, when the lure was about fifteen feet below the surface, the rod doubled over in that welcome and unmistakable arc. We had found the fish and they had moved up to take advantage of the warming rays of the sun. After that, we could use the countdown method to drop a lure to the fifteen-foot level and the fish would hit.

It has been our practice over the years to check for suspended fish by dropping a lure to the bottom and jigging it up in stages. This is very similar to the technique employed by fishermen who are trying to locate suspended schools of crappies. More important, before we leave an area for greener pastures, we'll usually steal a moment to try that type of retrieve once or twice. When it works, you've found the mother lode.

Understanding Shorelines

Traditionally, bass fishing has been a shoreline affair, and even the deepwater structure advocates make occasional sorties among the stumps, lily pads, fallen trees, and pockets in the banks. There's something exciting about working along the bank. Perhaps it's the constant anticipation that the dark little notch between the cypress tree and that stump next to it will produce a lunker bass. Maybe it's just the pleasure and solitude of being close to shore, listening to the many sounds, and quickening to the movement of birds and animals.

Shoreline fishing is a way of life in the northern

part of the United States and it is also practiced extensively in the South. The original techniques, however, have been modified slightly, and anglers are now attempting to turn experience into a more scientific approach. Casting is not as haphazard as it once was, and there's a way to fish each type of object.

Pinpoint accuracy is especially important for this type of fishing. Being able to drop a lure exactly where you want it to land is part of the fun and excitement of fishing the banks—and it will produce more fish for you in the long run. Nothing is more frustrating to a shoreline fisherman than the constant need to ease into the bushes to release a lure that managed to impale itself on an overhanging limb.

READING THE BANK

The new breed of shoreline fisherman wants to have the total picture at all times. He is vitally concerned with structure along the bank and he knows the depth at which his lure is working. If, for example, a bass crashes a bait halfway between the shore and the boat, he immediately surmises that the fish are deeper and are coming topside to catch that bait. This type of alertness is crucial to successful shoreline fishing and it goes well beyond varying the retrieve or changing lures.

The major concept of shoreline fishing is that the configuration of the visible bank and ground behind the bank does not stop at the water's edge. It really doesn't matter whether you are fishing a man-made impoundment or plying along on a natural lake; the lake floor should be a continuation of the surrounding area. As you cruise along the shoreline, look at it closely. If you see a ridge shoulder its way across a field and bow down toward the shoreline, you can assume that it continues under the surface of the water.

There might be a gully running between two "sheepbacks" and there is every indication that the gully will continue. If the bank is rocky, the rocks should also be under water. Mud shorelines usually mean mud beneath the surface. Remember we suggested that you study fields and countryside as you drive along in your car; when you do this, select an imaginary water level and then try to picture how the land would appear below that level.

Reading the shoreline will give you a good idea of what you can expect right up to the bank and it will provide the clues to the type of structure dropping off into the deeper portions of the lake. As you fish the shoreline, you must continue to search for irregular features. They may be the edge of a tree line, the beginning of a bluff, a place where a mudbank ends and gravel begins, or anything else where a change takes place. Bass like to hang out along marginal territory where the land is changing.

THE BOTTOM

Lake bottoms are formed from a variety of materials that include mud, sand, clay, rock, gravel, grass, and even boulders. In most lakes, bottom materials change as you travel the shoreline and they generally reflect the adjacent terrain. Look at the bank and you have a fair picture of the bottom structure. If the bank is sandy, the sand should extend into the water; and if there is small rock or gravel, the same material will be on the lake floor.

The majority of shorelines have transitional zones where mud might change to sand or gravel and rock might ease into a clay bottom. It's easy for anglers to let these changes pass unnoticed or to disregard them, but they can be prime fish habitat (Illustration 18). Bass love to lie along the transitional zone. They may feed on minnows, crawfish, and water lizards on a pebble bottom and then move just over the border to rest on a bottom formed from large rocks. When you work a shoreline, watch the bottom changes and try to relate them to a pattern. If you have a hit or hook a fish, check immediately to see if the bottom material changes; just glance at the bank and you'll have the answer.

If you do notice that the bottom changes where you hooked your fish, this might be the beginning of a pattern. Move down the shoreline until the

18 CHANGING SHORE LINE

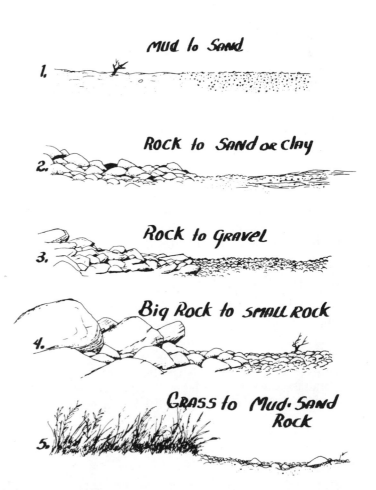

1. Mud to Sand

2. Rock to Sand or Clay

3. Rock to Gravel

4. Big Rock to small Rock

5. Grass to Mud·Sand Rock

same condition exists again. Let's say the bottom changed from sand to grass and you fish another changeover spot and catch a second fish. Don't waste any more time puttering down the shoreline. Move directly to the next area where sand changes to grass or grass changes back to sand and fish there.

THE HOME RANGE TENDENCY

Anglers have disagreed on whether or not largemouth bass exhibit a home range tendency. That is, when the bass move into the shoreline, do they continue to occupy the same relative place repeatedly or do they pick new sections of shoreline at random, based on where they happen to be at the moment? Under the auspices of Southern Illinois University, two scientists studied the bass population in a farm pond in Illinois and came to the conclusion that bass *do* have a home range.

The technique employed was to cover the shoreline in a boat and, using electrical shocking equipment, capture the bass on shoreline cover. The bass were then marked for identification and returned to the water. Over the course of several months, the procedure was repeated a number of times and records kept of where each marked bass was found.

One of the more interesting facts to come from this study was that only 1.2 percent of the bass were on the shoreline at any one time, on the average. That meant that most of the bass population—over 98 percent of it—was in deep water the majority of the time. Recaptures indicated that 96 percent of the fish that did invade the shallows or shoreline were recaptured within three hundred feet of the spot where they were first captured and marked for identification. With some fish, recapture took place three or four times, yet they were always within the same area. After wintering in deep water, the same bass returned to the same segment of shoreline.

FISHING BLUFFS AND LEDGES

There is no single method for fishing bluffs and ledges. Your approach must be varied simply because old Mr. Bucketmouth is so unpredictable at times. The best way to fish a bluff—at least on the initial pass—is to parallel it (Illustration 19). With a series of fan casts and the boat in a parallel

position, you can fish it more thoroughly and faster than by casting into it.

If the ledges extend way out into the lake, there are times when you might want to put the boat right under the bluff and cast outward toward open water. This, of course, will move the lure from deep to shallow. We have seen times when a creek channel shoulders up to a bluff and you could sit beyond the creek channel casting toward the bluff without a strike. Reverse the boat and cast over the creek channel from under the bluff. The fish will hit anything you throw. We mention this because direction of retrieve can be important and you should be aware that if the retrieve doesn't produce fish from one direction, it could do the job from the opposite direction.

There are other instances when the only way you're going to catch fish on a bluff is to cast directly into it and work the lure from ledge to ledge (Illustration 20). Walking a lure down the ledges takes a certain amount of practice and skill; if you lift your rod tip too much, the lure will probably move too far and miss a few ledges in between. The trick is to move the lure only a few inches and let it drop a foot or two to the next ledge. If you pulled the lure a couple of feet, it might fall ten feet before striking a ledge and you would pass up all the water between the two.

It is somewhat easier to fish the ledges at a 45° angle or by keeping the boat parallel. Make a cast and allow enough line for the jig to fall on the ledge, but follow the free fall of the lure with your rod tip. Remember, there could be suspended bass right here, and unless you watch the line you may never realize a fish picked up the lure. When the lure hits the ledge, flick the rod tip slightly and drop the lure to the next ledge. Continue the same procedure as you walk the lure down the steps.

By keeping the boat parallel to the ledges, you can also cast down one ledge and retrieve, then work the next ledge, and so forth; or you can walk the lure down the ledges on a 45° angle. If you do fish directly into the ledges, you must be careful that you don't drag the lure back to the boat without letting it fall to each successive level. Bouncing a jig-and-eel from ledge to ledge is not

19 PARALLELING A BLUFF

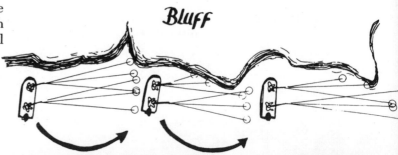

20 BOUNCING A LURE DOWN A LEDGE

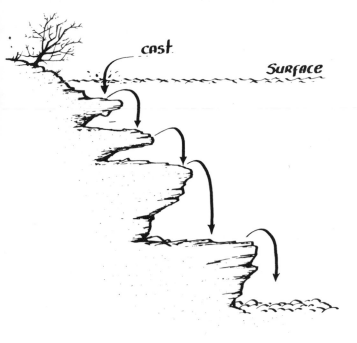

cast

Surface

the fastest fishing method ever devised, but it is an extremely effective one and a technique that could find bass for you at any level.

SHADE

Almost every bass angler learns early in the game that bass are constantly seeking cover, and the best cover we can recommend is subdued light. For one thing, bright light seems to bother their eyes; for another, shade offers protection from predators and camouflage when feeding. A bass can hang in a shady area and gaze into a brightly lit area as if the fish were peering into a well-lit room on a dark night.

Most fishermen are visually oriented and are much more comfortable and far more confident when they can see their target. Shade offers this approach to fishing. We use the term shade, but we also refer to shadow as well. Even on a cloudy day, there can be an almost imperceptible shadow coming from a bluff, tree, or rock on shore or in the water. As long as the spot you select for your next cast is a bit darker than the surrounding water, there could be fish in that spot. Make it a rule never to pass up shade. It's worth at least a couple of casts to satisfy your curiosity and perhaps that of the bass as well.

The clearer the lake, the more important shade and shadows can be. Naturally they will change as the sun swings around during the day. The fish will continue to reorient their position as the shadow line moves. Be alert to shadows, such as those from a tree or bluff, cast far out from the shoreline (Illustration 21). We have seen times when you could cast to the base of a cypress tree and hook a bass; then turn around and toss the lure into open water where the shade from that same tree offers cover. Another bass would be in the shaded patch almost fifty feet from shore.

DOCKS AND PIERS

The most noticeable feature on any shoreline is a dock or pier. In fact, it is so obvious that most anglers either overlook it or pass it up. Docks offer shade and cover, and, for that reason, you'll almost always find schools of baitfish patrolling the area, darting in and out among the supports or simply

21 SHORELINE SHADOWS

Shadow side

SUN

The area around a dam is often a favorite haunt of the bait fisherman, but it can also be productive for the artificial lure enthusiast. The key is to look at the dam as shoreline structure, taking maximum advantage of shadows, water flow (if there is any), channels, cuts, sloughs, and the edges where the dam meets the shoreline.

You can alternate your fishing from shallow to deep and deep to shallow. If the water channel cuts an edge along a shoal, you may want to parallel it and fan cast. When water if being pulled through the dam, baitfish are sometimes taken along for the ride or, at least, they become disoriented in the flow of water. Bass could be on the prowl just out of the main current, picking off the hapless minnows as they struggle against the water flow. Moving water also carries more oxygen and this could be an important consideration during the warm months when oxygen content could become critical.

Ripraps are rock walls that help to hold back the water on the sides of a dam or where a bridge might cross the impoundment. They are designed to resist erosion and when these walls were constructed, the basic material came from the lake bottom. That means that there will be a trough or a drop-off nearby.

You can fish a riprap in any one of three ways. The most common approach is to hang over the deeper water and cast the lure into the riprap. If you prefer this method, try some casts at a 45° angle as well as straight in to the target. You may also want to parallel the riprap, casting up and down. Be particularly alert to the corners of the riprap where it joins the normal shoreline. If all else fails, you could get out of the boat and walk along the riprap, casting on a 45° angle and straight out into the deeper water. Very often a riprap wall can be fished better from shore than from a boat.

When you fish this type of structure, you should be alert to other forms of substructure. Perhaps you find a break in the wall or a minor slide where some rocks fell into the water. Maybe it's a log or a stump or simply a large rock. Whatever the substructure, it's worth your time because, if fish are along the wall, they should be near the substructure.

STUMPS

Of all the objects in the water, none seem to arouse the confidence of a bass fisherman more than an

under the floating docks. No one need tell you that where you find food and cover, you find bass. If it is a big dock that is used constantly, the bass might move off during the daytime when there is a lot of traffic, but they could be on hand at daybreak before any commotion begins or late in the afternoon when the last boat is tied up for the night.

Bass can be on any side of a dock or pier, but they will be back in the shade. At times they might limit their activities to the shady side (Illustration 22) or they could be on the bright side but back under the dock. If your experience is similar to ours, you'll find these docks and piers best in the fall of the year. We can't tell you why, but we know we catch more fish from this type of shoreline structure when the leaves start to turn.

If you don't limit your bass fishing simply to casting the shoreline, there's one other aspect of docks and piers that you should keep in mind. Study a contour map of the marina and dock sites. If there is a creek channel nearby or a deep hole, the bass might stay there during most of the day, moving into the dock area at dawn and again at dusk. It's worth a try to locate deep structure near a dock. Most anglers are too busy heading for the other end of the lake.

Launching ramps are another place frequently passed up. Bass will sometimes move right up on the concrete ramp or they could stay right along the edges. Most ramps drop off into relatively deep water, so the escape routes are right there.

In fishing docks, piers, or ramps, you can use almost any type of lure that you would normally fish; and you'll soon learn that docks that have brush piled under them or nearby are better choices.

exciting-looking stump. For some reason, we all associate largemouths with stumps. On the other hand, some stumps can be more productive than others. As an example, a stump that sits on the edge of a drop-off will usually be better than a stump way back up in the shallows, if the depth is correct. When we say *usually* better, we mean on a consistent basis rather than a single experience.

Remember that the shady side of an object is normally better than the brighter side. Therefore, your first cast should always explore the shady side. At one time, bass fishermen always tried to drop a lure right on the object they were fishing. If the object was a stump, they would try to hit the stump on the cast and let the lure fall alongside. By doing this, they passed up a lot of productive water behind and alongside the object, and the sound of a lure falling over the head of a bass could spook the fish into deep water (Illustration 23).

We prefer to make our first cast on the side and beyond the object. Sometimes a bass won't be right on the object, but near it. By casting in this manner, we can cover the back, side, and the front with a single cast. Once the lure passes the object and is well on its way toward the boat, you might as well crank it in and cast again. Big bass will seldom follow a lure any distance. If they want your offering, they'll hit it as it comes by.

You can fish a variety of lures around stumps. Topwater, spinnerbaits, worms, jig-and-eels, swimming lures, and diving lures can all be good choices. You're going to have to experiment to find out which ones are best for you. Keep in mind

23 FISHING A STUMP

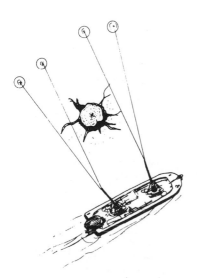

that you may have to vary the retrieve to catch fish. We have seen times when you can cast a spinnerbait past a stump and buzz it by quickly; a bass would nail it before it even reached the stump. The next day in the same area the bass wouldn't hit a spinnerbait unless you buzzed it up to the stump, stopped the lure dead, and let it fall. They would have it in their mouth before it dropped a foot.

The second cast around a stump should still be beyond it, but the lure should brush the object as it passes. There's no guarantee that a bass will hit your lure on the first or second cast, even if the fish is right there. You may have to cast six or eight times before you get a strike, and change lures in the process. That's bass fishing and there is no shortcut to success.

TREES

Some old-timer once theorized that "if you ain't hangin', you ain't fishin'." When he uttered those immortal words, he must have been talking about treetops, because it is easy to hang up in this type of structure. If trees are left standing, the branches may protrude above the surface or they could be just under the surface. The way we prefer to work a treetop is from the branches to the trunk (Illustration 24).

Start with a spinnerbait and buzz it through the branches. You know, of course, that those trees with more branches and limbs offer better cover for bass and should be fished first. After you've tried the spinnerbait across the top, you could let it drop in the branches and work it carefully. Another choice would be to make a commotion with a topwater bait around the edges of the branches and then toss a worm into the middle of the limbs, letting it fall around the cover. Considerations include the time of year, clarity of the water, depth of the tree, preferred temperature, and similar factors. It's almost impossible to list all the variables, but you know from an earlier section that, on a sunny day in the winter, the bass could be right up near the top of the tree.

If the tree is under water, you might want to get the boat right over the top and use a structure spoon, if the time of the year is right. Or, you could choose a fall bait and work it right down around the base of the tree. There's no single formula, but we hope these suggestions will trigger ideas of your own.

Shallow-water, light-tackle saltwater fishermen

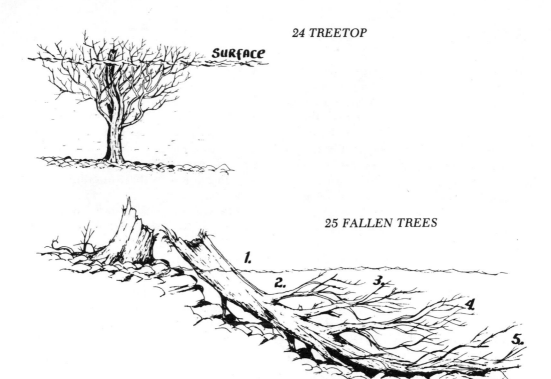

24 TREETOP

25 FALLEN TREES

learned the value of polarized sunglasses a long time ago. They make quite a difference in looking through the surface of the water and they can be invaluable in spotting objects below the surface. They are not miracle glasses, but rather a type of glass that eliminates surface glare, enabling you to see better. Many models are inexpensive and they would be worth a try.

Frequently, a tree blows down in a storm or rots out and comes crashing into the water. All that remains on the bank or in the shallows is a stump and a short end of the tree base (Illustration 25). The spot looks perfect and it probably is. Most fishermen will immediately begin to cast around the stump and the portion of the tree protruding above the surface, but, for some reason, the average angler will totally ignore the fact that the rest of that tree is probably under the surface. The part of the tree extending above the surface can give you an idea of the underwater terrain. If it seems to stand almost straight up (upside down), you know that there is a major drop-off. If the log appears to lie flat, you'll probably see the branches at the other end and know that a drop-off isn't present.

It's not always easy to tell if there are limbs and branches left on the deep end of the tree, but it is certainly worth investigating. There are several different ways that this structure can be fished. If you are using a topwater bait, start a series of fan casts from the stump and stub of the tree across the area where the rest of the tree should lie. Then switch to a spinnerbait and follow the same series of casts, allowing the lure to fall deeper on each succeeding cast (from the shallow end to the deep end). You might also try a jig-and-eel or a worm and toss it back into the section of the tree that has branches.

Once you know that a particular blowdown has branches, a better way of fishing it is to position the boat out in deep water and fan cast along the length of the tree. The idea is to cast into the tree and retrieve in the direction the branches point. By doing this, you will minimize the chances of hanging up.

If the tree plummets almost straight down, you may want to electric motor over it and use a structure spoon or jig-and-eel to probe the bottom branches. Each tree should be analyzed individually and fished according to time of year and the way it lies in the water.

STICKUPS

Stickups don't provide very much cover for a bass, but they are significant structure in the spring of the year when the bass move into the shallows to spawn. At that time, the fish are willing to sacrifice habit and ignore cover. One reason is that bass require sunlight in spawning, at least to keep the water warm so the eggs will hatch in the normal length of time. Rather than just stay out in the

26 STICKUPS

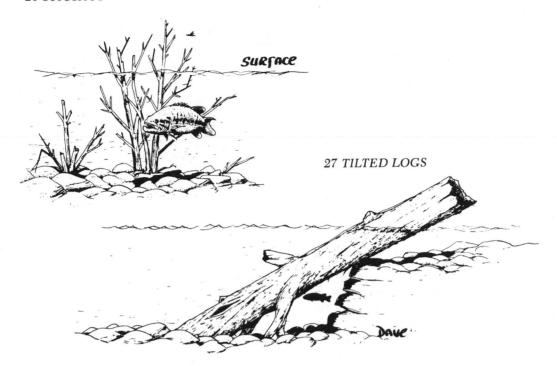

SURFACE

27 TILTED LOGS

DAVE

open, the bass will shoulder up to a stickup. Stickups on hard bottoms such as sand or gravel are usually the most productive.

A plastic worm or a spinnerbait is relatively hang proof and is an excellent choice for this type of fishing. The best way to cover a stickup is by casting to the left side, right side, and down the middle. If a bass is nearby, the lure will be seen (Illustration 26).

Since stickups are in relatively shallow water, a quiet approach is necessary; any noise from a motor or noise that is transmitted through the hull will chase the fish into deeper water. However, since the fish are either spawning or guarding the nest when they are among the stickups, they are very aggressive and will come back very quickly.

TILTED LOGS

Anytime you see a log in open water with one end reaching above the surface, you can assume that the log is waterlogged on the larger end and has floated up against a ledge or drop-off. It's a good visual clue to structure and certainly worth investigating (Illustration 27). The fish may be near the log, or other parts of the drop-off could be even more productive.

To fish a tilted log, you can apply about the same approach as you would use on a fallen tree. The log may or may not have limbs left on it, but you can determine this by working a lure through the

deeper portion. If there are limbs, you'll feel a lure brush by. And you could use a structure spoon in this type of situation.

LILY PADS

The words "bass" and "lily pads" are almost synonymous. From the time a youngster begins his fishing career, he learns that bass hang out around the lily pads waiting for a minnow, frog, or crawfish to happen by. Lily-pad fishing requires a lot of patience because there are usually large areas of pads and it takes time to find the fish. Pads grow in the shallows, which makes the area somewhat sensitive and dictates a quiet approach.

Take a look at Illustration 28. We have created a typical lily-pad setup, and experience has shown that there are certain areas among the pads more prone to hold fish than are other areas. Concentrate your fishing on these key spots and then move on to the next set of pads. If you happen to establish a pattern in the pads, then you would naturally fish your pattern in every set of pads you could find.

You already know that anytime there is a change in the shoreline or the bottom material changes, you could find bass. The same theory holds true when lily pads are present. There could be fish at Spots 1 and 10, where the pads start and where they stop. Try the corners and then move out to the first major point indicated as Spot 2. Spot 8 would

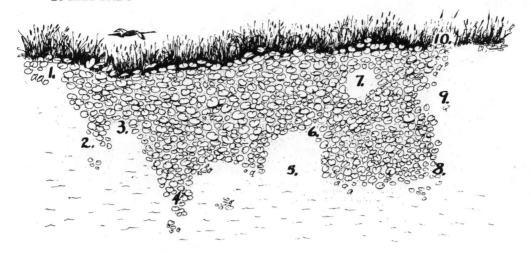

be the first point if you approached the pads from the other direction and could be equally good, regardless of whether you were fishing the shoreline from right to left or left to right.

When you find small pockets reaching back among the pads, it can produce a fish or two and is worth a few casts. Spot 3 is typical of this type of structure among lily pads. One or two points that extend farthest into the lake might be good (Spot 4). Work either side of the point and back into those pads.

When you've found a pocket going back into the pads from the outer edge, give it a good working over. Spot 5 shows this type of pocket, and it should be fished at the points on either side as well as the mouth. Then you can move into the pocket and fish it. Any tiny offshoots such as Spot 6 warrant a cast or two.

Many assortments of lily pads have small circular openings completely surrounded by pads. It's tough to get a fish out of this type of real estate, but you can certainly get them to hit. Cast back and across these openings and work the lure through them.

Finally, don't forget to consider the direction of the sun. Indentations on the shady side such as Spot 9 could harbor a fish. You can easily spend most of the day around a set of pads, but the better approach is to concentrate on the highlights and high spots and then move on to different structure or another set of pads.

PART TWO

BASSING

Now it's time to get on the water and start fishing.

In the arcane world of lure selection, knowing the right bait to use at any particular time is about as useful as knowing how Catfish Hunter holds the ball for a down and in. You still have to make the thing go. That's why our contributors have concentrated so heavily on the techniques of actually fishing the lures.

I hope you won't be surprised or put off by the occasional contradictions and disagreements that surface in this section. As you read on, and then fish on, you'll take sides yourself as you learn what's right for you.

Prejudices toward certain basic baits run high. My old buddy Homer Circle, for instance, considers his old favorites downright unfriendly when they fail to get the job done for him, which isn't often by the way. But when a bait does hit a dry run, Homer will squint at it like he's looking at a roach, reach for his clippers and say, "Sorry, friend, but you've let me down. Got to send you back to that dark old tackle box."

My favorite story on lure selection is a true one. A few years ago one of our largest sporting goods manufacturers hosted the head buyer for a huge discount chain to some Canadian smallmouth fishing. The buyer was an absolute bass-fishing fanatic, and naturally the hosts arranged for Mr. Big to have the best Indian guide and boat. Risking a double hernia, the buyer deposited one of the largest tackle boxes made into the bottom of the boat. The buyer regarded the guide with interest. He thought the elderly guide's face, brown as pine spills and deeply lined from the lash of sun and weather, showed a look of eagles and oneness with nature. Beaming proudly, he began opening the tackle box. Layer after layer of bright lures gleamed in the sun as the trays were extended. Finally he looked into the stoic face of the Indian and said: "All right, Chief. What will it be?"

Without changing expression, the Indian shook his head and said, "No good! Close up!" From his mackinaw, he retrieved a battered white jig festooned with half a purple worm. He held it out.

The buyer did not laugh.

There was no sale.

7

Plastic Worm Fishing
A Complete Guide to Bass Fishing's Most Deadly Weapon

JERRY GIBBS with contributions by
**BILL DANCE, PAUL CHAMBLEE, AL LINDNER,
TOM MANN, STAN SLOAN, LAMAR UNDERWOOD**

The other day my black Lab, Gypsy, came snorting into the house, wet from rain, holding an eight-inch plastic worm in her mouth. The worm was still in pretty good shape, which surprised me because Gypsy likes to eat soft plastic. As I took the lure from her I began thinking that we've pretty much come full circle in the use of these snaky critters.

Not long ago anybody who'd play a worm on the surface was considered a real tyro. Now that method is back in style again, sometimes. I recalled that it was the way I first started catching fish on the plastics, a long time ago.

It was a hot spring day, and I was pushing along an overgrown path around a farm pond in Sussex County, New Jersey. A lot of big bass were in that pond.

A snoozing garter snake that I disturbed by the path made me think of the plastic worms so long ignored in the bottom of my kit. The last time I had tried one I had hooked it through the middle (the way I sometimes hook real worms), plopped it in, and jiggled it around, feeling a little foolish. It was the color of a bruised peach, and after catching nothing with it I had thrown it away because of the dreadful things the unwrapped plastic worms did to the rest of my tackle.

I had some more worms (well wrapped) in my box, and after seeing the snake I decided to try one.

I hooked the worm at the head (the other way I fish real crawlers), worked it in the shallows, liked its sneaky wiggle, and waded out. Those early worms sank slowly, but if you started retrieving immediately they would ride just under the surface, twisting like a whirligig. I used no weight.

After I'd made three casts out into the midpond weeds, my line was twisting so badly that I thought I'd better put on a swivel. Also, the hook stuck out at the side of the worm and was picking up muck. I tried one more cast. I brought the lure out of the salad patch, and suddenly it stopped in a way that couldn't be weeds. I set the hook hard. The fish tore around out there, but I eventually got him in—a largemouth with a snout full of weeds and that bruised-peach-color worm hanging from his jaw.

Eureka! More fish followed until my line wouldn't have any more of it.

The addition of a barrel swivel about 15 inches in front of the worm was my first real improvement on the rig. As the weeks passed I began fooling with large split shot to get the plastics down faster when bass wouldn't hit on top.

Early Worms: Improvements and Problems

In the late 1940s and early 1950s, real progress was made in rigging plastic worms. The worms were harder then, and available only in a few solid colors. I learned to bury my hook in the side of a worm to keep it weedless. Then I really started losing fish. I found that I had to sock them hard in order to get the hook through the balled-up wad the fish made of my worm. That hard yank required heavier tackle, so I went back to plug-casting gear and found that I couldn't cast far enough without more weight.

Eventually I started using a bank-type sinker rigged ahead of my swivel. I put on a bigger swivel to prevent the sinker from sliding down to the worm. In effect, I had a clunky version of the bullet-head Texas rig I use today.

The sliding-sinker rig allowed the bass to suck up my worm and start moving away without feeling any resistance. I would usually let them go a little before I struck. Sometimes I lost no fish that way. Other times I had to set my hook as soon as I felt a tap. It's the same today. I'm convinced that anybody who *always* lets bass run with the worm a little or *always* hits them right away is going to miss plenty of strikes. It depends on how the fish are taking.

Breakthroughs in the manufacture of soft plastic worms and the development of superior techniques for fishing them have led to more bass-fishing action than any other factor. Glen Lau

During those early years I hooked my plastic worms any old way around the head, and they went right on spinning like crazy and catching fish. Maybe those Yankee bass were stupid, because when I went South later my Uncle Andy, who lived in West Palm Beach, Florida, told me that I was rigging my worms all wrong.

"See here, Cousin," he said (he always called me Cousin, though I was his nephew-in-law), "you've got to keep these worms from going round like that. You got to keep 'em on the bottom all the time too. It's the only way to catch bigmouths consistently."

I told him that in the North we had smallmouth bass too, and that the spinning worms sometimes worked on them as well as on largemouths. He ignored the comment.

"The way we catch *real* bass down here," said Uncle Andy, "is with the sliding weight snubbed up against the worm nose. Those hooks you use are too small. They got to be 5/0–3/0 minimum—and you don't want 'em straight at the shank. Look here. With a bentup shank the worm lies straighter. Another thing—the point is in direct line with the direction you pull, and you get quicker penetration."

He showed me how to thread the hook point through the worm's nose, work it out the bottom about a half-inch below the head, pull the shank out until the eye is buried, and then twist the hook around and bury the barb in the worm from the bottom. The worm lay straight.

That rig worked fine, and I usually hook worms that way today. Sometimes I push a toothpick through the buried hook eye and clip it flush on either side; or I stick a short piece of flexible wire through the eye, bend the ends around the worm's head, and bury them too. These tricks help keep the eye from tearing through the worm's head. Some of the hooks I now use have either a little barb near the eye or an S-shaped eye that helps do the same thing.

I took Uncle Andy's tactics seriously, and I caught fish. But I didn't forget about my spinning worms. I found that when bass were in shallow water or close to the surface in deeper water they would often hit the spinning worms far better than the bottom-worked baits. I also found that by rigging worms the "wrong way" on bent-shank (central draught) hooks I got a wilder spin than ever.

The way I rig the spinner is to run the hook point through the center of the worm's nose and on down inside the worm three to three-and-one-half inches before pushing it out the bottom. Only the point and maybe one-eighth of an inch more stick out, so you can't turn the hook around to make it weedless. What you have is a worm with a humped back. It spins ferociously.

Before threading the worm this way, I tie sixteen to eighteen inches of monofilament to the hook, slide on a cone-shaped or bullet-shaped slip sinker, and then tie on a good ball-bearing swivel to prevent line twist.

Sometimes with the humpback, as well as with the Texas rig, I keep the worm coming steadily, varying the speed but generally maintaining a medium-slow retrieve. No stop-and-go. Often with the standard, or Texas, slip-sinker rig I give the worm an occasional twitch or hop.

There are other ways to retrieve the standard rig. The ones I often use include: 1) cranking the reel slowly while slowly raising the rod tip, then dropping the rod back without reeling; 2) sweeping the worm off the bottom by raising the rod, then cranking very slowly while lowering the rod; 3) sweeping with the rod, dropping back without cranking, and then crawling or hopping the worm along a bit before sweeping again.

With all methods the key element is keeping the line taut. Allow no slack to occur, ever, or you'll miss pickups.

Softer Worms: The Breakthrough

As I was learning how to fish plastic worms the right way (and the "wrong" way that was still producing fish), the worm makers began to use softer and eventually translucent plastics. Beautiful. The new worms glowed in the proper light. The slightest twitch caused their tails to pulsate. But these worms ripped apart in the brush where the bass hung out. Well, you had to compromise somewhere.

Then somebody got smart again and started attaching the worm to a bare jig hook whose lead head was bent up like a ski. I used the things, which ended up being called jig-'n-eel baits. I skidded them through heavy vegetation on the bottom and through weeds that grew to the surface. They worked. Later I experimented with hair dressing that stuck out around the jig and encircled the nose of the worm. This worked too.

As the worm improved, so did the plastics in tackle boxes. I found that my worms no longer melted and ruined my plastic boxes. We had reached the pinnacle in plastic-worm development, I thought. I could run a worm along the bottom with weight, rig it to spin if I thought my fishing partners wouldn't be offended, or retrieve it without weight a few feet below the surface, its

A worming master in action: Tom Mann works his floater worm along a weedy edge. B.A.S.S.

tail floating high and wagging, its nose down, the whole worm sinking slowly.

But what about those times when a real snake wiggles back in among the lily pads and is picked off by a behemoth bass? How about a plastic worm that would duplicate the situation? I remembered that some true floating worms had been made a while back, but they had gone the way of the Stanley Steamer. Now they are back.

When I worked a floating worm in the lily pads it snaked beautifully, right on top, and in the spring, after their winter fast, the fish gobbled it. The floater, I have found, also works in deeper water with the standard slip sinker. I bring it back a little, let it settle, and then ease up so that the worm begins rising as it pulls line through the sinker. Then I twitch the rod to jerk it down again.

I repeat the same action throughout the retrieve. It's dynamite.

I have also tried using a three-way swivel with a dipsey sinker hanging on six to eight inches of light leader attached to one eye, the worm on twelve to sixteen inches of leader attached to another eye, and the main line attached to the third eye. Where the bottom is very mucky, I use this rig with the floater trailing just over the bottom. If I get hung up, the sinker breaks off, not the rigged worm.

I find that the high floaters have a less-sensitive tail action than some of the very soft slow sinkers. Because of the hundreds of air bubbles impregnated into the floating plastics, they tend to lack that appealing translucence. But at times you need a real floating worm, and now you can get it.

Colors, Scents, Noise: The Guessing Game

I fish worms of many colors, and though most of my warm-weather fishing is done with purple or black—especially in dark water—I don't limit my chances by stubbornly sticking to those favorites. In clearer water I go to a pink or a light-blue worm. In spring a light gray or a light green worm often is successful. I use reds and naturals too, especially in the fall. And in muddy water a yellowish shade sometimes produces. When all else fails, I try the changeable worms that appear as different shades under various light.

Largemouths in clear water respond differently to plastic worms. In diving experiments to observe bass, I watched worms of various colors descend near good bass-holding places. Those bass that were interested would rush over, assume a head-down attitude hovering over the worm, and watch it carefully. If the worm was hopped—which normally produces good strikes in dingy water—the largemouths would turn away. If the worm was raised slowly, then made to swim, sometimes the bass would strike. But the retrieve that best induced strikes in the clear-water situations was performed like this. Let the worm remain motionless on the bottom for a few moments after it settles. Next crawl it forward no more than half an inch. Pause, then bring it slowly forward again that short distance. Keep this slow retrieve going and very likely one of the big fish that has been hovering over the plastic crawler will crash

down, nail the worm, and veer away.

When the water is extremely murky, I often insert a rattler into my worm. This is a bean-shaped plastic capsule containing tiny lead shot. It is inserted into the worm's collar to act as an added attractor.

I also like scented worms. In the beginning I rubbed my worms with fish oil or oil of anise, or I kept them in a closed compartment with a wad of cotton saturated with anise, rum, or bourbon.

My wife Judy triggered the idea of the whisky by complaining one day about the wretched odor emanating from my favorite pipe. I promptly soaked some pipe cleaners in a little bourbon and stuck one of them down the pipe stem. Instant sweetness. Then I began thinking that maybe I smelled pretty poor too. To counteract the pipe odor on my hands, I invested in some high-potency "mouthwash" and a scent jar for my worms. It seems to work.

I think that the scent saturating plastic worms, rather than acting as an additional attractor, primarily disguises odors—human, tobacco, gasoline, and oil—that repel fish. I've had success with unscented worms just by periodically rubbing my hands with anise during a day of handling lures. Today, worms that are already scented are available. These too camouflage human-associated odors.

Worming Tackle That Works

My choice of worming tackle varies with conditions. When I'm working shallow water with no lead weight or when I'm using sinkers of one-eighth, three-sixteenths, or one-quarter ounce, I use spinning gear—often a five-foot nine-inch one-piece rod with stiff, so-called worm action. I always use a heavy-duty reel with a high gear ratio.

I most often use ten-pound-test line, but I go to fifteen-pound-test in heavy cover and as light as eight-pound-test in clear Northern waters. With the lighter line I use a hook of finer wire in order to get easier penetration of the plastic and the fish's mouth.

When casting sinkers of more than one-quarter ounce I use a stiff five-and-one-half-to-six-foot plugcasting rod, a top-quality, high-geared, revolving-spool reel, and ten-to-twenty-pound-test line. A stretchy line and an ultra-whippy rod will result in a lot of lost fish.

I remember times during my early days of using plastics when I thought I had really hit a bass solidly. But when I'd get him close and he would open his mouth, I could see that the hook had penetrated only barb-deep. The result was usually a lost fish. Other times I'd start to bring a fish in and suddenly the line would go slack. Upon examining the worm I'd find that the hook had never penetrated the plastic; the fish had simply been holding on.

When fishing for Yankee bass, which generally run smaller than their Southern relatives, I rig my worms on hooks as small as No. 1/0 or even No. 2. I also use the smaller hooks for smallmouths. Walleyes and panfish will hit the two-and-one-half and three-inch worms—especially those rigged on a No. 8 hook below beads and a propeller-type spinner. Without weight, these miniworms can be used effectively on an eight to eight-and-one-half-foot bass-bug flyrod designed for a No. 7 or No. 8 line. I leave the hook barb exposed when using a fly rod.

I was experimenting with weedless hooks about the time those plastic worms rigged with a propeller on a double-weedless hook hit the market. I gave up on the weedless hooks, and a lot of other people did too. My main objection to them, other than just not liking weedless hooks for most of my fishing, is that you cannot fully bury the eye of a weedless hook in a worm. In addition, I find that the larger eye of a weedless hook collects more debris than does a blunt-nosed worm. And unless it has barbs on the shank, a weedless hook tends to pull through the worm, causing the artificial to slip down the shank.

For smallmouth fishing, and where largemouths run only to about two pounds, I prefer the six-inch worms. I also use the six-incher for the humpback worm rig. Where the fish run into the four-pound range, I like worms of six to eight inches. Where the bass run bigger, I use worms at least eight inches long.

I know many anglers who have tried molding their own worms, only to give it up. It takes a lot of experimenting to come up with a worm that's just soft enough, floats or sinks in precisely the right way, and produces the desired amount of wiggle. To get a high floater, for example, you would have to obtain a blowing agent for polyvinyl chloride plastics. This chemical, used in foam playballs, creates little gas bubbles in the PVC.

A fine-quality plastic worm is made of mineral oils, soybean and peanut oils, special plastic oils, and sometimes scents. Soybean oil and the special plastic oils are currently in short supply.

New Breeds of Worms and Tactics

Traditionally most plastic worms have been designed to resemble earthworms, though to the best of my knowledge you never see nightcrawlers swimming around in the water. The newer plastic crawlers have departed from tradition, incorporating various tail styles and unique body structures, and that is good. The long cylindrical shape of worms probably represents eels or various salamanders to bass. These creatures eat bass eggs and are natural forage for largemouths, giving them double-barrel impact as a bait.

The innovation of the so-called curly tail that undulates through the water has been responsible for a change in the way we've begun fishing all

types of plastic crawlers. The change has been for the better. The old raise-and-settle method of fishing a plastic worm will take bass but it is far from being the most effective. In most cases, especially in normal (dingy) bass water, the faster swimming retrieve takes more bass. Average bass. For the biggest fish the best retrieve seems to be a fairly swift hop-swim action. Big bass are also likely to hit a plastic worm as it is dropping—frequently just after it has entered the water following the first cast to a holding spot. Many anglers miss these takes because they are not prepared to strike the instant the worm enters. In this situation a bass will not hold the worm in his mouth for over seven-and-one-half seconds. You can make these strikes result in hooked fish by using the following technique.

First, your spinning-reel bail should close or your level-wind reel engage the moment the worm touches the water following a cast. Keep all slack from your line by raising your rod tip slowly—often referred to as backpressure or tightlining your lure as it sinks. It is the only way to see your line twitch (frequently the only signal that a bass has grabbed your crawler), or feel the slight tightening of line or sharp tug that indicates a bass is there.

Be aware of the water depth in the various good holes you'll regularly fish. In this way, should your line stop settling at three feet, for example, when you know the water depth is seven, you will be alerted to set the hook immediately. If you do not receive a hit on the initial drop, then begin the hop-swim or swimming retrieve.

In most cases there is no doubt when a bass hits a swimming worm. You'll feel a sudden thunk. And you should strike quickly. More often, though, you'll experience the familiar subtle tap-tap sensation or (if you've been concentrating on the line where it enters the water) you'll see your line kick. This will occur when the worm is drop-ping after a hop. Here's what's happening underwater at these times.

By the time you receive the tapping message a bass will more than likely have your entire worm in his mouth. In the old style of worm fishing we believed that it was best to give the largemouth slack and let him run for a few moments before striking. We caught bass this way, but only because the largemouth was with his fellows and ran to prevent other bass from stealing his worm. If a bass is not being pressured by his fellows he'll usually do one of two things. First, once he has the worm in his mouth he'll maul it. If you let him hold that artificial for too long he's going to detect that something is wrong and expel it. Therefore you should strike immediately upon feeling that tapping sensation. The second thing a bass will do is grab a plastic crawler, blow it out, inhale it, blow it out several times. What he is doing is trying to kill the worm. Your signal that this is happening will more than likely be line twitch. Too often fishermen wait until they see several twitches before attempting to set their hook. This is a good way to miss a bass. Often the fish is really not interested in eating the worm, but only in destroying the eel-shaped predator to their eggs. After a couple of quick in-and-out gobbles it's had enough. Satisfied the creature is dead the fish will cut off the attack.

To be successful when bass are striking this way, you should strike with a short, sharp, stabbing movement (as opposed to a long sweep), the moment the line twitches. If you miss, your worm may still remain in the action zone for the bass to hit again. If your worm has not become wadded on the hook from the setting action, you may get a second chance. If you do connect using the short stab, stick him again to make sure the hook is in. If you've been a trifle slow and have waited past the moment of the first line twitch, be prepared to hit at the very next movement of the line—if it comes.

How Bass Hit Worms

Contrary to popular belief, bass do not take a worm only from the head end or as other stories have it, only from the tail end. Largemouths will attack plastic worms from any angle. They'll be more likely to take in and expel the larger worms, while the smaller worms will most often be mouthed entirely. The most difficult strike to turn into a hookup occurs when you are using a slip sinker of three-eighths ounces or heavier. The bass grabs your worm, then darts off at close to a right angle. The cone slip sinker stays put. When you set the hook you are doing so first against the sinker. The result is a lot of missed fish. Because of this, many fishermen are now sticking a small

Bottom-hopping worm lures a bass from cover. The pickup can be so soft—and fast— that it may not even be felt by the angler. Glen Lau

section of wooden or plastic toothpick in the hole of the slip sinker. Such pegging keeps the sinker up against the worm. A jig head or one of the worm weights with metal eyes at both ends will do the same thing. There's no need to worry that bass will not take a worm well because they feel the weight of the sinker. As long as the sinker is not too heavy a bass will take it up along with the artificial, and with an integral hook-weight, you'll stand a far greater chance of hooking up.

Sometimes bass do nip at the tail of a plastic worm. These are mostly small bass. Such a strike will be felt as a rapid rat-a-tat-tat. Panfish, too, nip at a worm like this, causing the same sensation. To determine which species are there, switch to a small three-and-a-half or four-inch worm. If the bass are small you should soon catch them.

PLASTIC LIZARDS: A SWITCH IN STRATEGY

In the early spring from the time bass start to spawn until early May in the South, and as late as June in the North, one plastic lure will take more fish than the worm — one that in shape resembles a lizard. Using a lizard you'll have to react even faster to a strike. Largemouths do not hold a lizard in their mouths even for the short time that they

hold a worm. Their sole intent is to kill these egg-predators. When a lure resembling a lizard approaches, all bass become alert. When he strikes a plastic lizard, a largemouth will shoot forward and drive the lure into the bottom. He'll go down into the timber or weeds, crush the lure so hard the corners of his mouth will flare out white. As soon as he feels he's mangled the lizard he'll expel it, then back off. The action happens like lightning. The only consistent way to hook fish that are attacking lizards is to keep slack from your line and set the hook the moment you feel the slightest difference in the way the lure is reacting underwater.

Plastic-tail grubs and feather or hair jigs are also excellent early-season lures. You can use jigs as small as those normally used by crappie fishermen. During the prespawn period, which is marked by erratic warm-cold weather, I've had excellent success using jigs as light as one-quarter to one-eighth of an ounce. As the season progresses you should fish the larger grubs.

Bass can take jigs and grubs so gently that you may never become aware of the strike. Largemouths do not really strike a jig. They position themselves close to it and flare their gills to pump it into their open mouths. When they do this a bit of line moves in, too, and that movement is

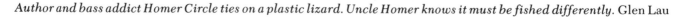

Author and bass addict Homer Circle ties on a plastic lizard. Uncle Homer knows it must be fished differently. Glen Lau

often telegraphed as line kick; you may also receive a slight sensation of slack. When using a light line these two reactions may be your only indication that a bass is taking. Keep reminding yourself that a bass will be taking the jig or grub as it drops rather than as it's moving upward.

I once watched underwater while experimental psychologist Don McCoy threaded a tiny crappie-size jig down through a tangle of timber to where a group of huge largemouths were holding. It was a bright sunny day and these fish, so deep beneath the supercover, would have been impossible to reach through normal casting. Using a modified flippin' technique such as that made popular by Dee Thomas, Dr. McCoy jigged and gently vibrated his little lure as near as possible to the big fish. Soon a huge fish shot toward the lure. He paused inches away, opened his mouth, and flared his gills in a single movement. I wanted to yell to Don. Then the big bass pumped his gills once more and the yellow jig flew out.

I asked McCoy if he had felt anything. "Not a thing," he said. No matter how fine your concentration and reflexes, bass have a habit of doing that kind of thing with disgusting regularity. It helps greatly if you are using a jig heavy enough to hold your line straight. A jig that's too light will let the line hang in kinks or coils. While it's possible that the straightening of a line coil could indicate a taking fish, you have more control over your line and lure when the connection between the two is taut.

Six All-time Great Worm Rigs

No top bass angler uses only one style plastic-worm rig. If he did he'd find the number of largemouths he hooked in a season falling off drastically. Yet when I asked six good bass fishermen what single rig they would use if they were forced to fish just one, we suddenly found ourselves in a crossfire of opinion. When the flack settled it became evident that the pros were picking the rig best suited to their home waters—the lakes they most often fished.

So varied are the rig types, at least one is sure to be right for your kind of bass fishing.

Texas Rig/Bill Dance

The Texas rig may be the world's most popular rigging for the plastic worm. Though some anglers find fault with the method, 1977 B.A.S.S. Angler of the Year Bill Dance calls the Texas technique the best all-around rigging method.

"Year in and year out the slip-sinker Texas rig catches more and bigger fish for more people than any other single lure on the American market," he says. Why?

"The rig is simple to use," Dance says. "It feels and looks natural and, with different weights, it can be fished from the surface to great depths. Here's how I rig with various weights.

"With a heavy three-eighths to one-half-ounce sinker, I use the weight as a free slider. The sinker will slip two to three feet up the line when you hook a fish. With no weight around his mouth, a bass has a heckuva job throwing the hook. When I fish grassy or mossy areas, I sometimes peg the sinker with a flat wood toothpick to keep it from sliding. I peg in grass because I'm usually using a light weight, which makes it difficult to feel bottom. If the weight slides far ahead of the worm in such situations, I might strike too late.

"I use the lightest possible weight in most situations. A light weight gives the worm the most natural appearance, despite the fact that it's harder to cast and work. By light weight, I mean one-sixteenth to one-eighth ounce. With a lot of current, wind, or deep water you'll have to go to heavier weights to feel bottom.

"Though some fishermen complain about the worm and slip sinker getting separated, I like that to happen at times. When I'm using a heavier weight in a bush, for example, the sinker will drop from a branch while the worm will hang in the bush. When I work the sinker a little, the worm will come off and begin to sink slowly. I've caught a lot of good fish at that moment.

"When you're rigging up Texas style, it's important to pull down the knot at the hook eye so it's buried in the worm's plastic head. You don't want any part of the knot exposed. A sinker rubbing over an exposed knot can wear it through—

especially if the inside diameter of the sinker is fairly large and you're using light line.

"I use two hooks: the straight-shank Mustad #33637 with two little barbs in sizes 3/0 to 6/0 for seven to ten-inch worms, and the #295 JBL Eagle Claw in size No. 1 for four to six-inch worms. The latter hook has a little stair-step bend at the eye. If I'm tournament fishing, I'll sharpen the inside and outside of the barb with a little pencil-shaped Arkansas stone or fine metal file.

"I use a six-inch worm most of the time, but go bigger in Florida. In the spring I like the smaller worms.

"An important thing to know about the Texas rig is that the worm should be straight. It'll twist if there's the slightest bend, which is desirable in the spinning rig, but not in the Texas rig. Also, if there's a concave bend in the worm between hook eye and hook point, the worm will slide up the hook when it hits an object.

"I don't think there's a color made that won't catch fish, but I use basic blue, red, black, purple, and green. The translucent colors reflect light in

Bill Dance

Bury knot in head of worm

Sinker slides up to head of plastic worm

Hook buried in worm

Drawings by Dana Rassmussen

bright weather. I use darker colors early in the morning, late in the day, at night, or in cloudy weather. My cone sinkers are unpainted.

"The Texas rig will snake over every bottom and structure contour. Have confidence in it. And don't forget that light slip sinker. It's most important in spring, when you'll double your catch if you use it instead of a heavy lead."

South Carolina Rig/Paul Chamblee

Though the South Carolina rig won't work through the heavy cover a Texas rig can handle, it's great in deep water and when fish are suspended. Raleigh, North Carolina, bass expert Paul Chamblee has some new twists for using the rig.

"The South Carolina rig shines when your fish are a little off bottom or when other rigs won't produce," Paul says. "I use it with a leader up to three feet long, depending on the depth of the

fish. The leader is normally the same material as my line, which is usually fourteen-pound test. I'll drop to eight-pound test when I'm fishing clear water or when I'm using a small worm.

"I usually use an Eagle Claw 1/0 295 XBL light-wire hook. Sometimes I'll use a light-wire weedguard-type hook. With that, I run the point right through the center of the head, bringing the barb out away from the side. The eye of the hook and wire weedguard remain outside the worm. You can use a barrel or cone sinker. I prefer the barrel-shape sinker because it doesn't wedge between rocks as a cone-shape sinker sometimes will. It also has a larger hole than a cone sinker. This lets the line slip through easily when a bass grabs the worm. I use a medium-size barrel-type swivel as a sinker stop. Occasionally I'll put a small bead between the swivel and the barrel sinker to prevent knot wear.

"The idea behind the rig is to get your sinker bumping along bottom with your worm floating up behind. You normally use a high-floating worm. As you pull the sinker, the worm moves along behind. When you stop cranking, the worm starts floating up. Feed line and the worm will go higher. In working this rig you want to pick it up easily, swing it slowly in a waving motion, then drop the sinker down and let it set for a moment. This gives the worm a chance to float up and the fish a chance to get there and grab it. With this rig, bass see the worm coming from a longer distance than with the Texas rig. You're mainly working

Paul Chamblee

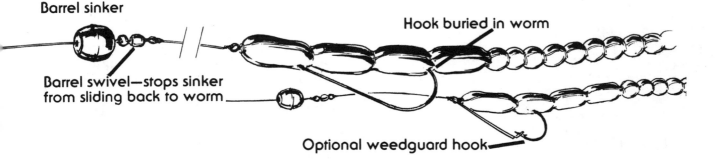

Barrel sinker

Barrel swivel—stops sinker from sliding back to worm

Hook buried in worm

Optional weedguard hook

more open structure—sandbars, clay banks, deltas, and so on.

"I've also been experimenting with a slow-sinker worm. With this you lift up the weight and worm, then let the weight drop rapidly to the bottom. The line will pull through the sinker and the worm will slowly sink. I haven't decided whether I'm getting more strikes on a high floater or a sinker worm.

"Whatever worms you use, bumping bottom is critical. This is why you need a heavy weight. Where you'd be using a one-quarter-ounce weight on the Texas rig, for example, you'd be using a three-eighths to three-quarter-ounce weight with the South Carolina rig. You sometimes have to go

to one ounce in water over thirty feet deep. I've caught fish on this rig in fifty-five feet of water. You have to jig the rig at such depths.

"With the South Carolina rig, you move your worm up and over structure rather than dragging it through cover as you do with the Texas rig. The South Carolina rig originated on Clark Hill Reservoir, South Carolina, where there's a lot of grass and moss on bottom. The idea was to keep the worm above the vegetation, where the bass could see it.

"Because you're basically fishing open water, you're not concerned about pinpoint casting to targets. That's good because the South Carolina rig is difficult to cast. It's best thrown with a six to seven-foot rod—or something such as the Flippin' Stik.

"It'll also pay to remember that you don't feel the usual tap-tap when a bass hits. Rather you feel resistance when you start to pick up. Hold what you've got, get out the slack, and then hit.

"This is a great rig to check out structure in a hurry. You also can get into suspended fish quite easily with the floater worm. It's a fine coldwater rig too. Just remember that you don't need big worms."

Exposed Hook Rig/Al Lindner

Al Lindner of Brainerd, Minnesota, is one of the nation's most versatile fishermen. A tournament angler and producer of home-study fishing techniques and television shows, his chief love is experimental fishing. One of his specialities is weed fishing for bass. He often chooses an exposed-hook worm rig for this assignment. These are his reasons:

Al Lindner

"The whole thing in a nutshell is how many more fish you'll hook with the open jig-head hook compared with the Texas rig. With the weedless method, a bass can clear the worm from his mouth quickly. An open hook will often grab in those sandpapery teeth. The open hook also gives you up to a full second longer to strike. When he's learned to use it, the average fisherman will catch 50 to 60 percent more fish with the exposed-hook jig than with the Texas rig.

"When you're fishing the big weedbeds with the exposed-hook rig, you need a jig head with the shortest shank hook you can find. You need a thin hook that can be ripped through the weeds. And you need one with the eye coming right out of the nose to prevent weeds from wrapping around the eye. The model I use is the spear-shaped head with scooped-up bottom made by Mr. Twister.

"With this arrangement, the jig and worm will sort of lay there in the weeds. You can pull it off the weeds by easing back on your rod. If it gets stuck, give it a little snap. A long-shank hook will always catch the weeds. When the rig reaches the edge of the weeds or a pocket, let it drop. If you put a live redtail chub minnow or a fathead minnow on the back, you'll catch a larger variety of fish.

"Weight is important, too. The longer the rig stays up in the weeds, the better: so I use the lightest jig I can. I use a one-eighth-ounce head in four to eight-foot water. In eight to fifteen-foot water I'll go to a quarter-ounce head if there's a little wind. Rarely, except in heavy wind, will I go

Spear-shaped jig head

Twister SinSation

Hook has short shank

to a three-eighths-ounce head. Your line must be matched to the jig. I generally use ten pound test as an all-round line.

"I like the exposed-hook rig in timber. I go down to six-pound-test line in highland reservoirs, especially when I'm working smallmouths along a rock wall.

"So far as plastics go, for bass I use the Twister SinSation in solid colors. If I'm going for numbers of fish, I'll use a firetail. I use the black jig heads about 60 percent of the time. Occasionally I'll use white, yellow, and brown.

"I prefer to cast rather than flip because I fish a lot of clear natural lakes. If I'm working the bulrushes or a flat in three to four feet of water, I usually spook too many fish by the time I get in there to flip.

"In big weedbeds—which I prefer to fish—I sometimes set markers along the points and edges of the weeds. Then I get back into the weeds with the boat, cast out, and bring the rig back to the base of the weeds. If you're on a new lake and don't know where all the pockets in the weeds are, your best bet is casting into the vegetation and then working your way back, feeling your way until the rig comes off the edge.

"It's often difficult to detect a strike in the weeds. If you suspect a fish has hit, give the hook a short snap. If a fish has hit, you'll have enough leverage to come back and bury the steel.

"The most important things in this type of fishing are perfecting the hooking and slow-dropping techniques. Use the lightest jig you can get by with, and match the line to the head."

Floater Rigs/Tom Mann

Alabama luremaker and top competitive bass angler Tom Mann doesn't like the South Carolina rig. If he's going to fish suspended bass, he'd rather rig Texas-style and just rip the worm up—jump it from the bottom three to four feet, and then let it drop. But Mann prefers fishing plastics other ways. Here is his pick for the most effective rig.

"In the right conditions, topwater or floating rigs can be the deadliest of all," Mann says. "They're especially good in spring, before and after spawning, but you can use them all year. Cloudy, fairly calm days seem best.

"I use several topwater worm rigs. The first is for lakes with a lot of moss and thick grassbeds with little pockets. I use a big eight or nine-inch worm for extra flotation and for casting weight; I don't use a sinker. I push the hook point back in the worm Texas-style to make it weedless. I throw out past my target, right on the lily pads or moss. Then I start snaking the worm back. The strikes usually come when the worm reaches a pocket in the weeds. The Eagle Claw 295 JBL is my favorite hook for this type of fishing.

"A lot of folk think a bass will just hit the tail of a nine-inch worm, but that's not so. They'll hit it right in the head unless you're snaking it too fast. You'll land as many on this big worm as you will on anything else.

"My second rig is a super-high-floater worm.

This worm gets the hook—a plain Sproat hook—right in the nose, in and out so the barb is exposed. I use this rig in clear lakes in open water over vegetation—over grass flats, for example. The hook barely sinks the worm nose and helps the worm wiggle when you pull on it. I work this rig the same way I'd work a Rapala—just a slow-twitch retrieve. If there's current I cast upstream and let the current float the worm down, twitching it every once in awhile. This is one deadly rig. You have to get used to how bass strike it, however, because they don't hit it like a plug. They just slowly suck it in.

"A lot of people don't like the real high-floating worms because they're stiff. But on some days the fish want a worm that has absolutely no action. That's when they'll hit a super-high-floating worm that's just moving along like a stick.

"I occasionally use the high floaters with a split-shot. I put the shot on at the head rather than six inches up the line, because it improves my casting accuracy. This weighted set-up will sink a worm ever so slowly. I use the rig in a couple of ways.

"I use the first method when there is three or four feet of grass growing in ten feet of water. I can feel the worm riding along the grass tops with this rig. I'll use the split-shot and high floater under boat docks or in standing timber when I'm after

Tom Mann

suspended bass. They may be hanging one or two feet deep, though you can't see them. When you pitch the worm in you don't want a big splash, which is one reason for using a small split-shot. The other reason is to get a very slow head-first sink. Use an exposed hook on this rig when you can.

"The last topwater worm rig I use is the popping rig. I get an unpainted cork, make a slit in it, and slip the line into the slit. The worm is hooked as a natural worm would be. I use a Sproat hook and thread the worm up the shank of the hook and stick the point through. When the water's very clear and you've got just a little chop on the surface, you need something to bring the bass up if they're down four to six feet. The rig's also good on schooling bass. You need that exposed hook because you've got to hit fast.

"A flat-tail worm is as good or better than a curlytail with all these rigs. I use spinning tackle all the time."

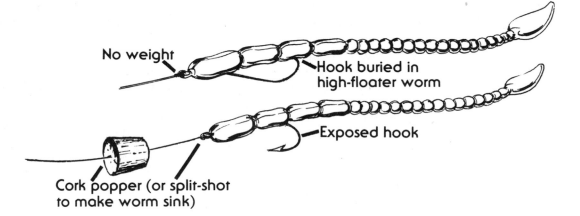

No weight

Hook buried in high-floater worm

Exposed hook

Cork popper (or split-shot to make worm sink)

Weedless Jig Rig/Stan Sloan

Stan Sloan of Nashville, Tennessee, is known in bass-fishing circles as a hard-fishing competitor and maker of the Aggravator line of spinnerbaits. When the Flippin' technique gained popularity, Stan devised a new lure that is well-suited to underhand presentation. It is readily adaptable to normal casting methods too. Sloan calls his weedless-worm-plus-jig technique the "art of positive worm fishing."

"When you're using a slip-sinker rig, you usually have to guess where the worm is," Sloan says. "Most times you have a mental picture of the worm following the sinker as it drops. But more times than you'd care to believe, the worm is hanging up in a branch somewhere. My method includes the only jig that can be rigged Texas-weedless-style, perfectly straight. It gives you a continual feel of what's happening.

"The secret is that the worm is slipped over a little spur on the jig head so it's held in perfect position for hook insertion. This rig helps you identify the strike. If you come over just a little two-inch limb with the Texas rig, the sinker will slip over the limb and leave your worm unprotected. If your exposed worm hits that branch, it can work back up the hook. That puts a little bow in the worm and increases the chances of hanging up the next time it hits a branch.

"This Flippin' jig is designed for cover—the tougher the better. It's especially good in bug brush—that green brier-patch brush growing out of the water near shore in some lakes. You've got to think of that cover as the bass's sanctuary. He's inside it, and you won't catch him by casting behind or to either side of the cover.

"I work this weedless jig in the normal way I work a worm. Lots of people have trouble setting the hook when they're worm fishing. With this rig, you just stick the fish as soon as you feel a hit. You'll generally get him in the top jaw.

"I customize the jig by bending the point upward, opening the gap or throat a little, and then bending the point out to one side. Once you bend the hook, you'll catch 99 percent of the fish you hook.

"It's important to match your line to the jig weight too. With the one-eighth-ounce jig I like four to ten-pound line. I use eight to twelve-pound test—you could go up to twenty with the three-sixteenth-ounce head. In very deep cover you need a heavy head—about one-half ounce—to pull the seventeen-to-twenty-five-pound line through the guides. Around stumps, however, a heavy jig may hang in the roots. In shallow water you've got to get a way off and cast in or you'll spook the fish. In deeper water you can jig this rig vertically, below your boat.

"You can put a skirt and a worm on this head the way they like to do in California, or you can use a grub. Still, I'd rather use a plastic worm. My favorite color is blue—it's the only one that really

Stan Sloan (right)

stands out in depths. I'll choose purple as a second and black as a third choice. I prefer a six to eight-inch worm, and like a long two-handed rod because I pitch underhand. You can throw this rig any way you want, however. Just make sure you get it into the thickest cover you can find."

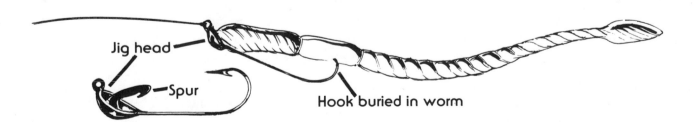

Jig head — Spur — Hook buried in worm

The Florida Rig/Lamar Underwood

Lamar Underwood, who asked me to contribute this chapter to his *Bass Almanac*, is convinced that his own favorite worm rig, though unproven in tournament competition, is absolutely tops for shallow-water bass fishing. Lamar's enthusiasm is contagious, as you'll see here.

"In 1970, after I became editor of *Sports Afield*, one of the regular contributors urged me to try a new bass worm rig. Colonel Dave Harbour, who was to make the rig nationally famous through the magazine and his book *Super Freshwater Fishing Systems*, was positive I would never go back to standard worming schemes.

"Dave was living in Florida at the time and had run across the rig down there. I started fishing it in Virginia, Maryland, Georgia, and New Jersey. My usually spotty record changed overnight. I found I could catch bass consistently if I could locate them in five feet of water or less. I frequently outfished my companions.

"Today my opinion has not changed. If bass are moving at all, and I can find them, I'll have more strikes on this rig. I depend upon it more than any other single bass fishing method! Give it a try, and you'll become a believer. Here's how it works. The rig consists of two No. 7 black Sampoo swivels, a fourteen-inch section of leader the same test as your line, a short-shank No. 1 hook with shank barbs but no weed guard, and a soft, six-inch, straight-tail purple worm.

"Dave recommended strongly that the worm used be the Creme Wiggle Worm, Series #100, color No. 36. He was right. This rig has outfished all others for me, but you may want to experiment with different colors in different conditions. If you have to substitute a style of worm, go for the softest six-incher you can find.

"The point of the hook should be brought out the worm's flat underside, leaving an exaggerated bow in the body. About half the hook curve should be exposed. The head of the worm is pulled slightly over the eye of the hook onto the leader.

"Retrieve the worm slowly with soft twitches. If the strike comes as a hard, dramatic smash, try to set the hook immediately. Usually, the take will be a gentle tug. In that case, lower your rod and let the fish swim away for several seconds. Then hit him hard. The slow-mouthers are tough to hook. Discipline yourself—if you can—to continue reeling slowly while the slow-mouther toys with the worm, then set the hook."

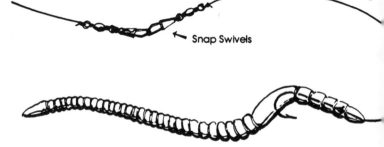

← Snap Swivels

Lamar Underwood (right) with Grits Gresham

8

Plugging

ROLAND MARTIN as told to LARRY MAYER

Spanning the Chattahoochee River at the town with the same name in northern Florida is a dam and a reservoir formally named Jim Woodruff. To bass fishermen nationwide, the 37,000 acres of impounded water is known simply as Lake Seminole.

This huge body of water has monstrous rocks and boulders tapering off the dam face on the Florida side. Every time I see those boulders, I think, "What a spot to toss a crankbait!"

Though most of Seminole lies in Georgia, many bays and cover filled with lily pads and moss patches are on the Florida side. When I see them I instantly conjure up the image of fat six-pound largemouths smashing topwater plugs close to this aquatic vegetation.

On up the northeast side—the Flint River side—are steep, clay banks with a lot of fallen trees in the water. I wonder what I could provoke by twitching a Rapala past these submerged limbs tomorrow morning during the first hour of daylight.

The access road I'm traveling winds through huge oak trees on up the northeast side of Seminole. Many of the deeper coves are filled with the flooded remains of these hardwoods. I hardly can wait until tomorrow when I'll bump a Bomber plug through the submerged branches in this standing timber.

A little while later I arrive at Jack Wingate's Lunker Lodge on the Flint River arm. It's late afternoon, and I can't wait to get out on the water, and my mind is racing through all my bass-catching possibilities for this evening. A couple of bass boats are bobbing slowly in their stalls. Some hopeful fishermen are loading their tackle into Wingate's aluminum rental boats pulled up on the bank.

Although I'm full of enthusiasm, I get second thoughts about my chances when I read that old arched sign over the walkway to Wingate's main dock. It says: "I know they'll bite tomorrow, cuz they bit yesterday."

Before I walk into Jack's tackle shop, something else catches my eye. Two elderly gentlemen are cleaning big crappies at the fish-cleaning table. Next to one of them is the garbage can, and protruding over the rim of it are two enormous bass heads. Gosh! Those two were big enough to send to the taxidermist! They appeared to have been largemouths in the nine to ten-pound range, but whoever caught 'em had worked 'em over with a filleting knife.

Like ol' Fred Sanford might have done, I pick up a stick and begin stirring the carcasses in the can. I find the skeletons of a couple of respectable spotted bass in addition to several two- to four-pound largemouths.

A noisy splash out in the water diverts my attention. Out in the cove past the boats, a school of shad is breaking the water ahead of the boil created by a good-sized bass. What I would give to twitch a Devils Horse plug through there at this moment!

Finally I enter the store while trying to hide my anticipation, and I greet my old friend, Jack. "How're the bass doing?" I ask.

Wingate, a typically slow-talking native south Georgian, pauses and spits tobacco juice into a Styrofoam cup. Then he drawls: "Roland, ol' buddy, they're flat tearin' it up! They're hittin' topwater early, and they're gittin' 'em on crankbaits in the timber and on the points. And some of the boys are even catchin' 'em trollin'. I've been so dadburned busy I ain't got to go much lately, but we've had locals who don't catch no bass to speak of go out and bring in some danged good strings."

I've been fishing Lake Seminole since 1970, and know it well. I make one or two annual trips down here. The beauty of Seminole is that it has just about every conceivable type of cover, structure, and bassing possibility I've ever found in a single lake.

Up in the Spring Creek area, the water is swimming-pool clear and full of grass; it looks like a northern lake. The Chattahoochee side is muddy and full of trees, and it resembles many Texas and

All-time pro bass tournament money winner Roland Martin ($95,230 since 1968) matches his plug selection to light conditions. Here his choice of a small, big-lipped diving plug fished deep earned a strike and some anxious moments in the brushpile.

Oklahoma impoundments. Up the Flint River are reeds and rocks, and near the town of Bainbridge you can find redeyed or Coosae bass. They behave similarly to smallmouths in Minnesota streams.

Down near the dam are rocks and rip-rap, and the deepwater structure is what many bassers in mid-America can identify with. Unlike many of the Florida lakes, which are live-shiner or plastic-worm lakes, Lake Seminole is excellent for plug fishing. I've caught five largemouths over ten pounds at Seminole, and *all of 'em* were taken on plugs.

This is not a story about Lake Seminole; this impoundment merely has the type of water where I usually fish plugs for bass. Seminole could be Monroe Reservoir in Indiana, Kerr Reservoir on the North Carolina-Virginia line, or one of the lakes near my Oklahoma home, such as Lake Eufaula. Seminole has a little of the character of all of these lakes in its makeup.

For every ten Lake Seminole fishermen you ask, you'll likely get ten different answers for what they caught their bass on and how. Basically there are at least a dozen different ways to catch a bass on that lake on any given day.

One of the most noticeable features of Wingate's store is the huge fish net draped around the ceiling. On it are a lot of ole reliable standby bass plugs, such as the Lucky 13, Devils Horse, Big-O, new crankbaits—dozens of lures. Each has a history on Lake Seminole.

Sorting Out the Plug Options

In the mouth of Jack Wingate's biggest bass—a fourteen and three-quarter-pounder—hangs a big diving plug. Many novice fishermen stand at his counter looking at the huge array of bass lures; deciding what they need is often a bewildering dilemma for them. Actually, all of these baits fall into four categories.

First is the topwater-plug group. These float on top throughout the retrieve. Devils Horses, Injured Minnows, Diamond Rattlers, Chuggers, Hula Poppers, Jitterbugs, and Crazy Crawlers are some of the many brand names and types of surface baits.

The surface-diving or floating-diving plugs comprise the second category. They can be twitched on the surface during the early part of the retrieve and then pulled beneath the top to imitate a swimming minnow. Plugs such as the Rapala, Rebel, Bang-O-Lure, River Runt, Bass Oreno, and Lucky 13 are a few in this family.

Swimming plugs, which sink, are another type. These are shallow plugs, although they can be worked deep on a slow retrieve. They're the "countdown" type of lures—you throw them out and count for a few seconds as they sink to mid-depths. In this bunch are lures such as the Countdown Rapala, Hot Spot, Sonic, Sonar, and Gay Blade. They have fast, vibrating actions when reeled in swiftly, although they can be cranked slower and thereby fished deeper.

The fourth category—and one of the best for big bass—are the crankbaits. Years ago they were called deep-diving baits, and favorites back then (and still today) were the Bomber, Waterdog, Hellbender, and Arbo-gaster. Many modern bassers have replaced these old standbys with the newer series of "alphabet plugs," such as the Big-O, Big-N, Balsa B, Fat Rap, Model A, and Deep Wee-R. Some, such as the original Big-O, Balsa B, and Fat Rap, are made of balsawood, whereas others are plastic.

Diving plugs are very efficient in bumping their way snaglessly through submerged stumps, branches, and bushes in many impoundments. The advantage of a crankbait is the lip. It creates an almost snagless bait. You can bump crankbaits into a stump, boulder and often through weeds without hanging it up much, whereas the regular swimming types of lures have more exposed treble hooks and get snagged up frequently.

I'm talking here mainly about my experiences with various plug patterns. Don't be misled into thinking I don't use other lures. I use plenty of plastic worms, spinnerbaits, spoons, jigs and grubs. In fact, in tournament competition I probably use a plastic worm one third of the time for efficiency. But I usually locate the bass with a plug such as a Countdown Rapala. That's the lure I used to find largemouths in B.A.S.S.'s New York Invitational Tournament in June of 1978 on the St.

Swimming plugs include newer entries (left, top to bottom) Devils Horse Rogue, Bomber's Speed Shad, and Jointed Rapala. Older favorites (right, top to bottom) are Crab Wiggler, Heddon Vamp, Heddon Zig-Wag.

Diving plugs include newer entries (left, top to bottom): Cordell's Spot, Heddon Sonar, Countdown Rapala, Heddon Sonic. Older plugs (right, top to bottom) are Shakespeare River Pup, Heddon 00, Heddon 150.

Lawrence Seaway. I went back to those fish, caught them on plastic worms, and ended up winning the tourney.

Plastic worms and spinnerbaits are more snagless than most plugs, and these are about the only lures you can get through heavy cover: so you have to use them to fish such cover. But worm and spinnerbait fishing aren't as much fun as plug fishing, because plugs offer the visual contact of the topwater strikes and provoke hard-hitting strikes beneath the surface. Plug fishermen feel a little more contact with the bass, whereas plastic worms are more like live bait. Also, more innovations are available to the plug fisherman. He has more colors, sizes, and actions to choose from. To me, it's more of a challenge to discover some truly strong plug patterns for bass. And more nostalgia is associated with plug fishing. Any time you're around a group of fishermen, someone always pulls out an old favorite plug with cracked paint, rusty hooks, and his story behind it. Plugs are big parts of these stories.

Some anglers collect antique plugs, whereas others, like me, "retire" sentimental favorites. Encased in a glass box on my desk are my sentimental baits, including one which caught my biggest plug bass—a twelve and three-quarter pounder. Another plug there won me two different tournaments, and another has teeth marks from a bass I believe was close to the world record.

Like you, I have my nostalgic memories and favorite stories about plugs and bass.

Let's Go Plugging

I'm going fishing, and I'd like to take you with me. Although we'll be fishing Seminole, you can apply the tricks and techniques to many of your favorite spots—farm ponds, gravel pits, impoundments, or natural lakes.

It's a typical day, and there are several things we should try. Now that it's early in the morning, let's first try what I call my "topwater treat." This is fishing the points at dawn with propeller-type topwater plugs, such as the Injured Minnow and the Devils Horse. This is a beautiful pattern because the lake is calm, the water's fairly clear, and the surface temperature's about 70°. The bass are fairly active, and they're feeding. We're fishing during the magical hour when several bass have moved up from deep water and are having breakfast on these points.

We'll select several main lake points and make only two or three casts at each, unless we find several bass on a point. Our main technique will be to throw to what appears to be a good ambush point, such as a good stick, log, or bush. Bass are predators; they like to conceal themselves and dart out at unsuspecting prey, and these ambush points give them good hiding places. We'll cast to these ambush points and let our plugs rest for five to ten seconds. This quiet, slow-retrieve approach often pays off, and we're apt to catch bass from a pound and one-half to nine pounds with this technique.

After the plugs sit there for about ten seconds, we'll give them only slight single twitches so that the propeller blades barely rotate. After five more seconds, our second twitches might move the plugs three or four inches and throw off a few bubbles. The third and fourth twitches might be double pops and move the baits two to three inches each time. If we haven't had a strike after the plugs have moved two to three feet, we probably should reel in quickly and cast again to other ambush points.

If we don't get a strike after three or four casts, we'll crank up and move to another good-looking point. Points early in the morning often spell *concentrations* of bass: if we catch one, usually we'll catch several. Frequently we'll try several points where we don't catch any. Two points over from us might have more baitfish, and that's where the bass likely will be. This topwater treat is apt to last until the sun gets on the water.

Switching to Deepwater Tactics

An hour has passed, and we've had some strikes and caught a few bass. The second pattern we'll try is what I call the "subsurface spectacle." We'll use the slender, floating-diving plugs like the Rapalas and Rebels. A little breeze has kicked up, and when I fish these types of plugs, I like to find calm, shaded water. So let's head into a sheltered cove with tall trees on the east side of the lake.

Why the east side? That's where there'll be long shadows from the trees, as the sun is climbing behind them. We'll fish the secondary points back in these coves and throw our plugs past likely looking stickups and patches of grass. We'll work those plugs slowly and twitch them for the initial two to three feet of the retrieve just like we did the prop plugs. If we don't get a strike this way, we'll swim the plugs back to the boat.

The advantage with these floating-diving plugs is that perhaps half the bass we catch will be on the swimming retrieve. We'll actually "work" these plugs back to the boat instead of merely swimming them steadily. Every five to ten feet during the retrieve, we'll twitch, pause, and jerk the baits to try to provoke strikes from bass that might be following the lures. While we're swimming the Rapalas back, we might be coming past ambush points we don't see. Even though we're in clear water, the sun is not on the surface, and, therefore, is not revealing the underwater cover. Likely there'll be ambush points hidden from us, and we're apt to get many unexpected strikes.

"Counting down" will be the third pattern we should try. It's a great pattern for the early mid-morning period shortly after the sun is bright on the water. Bass seldom will hit our topwater and floating-diving plugs as well as they did earlier, but at this time they'll hit a subsurface bait that runs from two to five feet deep and resembles a minnow or small baitfish. We'll use swimming plugs that sink, such as the Countdown Rapala, Hot Spot, and Bomber Pinfish. The surface isn't as calm, because the rising sun usually creates convection currents that normally cause wind after the first couple hours of the morning.

Our boat is positioned in about ten feet of water, so let's throw toward the point. For the initial five or six feet, we'll be swimming the plugs in fairly shallow water, and then as we hit the deeper edges or dropoff on the point, we'll pause and count slowly to let the plugs sink and settle down toward the bottom. For this pattern use a varied retrieve, because gamefish in general and bass in particular don't get as excited over a steady retrieve. Stopping or hesitating the plug is important.

Roland stalks stumpy water with a floating-diving plug that he twitches on surface, then pulls under for a swimming retrieve.

Buzzing with Propeller Plugs

Now that the sun's up more and the shadows are shorter, let's try buzzing. I love to buzz! A buzzing lure is like a spinnerbait except that the buzzer has a big propeller that chugs along the surface on the retrieve. It actually sinks, but it's run on top as a surface lure. Examples are Floyd's Buzzer, the Lunker Lure, and the Dedly Dudley; the old Arbogast Sputterfuss has been around for years—and it's still a good buzzer, too.

I got on to the buzzing technique a couple of years ago and immediately saw the advantage: buzzing lures can catch bass faster than can standard surface plugs. I went to Oklahoma's Grand Lake, which has clear portions much like Seminole does and a lot of willows along the shoreline. I'd been catching largemouths early on topwater plugs, but these take a long time to retrieve. An entire retrieve sometimes takes a minute with a regular surface bait, but a buzzer can be thrown out and cranked across the top in approximately ten seconds. With a buzz bait you can cover five or six times as much water in a given period of time as you can fish with a topwater plug. Therefore, if an early-morning feeding spree lasts only forty-five minutes, as often happens, you can get more strikes and catch more bass on the buzzer because you're showing the lure to more fish. When they're hitting topwater lures and are looking up, the buzzer sometimes is the fastest way to catch them once you've established where they are.

On Lake Seminole some of our best places to run buzzer lures are around big trees lying in the water. On the northeast shore of the lake are numerous fallen big trees, and this section is a perfect spot to throw our buzzers. Remember again: this same technique applies to other lakes and farm ponds you fish where big trees have fallen into the water.

Other good buzzing places on Seminole are grass points. Many points in Seminole's Spring Creek sector have grass and resemble the natural lakes in Minnesota and Michigan with elodea and coontail moss on points. Even though the points might only be two feet deep, bass concentrate on them, and these spots are perfect for buzzing.

Standard buzzer lures have only one single hook as do regular spinnerbaits. I usually add a trailer hook to my buzzers. If the water is fairly open, without a lot of grass and stickups, I use a treble-hook trailer. I use the single-hook trailer, which rides upright in water, with a lot of brush, lily pads and weeds.

Some of the bigger bass in the lake really get excited by that lure sputtering over them; the biggest bass in an area hit the buzzer early in the morning or during periods of cloud cover, another good time for topwater bassing. Strikes are visual, and they're often explosive and thrilling. Although we don't have a lot of big bass in Oklahoma, several times this past year I caught five, six, and seven-pounders where before with standard topwater plugs I caught only two and three-pounders.

Fishing the Deep, Brushy Lunker Lairs

Well into the midmorning hours when there's little shade, bass start to seek heavier cover. This is when I start "bombering the brush." Bass have been spread out on the points and banks, but now the sunlight has begun to concentrate them. So we'll look for brush. The term "bombering" comes from the use of an oldtime standard crankbait that has been a favorite for most of the past four decades. It's the Texas-made plug named the Bomber.

So we'll look for logs, trees, and stickups with shade, and we'll crank Bombers, Fat Raps, and Hellbenders or some other deep-diving plugs through these areas. The big advantage to a crankbait in these circumstances is its relatively snagless lip, which helps guard the treble hooks. Like the buzzer baits, crankbaits are fast-moving lures, and we can cover a lot of water quickly. These are great lures for locating fish. We can put the trolling motor on a medium-high speed and go down a bank, a timberline, or the edge of the grass and cover an entire mile of potentially good water. If we locate a school of fish, we can stop and start casting to them with a variety of slower-moving lures and likely catch more bass.

One trick we need with the crankbaits is "bump

Smallmouth action on Minnesota's Lac La Croix, as Roland invades northern waters with his army of crankbaits.

the stump." Although it might be a bush instead of a stump, we'll actually make contact with the shady side of the object with our plugs. We'll tempt the bass through their own reflex action; they're in the shadows of the ambush point, and they're probably resting and hiding in the cover instead of feeding. Our plugs are intruders bumping through the cover, and those bass can often be *provoked* to strike. We'll conjure up an image of where the bass are by studying the cover and wind direction and looking at the sun angle and the shade from the cover. We need to figure out where they're apt to be lying, and then we need to throw to that precise target. But we'll never snag them; at the last second the bass will whirl around and almost out of self-defense or reflex action grab the lure.

Bass anglers can choose from a huge variety of crankbaits. Often I prefer the balsawood models, such as the Fat Rap, Estep, Balsa B, and the original Big-O. Fred Young of Oak Ridge, Tennessee, pioneered the balsawood crankbait craze with his handcarved original Big-O, which became highly popular in the early 1970s. Local varieties of balsawood crankbaits are carved in many regions; these lures usually run from four to seven feet deep.

Crankbaits also come in big-lipped models—including the 600 series Bombers and 900 series Hellbenders. On the average retrieve these models run from eight to eleven feet deep; they're good for trolling as well as casting. They're used in the deeper timbered areas. Lake Seminole has thousands of acres of flooded hardwood (cypress and oak) trees standing in four to forty feet of water; largemouths often suspend in the shade of these big trees and with the big-lipped crankbaits we can bump through the shady side and catch some lunkers.

My biggest bass in a tournament was at Seminole in 1972. I was in ninth place, and at one o'clock in the final round, I put on the biggest lure in my tacklebox—a Magnum Hellbender—out of desperation. A big bass was my only chance of winning. I stopped along some huge oak trees out in the Spring Creek flats directly on the edge of the channel. On my first cast I cranked this plug down in the shadow of a big tree. I paused it for a second and the bait just stopped. I set the hook hard and caught a ten-pound, three-ounce largemouth that not only won me the tournament but also was the big bass of the event and earned me a new bass boat as well.

I noticed another big bass following the one I'd hooked, and on my second cast I got a seven-pounder; on the third cast, a six-pounder struck. Following that, my partner caught a couple of big ones there. After the spree was over, I'd caught nearly thirty pounds of bass in fifteen minutes with this large deep-diving plug.

Crankbaits Over Structure

Now that midday has arrived, many of the bass have left the shallow water and have migrated out to the center of the cove where a submerged creek channel runs. One of the best strategies now is cranking the structure.

Back before the 1950s, bass fishing was primarily a shallow-water sport. Most bass anglers back then fished until about nine o'clock in the morning and then left the lake and didn't return until five or six that evening. This was the typical summer approach. I've found that some big bass and concentrations of bass can be caught on deep-

diving crankbaits at midday by cranking through structure, such as creek channels, old house foundations, road beds, rock piles, and deep edges of submerged grass. These potential hotspots are anything with an irregular feature, and usually the best structure is connected with deeper water. Tournament fishermen from the club to national level need to find such spots, because tournaments almost always are in the daytime hours.

A good contour map (along with our depthfinder) will help locate these prime areas, and the map will also designate any sharp bends

What rarer fishing moment than to get your surface plug into a good-looking hole and have it receive a savage, instantaneous strike? Erwin Bauer

in the creek. These bends normally are the best spots on the creek because a straight channel doesn't hold bass as well. Deeper banks were formed on the outside parts of the bends by creek water undercutting the banks before the lake was inundated. These more vertical dropoffs usually offer the bass more shade. We need to crank our plugs through the shady portions of these creek channels. We'll keep the boat in deep water and make long casts to shallow water and thirty to forty feet beyond where we think the creek ledges are. We need to crank very fast to make our lures dive to that eight to ten-foot depth, and when we believe we're near the ledge, we'll slow up the plugs and maybe even stop the retrieves momentarily. We'll also bump the bottom with the plugs. This is important because bass in such spots during the summer often are feeding on crawfish, and deep-diving plugs imitate crawfish kicking up mud while scurrying backward across the bottom.

We're in a schooling-bass situation here, so when the first bass is caught along a creek channel, we'll throw out a fish-marker buoy and keep fishing the same area from different angles and even with different plugs.

I like to try to do what trout fishermen call "match the hatch." If I think bass are feeding on crawfish, I'll try a brown or crawfish color initially. I'll go to the shad colors if I think they're feeding on shad. In northern lakes when I think they're feeding on perch or bluegills, I'll fish the new natural finishes as first choices. The many sizes and colors of lures can easily confuse novices. Brochures listing popular baits reveal that plugs such as the Bomber are made in five or six sizes and more than a dozen colors. So there might be seventy or more different Bombers to choose from. I don't think you need this many different Bombers. I try to determine if the water I'm fishing is a crawfish, shad, or perch lake. Then I'll want lures in these certain finishes. Possibly in a muddy lake in early spring, I'll need brighter colors, and I narrow my selection of lure sizes to about three. I need plugs that will dive fairly shallow—five to six feet—and those are the smaller, short-lipped models. I also need intermediate-depth lures, which run seven or eight feet deep, such as the longer-lipped Fat Raps and Little N's. Then I need some deep hummers, such as the large Fat Raps, 600 series Bombers, and Magnum Hellbenders. Some of the latter dive eleven or twelve feet on fourteen to seventeen-pound-test line on average retrieves.

During the midday period I also "crank the mud line" on the windy shorelines. I'll throw a crankbait into the mud and retrieve it out. When I reach the clear water, I'll pause and twitch the lure. Where possible, I'll line my boat parallel along the mud line and make parallel casts barely on the clearwater side of the line. Some of my crankbaits have rattling devices and thereby make noises; sometimes this extra feature gets attention.

Trolling Deep Water: A Locator Technique

In summer, when fishermen try several techniques and don't catch many bass, they're probably not getting deep enough. Often in the summer, bass go deep on the thermocline, which on larger lakes throughout the country is too deep to reach by casting a plug. Trolling a crankbait is the way to get down to these bass. I can take that same Bomber, Fat Rap, or Hellbender which runs ten to eleven feet down on a cast, let out twice as much line, troll it at two miles per hour, and get it twice as deep. By using lighter ten-pound-test line and letting out greater lengths, I can get deep-divers down as far as twenty-five feet.

At Seminole, some sections down by the dam on the Chattahoochee side have been cleared of brush and timber. These are the types of places we want to troll. If we troll the brush or timber areas, we're going to get hung up frequently. We're really looking for sandbars and shoals off the main river channel. The bass are there because they're seeking the cooler waters along the thermocline and also because the deeper water filters out the sunlight.

With large, deep-diving crankbaits we can catch some bass by trolling at fifteen to twenty-five-foot depths. This also is a great way to locate bass because at two miles per hour we can cover several miles of river channel and dropoffs or bars in the center of the lake in just a few hours. When we locate a school, we'll throw out markers and make repeated trolls. One thing to note carefully is the direction we're trolling. The wind might be blowing, and the current created by the wind might be pushing around the water, so the bass could be facing the current the way trout do in a stream. If they're facing the current, they'll be expecting shad, bluegills, or minnows to be coming down current to them. If our crankbaits are going the *opposite* way, we probably won't get a strike. Often when you're trolling deep water, you can catch 'em only by going one way.

Trolling is an easy way to fish, and trollers don't need sophisticated, expensive equipment. They do need a good fish locator, a good contour map to find bars and shoals, and good marker buoys to mark the spots.

Schooling Bass: A Different Plugging Game

Quite often on a southern lake with shad, I'll see schooling bass. In the northern lakes where bass school, they don't break the surface as much. In southern lakes concentrations of bass often follow schools of shad that are swimming at five to ten-foot depths. The bass are deeper, perhaps down near the thermocline. Occasionally the entire bass school will come up and tear into the shad.

Keeping in mind the "match the hatch" concept, I'll use a swimming-type plug. At first when they start breaking, a standard topwater plug that imitates small shad works well. Good examples are small Rapalas and Tiny Torpedos the size and color of the bait fish. Often I'll go to a huge topwater lure such as the big Zara Spook to try to catch the biggest bass in the school. Not many one to two-pounders will hit it, but if you twitch such a plug, you're apt to catch one of the bigger bass.

When the bass drop below the surface, they must be followed down. Two of the most effective lures for doing this are the Countdown Rapala and the Hot Spot. The depth-finder reveals the depth the bass go to, then lures can be counted down to the school. When the bait gets to the school, run it in the direction the bass are traveling. If the bait fish are moving east, the bass will be doing likewise, and your lure needs to move east. In southern impoundments, white bass and striped bass school in addition to black bass. Big largemouths, smallmouths and Kentucky (spotted) bass often lie a few feet beneath the white bass and striped bass. They're waiting for crippled shad to filter down to them. The larger, deeper countdown lures are my choices to get down below the white bass; I retrieve them slowly for these big black bass.

Sundown: Back to Surface Action

By late afternoon, the wind dies and Seminole begins to calm down. Shadows begin to lengthen. Many of the early-morning patterns will work again this evening. Dawn and dusk are synonymous with topwater and near-surface action. We'll try the prop and chugging-type baits and the shallow surface-diving plugs until nearly dark.

At dark I like to go after some truly big bass, and I like to call 'em up with a Jitterbug. A big black Jitterbug, Sputterbug, or Plunker should be retrieved rhythmically because bass don't have all their abilities at night and cannot hit a creature accurately. The lure moves at a steady pace with a rhythmic retrieve, and the bass can zero in on it more accurately than if the retrieve were erratic.

We'll look for shallow points and shallow grass flats and also for shallow moss, lily pads, and shallow brush. Our casting rods need to be stiff and our reels equipped with twenty or twenty-five-pound line because these plugs have big hooks and we're after big bass. Also, we must find clear water and preferably a calm surface. A key trick for this type of night fishing is *not* to set the hook until you feel the fish after he strikes. Often the bass hits but actually misses the plug. He's not nearly as accurate at night, and if you hear the big strike and immediately set the hook, lots of times you'll miss him. So you want to wait until you feel the fish on your line and then set the hook.

Pursuing lunkers with Musky Jitterbugs and other big topwater plugs after dark will be a perfect ending to our fishing day. Surface strikes from huge bass at night are thrilling and often unnerving.

9

Spinnerbaits
The One-Lure Arsenal

DAVID E. MORRIS

Today's spinnerbaits come in all shapes and sizes. Some are homely workhorses, while others are flashy specialists. But they all have one thing in common: when their flashing blades are splashing the surface or humming in the depths, they bring fierce strikes from bass. Even when these baits are in free-fall, tumbling toward the bottom, gleaming and woobling, bass strike them savagely.

As far back as 1881, Dr. J. A. Henshall, in *Book of the Black Bass*, had this to say about spinners, which he called "spoon-baits," reflecting their recent kinship to spoons. The spinner "revolves gracefully beneath the surface of the water, the burnished surface flashing at each revolution, and proves quite an effective lure." Since Henshall's time, many modifications and additions have been tried, but not until the mid-forties did any significant improvements in the spinner design take place. The breakthrough came in the form of the so-called "safety-pin" spinner when the Howser Helldiver from St. Louis, Missouri, was introduced. It quickly became known as the "spinnerbait." The design was typical of spinnerbaits popular today. It had a spinner on one end of the V-shaped wire and on the other end a leadhead hook adorned with a rubber skirt. Many other spinnerbaits soon followed the Helldiver,

and this type of lure quickly gained popularity and became one of the favorite and most versatile bass baits. National tournament records show that spinnerbaits are pushing worms for the top spot with pro bassers.

Fishermen today have five basic types of spinnerbaits to choose from, including the older, in-line style. They range in size from one-thirty-second ounce to one ounce. The in-line type are commonly called simply "spinners." Mepps spinners, Shysters, Snagless Sallys, and Roostertails are well-known spinners. They are very effective when used with light tackle in relatively open water, but they do not offer the versatility of certain other types of spinnerbaits.

A second type of spinnerbait is the twin-spin, which has two shafts with a spinner on each one. Shannon spinners and twin-spin Bushwackers fall into this category. Though these lures offer little advantage over the other types of spinnerbaits, they will catch bass and are probably at their best when fished rapidly over grass or moss.

A third type is the new surface spinnerbait. The best-known example is probably the Lunker Lure. Unlike the other baits, the blade is a broad, triangular slab of metal with two of the ends bent in opposite directions to catch water when pulled along. A wire shaft runs through the middle of the blade. This is strictly a topwater lure and can be very effective under the right conditions.

The last two types of spinnerbaits are the most popular, versatile, and useful. They are single spins and tandem spins. Nearly every manufacturer of spinnerbaits has a wide selection of both.

Single spins, one-bladed baits, are the most widely used of the two and have greater application in most fishing situations. Tandem spins have two blades and are better suited for specialized use, like buzzing. Single spins and tandems get the main play in my fishing.

Buzzing: Spinnerbait Fishing's Deadliest Art

Of all the ways to use spinnerbaits, the most exciting and one of the most effective techniques is "buzzing," sometimes called "bulging." This warm-water tactic, generally most productive in water over 65°, supposedly originated in east Texas, Arkansas, and Oklahoma; it was a closely guarded secret for several years. In buzzing, you retrieve the spinnerbait at a speed fast enough to keep it just under the surface so that a bulging wake is created. I used this method in the grassbeds of Lake Eufaula, Alabama, a few years ago to catch one of the best stringers of bass ever caught anywhere.

During that early June I expected the bass to follow their normal pattern of abandoning the shallows in favor of deep ledges and channels. For several days, I had guided parties with only moderate success while working the usually productive ledges. I was determined to try something different to find the bass. Everything seemed right, and I felt sure the fish would bite if we could find them. Gambling, I decided to spend the next day working shallow water, where everybody knew no self-respecting bass would be.

When I met my party, a doctor from Birmingham, Alabama and his son, at Chewalla Marina the next morning, I had to do a little back-peddling when asked, "Got some bass located?"

"Well, it's been kinda slow, but I think we can catch a mess of fish before the day is over," I answered weakly.

With that, we loaded the boat up and headed to

The flashing, splashing action of modern spinnerbaits can bring the wisest bass from their lairs with murder in their hearts. Glen Lau

the big flats just south of Cowikee Creek. We didn't leave the shallows all day. The bass were there, and we caught plenty of fish, thirty-two of them. Five topped the five-pound mark. Grassbeds seemed to be the key, and worms were the bait.

But that night, as I thought about the day, I was haunted by the feeling that our catch didn't reflect the number of bass we had found. I was sure we should have caught more bass from the grass than we did on worms. The bass were fresh off the beds, lean, and hungry. Worms were productive, but the slow retrieve and passive nature of worm techniques didn't allow us to cover the territory quickly. The largemouths were aggressive, and our success seemed directly related to the number of casts made. The grass was thick, and the fish were well back inside the grassline. A topwater lure wouldn't do, crankbaits were out of the ques-

Spinner buzzed through lily pads so that blades barely break the surface.

tion, but spinnerbaits seemed made to order. They were weedless and could be fished rapidly. In addition, the flashing blade sent vibrations out that hungry bass in shallow water and heavy cover could not turn down.

When dawn brightened the eastern sky the next morning, my dad, Flynn Morris, Sr., Don Simmons, one of Lake Eufaula's best guides, and I headed for the grassbeds armed with spinnerbaits. It didn't take long to see that our strategy was right. All day we caught big bass. Our white, tandem Wooly Bullys proved deadly when cast far back into the grass and retrieved just under the water. If a bass hadn't blown a hole in the grass by the time the spinnerbait reached the outside grassline, we would let the lure drop deeper in the open water. Many times this brought a jarring strike. We ended the day with aching arms, bruised ribs, and forty-five bass. Seventeen of them weighed between five and eight pounds!

Buzzing is at its best around such cover as stickups, brush piles, logs, grass, rock piles, stumprows, or any object that may be harboring a bass. Bass tend to strike the buzz bait out of reflex, so it is most effective when the fish don't have long to look at it. For this reason, buzzing will take more fish in muddy or stained water unless the cover is thick. Don't be afraid to throw a spinnerbait into the thickest cover. They are snagless as long as you keep them moving.

Buzzing is fairly easy to master. First you cast to a target; if possible, cast *beyond* where bass are most likely holding to prevent spooking them. Start the retrieve the instant the lure hits the water. A smooth sweep of the rod just as the bait enters the water will give you time to engage the reel and start the retrieve. A high rod tip will help keep the bait near the surface. As the lure approaches the target, you can either keep it coming or let it drop as it passes. Either option can be deadly on a given day.

One note of caution: bass hit a buzzed bait with savage enthusiasm, so you should always have a good grip on your rod and be ready to react. When a second wake appears behind the spinnerbait, try to keep your retrieve steady and wait until the fish actually hits the lure. I recommend a good, stiff rod and stout line.

Several wrinkles will give buzzing a little more spice. The retrieve can be sped up so that the blade breaks the water to make a sputtering, gurgling sound. Or a stop-and-go retrieve can be used that allows the lure to drop occasionally before

Spinner buzzed just beneath surface, creating "bulging" wake and explosive strikes.

returning to the surface. Another method would be to buzz the bait over a target, let it sink, and then work it back slow and deep. It pays to experiment. Let your imagination run wild.

Using a combination of these variations, I have taken bass up to eleven pounds in the weed-choked lakes of South Georgia and Florida. My favorite tactic is to cast beyond an opening in the grass and immediately start the retrieve. I make the spinnerbait sputter, gurgle, and "bulge" as it draws near the opening. Once the "pothole" is reached, I stop the retrieve and let the spinnerbait fall. If a bass has been aroused by the commotion, there's a good chance he'll nail the lure as it flutters downward. The flashing and woobling motion of a spinnerbait in free-fall is one of its most important characteristics.

Which is better, a tandem-spin or single-spin buzz bait? This question causes great disagreement. I think the single spin will do anything a tandem will under most circumstances. Single spins send off more vibrations, but tandems give more flash. Most times, it is the "sound" that ac-

counts for the action. However, tandem spins are easier to keep near the surface and can be worked slower. This can be a definite advantage at times. Even though my vote would go to a quarter-ounce single spin outfitted with a three-inch grub as the best all-around buzz bait, my favorite is an old quarter-ounce tandem-spin Wooly Bully with a vinyl skirt. It has put many big bass in my livewell, including an eleven-pound, two-ounce lunker from Lake Toho in Florida. Whatever an angler has confidence in is a good choice, but it pays to try different combinations and styles.

Spinnerbaits used for buzzing must be balanced and tuned to prevent them from rolling. You should check a bait as soon as it comes out of the package to be sure it runs true. If it doesn't, the top wire, the one with the spinner attached to it, should be bent so that it is centered with the hook point. This should correct the problem, but if it still rolls, bend the wire in the opposite direction from the roll until it runs true. In other words, if the spinnerbait rolls right, bend the top wire to the left, and vice versa.

When the Water Cools, Change Your Tactics

When the water cools and bass slow down, spinnerbait tactics have to change. Instead of the rapid retrieve that was effective when the water was above 62°, a slow retrieve now becomes the order of the day. Yet the spinnerbait makes the change gracefully and is just as potent.

It is essential to match the speed of retrieve with the temperature of the water. From about 50° to 62°, it's a little tricky trying to find just the right combination of speed and amount of "fall" during the retrieve. Though temperature and water color are important concerns, perhaps more important is whether the trend is toward cooling or warming water temperatures.

I had a frustrating experience on Lake Eufaula early one April, learning the importance of retrieve speed as it relates to temperature. A young man from Montgomery, Alabama, was fishing with me while I worked a shallow ditch just off the river channel above Cowikee Creek. During the past few days, I had enjoyed good fishing in this area by slowly working white grubtail Wooly Bullys through scattered stickups along the ditch. The weather had been bright and warm, and the water temperature had risen steadily to about 58° to 60°. My companion had little fishing experience but was quick to learn and had a knack for fishing. All day we had worked spinnerbaits slowly along ledges and stumprows, but fishing was slow. Finally, the fish began to show up in the ditch just as they had for the last few days. The only problem was that my inexperienced buddy was taking five fish to my one. Since I was supposed to be the guide and instructor, the situation became untenable! To make the situation worse, my partner began to tell me how to fish spinnerbaits and where to cast. But within the span of a few casts, he boated a six-pounder, a seven-and-three-quarter-pounder, and a five-and-a-half-pounder. Now I began to pay attention. I even started asking him questions. At first I could see nothing in his technique that differed from mine, yet he continued to outfish me by a ridiculous margin. Then it dawned on me: he was fishing with a Mitchell 410, a high-speed-retrieve spinning reel, while I was using an Ambassadeur 5000C, which takes in much less line per crank. The difference between his success and my failure was speed. I adjusted my retrieve but was too late with too little; my companion went home with tales of unmercifully licking his guide.

The situation now seems obvious. Although the very slow retrieve had been productive during the days that had preceded this trip, the warm weather and warming water had made the bass more active and the faster retrieve effective. It pays to experiment with various speeds, especially when the water temperature is changing.

When fishing "intermediate" temperatures, shallow creek ledges, hedgerows, stumprows along channels, steep banks with cover, stickups, and rip-rap have proven to be excellent places to prospect. I cast the spinnerbait toward the cover or structure and let it sink. If the fish are in water less than six feet deep, it is not necessary to let the bait fall all the way to the bottom before starting the retrieve. If a bass is nearby, he'll either see the flash of the blade or "hear" the vibration of the lure. Keep the lure in contact with or very near cover if it is present. In water over six feet deep, more fish will be caught if the lure hits the bottom before you retrieve. It is critical to keep a tight line and watchful eye as the lure falls. Many strikes come during this time.

The retrieve consists of pumping the lure and letting it free-fall. How fast should you pump the rod and how long should you allow the lure to fall? These are decisions that must be made on the spot, but as a general rule when the water is stained or toward the lower end of the temperature range, a slower retrieve will be more effective. Of course, clear water and warmer temperatures call for a faster retrieve. In all cases, you should work from shallow to deep water. This allows you to take full advantage of the free-fall and the weedless spinnerbait.

For this type of fishing, single spins will outperform tandems in just about every case. They are far superior free-fall baits and give off better vibrations. I prefer the grubtail over the skirt because of the improved sound and vibrations. A quarter-ounce single spin with a No. 4 Colorado spinner has proven hard to beat for this type of fishing, and believe me, this spinnerbait technique can be absolutely deadly in stained water near cover.

Strikes on buzzed spinners tend to be sudden and savage.

Spinnerbaits pictured here are (clockwise): tandem spin, in-line spinner, twin spinner, surface spinnerbait, single spin. Each lure is deadly in certain situations, but the tandem and single spins are the most versatile.

Cold-Water Fishing Can Be Hot

When the water temperature drops below 50°, there is only one way to fish a spinnerbait—slow and deep. Even under these conditions, the spinnerbait shines. It is hard to beat as a cold-water bait.

Now a depthfinder becomes indispensible. Deep creek ledges and river channels are the best places to start your search. Standing timber and submerged islands can also pay off.

Now's the time to get down in the tackle box and pull out the heavier spinnerbaits, because the fish are sure to be at least fifteen feet deep and usually deeper. A three-eighth-ounce bait is the minimum size needed, and one-half and five-eighths ounce spinnerbaits are better. Skirts and grubs are good for this type of fishing. Skirts have more drag and fall slower, but grubs still have the "sound" advantage and "feel" better. Once again, it is important to fish from shallow to deep, near cover if possible.

Cecil Poss, a well-known Lake Eufaula guide, is a master of cold-water spinnerbait fishing. Cecil consistently takes good stringers of outsized Eufaula bass during the coldest months when most fishermen are huddled around a warm fire. Cecil's technique is simple, but it takes patience and a feel for the spinnerbait. His secret is to retrieve the lure with a very gentle pumping action that barely moves the spinnerbait forward as it falls. The blades of the better spinnerbaits spin as the lure free-falls, and the slight pumping action should do nothing more than keep the slack out of the line and add a little change of pace to the speed of the slowly whirling blade. Complete lure control is essential to fish the spinnerbait properly and to detect the faint tap of a bass.

The effectiveness of Cecil's technique was graphically illustrated by an unusual incident that happened to him while fishing on Lake Eufaula one cold winter day. He had been working the heavy brush in twenty feet of water along the old Chattahoochee River channel near the mouth of Chewalla Creek. His half-ounce Bushwacker had accounted for a couple of good bass, but now Cecil was hung tight to the brush along the ledge. A fair amount of pulling, rod jerking, and maneuvering of the boat failed to free the spinnerbait. Cecil was holding his Ambassadeur 5000 reel and Fenwick rod in a relaxed position, with the butt of the rod resting just under the left side of his rib cage. Without warning, the tip of the rod dove toward the water as the weight of a big bass freed the lure and stretched the twenty-five-pound-test line. Cecil responded to the strike by coming back hard on his rod, which caused the butt of the rod to thrust upward into his ribs. The net results of dabbling his half-ounce spinnerbait in twenty feet of water were a cracked rib and an eight-and-three-quarter-pound bass.

Topwater Spinnerbaits

A new addition to the spinnerbait arsenal is the topwater version. This lure is a safety-pin-type spinnerbait with a broad, triangular blade that keeps the lure on top and gurgling, much like a Jitterbug. This special-purpose lure can be unbelievably effective at times, but it lacks the overall versatility of the single and tandem spin.

During the spring and fall when the water temperature is above 65°, the topwater spinnerbait is most effective. It should be worked around such cover as brush tops, stickups, logs, lily pads, and grass. The lure is particularly productive in shallow, weedy lakes with lots of grass and lily pads. Most of these lures are weedless and should be fished right in the cover. Fishermen often fish the baits too fast. As a rule, they should be worked just fast enough to keep them on top. However, bass are fickle and their taste varies, so try different retrieves.

Fishing the Ultralight Spinner

Spinners differ from the safety-pin-type spinnerbaits in that their spinner blades are in line with the body. These lures are small; they are most effective when fished with ultralight tackle.

Though they are not as versatile or as weedless as the safety-pin spinnerbaits, at times they can be lethal in shallow, open water. Many otherwise fishless days on farm ponds and streams have been saved by in-line spinners. They take not only bass but also bluegill, crappie, catfish, and pic-kerel. At times you can make them more effective by adding small strips of pork rind or such natural baits as worms or small minnows, but these little spinners are hard to beat straight out of the package. A swivel is almost mandatory with them since they have a tendency to roll.

How to Get the Most Action From Spinnerbaits

Spinnerbaits have basically two parts, the wire shaft with the blade or blades and the leadhead hook or body. The body offers the angler many options. Each adornment has its own place in the fisherman's tackle box; the most popular kind is the skirt or dress, which is avaiable in both rubber and vinyl. Rubber has more action, but vinyl is more durable.

Skirts are at their best with buzz baits. The added resistance they provide helps keep the lure near the surface and prevents it from rolling when retrieved at faster speeds. They are also popular as dresses for drop baits and provide a tantalizing wiggle when free-falling. Pork-rind strips and wiggle baits are often added to give skirted spin-nerbaits more appeal. Skirts are most useful with tandem-spin baits used for buzzing and with large spinnerbaits worked slow and deep for cold-weather bass.

Grubtails are gaining favor rapidly in bass-fishing circles. These three-inch plastic grubs, like Mann's Sting-Ray Grub, shine when fished slowly with single spins in cool weather. This combination free-falls with little resistance and emits greater vibrations than other baits. Grubs also look amazingly similar to the largemouth's favorite food—threadfin shad. I also use grubs while buzzing, especially in clear water. In fact, 75 percent of my spinnerbait fishing is done with a grubtail on the hook.

Pork rind and the new lifelike wiggle baits can also be effective on a spinnerbait at times. My best success with these "ribbon" baits, such as Mr. Twister and Jelly Wigglers, has been in the shallow, weedy lakes in the South. Black performs best in these lakes—probably because bass often feed on sirens, small snakelike amphibians that inhabit these lakes. Pork-rind strips and chunks can be equally potent, but they generally lack the simplicity of plastic baits. They are harder to store and use, and they dry out quickly when not in use.

Which color is best? This question is as old as the fish hook, but mystery still shrouds the answer. Every fisherman has his own opinion, but certain rules of thumb are standard with experienced anglers. White and green are good colors in clear water and bright weather. Yellow and chartreuse are good choices in stained water or on cloudy days. White is good in almost all conditions. Chartreuse produces well in all but the clearest water. Combination red, yellow, and black skirts are good in stained or off-color water. Blue and white bring good results in clear water. Yet the color preference of bass on a given day can be totally different from the expected, so you must be flexible.

Blades come in different sizes and shapes. The size must be matched to the bait so that balance is maintained. If the blade is too small, it will spin without imparting any action to the lure, losing the proper "feel." Blades that are too large cause the lure to roll and make the bait wobble instead of

Most spinners need subtle adjustments to bring out proper action.

quiver. However, oversized blades can be attractive to cold-weather bass when worked very slowly.

Each of the different types of blades available has its own characteristics. Long, narrow blades spin in tighter revolutions, imparting less action to the bait. Broad spinner blades revolve in wide circles and have much more action. The extremes are the narrow, willow-leaf spinners and the nearly round Colorado spinner blade. Popular Indiana blades fall in between. All will catch fish, but the Colorado is probably the best all-around spinner blade.

Every once in a while I run across a spinnerbait that outfishes the others. I can't look at it and see anything different, but when I retrieve it, the vibrations tell me that it is sending out fish-attracting sounds. The quiver and vibrations make it *feel* like it should catch fish. When one of these baits comes along, make it a prized possession.

The balance of a spinnerbait can sometimes be improved by shortening the length of the top wire. The weedless characteristics of the longer arm are lost, which is a trade-off not worthwhile in brushy or weedy waters. But it may pay to keep this in mind on lakes with little cover.

Spinnerbaits are at their best when fished around heavy brush. Even though they are basically weedless, unless the correct approach is taken when fishing cover an angler can find himself frustrated.

Always try to fish spinnerbaits "with the grain." For instance, if the angler is casting to a fallen tree, he should make every effort to retrieve the bait so that it returns with the angle of the limbs. The lure will flip over limbs but may become wedged. Keep the lure moving to minimize hangups.

I work around cover before working through it. There are two reasons for this. First, if a fish strikes, he will be much easier to boat if he's not buried in a brushtop. Second, I would rather be assured of a couple of outside casts before running the risk of ruining a piece of cover by hanging up.

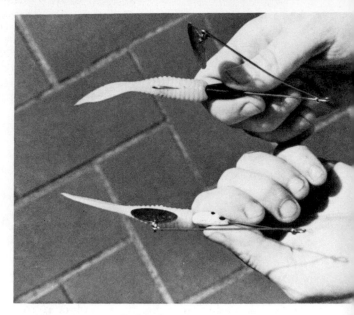

To stop spinner roll, bend top wire in opposite direction of roll.

After all, spinnerbaits can call fish up from quite a distance.

Tom Mann taught me the value of the first reason when he caught a nine-and-a-half-pound bass from a tangle of roots in Lake Eufaula. I had hung that bass three times within a week, but each time she wrapped me in the roots. I met Tom on the lake and told him my story.

"Mind if I try her?" he asked.

"Help yourself, she's more than I can handle," I answered.

I gave him directions and he took off. Five minutes later he was back.

"This your fish?" he said, holding up a huge bass.

"Great day! How'd you get her out of the roots?" I asked enviously.

"I called her out," Tom said.

"What do you mean?"

Tom said, "I just started buzzing a Wooly Bully about fifteen feet from the roots. Each cast, I'd bring the spinnerbait a little closer to cover. On the third throw and about ten feet from the roots, she nailed it."

That was a nine-and-a-half-pound lesson I'll never forget!

Little Things That Make a Difference

Despite all the knowledge and ability of a fisherman to locate bass and make them hit a spinnerbait, often it is attention to detail that actually puts fish in the boat. For instance, nicks and abrasions to the line cause many fish to be lost. Spinnerbaits are prone to damage line since they are often fished fast through heavy cover. In addition, line can become wrapped around the wire shaft,

Author David Morris (right) was a part-time guide and college student at Auburn University when he made this amazing catch with his father (left) and another guide on Lake Eufaula on the Georgia-Alabama border in 1969. The catch on buzzed spinnerbaits for one day totaled forty-five bass, with seventeen weighing between five and eight pounds. Today, with his degree in fisheries management, Morris says he would release the fish, even though they were not wasted back then.

which wedges the line into the backside of the tie-on eye when you apply pressure. Enough pressure can cause the line to shear. It pays to check the line often and to retie it if any roughness is present. This can put an otherwise lost trophy in the live well.

I'm often amazed that bass so consistently find the hook in the maze of wire, rubber, steel, and lead called spinnerbaits. Yet, a strike usually results in a hooked fish. That is, if the hook is sharp. Spinnerbaits, like most lures, often come with dull hooks. A few swipes with a small stone or file are all that is required to insure a greater number of hooked fish. There is one problem, however, that fishermen sometimes encounter when putting a point on chrome-plated hooks. If the chrome plating is chipped, the point can be seriously shortened and will then rust. Extra care must be taken not to file beyond the chrome plating. Once the hook is sharp, be sure that the spinner blade does not hit the point when it revolves. This, of course, can break or dull the point. Experienced anglers increase the hooking capability of spinnerbaits by bending or slightly springing the hook. Angling the hook point outward somewhat improves the "grabbing" qualities of the hook. But if the hook is bent too far, its strength can be lost, and a fish can straighten it out.

Bass often strike spinnerbaits short. They simply hit the bait below the hook, so there is little chance of hooking them. In this case, shorten the dressing, and if this doesn't solve the problem, attach a trailer hook. Although they won't be as weedless, spinnerbaits with trailer hooks can still be worked in cover.

The ease with which a blade spins is an important factor in the effectiveness of a bait. To improve this quality, a shot of WD-40 or Super Lube on the swivel will work wonders. Another way to make the blade revolve easier is to hold or devise a way to hold lures outside the car on the way to the lake. The wind will make the blades revolve, thus smoothing any rough edges that may impair their action. The best way to insure that blades will spin properly is to buy quality spinnerbaits with established reputations.

The spinnerbait may well be the most versatile lure in a bass fisherman's arsenal. In fact, an angler probably would not find himself seriously handicapped if spinnerbaits were all he had when he left the landing. His catch would stack up well day after day with that of worms and crankbaits.

If spinnerbaits have one weakness, it has to be during the heat of the summer when bass are deep. It is almost impossible to work them deep and fast, and for some reason, hot-weather bass tend to shun spinnerbaits worked slowly. But then, every lure has its weakness. Look at our number one bass bait, the plastic worm. It is kind of hard to buzz.

10

Jigs

HOMER CIRCLE

I once posed this question: "If you could have only one lure to catch food for survival, in both fresh and saltwater areas, what would it be?" The readers' preponderant answer came back: a *jig*.

That did not surprise me. In more than a half century of fishing over three continents, I have found jig-type lures to have universal appeal to a broad span of gamefish.

Yet the jig is one of the most underused and misused lures I can think of. Nearly every serious fisherman has some in his tackle box, but surprisingly few know when or how to use them.

So let's shed the light of experience and observation on this dark area of sportfishing in order to brighten more of your fishing days. And let's begin by taking a close look at jigs in all their varied forms.

On my office wall I have suspended some of the earliest and most primitive forms of jigs. Those made by Eskimos have fish-shaped bodies carved from walrus tusk, with bent nails inserted for hooks. Others are made of copper tubing filled with lead, or bits of colorful plastic, also with bent nails for hooks. From these have evolved the many modern counterparts made of all sorts of bodies and many designs of lead heads. But they all have two things in common: (1) they sink quickly, and (2) they catch bass—if you know the art of using them.

One of my early comeuppances in fishing jigs came at the hands of an old master, Billy Burns, a tobacco farmer from Lexington, Kentucky. Billy tied his own jigs during the winter season, then fought fish and farming from spring through fall.

His pet lure was a quarter-ounce black jig head molded on a gold 3/0 Model Perfect hook. The body was black-dyed polar bear hair. To this he added a three-inch strip of black pork eel. So it was all black except for that gold hook, which Billy said added a touch of class.

Here is his time-proved technique. He powers out a long cast, lets the jig sink until a slack line tells him it is on bottom. His left hand cradles, rather delicately, the foregrip of his lightweight rod. He holds the rod tip almost overhead and gently raises and lowers it while intermittently reeling just fast enough to maintain a slight tension on the line.

If you were down below where the fish are, you would see a black creature swimming with an up-and-down motion, provocatively lifelike. And Billy keeps it coming just over bottom cover, until it is directly below his boat. Here he gives it a few gyrations to tempt a following fish.

But, there's even more technique at work as Billy retrieves his melanistic jig. That left hand is sensitive to any change in the resistance of that lure as he swims it along. If he feels even a faint

111

Homer Circle's favorite jigs are designed to catch the eye of deep-sulking bass. They range in size from 1/64 ounce to 3/4 ounce. Glen Lau

degree of lessened or increased tension, he sets the hook.

Also, his eyes are locked on the line where it enters the water. Should it become minutely taut, or slack, or move laterally, he sets the hook. This is because when a fish takes a jig, it rarely is with a jolting strike as with other lures.

Fascinated, I have watched fish take jigs in clear water to ascertain how they do it so gently. They simply open their mouths, flare their gills at the same instant, and the jig gets sucked into their mouths.

If you ask Billy how he knows when to set the hook, he replies: "Well, it's hard to explain except if the tension feels different, or the line looks different, I give it to him. Sometimes I think I set the hook just on suspicion."

Another master jig fisherman is Billy Westmorland, a professional who makes a living in tournament fishing for bass. This affable Tennessean, who has caught tons of fish with his jig technique, describes his method in simple terms.

"The first thing I determine is the depth of the water where I'm about to fish. Say it's twenty feet. Through experience, by feel and by watching my jig, I can judge how deep the jig is every second it sinks until it finally rests on bottom.

"This way, if my jig hits something before I think it should be on the bottom, I set the hook because a fish has it in its mouth. Also, if I lose feel of the jig as it sinks, I know a fish has picked it up, so I stick him.

"This countdown, and feel, varies with the weight of the lure. An eighth ounce takes longer to reach bottom than a quarter ounce, logically. So you must learn to feel each lure all the way down.

"Once the lure reaches bottom, gently lift it off a few inches and let it drop back with a tight line. If you let slack into your line, you can't maintain feel of the jig. Just pick it up and drop it back under tension all the way back to you. I prefer a short, stiff lightweight rod for the best feel."

Now, let's look at jig fishing through the skilled hands of Cotton Cordell, who got started in the lure-making business by molding jigs in his kitchen near Hot Springs, Arkansas. He is the quiet type who sits there saying nothing and does it quite eloquently as he pulls in successive fish.

Nothing fancy about Cotton, either. When he goes jig fishing he carries along a brown paper sack with a couple hundred white jigs, and another with a couple dozen yellow ones.

I asked: "How do you know when to use yellow?"

He replied, "Oh, whenever I run out of white."

Here's his method, which takes bass and big crappies. He uses a seven-foot spinning rod and chunks the jig close to brush piles which he has previously buried. Some two dozen of them.

By counting down, he judges when the jig is just over the brush. Then he retrieves it just over the brush using one of two preferred procedures: (1) he reels so slowly you think he's dozing between turns of his reel handle; and (2) he still reels slowly but every third or fourth turn of his reel handle he gives the jig a sharp twitch.

Cotton explains: "There are times when a fish wants that jig doing nothin', and doing it real slow. Then, at times, the occasional twitch triggers a strike you wouldn't otherwise get. You show me a man who fishes a jig fast and I'll show you a man who'll never dull the edge of a fish-cleaning knife."

Then, take my longtime friend Glen Lau who has a touch with a jig that borders the uncanny. He

Author Homer Circle, veteran Sports Afield *Magazine Angling Editor, interviews one of his favorite subjects, a six-pound bigmouth that just couldn't leave a deep jig alone. "Tell me your secrets, old bass," says Uncle Homer, "and I'll put you back!"*

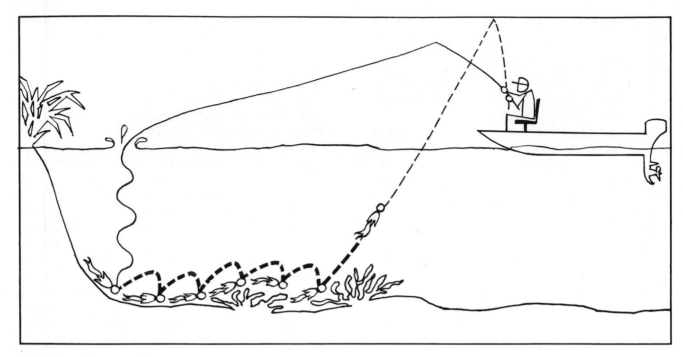

BOTTOM-HOPPING THE JIG: *Cast to target and let the jig fall on a tight or slack line. Raise the rod tip a few inches. The jig will swim forward until it hits bottom. Lower the rod tip, take up the slack and repeat.* Illustrations by Bill Bartlett.

SWIMMING THE JIG: *The jig should swim roughly parallel to the bottom as you keep a taut line and retrieve slowly. Try to feel the jig and watch the line.*

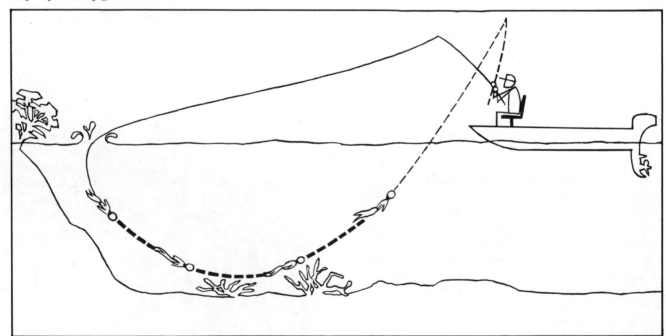

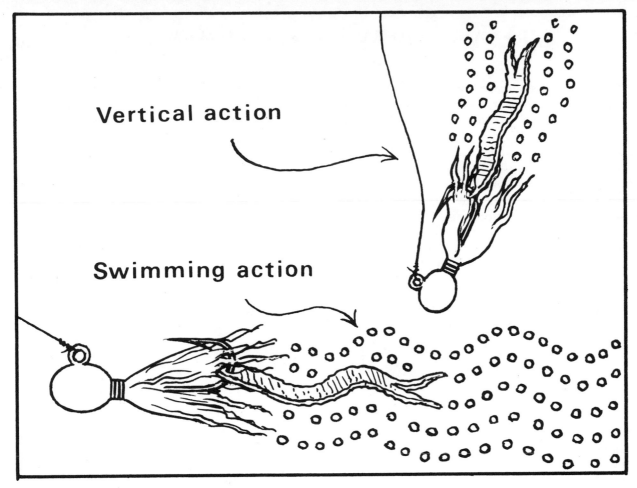

Vertical action

Swimming action

JIG ACTION: *A small piece of pork rind on the hook helps give the lure some natural action as it's falling, and also while hopping or swimming during the retrieve. This is the old "fly and rind" from the early 50s.*

is especially effective during the hot summer months when few fishermen bring in enough fish to eat. Glen goes for the ultralight touch both in a rod, line, and jigs.

For bass, Glen uses a responsive rod, six-pound mono, and jigs in the one-eighth to one-sixteenth-ounce class. Like Cotton, his most productive colors are white and yellow. He prefers to work the jig straight down, and *very* slowly, in dropoff water, rather than casting into distant holes. "The bigger fish of any species don't move much away from the hole in which they habitually lie," he says. "They are secure there. So, they won't pursue a fast-moving lure unless extremely hungry. But when a jig is gently lowered right in front of their eyes, it's so easy to suck in they usually do. The trick is to get it there, and that calls for patience and perseverance."

Well, there you have the successful methodology of three of the nation's best jig fishermen. While I agree that you should follow their proved methods, I can add a few suggestions that will broaden your success throughout a season's fishing.

When fishing a stream, anchor above a deep hole at the foot of a riffle. Use a jig heavy enough to take it down against the pull of the current. Cast slightly downstream, raise your rod tip and let the lure nudge bottom as you fish it downstream.

When fishing in a lake, imagine the shoreline is like a stairs or ramp because to varying degrees it is interspersed with weeds, rock formations, or other types of cover. Anchor your boat against shore and cast a jig for about fifty to seventy-five feet into deep water, and let it settle to bottom. Then, just hop it in by reeling steadily, slowly, and working it up the sloping bottom.

Conversely, anchor in the deeper offshore water and make your casts into shallow water. Then, just hop the jig down the sloping bottom. In either approach, remember to watch your line like a chicken ogling a bug. If it does anything unusual, *strike*.

And finally, here's a method of jig fishing so deadly I hesitate to tell you about it. It could get you snatched right over the gunnel of your boat. The only reason I feel justified in telling you is because I don't believe you will be using a line heavy enough to endanger you. Look around a lake until you find a stretch of weeds where they border deep water, say six to fifteen feet. Put on a half-ounce jig, sit in the rear of your boat, and run it backward. Either a small outboard or an electric motor does this job well.

As you slowly back your boat in and out of the curvatures of that weedy perimeter, imagine you are hemstitching the bottom with your lure. Just raise and lower it in and out of each nook and slot as you wend your way backward. Once you become adept at this method, which some call "backtrolling," you'll be both pleased and amazed at the variety of fish it will produce. If you do it against much wave action, you'll need splash boards mounted on your boat's transom.

Finally, here's a chart that will help you to correlate lure, line, and rod weight. Remember that a line too heavy for the jig you're using will retard its action just as too much tail will bog down a kite.

JIG WEIGHT IN OUNCES	LINE TEST IN POUNDS	ROD ACTION
one-sixty-fourth	2	ultralight
one-sixteenth	4	ultralight
one-eighth	6	light
one-fourth	8	light
one-half	10	medium-light
three-fourths	15	medium-heavy

The Fly Rod on Bass Water
A Modern Approach

DAVE WHITLOCK

Several years ago I voluntarily launched myself into a bass-fishing experiment that had some of my friends shaking their heads, wondering if Whitlock had fished through too many noons under the scalding sun. Actually, I was completely lucid, even though my notion seemed that of a dizzy child. My project was extreme in its intent: for seven years, when I went bass fishing anywhere, I was to leave my spinning and casting tackle at home. I was to fish with only two fly-rod outfits, no matter what the circumstances of season, weather, or water conditions!

This self-inflicted exile from normal methods changed my entire outlook and respect for bass fishing, a traumatic experience for an Okie who teethed on a cane pole, had his first backlash at age five, and fell in love with spinning when he was fifteen, back in 1949.

I have courted bass since childhood, first with the cane pole and line, then graduating to baitcasting, fly-rodding, ultralight baitcasting, spinning, spincasting, and the super-duper bass-hauling stud sticks and high rpm winches of the modern era. I've yet to abandon any of these proven methods. But I must admit, my talents with the fly rod and bass bug constituted the least of my angling skills but were what I loved best of all.

Like 99 percent of the other bass fishers who carry the three basic casting tools, my fly rod only got in the way in the bottom of the boat, usually tangling up with the other tackle. It was used only at those magical moments when wind and water were calm, and the back of Mr. Bass was pushing up against the warmwater surface curtain. If I was fishing with a friend unsympathetic to fly fishing, the first bug seldom got wet.

Each year that followed after I became the complete bass fisher, I fished bass less and trout more. I had great bass fishing right on my doorstep, as the filling reservoirs of Oklahoma, Texas, Arkansas, and Missouri became teeming with bonanzas of bass. But I'd drive 250 to 1,250 miles for a few days of wading and fly casting for eight to eighteen-inch trout—tame or wild.

Why? Well, that's what I asked myself. To a trout fisher the answer was obvious—more action, challenge, and pleasure per hour of fishing.

It's hard for most people to break old habits, and I'm no exception. Besides leaving the other rods home, I was faced with the limitations of fishing only topwater bugs to shoreline bass. I lacked the confidence and experience to start other fly-fishing methods when conditions indicated sub-surface bass. That's the time when you and I would generally reach for the worm rod or crankbait outfit. Even when I started this fly-

A modern assortment of bass bugs and flies contains shapes, materials, and colors that would have dazzled our bassing grandfathers.

rod-only thing, I'd find myself pounding away at barren shoreline with corkhead poppers as if I were a programmed machine. That sort of target shooting can be lots of fun passing time, but it can't produce bass when they are most comfortable at a ten-foot depth and forty yards out from shoreline cover.

Seven years of angling is a long time to practice breaking old habits and developing new ones. I'm pleased to say that under most circumstances now I can produce, cast for cast, as many and equal-size bass as the average good bassman using conventional methods.

Cast for cast is the key phrase in that broad statement of mine. Other than in topwater fishing, which on a twelve-month basis across North American bass water produces fewer than 20 percent of the bass take, a spin or baitcaster can fish more water in a given period than a fly fisherman. The reason? A great time efficiency in getting the lure down to the bass. Over a period of time he might fish four casts to my one, especially at the deeper depths. But I'm saying that of one thousand casts for each of us, I will catch about the same number and size of bass as the baitcaster or spinner in the same water.

Now a nonfly-fishing sceptic would most likely ask: "*Why* fly fish, then, if the other methods are so much more efficient?" The reason is, to quote the late Arnold Gingrich: "Fly fishing is the most fun a man can have standing up." Of all the popular methods of catching fish of any size, casting, hooking, and playing a fish on the fly is the most enjoyable, and *that* is the main reason most of us fly fish, despite reports to the contrary.

In the material to follow, I hope to share with you some of the experiences and observations stemming from my own fly-rodding for bass. You won't have to spend seven years learning how to make your fly rod a more-than-sometime angling tool.

Presentations and Retrieves: From Cast to Strike

Working a fly with line and rod motions to create the live deception is one of the greatest charms and challenges of bass fly-rodding. I use dozens of standard routines and probably make up more every year. Generally, certain bass foods—and the flies we use—have natural movement in patterns. Often the most unnatural retrieves turn on bass most. So often irregular moves and erratic noises trigger the bass's most primitive killer instincts on crippled or distressed creatures.

No other casting and fishing system even approaches fly fishing for manipulating artificial lures. Only the fisher's skill, imagination, and interest limit what he can do with flies.

Our first problem is to get our flies into and through the hazards that bass love to use for cover—rocks, moss, wire fences, brush, weeds, reeds, logs, lillies, boat docks, piers, and stumps. I'm not referring to *working* the flies, but how to get them in and out of the cover without spoiling the spot or losing your fly.

Always use a full side or three-quarter sidearm cast to present flies into or beneath overhanging cover: low-angle presentation avoids hangups and cuts the effect of cross winds. In these days of high fishing pressure, pinpoint accuracy is essential. Inches from the proper spot can make a huge difference in your day's catch. The bass willing to move out of his hole to a lure was probably caught the day before by a spincaster.

Whether you use a top, middle, or bottom retrieve, exactly the same technique must be used to accomplish a snag-free swim of the fly. This is also the best way to detect unseen bass strikes, and the best way to strike, hook, and control bass. Hold your rod low to the water and as nearly parallel and in line with the retrieve plane as practical; the rod and extended line, leader, and fly should form a straight path. In moving water this path will arch to the current's drag, but in still water it will be nearly straight.

Place the fly line over the index or second finger of your rod hand and retrieve with your other hand, pulling the line over the finger of your rod hand. When the fly lands on or in a potential snagup area, or is retrieved into an obstacle, you must pull it off, around, or over the spot by using only the slow handline pull with the rod pointed

Author Dave Whitlock has pioneered new techniques and lures for fly-rod bass fishing.

directly at the obstacle. *Do not give any assistance with your rod!* This is a hard habit to break but the pull of the rod—and its "loading"—against the resistant obstacle either causes the hook to embed or else spring uncontrollably away from the hot spot when the hook pulls free. A loop snag-guard will deflect the hook's point direction when you pull the fly over or through obstacles. The quick jerk or flip of a rod will often cause excess fly momentum, which causes the loop to collapse, exposing the hook's point for an unwanted hookup. On strikes, the bass will collapse the loop guard, whereupon a quick jerk of the rod or pull on the line will cause the point to penetrate the fish's mouth.

Even without a snag-guard, most flies can be worked through hangup hazards with this method. Another advantage to this method is that you *always* have a tense or tight line link between yourself and the fly. This makes striking sure and quick. If the bass should run directly toward you—which is often the case when fishing into shore from a boat or tube—you have the rod's full arch to take up slack.

Absolute control over fly movement on still waters is possible when you hold the rod tip close to the water. Any distance above the water creates an additional pulling effect, since the fly line seeks to form a perpendicular with the water's surface and rod tip. A rod tip held three feet above the surface when a bug is spot-cast—say, against a stump base—will cause the bug to pull about two feet away from the target without one inch of retrieve. So without realizing it, you may be moving the fly away from prime spots before you intend to do so. *A large amount of good bass fishing depends upon the lure staying in one spot to sink or float right there—not creeping away toward you unintentionally.*

When using the low rod-angle line retrieve, hook-setting is more efficient. By raising the rod butt with a locked wrist movement, you move the hook point with greatest authority. A rotating, or wrist-twist, back movement raises the more flexible tip through a long arch, which becomes *too* efficient a shock-absorbing device. Thus the hook is not moved briskly into the bass's tough mouth parts. Improper hooking usually results in the bass throwing the hook with a head-shaking surge or on the first jump.

An argument might be made that the rotational strike protects the tippet. This is only a problem with very light tippets—four to six pounds. But if you use a lighter rod, of 5 or 6 weight, even a four or six-pound tippet is safe if you use the lockwrist rod-butt strike with finesse. Remember: you are only moving the fly an inch or so with this method, and the line and leader's stretch is more than ample to absorb such a shock.

Bug and Fly Imitations: The New Realism

When I started my seven-year study, I took a long look into my suitcase-sized bass tackle box, and a short look into my cigar-box-sized fly box. My fly selection was miniscule compared to the twenty-five pounds of plugs, worms, spoons, jigs, eels, and spinnerbaits! If I was going to fly fish for bass, and do it successfully, all the fly rods, fly lines, and fly reels made weren't worth much without special flies that did a better job than the small bunch of popping bugs and spinners and bucktails I possessed then.

For the first three years, while doing routine water field studies, I kept notes on my catches, conditions of the waters, food patterns, and especially how other bassmen were doing in the same waters and situations with casting lures. To verify or disprove my thinking above the water, I did a lot of skin-diving, seining, and work with aquariums.

My fly-lure collection doubled and redoubled as I fished, observed, tied flies, fished, observed, and tied flies some more. I divided three large partitioned drawers of a tackle box for top, middle, and bottom flies. The shapes, sizes, colors, and numbers began to exceed even the carnival variety of my idle spin and bait-casting lures.

As I reviewed the range of flies I had tied to imitate the spectrum of bass foods, a new perspective struck me. With essentially one method (fly fishing) I could present the bass with all its foods, from a half-inch insect to a six-inch shad to a twelve-inch snake. Each could be cast and fished to fool even the most selective bass. No other single method could approach this. I could imitate

Imaginative bug creations like Whitlock's Nearnuf Hair Frog have opened new opportunities for bass fly fishing.

New bugs for deep fishing, like this Whitlock creation, give the fly rodder a lure with plastic worm potential.

the delicate, fluttering landing of a may fly or the desperate escape of a shad or the crawl of a big salamander with the same rod. Three fly patterns in three casts. My confidence and enthusiasm were fired.

Each time I tied new flies or fished them, I had a new sensation of playing the role of a master puppeteer. I made my puppets fly, flutter, skip, twitch, pop, shake, dive, wiggle, and swim with countless maneuvers of rod, line, and leader. My new flies were tied with special materials, shaped to accent the animations. The strikes I got from big bass were almost secondary to the fun I was having fishing with these new patterns.

The fly patterns I adapted or created still needed a lot of refinement. Beyond the right size, color, water action, and balance, these flies had to have the right hooking ability, and the right feel or texture. Bass have large mouth cavities that are lined with tough skin, reinforced with rubbery cartilage and bone. Their strikes, bites, and swallows often seemed violent and insensitive, but were they really that way? I wanted to know.

By watching wild bass in my aquariums strike natural and fake foods, I had some eye-opening experiences. First, they are extremely sensitive to food texture, prefering a firm meaty object to one that is very hard or mush-soft. In fact, they seem almost to detest a hard plastic, metal, or wood object unless they're extremely mad or excited. They quickly reject or eject them *faster* than they take them in. This was obviously the cause of a lot of my missed strikes on bugs, plugs, and spoons.

I improved the texture whenever possible by using deer or elk hair in place of cork or balsa on

my topwater bugs. Natural and synthetic furs on nymphs and streamer bodies were used instead of metallics and hard rubber or stiff plastic. I used flexible feathers and hair for streamer wings instead of stiffer ones.

Next I considered the hooking. Bass primarily strike by fast tail-and-fin forward thrusts while opening their mouths with closed gills to create a strong intake vacuum on instant contact with the prey. As the food is inhaled (not swallowed) they open their gill covers, exhausting the incoming rush of water but trapping and holding their catch with jaws, tongue, and gill rakers. Unless the lure is too big for the mouth cavity, the lips are closed over or bitten down upon the catch. The lure must be moved in the mouth to insure hook-point and barb penetration. Bass may initially prevent this, especially if the lure is completely inside closed lips. It merely butts up against them inside, stopping the movement.

To demonstrate this statement, take a bass bug or a small casting bait, attach a line to it, and place it between your thumb and index finger. Close your hand tightly to form an open chamber, but press your thumb and index finger together tightly. Pull or jerk on the line with your left hand as if setting the hook after receiving the strike from a bass. It's almost impossible to move the lure through the closed finger and therefore penetrate the hook point into your skin.

A good bass fly must have a hook point exposed, with excess gap past the widest part of the fly body or head, to make contact as the fly moves inside the mouth or out through the fish's lips. Soft materials, which collapse or compress under mouth pressure, aid in exposing more hook. They encourage the bass to maintain more mouth-retention time, which allows more time to strike with the hook point. I now make most of my bass flies snag-proof. A single nylon loop guards the hook; it is devised to discourage hangups and small-fish hookups but not affect the hooking of wanted fish.

Our bugs and flies fall into four major categories: (1) surface or topwater; (2) floating-diving flies; (3) swimming flies; and, (4) bottom-crawling flies.

If you could assemble a master bass menu of natural foods you would still only have less than half the items bass try to eat and can be caught on. Besides insects, crustaceans, reptiles, amphibians, fish, birds, and mammals, bass are always looking for new foods such as outboard motor propellers, rocks, beer cans, and sun glasses! This points up the wonderful predatory nature of the beast, the reason why bass are so much fun to tempt on artificial lures. Bass have true grit, for sure!

Topwater: The Ultimate Sport

Big, prime, adult bass like nothing better than to celebrate the rites of spring with a feast on shoreline delicacies. Consequently, this is the most advantageous period for a bug man to set his table with special recipes of hair and feathers. Spring's warm kiss of sunshine and showers awakens shoreline and aquatic life, creating a limited zone of prime environs that bass just can't resist moving up against for feasting and mating. The excitement of this good life dulls their normal selectivity and caution into a "devil may care" attitude.

As each spring day turns the landscape from a hazy winter dun brown to hues of pastels, then rich greens, shoreline surfaces are titillated with small frogs, little water snakes, baby turtles, fly hatches, biwinged dragon, and damsel flies. Small panfish and minnows dimple here and there as they sip down groggy ants, spiders, and aquatic insect hatches. The closer shallow shoreline waters of ponds and lakes warm quickly, deceiving the topwater bug fly fisher who waits until mid-June to begin his bugging season. Bass come into this narrow zone as if drawn and held by a magnetic force field and a properly fished topwater fly will often provide an early-season response that excells any other period of the season. Many calm sunny afternoons from late February through May, I have seen big bass, their backs out of the water, soaking up warmth in just inches of shoreline water.

Later, as temperatures climb and days lengthen, topwater action along shorelines will occur during the early morning or late afternoon. Until the waters begin to cool in the fall, bringing on a repeat of spring's surface-feeding frenzy, our bass will be holding in deep haunts. Then the topwater addict must join the dawn patrol or fish out the last light of the long summer evenings in hopes of presenting a buggy-acting topwater fly to a cruising fish. The extra effort will pay off, however, because a bass is truly at his best when attacking surface prey. A topwater strike can be as subtle as a raindrop ring or resemble a Polaris missile launch or fall of a bowling ball!

As popular as the bugs and poppers are, there has been almost no design development in the last fifty to one-hundred years. Bass topwater lures are classed as poppers, hairbugs, moths, frogs, and sliders. Few patterns actually look and fish like specific natural foods; most rely on the suggestiveness of fished action to create fish interest.

Cork, balsa, and light molded plastic are the most popular body materials for the poppers. I call these time-tested favorites "hard heads," and I have a pretty hard-headed dislike for them. They are usually complicated to make, heavy to cast, low in durability, and seldom held long by a sensitive-mouthed bass compared to the deer-hair-body counterparts. They usually require one or two line sizes larger than lines for hairbugs or streamers—if they're to be cast well. An almost universally common fault of most commercially available poppers is their poor hooking potential (the hook-body gap is too narrow), the lack of snag-guard devices, and a tendency to dive on pickup or drag in a dull manner while being worked. Homemade poppers are usually much better. There are special patterns and occasions, however, when some hard-head designs have no equal.

BASS BUGHEAD DESIGNS

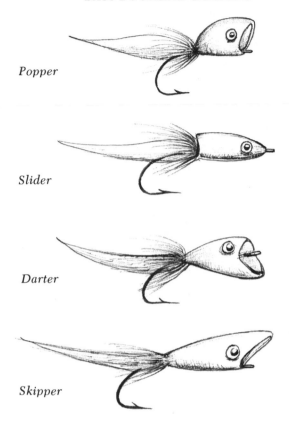

Popper

Slider

Darter

Skipper

the creatures that bass will strike or eat. Natural and dyed deer hair, chicken hackles, rubber hackle, and marabou feathers can be tied to an appropriate hook in a style that when carefully barbered with razor or scissors will become look-alike twins with almost any bass food. Not only in shape and action, but in texture, too, for a hairbug has a lifelike feel or texture most like the naturals bass frequently swallow.

Ah, now I've begun to touch this magical charm that hairbugs hold over their rigid bodied cousins . . . the popping bugs. The charm affects Mr. Bass and Mr. Flyfisher equally. First, when hairbugs fly over the water, land and settle, they excite the angler for they appear and sound so realistic that his confidence is instantly instilled. The flying silhouette, lifelike water impact, and realistic shape and action also begin working their charm on any bass in that area. But two factors must evolve before the magic spell is complete. First, you must manipulate the hairbug properly. The action is not a cast, pop, pop, pop, pop, cast routine

You can take bass with cork, balsa, or plastic-headed popping bugs, but using hairbugs is the way to go for premium quality action. Hairbugs enable us to tie and use a bug that closely simulates those soft live creatures that through their own will or accident, swim, struggle, or just float atop or just beneath the silvery curtain at the top of a bass's world.

I was fortunate enough a long time ago to discover the magical charms of bugs made from soft, hollow, bouyant hair and feathers. After experiencing how a smart bass reacted to the taste of a fuzzy bug, I easily forced myself to learn how to mate feathers and flare the hollow body hair of deer, elk, or caribou to the hook's shank. The first efforts were more weird than late Saturday night TV-movie horror creatures, but they caught bass almost as well as the more polished patterns I build now.

With a little imagination and innovation a hair-bug can be fashioned that imitates or suggests all

SPECIALIZED BUGS

Pencil Balsa Popper

Dipslipstick Slider

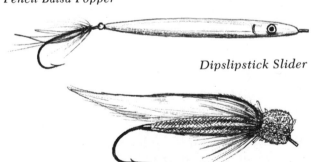

Marabou Muddler Cripple Minnow

Hair Frog

Moth Hairbug

commonly associated with popping bugs and plugs. No gentlemen, it is titillation to a fine degree. Don't think you have to pop a bug to announce its presence to a shallow-water bass. He is aware of the bug's intrusion the second it lands on his roof. Most of his victims are located by extremely subtle vibrations. Since we don't rely on our hearing to gather our food, it is hard for us to realize how acute hearing is in other creatures, that use this sense for survival and food. A good hair-bugger incorporates the actions and vibrations of real insects and other creatures a bass relies on to keep his tummy full.

This means a dead float, tiny twitches, slow steady or erratic swimming, crawling over pads, mosses, logs, off rocks. This game is not speed! Ninety-five percent of all topwater lures are cast and retrieved in a similar action and time span. Most natural topwater foods act exactly opposite of these popular popping, jerking, reeling, retrieves. Bass much over two years of age have seen enough of both to know the difference or they wind up as fillets in someone's freezer.

Second, these special finesse actions and techniques have dropped the bass's guard and raised his interest into a positive strike. This is perhaps the hairbug's charm. For the strike and reaction of a big bass will be so natural that it is like watching a Disney or Lau movie. The take of a hairbug by a big bass provides a neat sensation that gives twice the satisfaction of a bass striking a fast lure out of excited impulse, anger, or reflex. Hairbug takes will vary from subtle sips to noisy geysers to the perfectly timed out-of-water strike on a slow-landing hairwing bug.

Whatever way the bass might feel necessary to capture his prize, he will not suspect he has been duped until he's begun to be dragged toward your boat. Why? Because the hairbug, even more than a plastic worm, feels like live food to him. This fact gives the bass-bugger more advantages, for the bass will take the bug deeper, hold on to it longer, often swallowing it if the hooksetter isn't awake. On occasion I love to let a nice bass enjoy reacting to the idea he has got it made and allow him to swim back to cover on a slack line. Only about one out of three will volunteer to expel the bug after a few long seconds. Even those will often restrike it once it returns to the surface and I activate it again. A most enjoyable bonus!

Hairbugs are practical in sizes 12 through 3/0 and weigh from one-third to two-thirds less than their similar shaped hard-headed counterparts.

Now, that is not saying much when it comes to carrying them in a tackle box, vest, or on your hat band. But where it counts is in the casting. They are amazingly more easy to cast than the more common wood or plastic-bodied bug. They are equally as wind resistant but will fly much better with the same speed than brand X. This advantage allows a bass-bugger more latitude in size range of bugs he can cast with any given rod and line balance. He can cast further or use less line speed with this more efficient design. But perhaps the best advantage is that you can use considerably lighter tackle to fish effectively and efficiently.

I normally use a light to medium-light flyrod—a medium-action that handles 6 and 7 weight level or bass bug tapers. My favorite length for good line control is eight feet and I find rods from seven-and-one-half to eight-and-one-half-feet most practical. Harry Wilson of San Francisco, California, a custom rod-maker, designed me two beautiful hairbug rods of eight and eight-and-a-half-feet that have perfect bug action with a 7 weight bass-bug taper. The Scientific Anglers System 7 rod and Berkley eight-foot Gowdy Parametric are also perfect for bass bugging. Most bass-bug fishermen I know or read about use a gauge or two heavier outfit even for small bass.

Since the most common and abundant species (largemouth, smallmouth, spotted) seldom, if ever average two pounds across North America, why use Paul Bunyan sized rods and lines to enjoy effectively tossing bugs to them? I have the pleasure of introducing new fly-fishing friends regularly to bugging bass my way. Without exception, they find much easier casting and presentation than with their favorite hard heads. Hairbugs usually allow longer, more effortless, casting too!

I don't believe it necessary or practical to use fragile tippets on any bass bug. Typically, bass-bugging is a sport carried out in aquatic jungles of water plants, weeds, tree roots, dead trees, and other covers such as flooded duck blinds, boat docks, and barbed-wire fence rows. A heavy tippet will present a bug more accurately and allow it to be retrieved with or without bass from these jungles. Also, a good bass is hard-mouthed and you need a strong tippet to set the point past the barb in his jaw when he is biting down on the bug. I usually use tippets from eight to fifteen pounds depending on water clarity, bug size, and extent of water hazards. I never kill bass anyway but I do enjoy landing them.

Now back to topwater styles. When bass are

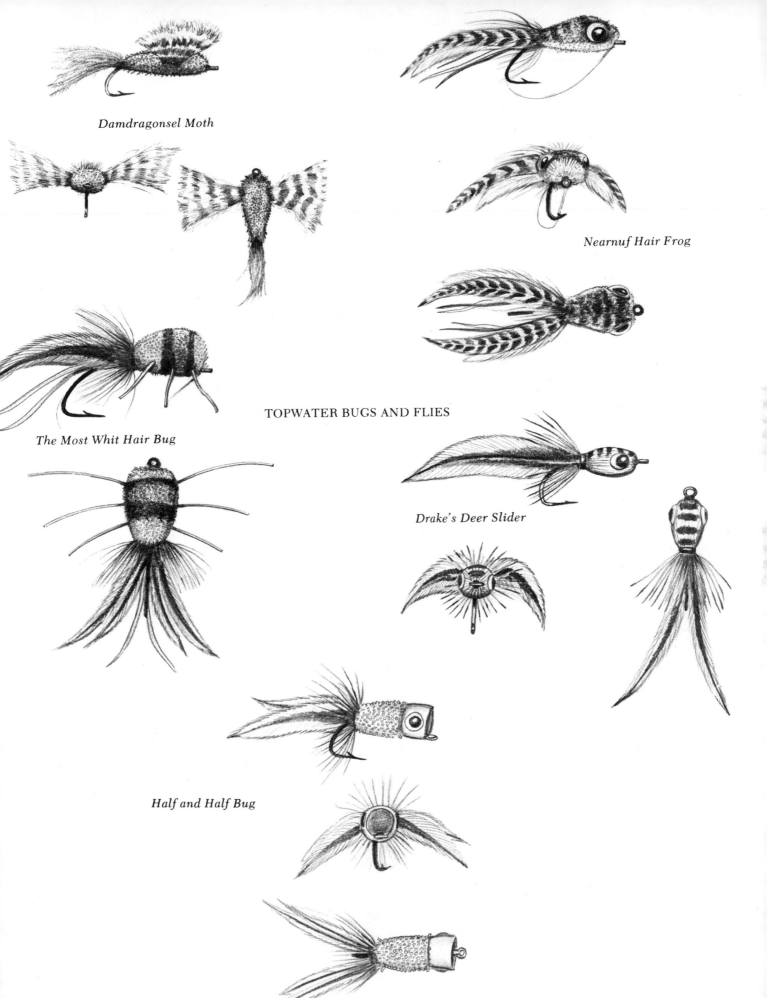

Damdragonsel Moth

Nearnuf Hair Frog

The Most Whit Hair Bug

TOPWATER BUGS AND FLIES

Drake's Deer Slider

Half and Half Bug

fresh out of their winter's deep dens, they want meat to dine on. They cruise the shoreline going in, out, under and through the cover in search of prey. Some will find an ambush spot if cover and food movement is just right. I have seen them backtail up against a shallow shoreline and soak up sun, snooze, and grab a softly cast bug, landing just out from them or carefully manipulated by the holding position. At this time, they will hit bugs that resemble almost any creature found living or falling into the shoreline areas. Perhaps, the best are frogs, small snakes, little green turtles, mice, and surface-swimming, small fish.

These spring-fever bass are usually spooky after months of deep-water living and will retreat to the depths if a sloppy cast or noisy approach is made. A small cartop boat, canoe, tube floater or waders are great to get shallow and quiet with. Today's throne bass boats make it rough to remain inconspicuous and quiet. I stay low and quiet and put my bugs down as softly as possible without lining the spot I think holds the bass. When possible, I put the bug down on pads, weeds, shoreline, or overhangs, and then slowly and gently pull it into the water. If the bug is shaped properly and has a loop nylon snag-guard, it will crawl and swim over

almost any obstacle. I love to manipulate these bugs through the cover.

The action changes when the water warms enough to trigger nest building, pairing, and spawning. Then bass become more stationary as they choose choice overhead cover areas in two to six feet of water to build a spawning nest. Mood, more than food, determines strikes now and I use an irritating action hairbug with more exotic color schemes that will squirm and dance over the nest without much retrieving. It should also pop without being moved much and float low in the surface.

When a bug plops down or swims over this private area, it seems to have a particular insulting effect, much more than a spinnerbait, worm, or topwater plug. I think it is a combination of being able to hold the bug in place for a long period and still have its rubber legs, fluffy tail, and noise create a teasing distraction. Whatever, during this period, I've seen hairbugs outfish hot-shot pluggers too often to be recorded as luck. Too, if you are aware of these shoreline honeymooners' love nest you can keep your bug over productive areas much longer than any other method except anchoring a live shiner.

Divers, Dippers, Darters, and Skippers

This group of bass flies departs from the popping bugs to more specialized actions. Some of these are more pluglike than typical flies but still cast and fish well on a 6-weight line and heavier. They all float on the surface and, upon activation, dive, dip, wiggle, or dart beneath the surface; then they either continue the up-and-down movement or swim deeper as the retrieve continues.

Both the floating weight-forward and the wet-tip or wet-belly lines are used with these patterns. I use the floating line for the up-down, up-down retrieves, very shallow swimming retrieves, or the dive. For most circumstances I prefer this line for working divers, dippers, and darters.

The sink-tip lines are truly effective when using the divers and darters along fast dropoff shorelines and when working river shorelines

while fishing from a boat or tube-floater. When the bug is cast, pause until the line tip sinks, then begin the retrieve. The fly will leave the surface to swim after the sunken line tip. The sinking tip with a floating diver is also a fine combination when working on schooling bass chasing schools of bait fish. Cast the fly across the surface commotion, twitch it quickly three times *across* the surface, then strip it fast *beneath* the surface.

Leaders for floating lines should be seven-and-a-half to nine feet. With the sink-tip line I much prefer a four to seven-and-a-half-foot length, which allows the sinking portion of the line to have maximum effect for pulling and holding the fly down in a deeper level. A long leader allows the fly too much play, and it might not even dive in shallow water.

Swimming Flies: Getting Down to Action

These designs are fished beneath the surface at various depths, with actions that usually attempt to depict a natural or distress swim. They imitate

such swimmers as minnows, shad, leeches, and aquatic insects. This group reflects still further adaptations I've made as a result of my fly-fishing-

DIVERS, DIPPERS, DARTERS, SKIPPERS

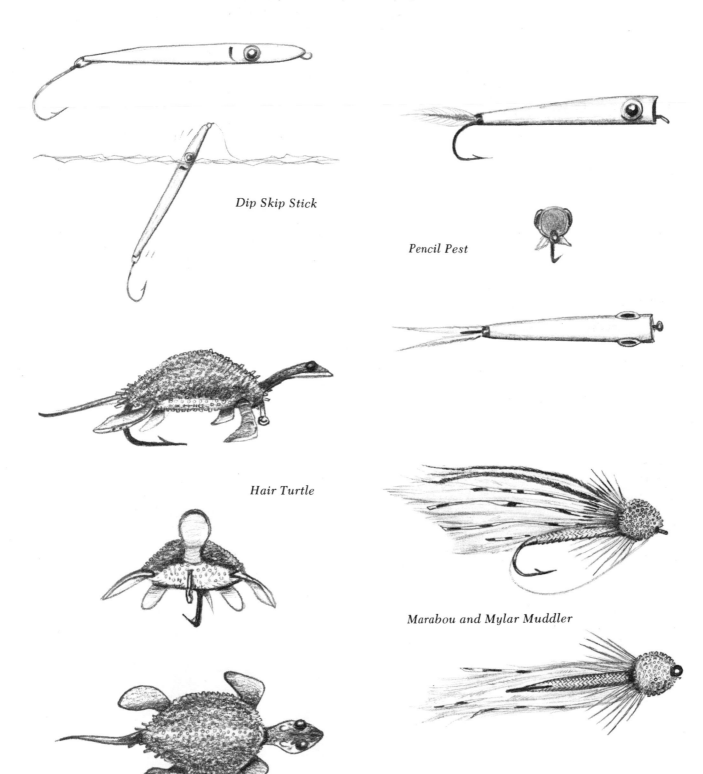

Dip Skip Stick

Pencil Pest

Hair Turtle

Marabou and Mylar Muddler

only study. Some patterns sharply depart from the accepted fly-fishing imitations of naturals and from materials traditionally used to make them. I had to be nonconventional to devise bass flies that would work as well as other methods. The use of straight and offset shafted spinners, rubber and plastic skirts, and such "sweeteners" as pork and plastic strips are examples of my unorthodox departures.

Both floating and sinking lines are useful for proper presentation, action, and retrieve for these swimming bass flies. I usually use floating lines for shallow or slow-sinking retrieves and the sink-tip and full-sinking lines for fast or deeper retrieves.

Using these swimming bass flies extends the daily and seasonal times for catching bass. Since 90 percent of the bass's diet is made up of subsurface food in streams and manmade lakes, and fish only occasionally come to the surface, these flies are imperative if you want to get regular action.

Even though the excitement of the visible top-water stroke is lost with the swimming flies, great enjoyment and fascination can be yours if you use the fly rod for this subsurface fishing.

SWIMMING FLIES

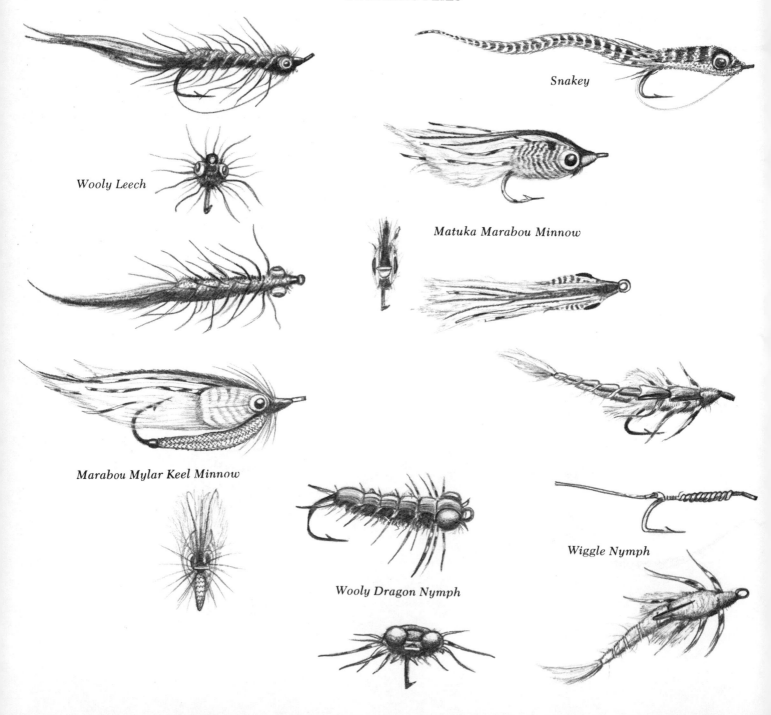

Snakey

Wooly Leech

Matuka Marabou Minnow

Marabou Mylar Keel Minnow

Wiggle Nymph

Wooly Dragon Nymph

Deep Stuff: Bottom-Swimming and Crawling Flies

Bottom-fished bass flies represent the most drastic departure I made in flies and techniques in my attempt to develop a system that would suit all forms of fly-rodding for bass. These flies are the most challenging and interesting and rewarding for me to tie and fish. And this ability to work the bottom effectively makes bass fly-rodding a year-round sport where season and temperature permit.

These flies usually imitate or represent such common bass foods as crayfish, worms, eels, water snakes, catfish, suckers, sculpin, crabs, waterdogs, and salamanders. Even those fly patterns that do not necessarily imitate any of those foods are readily attacked if crawled or hopped along the bottom of a lake or stream. Bass seem much less wary of artificial lures worked deep along the bottom.

BOTTOM-SWIMMING AND CRAWLING FLIES

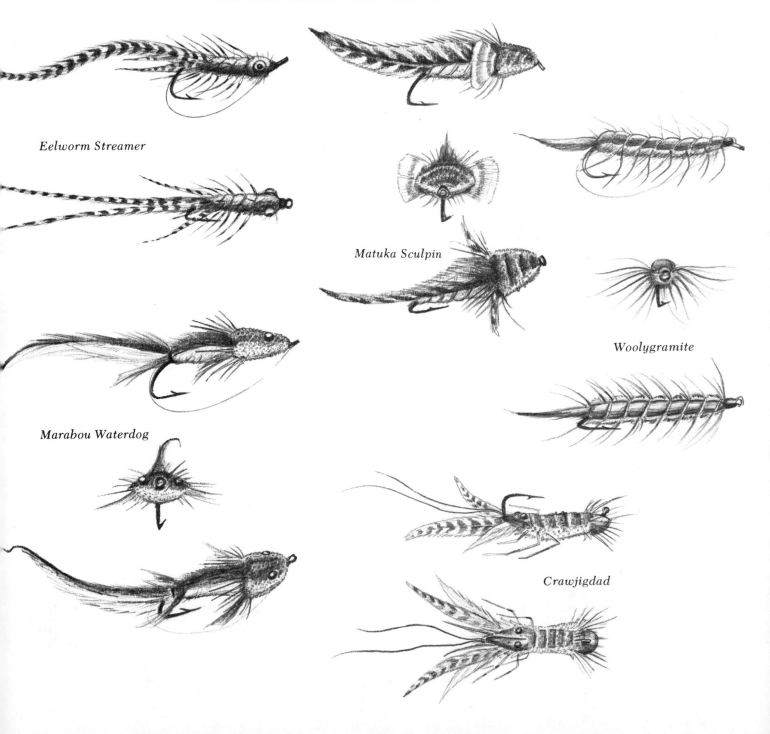

Eelworm Streamer

Matuka Sculpin

Woolygramite

Marabou Waterdog

Crawjigdad

Bottom fishing takes much more patience. It is also slower. But when it is done properly, it produces the largest fish.

The sink-tip, sink-belly, and full-sinking lines are most useful in still waters over three feet deep or in deep streams. I use the high-density lines as much as possible, but only resort to full-sinking lines when I have to fish in from fifteen to thirty feet of water. Fishing deeper than thirty feet renders most fly-fishing methods impractical.

In lakes, the bottom-dragging method works best on steep shorelines, sunken islands, channels, ledges, or over unusual structures such as submerged bridges, road beds, or artificial reefs. In rivers, it is good for working deep, slow pools, ledges, rubble-bottom runs, and the base of waterfalls.

I usually use a short leader—two and a half to seven feet—especially if the fly isn't heavily weighted. I try to adjust the density of the fly so that it sinks but still retains a slight bouyancy for better water action and fewer hangups. A very

heavy fly is mean to cast and drops into almost every crack and crevice it meets. Fly shape is another important aspect when considering sinking, snagging, and water and bottom action. The loop snag-guard is an absolute must for the bottom-retrieve flies, and I always set it extra-stiff for the fly is usually in constant contact with obstructions. For most bottom flies a head-heavy balance, for a jigging-action retrieve, is very effective for bass.

These flies *must* be fished from a *stationary position* to be most effective. A drifting boat drags them up and out of position, away from the fish. I either fish from an anchored boat, wade, or use a float tube and fins to assure that my retrieves are not supplemented by drifting drag. Whenever possible, cast the bottom flies into the shallowest water, then work them back into the deeper area. This is a more natural approach, saves a lot of waiting (since the fly sinks to the bottom sooner), and hangs up far less as it drops down than if it was pulled up over structure.

Fly Rods for Bass

Fly rods for bass fishing should be durable, light, powerful—and they should have a complete shaft action. Bamboo rods are often excellent—but glass rods in the 6 to 10-weight, seven-and-a-half to nine-and-a-half-foot lengths are much more practical. Most slow-action glass rods cast bugs fairly well but tend to overload badly under 7-weight sticks. Fast-tip glass rods are worthless. You want slow-bending rod action that you can feel right into the cork.

The new graphite rods are proving even better suited for bass fly-rod fishing than glass. Their greater power-to-weight ratio, slender shafts, and sensitivity make them really fine fishing tools. The characteristically higher line speeds and

tighter loops of the better graphites cast the larger, heavier, wind-resistant bugs with greater authority. They are exciting to use after a lifetime with glass. They snap line off the water well and allow one-cast line shooting. I also find the hook-setting qualities of graphite superior to those of glass.

For most of my bass fishing I prefer rods of eight to eight-and-one-half-foot lengths, calibrated for 6, 7, and 8-weight lines. Occasionally I'll use a 5-weight graphite with smaller flies for cover-free water in small lakes and streams. Bass can be a lot of excitement on trout-weight rods, and the always-present panfish are an extra bonus with lighter rods.

Fly Lines: One for Every Purpose

The floating and high-density sink-tip fly lines are the most useful and practical in ninety-five out of a hundred bass situations. I'll occasionally use full-sinkers, wet-bellys, wet-heads, and even

lead-heads; but day in, day out, I greatly prefer to use the other two.

Floating lines, especially the weight-forward bass-bug taper and level lines, are the most useful.

The level floater works well when short casts are most practical. Large and wind-resistant flies also work quite well with the level line, though complicated, delicate presentations are rarely possible.

The special weight-forward bass-bug taper developed by Scientific Anglers is the ultimate bass fly-fishing line. It was the first step toward revolutionizing this area of fly fishing. Its design allows efficient, trouble-free presentation of bass flies in a wide size range. It casts well in the wind with heavy and even wind-resistant flies—and at short, intermediate, and longer distances without false casting.

The weight-forward bass-bug taper allows a bass fly to be cast with great accuracy. Using a high-line-speed, tight-loop, shooting presentation, the fly is rifled low or high into the narrowest target paths, even exceeding the accuracy obtained by expert bait-casters. Even side-arm skip casting under and behind objects is duck soup with this line, as well as right and left curve-casts behind out-of-the-water obstacles such as stumps.

The floating line is used to fish dry flies, wet flies, nymphs, streamers, popping bugs, hairbugs, and diver-dipper bugs. It is thus practical when fish are feeding at the surface or in calm water three to five feet deep.

The high-density sink-tip made in the weight-forward bass-bug taper further extends your scope and season. It casts like the weight-forward bass-bug floater and can be used to fish all sorts of flies. I use it to fish diving topwater flies, crippled-minnow bugs, wooly worms, streamers, nymphs, bottom-crawling eel worms, crayfish flies, and spinner-fly combinations. It is especially effective in calm water; from the surface it can follow the bottom down to ten feet without long pauses while the fly sinks on its own. A three to six-foot leader should be used. By varying the speed of your retrieve, rod angle, fly weight, and leader length, the flies can be fished at appropriate depths from top to bottom with very little effort.

The wet-head, wet-belly, and full-sinking line allow the fly to be worked at depths of up to thirty feet.

Fly fishing for bass is attracting a growing number of addicts who like its quiet action and challenges. Erwin Bauer

Leaders That Make Sense

The final link in the tackle chain between you and your bass fly is the leader and its tippet. Like a real chain, it is only as strong as its weakest link. The leader provides the final phase in the cast-presentation sequence and serves to conceal the connection between fly and fly line. Most bass and bass flies require leaders somewhat heavier and less invisible than do trout.

Bass leaders for floating lines should be of the knotless variety and seven feet long; tippets should add another twelve to twenty-four inches. I recommend heavy-butt, magnum-butt, or salmon tapers. These have about two or three-thousandths-larger diameter than standard tapered leaders with similar size tips.

It is extremely important that your leaders be knotless tapers. Compound knotted leaders cause a lot of problems in most areas, since the knots hang up and tangle in the heavy covers bass hide in or dive into when hooked. Knots also accumulate aquatic algae and seem to seek out every crack and crevice in these bass covers. I use only two double surgeon's knots to attach a wear section and tippet to the main knotless tapered leader. These cause few problems.

Your leader tip and tippet material should test from six to fifteen pounds for most bass and streamer work. Eight pound is about ideal for most medium and small flies (10 to 4) in fairly open water. A ten to fifteen-pound-test tippet will turn over larger flies (2 to 3/0) better and allows them to be set firmly in the bass's jaw. Higher test tippets are practical in heavy cover areas, for proper presentation, hooking, and control of large fish. Bass are not polite, pretty rainbow trout. They're thugs. They use every dirty trick in their book to foul the leader on underwater obstacles where they live.

Duck blinds, pilings, lily stems, barbed-wire fences, boat docks, piers, old stumps, outboard motor shafts, and beaver dens are just a few underwater haunts a bass will use to cut off the tippet—if he hasn't already thrown the hook while jumping.

Bass in such dense-cover areas are usually not leader shy. Having a strong tippet prevents excessive abrasions as well as the frequent loss of hooked fish and flies. Most of us release our bass anyway, so it isn't unsportsmanlike to use such heavy leaders. I also choose the toughest, most durable tippet material I can find—not necessarily in the smallest diameter-to-weight ratio.

For sinking-tip fly lines I use shorter, simpler leaders; here the line tip or line belly actually assists in sinking or holding the fly at a particular depth. The sinking line is better able to influence the fly if the leader is from three to six feet long—and it usually does not scare off bass. The main exception might be when you are fishing a small nymph quite deep in very clear water to really hard-fished bass. Here a longer, lighter leader is called for.

A full-length level leader or two-part taper of butt and tippet is ample for most sinking-line bass work. I suggest a twenty-four-inch butt section of very flexible nylon of .018 diameter, and the rest a tippet section tied on with a double surgeon's knot. Balance and turnover for a delicate fly presentation are seldom needed for this type of bass fishing—but getting the fly down fast *is*. By varying fly bulk and weight, leader length and flexibility, and line-tip density, all sorts of underwater presentations and swimming retrieves can be used to interest bass.

Fly Reels for Bass

Both single-action and automatic fly reels should be considered for bass fishing. My strong preference is for the lighter, more versatile manual single action. These are less trouble, more fun to play a bass with, and usually far better for dealing with any fish that is boss enough to maneuver for cover by taking line against my will.

Automatics are heavier, more mechanically complicated and not as versatile as the single-action reel. Line cannot be pulled freely or with sensitive drag from automatics. The gearing and spring system of all the automatics I've used almost entirely eliminate this important option. Thus if you hook a big, strong, and active bass, you

HOW TO MAKE A LOOP SNAG GUARD

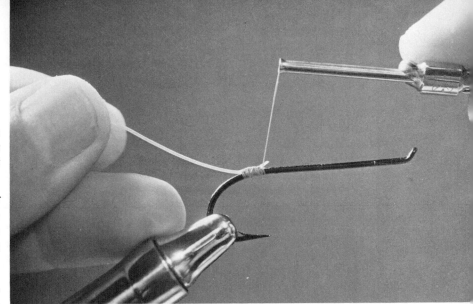

1. Place fly hook in vise just as you normally would to tie any standard hook pattern. Attach tying thread to shank just in front of hook's bend.

2. Cut a two- or three-inch section of stiff nylon monofilament approximately the same diameter or 1 ½ times larger than hook's wire diameter. Thus, nylon ranging from .015 to .024 inches in diameter.

3. With pliers or your front teeth, slightly flatten one end of the nylon section. Place this over thread base and tie down directly with thread on top of hook's shank with length extending back past hook's bend.

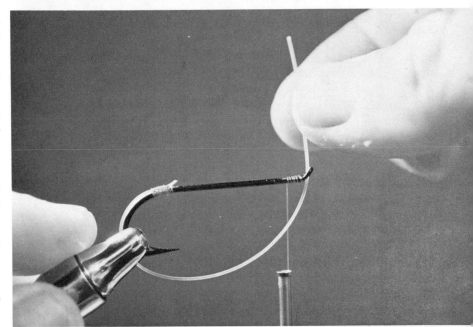

4. Place a small drop of cement on the tiedown area.

5. Proceed to tie fly as pattern requires with the nylon strand in material clip or just sticking back along vise sleeve.

6. Upon completion of the fly tying, finish the fly's head so that a little extra space is left to tie down other end of nylon strand.

7. Take nylon strand and loop it down and around hook's bend and pass end up through the hook's eye.

8. With tying thread, take several firm turns to bind down loosely to fly's head.

9. A closed loop is thus formed beneath the fly's hook. Now adjust its loop so that it extends ½ of the hook's gape below the point.

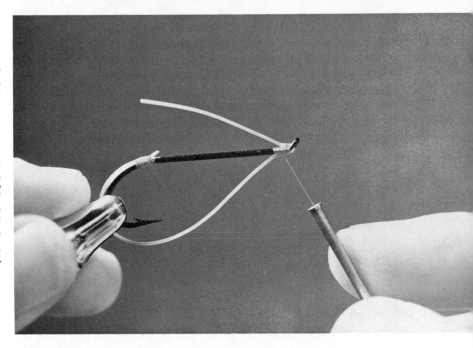

10. Bend loose end of nylon strand down over the top of the fly's head and securely wrap tying thread over it and whip finish. Clip excess nylon from head's top. Cement finished head.

The loop guard works well for most fishing as described above—with loop extending around hook's bend. However, to double its guard stiffness simply pull strand forward and set inside hook's bend. So set, it will allow the fly to be fished in the worst aquatic jungle if properly retrieved. This guard will discourage the smallest fish strikes . . . but won't hinder an eight-inch or larger bass from being hooked.

must resort to hand stripping to give line—or face a sure breakoff. Yet for short-line casting and short-distance retrieving from deeper water to shallow-water cover, automatics have their special usefulness. Some bass-buggers prefer them exclusively. They use their left hand to control and propel the boat with a small paddle as they cast, pop, and pick up their bugs in these areas. When a fish is hooked the brake is released by a little finger pressure, and slack line is zipped onto the reel by the spring recoil device. Tension is thus maintained until the boat is away from the cover and the paddle can be put aside for a good two-handed fight.

I suggest you try both reels before you make up your mind which is best for your temperament and area.

My seven years of fly-fishing-only for bass paid me great rewards. A great gamefish on any tackle, the bass seems even a bit greater when he's pursued and caught on flies and fly-fishing tackle.

WHERE TO GET WHITLOCK BUGS

The complete line of special bass bugs (and other flies) designed by Dave Whitlock are available from the following mail-order shops.

Fireside Angler
PO Box 823
Melville, NY 11740
Phone: 516 427-6881

Creative Sports Enterprises
PO Box 2157
Walnut Creek, CA 94595
Phone: 415 938-2255

The Millpond
59 North Santa Cruz Avenue
Los Gatos, CA 95030
Phone: 408 354-5291

Kaufmann's Streamborn Flies
PO Box 23022
Portland, OR 97223

Dealers interested in stocking Whitlock bugs and flies are invited to contact Dennis Black, Umpqua Feather Merchants, Inc., PO Box 72, Idleyld Park, OR 97447. Phone: 503 496-0297.

Erwin Bauer

12

Smallmouth Specialties

JERRY GIBBS

Documentary film producer Glen Lau is the former Lake Erie guide who achieved the incredible record of never having a fishless party in thirteen years. Though known to many anglers as the man who filmed *Bigmouth*, which traced the life cycle of largemouth bass, walleyes and smallmouth bass gave Lau his start.

During his guiding days, Lau got to the bottom of things when the fish came hard. On days when the fish weren't biting well, the Ohio-born angler would put on his scuba gear and go overboard to find out why. Long hours of underwater observation have taught him many little-known facts about fish behavior.

Let's let Lau take us into the fascinating world of smallmouth bass, a species he says is "about the most exciting I've fished for."

I hit him first with a question many anglers have asked me.

GIBBS: Why do so many fishermen find smallmouths hard to carch?

LAU: It's largely because of the tendency of smallmouths to roam open waters. They're definitely harder to find than largemouths, which you can pretty well depend on to be around some obstruction. Smallmouths are in a wide variety of areas during the year.

GIBBS: Would you describe some of your tech-

niques for finding smallmouths?

LAU: For open-water fishing in large waters you shouldn't look for individual fish. You want to find big schools because once fish in a school start striking lures or bait the action can go on for some time. But to find the fish you have to understand how they live in different places at different times. Smallmouths don't live the same way in little streams, a place like Lake St. Clare, the lakes in Maine, or a huge fertile body of water like Lake Erie. Though I've fished for smallmouths all over the country and Canada, my most intensive work was done in Erie. The fundamentals I learned there can form the base for smallmouth fishing methods everywhere. Let me tell you what happens early in the year in big water like Erie.

Let's take just one school. In 45° water all the smallmouths will be out around the thirty to thirty-five-foot contour. As the temperature goes up to 50° they start moving, congregating in the twenty-five-foot area. Then if you get a steady temperature rise of half a degree a day, all at once they'll move up to where the bottom drops from ten feet. They'll hold at the edges of this drop in twelve to fifteen feet of water. Here they engage in courtship. They do their picking of mates in a huge school. There may be one thousand to fifteen hundred smallmouths in that one place.

GIBBS: Just on the edge of that drop?

LAU: Right. Now when the water reaches about 54° the fish start coming up. At 55° they move into six or seven-foot shallows to spawn. Spawning will be done near a gradual sloping shoreline. The fish seem to know that an area with a steep shoreline will get too much wave action. Strong wave action will keep them off the beds. They'll pick coves and points, and they like to get up into dock areas. At 56 to 57° they spawn.

After the females spawn they stay near their beds for two to four days. Then they drop into twenty to twenty-two feet of water. They'll get on their bellies in mud or sand and lie there. They'll be concentrated in a narrow five-foot band at that depth on the dropoff. I've eased along wearing diving gear and seen hundreds of them just lying there.

GIBBS: Only the females?

LAU: Some males. The males will be from un-successful nests. The fish are completely exhausted. Half of them will be tilted over almost on one side. After a while a white mucous forms over their bodies. A coating like cataracts covers their eyes. Some—especially the four and five-pounders—will die. The others recover in eight days to two weeks. I call this the rehabilitation period, and I defy you to catch a good smallmouth during that time.

GIBBS: Have you caught them earlier out in that deep water before they spawn?

LAU: Out in that 45° water it's almost impossible to catch them unless you get a fast warming trend with the termperature climbing a degree a day. The coldest I've taken them in that thirty-foot water was 47°. Go out with live spottail minnows held in tight with a sinker no more than six inches from the hook, and you may catch some off the bottom. They'll be full of mud and clay.

GIBBS: In their body cavities? Why is that?

LAU: I'm not sure, but it must be from lying all winter on the bottom and absorbing it.

GIBBS: Let's go back to the smallmouths that have just made it through that recuperation period and are lying tilted over. What happens to them afterward?

LAU: Some of the fish slowly begin leaving the line of resting fish. They move up and down the line just outside the others. Day after day when I swam along just such a line with my scuba gear, I saw fewer fish resting on bottom. The ones that had recuperated were very curious. I'd look be-hind me and there would be hundreds of fish following. You can get smallmouths to come up by wiggling your fingers, and sometimes you can touch them on the nose. Not largemouths. They're a lot more cautious.

Some of the fish will break off and swim away. Those fish will take up residency alone in an area that has good cover. The males that have been guarding the fry also move into the concentration of recuperating fish at this time. The others will join the swimming fish that will begin forming into two or three groups. These groups eventually break off into what I call the wolf packs.

So now you have two groupings of bass. Just by looking at them I can tell which are the stay-at-home or resident fish and which will form hunting schools or wolf packs. The resident smallmouths have a different shape than the school fish. They're shorter and stockier. Some resident smallmouths develop black spots that are really like callouses from rubbing on rocks and debris. They get in their rock-hole areas and stay there. They're lazy fish. The school fish are longer, racier. The same is true of largemouths. These wolf-pack fish must be much faster to survive.

GIBBS: Where do these wolf packs go?

LAU: They travel for two or three weeks before settling into a home area for the summer. During the period when the packs are roaming you can have some of the best and some of the worst fishing of the season. When you run into one of these groups the fish are so hungry they'll hit anything.

GIBBS: Do they follow any particular behavior patterns?

LAU: You'll find them wherever you find bait-fish.

GIBBS: How do you find them?

LAU: It's hard. You've got to keep moving. If you're out every day you have the advantage of knowing what direction they were headed last. You have to keep an open mind. They can be in places where they won't be any other time of year.

I try islands, bays, and points. Sometimes a bay that wouldn't normally have fish in it will be full of smallmouths this time of year, and everywhere you cast in it you'll catch fish. I also like small rock reefs that just about break the surface. Especially the ends of them. The fish show up in the strangest places. The biggest mistake some people make is spending eight hours in a place where they caught a couple of fish. When you catch a few smallmouth from a school and then catch no more, you should immediately start casting in all directions to find them. Failing that you've got to move.

Author Glen Lau, documentary film producer and former Lake Erie guide, gives a hefty bronzeback a gentle lift before returning it to the water. As a guide, Glen established a record that has become a legend: not one fishless party taken out in thirteen years.

Around July Fourth in Lake Erie the packs have settled into home areas. They choose places around wrecks, lighthouses, and various rock formations. With the onset of warm weather they stop feeding on spottail minnows. This forage species is spawning and becomes less available. The smallmouths then turn to emerald shiners. Huge schools of these shiners will draw smallmouths from their home areas. The bass will follow shiner schools some distance and gorge on them, sometimes pushing the shiners up on offshore reefs.

Even after their bellies are full, the smallmouths will keep on tearing into those shiners. If you get a lure to them you won't be able to keep them away. At the deepest you only have to run a spinner or one of those Sonars five feet below the surface in maybe twelve to fifteen feet of water. Soon the bass drift back to their regular home areas.

Lau's intensive underwater filming and observation sessions taught him much about the secret ways of the wily smallmouth.

"The toughest thing about fishing for smallmouths is finding them," Glen confesses.

GIBBS: How deep do you normally fish around the home areas?

LAU: During the day I might fish at eighteen to twenty feet unless some heavy obstruction lets me fish shallower. The fish come out from hiding when the sun goes over the hill. The last hour and a half of evening I'd fish at about ten to fifteen feet. Sometimes in the day we'd have huge fish come out and follow a plastic grub up to the boat but refuse to hit. So we knew they were there. We'd just wait until evening and the action would start.

GIBBS: How was smallmouth behavior different in Lake St. Clare?

LAU: That's where you have a steep dropoff situation. The fish would come in and start their prespawning activities on the edge of the river channel dropoff. Then they'd move right into the shallows to spawn at 56°. They were either in deep water or in shallows. They could be in deep water just a few feet from the shallows. I found them by using a particular technique. There's a bank that drops out of a marsh into the Johnson River. It drops on a 45° angle into thirty-five feet of water. I put my anchor down in ten feet and moved along with the current and wind. I was bouncing a little plastic grub. I kept trying different drifts a little deeper each time. When I hit eighteen feet I connected. That little jig would go bump, bump, bump, then *pow*, a fish would hit. This was in

fairly cool water. The fish weighed four to five pounds.

The whole cycle reverses in autumn, no matter where you fish. In Erie the individual resident fish join the school fish again. They all move into areas that have large concentrations of food. All fish—minnows and gamefish—are gathering energy for the winter. Often the bass congregate on points in fifteen to twenty feet of water or shallower. These may not be the same kinds of places we talked about for spring. It may be a little reef that's twelve feet below the surface. You can experience a hit-or-miss situation again. Just prior to the water dropping below 50° they'll be in tremendous schools in one area—usually just off the area where they'll move in for the spring congregating.

GIBBS: How do they react in winter?

LAU: You can catch largemouths through ice. Smallmouths turn off completely when the temperature drops below 50°.

GIBBS: Do you feel smallmouths are more aggressive than largemouths?

LAU: Once you catch them in a feeding mood, I think they're more aggressive.

GIBBS: What about feeding moods and frequency compared to largemouths?

LAU: I think smallmouths feed oftener than largemouths. Largemouths sometimes don't feed at all. I've seen days when smallmouths were dormant, but not often. They like to feed. But they seem to want something to activate them, get them going. I've been out on a reef when we weren't catching anything. I knew the fish were there. I would have some crayfish with me. Smallmouths are suckers for softshell crayfish in summer. But at a buck a dozen you hate to do anything except put them on your hook for bait. Still, I've thrown a couple of dozen crayfish overboard. That was all it took to trigger those smallmouths. One crayfish at a time wouldn't have done it. It was really a form of chumming.

GIBBS: Could you do that with largemouths?

LAU: It might work, but I've never tried it. I'm sure they wouldn't get as excited as smallmouths. Almost everything a largemouth does is slower. He jumps slower, strikes slower. When filming smallmouths at the standard twenty-four frames a second it took just twenty-four frames per jump, and the jumps were higher than a largemouth's. It takes largemouths thirty-six frames per jump and the jumps aren't as high. A largemouth launches slower. Also with a smallmouth, you have to bow

your rod just as you do with a tarpon. If he jumps three feet high and lands on your light line and you haven't allowed any slack by bowing, he can break the line.

GIBBS: Did you ever keep smallmouths to study as you have largemouths?

LAU: Yes, but not in Florida. I had some in a horse trough once and they were vicious. You put any other fish in there and they'd just harass it, chew the fins off it. They really protect their domain.

GIBBS: And they're really curious?

LAU: Right. Let me give you an example. We were out fishing one day without having much luck. We were over a wreck that was a good home area. So I put on my tank and went over to see what was going on. I didn't see any bass. I'd noticed once before when exploring another wreck that when I chipped away at some brass fittings the bass seemed very curious about the noise. So when I found an old metal rod I picked it up and began banging it on my tank. All at once the smallmouths started coming from the wreck. They came from all over the place. Soon I had two to three hundred bass around me. The more tapping I did the more they gathered. Some would come up and take a look and swim away. Others stayed right there. I went topside and we started fishing. The bass had taken to feeding and we caught several.

Wrecks, incidentally, are excellent holding places. There's so much life around them. But they're in different water depths, so you have to know which ones to fish at various times.

GIBBS: How much visibility did you have in Erie?

LAU: Fifteen to twenty-five feet. That's a long way looking off like that. Lake Erie often has surprising visibility. The second week of June is when it's clearest. Then algae starts growing.

GIBBS: Did you find most of your wrecks with charts?

LAU: Every wreck I knew was virtually unknown to anyone else. Most of them probably still are. I found them just by being out there so much. Some are right in the middle of nowhere.

GIBBS: What things helped you the most when fishing for smallmouths?

LAU: A combination of things. A fast boat to cover a lot of areas, and the underwater observations were very, very important. For example, I could have fished for years wasting time during that recuperation period smallmouths go through.

Lau's slow-motion movies have proven that smallmouths leap higher and faster. Erwin Bauer

The other thing that helped me was just being out there a lot and learning how those fish behave. A good smallmouth fisherman is rare. Anglers who can consistently catch smallmouths—except during that recuperation period—are among the smartest fishermen I know.

GIBBS: What was your best year guiding—about how many fish did you catch?

LAU: Exactly 3,388. They averaged just under three pounds a fish. That's not counting all the small ones. It was all based around the theory of not fishing for individual fish but fishing the schools.

GIBBS: Do you have any other thoughts about smallmouths?

LAU: Yes. I think there ought to be limits on smallmouths everywhere. I feel they ought to be protected during the spawning season, and that the spawning season ought to be determined by notice each year based on water temperature that governs just when the fish spawn. Each year can be different. If you know what you're doing you can really do a job on spawning smallmouths, and they're too great a fish to hurt.

Glen Lau's Best Smallmouth Tips

EARLY SEASON: Drift with live spottail minnows using a sinker six inches from the hook. Line is run through one end of an "earflap" sinker, wrapped three times around sinker body, then run out the other end. The sinker flaps are folded over the line. Fish on the bottom while drifting. Raise sinker off bottom two inches every fifteen seconds, then drop it back down. As soon as fish contact is made, throw out a marker buoy where the fish struck. Continue drifting to establish the size of the school. Fifty yards past the marker start your motor and move upwind of marker. Drift to within twenty yards of the marker. Lower the anchor over the stern, let out the anchor line until the marker is reached, then pick up the marker. Tie anchor line to one side of stern. Changing anchor tie to opposite stern side will give a new swing to boat. Adjust boat position by letting out or pulling in anchor line.

PRESPAWN—FISH IN LARGE GROUP: Use spottail minnows, green Stingray grubs and leadheads, black jig-and-eels, four-inch yellow floating worms, and horse-hoof-shaped standup jigs. When water temperature reaches 52 to 53°, Rapalas or green grubs. Using minnows, drift with enough weight so your light line runs down from boat at nearly a 90° angle. Drift with minnows to find fish, then switch to artificials if desired. Using artificials, jig vertically over fish. Jig just four inches off bottom. Fish will hit on the drop. Instead of sharply setting hook, lift fish up (they will hold on) and set, thus keeping hooked fish from fighting in the school.

POSTSPAWN: Lau Lure or other spinners.

Rapalas—countdown or floater-diver model with lead weight ahead of it. Use Heddon Sonar when contact has been made with schooling fish. All silver finish, except red and white for Sonar. Try both drifting and casting methods. Emerald shiners are now the natural bait.

HOME AREAS (WARM WEATHER): Jigs and grubs. Mann's Razorback without rattle. Rebel deep divers. Half-ounce Heddon Sonar on schooling fish. Natural baits include emerald shiners, softshell crayfish. Work home areas—wrecks, reefs, rubble, lighthouses—by casting or drifting. Some days fish may be found by drifting but will not take cast lures or baits from anchored boat. Then you must continue drift pattern through "hot" area.

FALL: Water temperature in high 50's. Use yellow horse-hoof-shaped jig with a four-inch floater worm. Green grub. Spottail minnows or large four to five-inch shiners. Work edges and points. Cast or drift.

TACKLE: Lau uses a tackle formula based on lure size, type and hook. The lure determines the line size, the line size determines the rod action and reel. For a quarter-ounce spinner with No. 8 hook Lau chooses four-pound-test line, a light action rod, small reel. For a half-ounce spinner with No. 6 hook he chooses eight-pound-test line, a rod that will enable a good snap to be put into the cast, a reel with larger line capacity because casting will be farther. To get spinners down and vibrating fast, Lau sometimes attaches a quarter or half-ounce weight to the lures. With such rigs he recommends eight-pound line. Some anglers use as much as ten pound. Reels with high retrieve ratios are an advantage with weighted spinners, which should be retrieved quickly. A slightly heavier action rod is needed.

GENERAL TIPS

● For smallmouths, as with walleyes, think in terms of schools rather than individual fish. Don't fish for the singles.

● Smallmouths are far more curious fish than largemouth bass. They are also more excitable. It may be hard to get them feeding but once you do they make gluttons of themselves. They need something that intrigues them or triggers their feeding.

● For eight days to two weeks after actual spawning, smallmouth females and some males go through a recuperation period, dropping into twenty to twenty-two-foot water. You cannot catch smallmouths then.

● On the beds in shallow water smallmouths are extremely vulnerable. They can be decimated by a fisherman who knows what he's doing. All smallmouths should be protected at this time. Seasons should vary each year based on water temperature, which governs just when the bass will spawn. Fifty-six degrees marks the actual spawning but fish move into the shallows before the water reaches that temperature.

● Unlike largemouths, smallmouths virtually cease feeding when the water drops to around 50°.

● Especially in the early part of year, if you caught smallies in one place last week or even yesterday don't expect them to be there today. In summer the smallmouths take up home areas but they can move from these places as far as a mile, lured by an especially thick concentration of bait fish. After feeding they'll return to the home area.

● An angler who uses only bait or only lures for smallmouths is really half a fisherman. There are times when natural bait is the only thing to use and times when lures are better.

● The very best and worst fishing for smallmouths can occur after the postspawn recuperation period when some of the fish form "wolf" packs. These schools rip into every concentration of bait fish they can find. Fish such a school and the action is hard to believe. But you can have the devil's own time finding these packs because they're on the move so much.

● My favorite baits and lures for smallmouth include: spottail minnows, emerald shiners, soft-shell crayfish, various types of jigs like the green Stingray grub and the Marlynn horse-hoof jig with a four-inch yellow floater worm, Rapalas, diving Rebels, the Razorback without a rattle, Heddon's Sonar, spinners like my Lau Lure.

● The toughest thing about fishing for smallmouths is *finding them*.

13

River Bass
The Magic of Float Fishing

CHARLES ELLIOTT

Like many another Cracker boy who came along in my generation some few odd and then some more few odd years ago, I was raised on a middle-Georgia bass river. I didn't hatch out in a burrow or grow up in a hollow tree, like a coon, but almost from the time I could toddle, I was on that river bank with a cane pole and baited hook. Someone upstairs kept an eye on me, for I was never chewed on by a moccasin, or eaten up by a pack of wild dogs, which were our worst predators even in those days. Once I slid down a slippery bank into the river, but He had arranged that as a lesson in caution, for the water was only chest-deep and I was able to pull myself by roots and bushes back to semidry ground. Only once when I was hardly out of the lisping stage, and the fish were biting good, I overstayed my leave and a search party was sent to find my body and bring it home.

Later in my teens, when I decided to build a fire and spend the night on the river bank, no one came looking for me. After all these years it just now occurs to me to wonder why.

By awkward stages I graduated from a wet rear end on the muddy bank to a crude raft and then an old bateau; from a cane pole cut in the swamp to a cheap rod and reel—and then, as the pittance from my newspaper route increased, to slightly improved equipment. Naturally, the casting outfit called for artificials. With nothing that would pass for money, but with instructions from an old riverman friend, I whittled out and painted my own lures.

With such a background, I suppose I might claim to have been born a river fisherman. The sport was glamourous then, and it has never lost its charm. In spite of the spread of power impoundments and other manmade lakes and ponds that now dot our countryside, and in spite of the countless hours I have devoted to them in search of bass and other fish, eternally I come back to my first love, a flowing stream, overhung with canopies of foliage, or flanked by tall rock walls or sandbars, or with hillsides of trees marching down to the water.

First of all, I feel that I am touching elbows with history. The rivers of America were our first highways. They were the main arteries of travel and commerce, safer than the roadless wilderness, and at that time a much faster means of transportation from one point to another. The first forts for protection, the first homes, the first settlements were built along the rivers. These were the pathways by which those ahead of us penetrated the interior of our nation.

The railroads came. The settlements moved

away from the waterways and towns and cities grew around the railway stations. Then came the automobile and roads and eventually superhighways, and the focal points of the towns shifted again, spreading around the most convenient transportation.

Except in those places where a settlement had expanded into a megalopolis with the help of water transportation, or their shores converted into expansive agricultural lands, the rivers went back to wilderness. Today they make up some of our back-of-beyond country closest to what we term civilization. They are hunting and fishing trails supreme, yet strangely enough are overlooked by a sizable majority of our hunters and fishermen.

I do not by any means decry or discourage lake fishing for bass, or any other species. I've put in pleasant and profitable hours on the open water, seeking out points on which a school of largemouths had gathered, or casting the ends of remote coves away from the turbulence of high-powered motors and water skiers, whose sport I am sure is as relaxing to them as fishing is to any old dyed-in-the-hackle Waltonite.

Lake fishing has a fascination of its own. Before he can catch a bass, or more than one, an angler must first find the fish. The thermocline or freshwater layer temperatures at varying depths, water color, food concentration and other conditions, more than often determine where you'll locate bass, either singly or in schools. Whether you go about it with a depth finder, temperature gauge, or by trolling plugs that run at different depths, pinpointing fish in a lake is part of the fun.

On a running stream, you are likely to find the bass scattered out along the shoreline, taking advantage of cover and the eddies in the current. You won't find fish in the same type of cover in each river. Old logs, rocks, stumps, and undercut banks are usually good for largemouths. Others, like the smallmouth, redeye, and spotted bass, may prefer to hang around the eddies below shoals, where they feed on the morsel of food washing by.

Whether the streams are the same after half a century I have no idea, but I recall two south-Georgia rivers that I fished often with my old friend and college roommate, Cowboy Stephens. On one, the most likely spot to tie into a scrappy largemouth was below a big cypress tree or around a cluster of cypress knees. On the next river, which paralleled it a couple of dozen miles away, the fishing was every bit as good, but we couldn't buy a bass from the base of a cypress at any price or by any device.

I have no idea who coined the phrase "float-fishing," or when. It's a picturesque word combination that tells a story, but not the whole story. You are in a world of your own. The river is yours, whether you are there for a day or a week. Even on a stream that's popular for this type of angling, you seldom encounter another boat, for whoever might be behind you, or ahead, is traveling in the same direction and with the current at the same rate of speed.

Somewhere beyond, the affairs of a troubled world roll on. Your own problems are no longer as important as once they seemed. Here you can readjust your sense of values.

The float itself, with nothing added, would be an adventure in wilderness living. On almost any river there is more beauty than your eyes can fully absorb. You are wrapped up in a wilderness symphony. The music of the river may range from soft, liquid notes to a crashing crescendo where the current hurls itself against or over a wall of rock. You find fellowship with creatures you would never see if you were stalking through brush along the shore. You are a part of this wild place—the sights and sounds, the wind that touches your cheek, the storm that roars over you, the swinging blanket of stars never seen by those who live under artificial light. Your campfire on some lonely beach or gravel bar isolates you from the rest of the world.

The fishing is a bonus of your affair with the river. The largemouths, and usually the smallmouths, hang close under the cover of the shoreline, and you must be accurate enough in the presentation of your lure to put it into the tight corners and cracks within inches of the bank. With each cast you have to figure on the flow of the current. In this type of fishing there is a premium on your skill with a rod and reel.

I've listened to guides, who spent too large a percentage of their fishing time back-paddling to retrieve a lure that had snagged a hanging limb or some object ashore, grumble that their dude should either confine his casting to an open lake or take lessons on how to cast. Even the most precise angler, in trying to get within that inch or two of the bank, gets hung up occasionally, but he seldom throws his lure into the tree tops, as though he were after squirrels instead of bass.

One trick that seems to be the most difficult to teach a novice river fisherman is to cast in front

Arkansas' Buffalo River, with its bluffs, shady shorelines and fast water, is a wilderness float-fishing stream supreme.

Surrounded by bassy pockets, the author fishes the Suwannee River on the Georgia-Florida border. This is isolated water, with excellent camping.

instead of behind a moving boat. If you get hung up ahead of the boat, the lure is more quickly and easily retrieved. I've paddled for fellows who used up half our fishing time by casting behind the boat and getting hung. While working out your retrieve on one cast, watch the cover ahead for your next target. Anticipate the position you want to be in for the next cast.

Most of the guides with whom I've fished, from Canada to Florida's Cape Sable, hang small outboard motors on the stern. They ply a paddle and fish with the current, using the motor only to back up to retrieve a lure, refish a stretch of river where the bass are hot and hungry, or outrun the darkness to a good campsite ahead. And therein lies a big advantage of camping on a stream. You are there when the fishing is at its best at dawn and

dusk, without having to travel long miles to launch your boat.

If you've fished enough rivers, you know that each has its own characteristics and offers its own variety of experiences.

How could anyone ever forget a week on the Buffalo River in north-central Arkansas? Ed Dodd, father of the comic-strip character Mark Trail, Harold Ensley, Kansas City's famous outdoor television star, and I fished it with G. O. Tilley when he was an outfitter on the White River and Bull Shoals Lake. We remember the Buffalo for its cold, clear water and massive, picturesque cliffs. We remember it for its long stretches of quiet water, curtained with overhanging emerald hardwoods, and for its plunging, swift-water chutes through which the rapids boiled. The picture is vividly there of the wide, white gravel bars strung with tents and with smallmouth fillets sizzling over a campfire.

One outstanding memory that has stayed with me through the years is the size and number of the Buffalo's bullfrogs and how they added immeasurably to the excitement of our trip.

We had taken an abundance of smallmouths on underwater lures with ultralight spinning gear and I switched to a fly rod with a popping bug that Tilley had made to resemble a small, white caterpillar abundant along the stream and apparently a chief item of smallmouth-bass forage. He had shaped the lure in such fashion that it floated and half rolled on the surface with a twitch of the rod tip. He passed one of these to me and I tied it on. "Cast just under that limb, right up against the bank," he said, with a half-amused smile.

My caterpillar fell inches from the bank. I let it float a few seconds until Tilley said, "Now roll it over slowly."

I twitched the rod tip and the lure half turned on the surface. I got one of the surprises of my life. A huge bullfrog jumped off the bank with its mouth open and gobbled up the caterpillar. Tilley laughed. "Bring him in. He'll go good for supper."

I quit fishing for bass and went to looking for bullfrogs. The result was one of the most exciting afternoons I've had with a fly rod, and a supper of outsized bullfrog legs that would have made the head chef at Antoine's throw away his cookbook.

Who could ever forget an entirely different experience such as I had on Daddy's Creek near Crossville, in east-central Tennessee? John Jared, a colorful hunting and fishing partner over many years, and known over his Nashville radio show as "The Old Guide," had told me in glowing terms about Daddy's Creek.

"It's loaded with muskies," he said, "and nobody ever fishes for them. In a couple of days we can get into more action than you've ever found by float-fishing anywhere."

He didn't have to twist my pectoral fin any further. We made a date to float the creek, and before the trip was over I was convinced that his statement about the amount of action we would encounter was the truest I ever heard him or anyone else make.

A map showed the length of our float to be about seven and a half miles. Ralph Plumb, who was then manager of the Catoosa Wildlife Management Area through which the creek flows, hauled us and our boat to one of the bridges and planned to pick us up at another.

"If it's only seven and a half miles," I said, "we'll probably be there tonight."

"You'd better make it a couple of days anyway," he replied with a wry grin.

In less than an hour the full impact of his words began to sink in. Although the creek was low, we launched in water deep enough to man our paddles and float quietly along. Within two hundred yards the creek spread out into a skim of water, at no place more than three inches deep and flowing over solid rock. Our transportation was a new fourteen-foot metal johnboat that a dealer in Nashville had loaned to Jared. We had it loaded with food, tackle, and other gear. There was no way to move it except by dragging so we stepped out and began to heave at the bow. The sheet of water was so thin that we could well have been dragging it over solid rock. We made inches at a time. This went on for half an hour or more. I finally straightened up for a breather and asked Jared, "Did you tell me you'd been down this stretch of water?"

"Yeah," he said, "about twenty or more years ago."

We went back to work and finally got our craft into water deep enough to float it as long as we walked and led it. At the next shallow stretch, I stood up, sweating, and said, "Well, put your guts into this, or we'll be all summer getting to the next bridge."

"Guess I'll have to take it a little easier," John said. "I didn't tell you, but I had a heart attack a couple of months back."

From that moment on, a blow-by-blow account of that float trip would fill a book. I learned a lot of things about Daddy's Creek. One was that it flowed through a narrow canyon with walls that must have been from one hundred to two hundred feet high. In places huge slabs of stone had broken off the canyon walls and piled up in the canyon to block the flow of the stream. The creek went under these. We had to go over, pulling our boat up a few inches at a time, then letting it down on the other side, then portaging our gear by the armsful.

Night caught us worn down to a whisper, less than a mile from where we'd started. As I lay in my blanket on a shelf above the flow of water, listening to an occasional rock break off one of the high walls, rattle and crash to the bottom of the canyon, I remember thinking, "Lord, if you'll just get me out of this one, I promise to get out of the next one by myself."

We took time out between the periods of toil to get that boat downstream, to fish where the creek was deep enough or when we found a deep turquoise pool, so inaccessible in a tremendous cluster of boulders that the only way anyone could have reached it was the way we did, or with wings. We caught fish. The muskies weren't as plentiful as John had thought they would be, but the smallmouths were there and hungry for anything we fed them. Under more moderate circumstances, we would have considered this bronze back fishing fantastic. I was unable to enjoy it to the fullest for thinking about what we might find around the next bend.

We didn't sink the boat but twice, trying to let it down low waterfalls, but managed to salvage most of our equipment and food by grabbing that which floated away and diving for the rest.

About the fourth day, a plane flew over the canyon a few times, but we didn't pay much attention. The next day when it came back, it occurred to me that Ralph Plumb, who had agreed to meet us three days earlier, might be looking for us. I tied a white handkerchief to the handle of my paddle, found a sunny spot that could be seen from above, and when the plane came over again waved the makeshift flag. The wings dipped a couple of times to show that we'd been seen and the plane flew on.

We were longer than seven days making that one-day trip. When we returned the metal boat to the dealer in Nashville, he walked around it for a full inspection of the scratches, dents, and what little paint was left, and looked at Jared.

"Tell you what," he said, "you'd better keep this one. You might need it again."

I tell the Daddy's Creek story to suggest that before you attempt a float-fishing trip, you should be somewhat familiar with the territory you will cover. A majority of our bass streams are navigable with no difficulty and offer good fishing, but before you try one on your own or with a partner, know what lies ahead of you. You can get this information from local residents or the game conservation officers in the region.

After Daddy's Creek, I took more time to make inquiries about a stream. A friend invited me to float-fish the wild Chattooga River on the Georgia-South Carolina line, which has since become famous as the river in the film version of the novel *Deliverance,* and as a dangerous whitewater stream. I declined his invitation and told him why. He made the trip anyway, lost his boat and all of his equipment and had to walk his skinned carcass out over six or seven miles of rugged mountain terrain.

Most bass rivers in flat or slightly rolling country are not too difficult to navigate, provided a boatman has any experience at all. About the only danger you find in these are snags or tree trunks across the stream where your boat will be hung up and then pulled under by a powerful current. It's best to go ashore above these and go around them with solid ground under you.

Some flat-water rivers can hold surprises, even in the South. The Suwannee River near White Springs in northern Florida pours over a shoals some twelve or fifteen feet high. This is dangerous to navigate at certain stages of river level. I once found where the Alapaha River, near the Georgia-Florida line, turned out of its bed and the entire river, when it was low, poured into a limestone cavern. I'd hate to try a trip through that to where it again comes to the surface. Most rivers have their danger spots.

For the ordinary river, knowing the distance between bridges where you can launch and take out your boat and the number of float hours from one to the other is always valuable information when you plan your trip. Whether you float and fish for only half a day or a week, it's wise to have someone put you in at one point and meet you at another. A good trick is to use two cars. Park one—if you can find a safe place where it won't be disturbed—at your point of debarkation and leave the other where you launch. In this way you don't have to depend on a third party to put you in the river and then possibly have a long wait to pick you up. Your hours on the water are likely to be uncertain, depending on many circumstances. Good maps make the planning easier.

Allow enough time to cover the water properly. On most bass rivers, certain stretches are more productive than others, and you'll need time to try different lures and retrieves. On smallmouth streams, you may want to slide your boat or canoe ashore and wade some of those nice rocky sections, working your lures carefully into the pockets. You just can't fish areas like that well when the strong current is pulling you along.

Tube floats are a handy accessory for float-tripping both largemouth and smallmouth waters. While your partner takes your boat downstream, you can slip up to bassy bank-pockets and midstream boulders with more stealth than you

Good float-fishing streams carry anglers into places never touched by the crowds. Erwin Bauer

ever could from a boat. By the time you rejoin your buddy downstream, you should have some marvelous action to talk about.

The species of bass you encounter naturally depends on the location of the river. Generally in the North it's the smallmouth and in the South the largemouth, with a sprinkling of other species. Best known of these is the Kentucky or spotted bass that ranges generally in the Ohio-Mississippi drainage but is found south to western Florida, and westward to Kansas, Oklahoma, and Texas; the redeye or coosa bass that is generally a southern fish; and a number of subspecies closely related to these two.

I've taken the redeye throughout its range from east-Tennessee southward through Georgia and Alabama, but possibly my most interesting experience was in the Chipola River in northwest Florida, where the redeye is known as the shoal bass because of its nature to inhabit—as it does throughout its range—both the shoreline and shoal water of fast-moving streams.

We found the Chipola an intriguing stream. It flows out of limestone caverns near the town of Marianna, Florida, and roughly parallels the mighty Apalachicola before it pours into Dead Lakes above Wewahitchka. Except for its fast current and limestone shoals, the Chipola is a typical southern stream, crowded with cypress and gum and overhung with magnolias, hickories and oaks, many draped with long streamers of Spanish moss. The river's trail around the bluffs and through the swamps is as tortuous as that of a drunken black snake.

When we first went to the Chipola, the local fishermen would stand you down that the shoal bass had an identity of its own and that no other fish of the same size and weight was comparable to it in fighting heart. The first bass we caught made us inclined to agree with this. I dropped the topwater lure with one spinner behind it, against an old log, let it lie until the ripples died, and twitched it slightly. The bass hit it in a blur of speed that threw water over the log and set the hook without any help from me. The line sang in the current and when my fish jumped, he was on the other side of the boat from where I had hooked him. He made my four-pound drag squeal then and jumped again down river. I'd had only a couple of glimpses of him and when we finally got the fish in our boat, I'm sure my jaw popped open. I had expected at least a five-pounder and this one wouldn't go much over two.

"They're strong," the guide commented, noting my astonishment.

Where the swift Chipola spread out into the waters of Dead Lakes, the shoal-bass fishing ended and the largemouths took over. Later we sent specimens of the shoal bass to the fisheries biologists, who identified the fish as redeye bass—not a brand new species after all.

My most memorable day of floating for spotted bass on the Coosa River was with Charles Kelley, director of Alabama's game and fish division, and Jake Adams, one of his conservation officers. We fished the stretch of river between Jordan Dam and Wetumpka, as rocky and rough as any trout stream I ever encountered, but with a difference. This one was a hundred yards wide. Half a dozen currents raced back and forth across it, dodging tremendous boulders, pouring over ledges, sweeping through deep pools. The water was too fast for largemouths and too warm for the bronzies.

Below Wetumpka the river slows down and spreads out into largemouth habitat. "This is a subspecies known as the Alabama spotted bass. It's one of the best places for spotteds I ever found," Kelley told me.

Then he proved his statement. The water was too fast to fish as we drifted on the current. In some pools we could hold the boat in the eddy water with the paddle or an anchor. In others we had to cling to the tops and corners of boulders while we fished out the edges and tails of the flow.

Some of the ledges over which the river poured were ten feet or more in height, and we had to pick the deepest flow of water over them. Any canoeist would have found this white water supreme.

"Do you ever spill into this stuff?" I asked.

"I average about once a trip," Kelley said. "Only a few fishermen I know will tackle this stretch of river in a boat."

I put the camera strap over my shoulder and closed my tackle box, hoping it would float until I got to it.

We used light spinning gear and, since it was early summer, underwater lures. My choice was the small crystal spoon and it proved effective, as did the variety of small spinnerbaits and broken-back plugs that my two partners used.

We caught bass. We took a lot of bass, and got breathtaking jumps out of them. Most were small, around a couple of pounds. We returned all to the water.

"In the fall, we take some fine catches on the fly rod with popping bugs and flies," Charles said. "This time of year if we want big bass, we go to live shiners. We'll try that tomorrow."

The next morning we caught the shad minnows at the base of the dam with a wire net, placed them in his boatwell and spent that day fishing the holes and runs with live bait. Sinking the minnows in the right spots took a little longer, but the fish we caught averaged larger than the day before. The largest was over five pounds, and we took many almost as large.

When I remarked that some of these fish might pass for bronzebacks or even redeyes, Kelley pointed out a couple of unmistakable marks of identification. The black spot on the tail and gill cover are more prominent than in the other species of small bass, and the Kentucky has one distinguishing characteristic not found in the others. It is his "tooth," a small, rough projection on the tip of the tongue.

One should not expect the optimum conditions

Affectionately called "dough-nuts," the modern inflatable float tubes are perfect for float fishing. The good ones contain pockets for grub and gear and can be used in conjunction with a boat or for an interesting one-day-float alone.
Glen Lau

and luck on every float-fishing trip for bass, any more than he has a right to find perfect fishing every time he pulls his boat out on a lake. You can count on unexpected rainstorms that will catch you days away from your destination. If you are any sort of woodsman at all, you'll have your rain-suit along and a tarp for shelter at night, and the rain won't bother you. The rising and muddy water will put a damper on the fishing, though.

The best float-fishing usually comes at bug time, so don't fail to include insect repellant in your pack. Once when I fished with Bill Rae on the Suwannee River, we left home in such a hurry that I forgot the bug juice. We didn't even have mosquito netting. After supper, being an old Cracker boy, I took another big drink before I rolled into my blanket and went to sleep. My Yankee friend took a big drink too, but it didn't anesthetize him. He fought mosquitoes all night long and spent most of the next day trying to keep his head from falling off into his lap.

Snakes are no menace except under unusual conditions. On a float trip, most of the snakes you'll see are water snakes of the harmless variety. In the very deep South you must keep an eye out

for cottonmouth mocassins, which constitute an entirely different ballgame. Once on a south-Florida river that was very narrow and overhung with limbs, we often had to push against them to help us through a tight spot. In one such place I reached up to grab an overhanging limb and my guide in the back of the boat, almost broke my arm knocking it away with the paddle. When we were past the limb, he pointed out a deadly cotton-mouth stretched out just where I would have put my hand.

In close places, snakes that are disturbed often drop off limbs into the boat, but they can be more easily removed alive than by beating the bottom out of your craft with a paddle or an axe, trying to kill one. It is most likely a harmless water snake anyway.

When you plan to camp overnight, it's a good idea to find a suitable campsite well before dark. A sandbar or gravel bar is good, as is a low, flat bluff with a dry landing site and plenty of firewood.

On some rivers, clear, unpolluted drinking water is a problem. Unless you are familiar with the stream, carry along a jug of clean water. In an emergency, boil the water you find in a creek or spring branch. Don't take a chance.

In addition to my bed roll and light air-mattress, I have with me a ground cloth, tarpaulin for shelter in case I need it, and a light canvas to cover my boat to keep the supplies dry. The air along a river gets mighty damp at night. A number of times, for one reason or another, I've been caught on a float trip in the rain without any of these conveniences. When this happened, I pulled my canoe or bateau ashore, turned it over, and slept under it. In an emergency, it's a good shelter if you remember to dig a ditch around it.

A gas lantern makes your camping more enjoyable, but have a flashlight with you too, as well as a light axe and plenty of stout cord, which will come in handy for every purpose. I carry a supply of plastic bags that I may need to keep my food, clothing, and camera equipment dry.

For the convenience of cooking over the campfire, I built a grill out of a light rack I salvaged from an old refrigerator. To each corner I attached a light metal rod in such a manner that it would fold against the rack to form a flat pocket. Lying flat in the bottom of the boat, it's not in the way when traveling and has saved many a pot of coffee or pan of vittles sitting on the coals from suddenly shifting and tipping over into the fire.

For river fishing I carry a slightly different assortment of lures than I haul around on a lake. The old standbys are with me—topwater, spinnerbaits, jointed plugs, spoons, feathers—but the size is generally a little smaller, especially if I know I'll be fishing clear water. You don't need artificials that dig down twenty feet under the surface or make a dive for the bottom. A majority of your feeding fish lie within a few feet of the surface, usually around cover. The bait that runs above them is more likely to attract their attention.

As in a lake, you score better if you present the type of food the bass is accustomed to going after.

Artificials that resemble frogs, minnows, and large insects are good. A bronzeback will go for anything that looks to him like a crawfish. Fly-rodders find popping bugs effective. I also have several mouselike plugs. In these I like the floater. I cast it close against the bank, let it drift with the current along the shore, and twitch my rod tip every few seconds to turn it at a different angle on the surface. When the lure drifts two or three feet away from the bank and I bring it in for another cast, it dives and swims with a tantalizing motion.

Spinnerbaits are generally good in flowing water and I am partial to the seductive action of a pork rind wherever I can use one of the strips on a lure. As elsewhere, it is a matter of experimenting with your various artificials until you find one attractive to the fish.

Guiding and outfitting for float-fishing trips is said to have originated in Arkansas and Missouri many decades ago. The practice is now reasonably widespread, but seems to exist only in certain regions. If you can find a guide for the river you'd like to fish, this is by far the best way to learn the stream, the type of cover that provides the best fishing, the most successful lures, the preferred camping places, the time and distance between launch and take-out areas. From any pro in the business, you'll also glean information on the most useful equipment and what you might need when you make the next trip on your own. If your state game and fish department has no record or listing of such guides, it should be able to refer you to someone who is familiar with the river and does have that information.

Once you try it, I predict that you'll be hooked on float-fishing for bass.

Smallmouth streams are particularly nice for float fishing, once you learn to negotiate the currents and identify the best lies for the fish. Dave Richey

14

Better Baitfishing
A Practical Guide

BYRON W. DALRYMPLE

As a young fisherman, whenever I went after bass in the small lakes and slow rivers around my boyhood home the most important part of the project was gathering the bait, usually green meadow frogs or fat nightcrawlers. Most of today's bass fishermen wouldn't have any idea how to catch—or fish with them! The flurry and bustle of modern bass fishing, with its zooming big boats and gadgets galore, long ago sidetracked bait. And that's unfortunate, because bait will catch more and bigger bass more consistently than all the lures ever invented.

It's true that endless improvements in artificial lure designs and the massive accrued knowledge about how to fish them have to some extent cancelled the need for bait. Granted, lures eliminate the problems of acquiring, keeping alive, and handling natural baits. I like that part as well as anybody. Artificials, however, are all attempts at simulation in one way or another of basic bass forage. It therefore follows that the natural with a hook in it and a line attached must be sensationally persuasive, or else the ever-more-refined mimicry—basically to eliminate the bother of bait—would not have evolved, or continued.

The fact is, our forebears caught bushels of bass with bait long before there were bass lures, and a scattering of present-day bass fishermen wise to

the supereffectiveness of bait-fishing still do. A friend of mine who fishes numerous tournaments chuckled as he told me recently of an incident that proves the point of how bait delivers in the clinch.

It was one of those tough tourney days, he told me, when all the guys were applying all their machinery and know-how and playing hunches to boot, and the bass were keeping their mouths shut. At weigh-in time, he allowed, all the boats together had run up probably several hundred miles of travel, and tens of thousands of casts had been made. The best fish was a four-pounder, and it was the only one that fisherman had. The heaviest string was an embarrassing six-plus.

During the gloomy post-mortems a wooden rowboat with an oldtime native in it pulled up to the dock. He came along carrying a ten-fish limit on a stringer, all of 'em of envy size. Somebody said to him, "Where the heck did you catch them, Dad?"

The man replied with a nod, "Over yonder right across the channel around them stumps."

It was real quiet for a minute, my friend told me. "All us overequipped experts had our jaws down. Then of course somebody couldn't resist asking, 'What you catch 'em on?' The old gent just said, 'Crawdads,' and kept on walking up the dock."

It is perfectly logical that bait is the best bass

insurance. It has authentic appeal. Work an artificial crayfish with your most tantalizing action in front of a disinclined bass, and the fish will probably turn it down. Dangle the real thing in front of it and just leave it alone, and your chances will be high of convincing the fish. Living bait is authentic in appearance, in the sounds of its movements, in the scent it gives off, and in the feel and taste when a bass mouths it. It not only looks good, it *is* good. A bass that grabs it won't spit it out. The action of an artificial may fool an eager bass, but not an exceptionally shy or disinterested one. Bait, even without any action, is easily recognized by a bass as real food.

The fact is, a good many serious—and open-minded—bass fishermen are convinced that if and when a new world record is caught it will be on bait. A substantial number of bass enthusiasts suspect that a new record may come from one of the several small lakes of southern California that have grabbed the spotlight over the past few years for the astonishing number of outsized largemouths they're producing. A high percentage of these big bass are caught on bait. Over a period of a few weeks last year, for example, from one of these lakes twenty-seven bass above ten pounds and a total of more than eighty above six pounds were caught. Several kinds of bait took the majority of them.

Bear in mind that the largest bass are also the oldest, even in waters where bass grow swiftly. Unlike warm-blooded creatures, fish continue to grow until they die, so any bass of near-record proportions is likely to be old and to have looked at a lot of forage, and its imitations. Its judgment is honed as fine as it will ever get. To trophy bass, an authentic food item has the edge over a facsimile.

Many a guide and big-bass fisherman in Florida has for years sneaked off to use bait when he wanted to show off a big fish. Quite a number habitually fish with extralarge minnows to entice trophies. I fished all one winter with a guide in Florida who used golden shiners eight to ten inches long. On my first day with him he asked if I'd like to catch a really *big* bass and told me if so to put away my lures. I could hardly believe the size of the bait he produced from the live well. The first two bass caught on these huge minnows weighed seven-and-one-half and nine pounds. I needed no further convincing.

Several lure manufacturers are currently turning to smaller lures, because in so many impoundments nowadays fishermen are catching

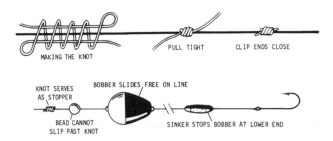

How to make a standard baitfishing rig.

bass of only moderate size. Some lure makers, and widely experienced tourney anglers, suspect there may not be very many large bass left. That hardly seems logical. Could it be that bait is the key to the big ones that have been endlessly fished over with lures? Most bass anglers don't know that this *isn't* true—because they never fish with bait.

This is like claiming that plastic worms are equally as productive as nightcrawlers. They are certainly less bother, easier to acquire and handle. But only a few bass fishermen today, chiefly older ones, have ever used a nightcrawler. Plastic worms are probably the closest simulations of any artificial lures. They catch a lot of bass. The fact still remains—and has been proved by quite a few anglers willing to use both—that when things are so tough that bass shun plastic worms, one here and there still will grab a crawler.

Curiously, bait fishing for bass today has the most adherents in two widely separated areas of the country, the western and northeastern states. The Great Lakes region is not far behind. Over the vast area of the so-called best bass states bait is least used. This may be due to the hundreds of large impoundments, and the publicity that has attended tournament and club fishing. It's a cinch that what catches bass in any given region is what the bass fishermen offer 'em. Darned few nowadays give bass a chance at bait.

Following are the best of the bass baits, and brief basics of how to fish them. Make sure that using bait is legal in any particular water you intend to fish. In some states either all baits or specified ones are prohibited in certain lakes and streams.

Minnows

Fish of modest size are one of the mainstays of bass diet, for both largemouths and smallmouths. Although technically the term "minnow" refers to species belonging to the large family *Cyprinidae*, to a fisherman any baitfish is a "minnow." Bait minnows are available everywhere bass are found. What baitfish species you use depends on what is obtainable from bait dealers or what you can gather in your own area.

Chubs, shiners, suckers, gizzard and threadfin shad are classic examples of the best bass catchers. Freshwater sculpin also are excellent, but not as easily acquired. Various sunfishes, on which bass feed naturally in many waters, can be used productively, too. But shiners, suckers, and chubs are forage fish with strong odor and without a lot of the fin spines that make them difficult to swallow.

Minnows native to the water where you'll fish probably have a slight edge over some of the non-native species sold by dealers. But bass are opportunists and not very selective. Golden shiners and shad are especially appealing to bass because they are soft, oily, and odoriferous. Big bass seem to know instinctively that these are rich and easily killed fare.

"Bass minnows" sold by dealers are usually two, three, or four inches long. Two-inchers will catch lots of bass, but not many big bass. For large bass you should use minnows at least four inches long, and if you are after true trophy specimens you can discourage interlopers and intrigue a lair-loving oldster by offering a baitfish six or eight inches long. In the North, where a six-pound bass is an authentic trophy, stay with four to five-inchers. In the South, and especially where Florida-strain or hybrid bass that grow extra-large are native or have been introduced, try anything up to ten-inchers for a fling at a wallhanger.

Near floating vegetation, such as water hyacinths, using a bobber of a size the baitfish can't hold down, and no sinker, was the technique the Florida guide sold me on using. For this fishing it's best to hook the bait under the back fin. This allows it total freedom. Drop it at the edge of a floating patch. The bait will run underneath but can't go down to bottom. It is in plain sight of a lurking bass. Or, drop it close to large stumps or submerged snags. A bass sees the bait as encumbered or injured. When one takes it, let out line as it runs. When it stops, snug up deftly and gently, then set the hook.

It's hard to beat fishing minnows under a bobber in any kind of bass habitat. Except near floating vegetation cover, use a sinker, of a weight just enough to keep the bait from coming to surface. A slip-type bobber arrangement allows you to cast and places the bait at any depth required. A pull of a few inches on the line every minute or so keeps the minnow from hiding, and also keeps it active. Or, cast the rig out parallel to the edge of cover, always close to it because large bass won't leave a favored lair to move any great distance. Retrieve very slowly, parallel to the cover edge. This presents the bait along an edge that may have several large bass spaced at intervals in lie-ups.

Drifting a minnow beneath a bobber on a current is deadly. Steer it into likely looking slicks and pockets near cover objects. But whenever a minnow must be cast, regardless of the rig used, you have to be careful not to kill it or throw it off the hook. An excellent bottom-fishing minnow rig can be made with a bell sinker at line's end and a dropper tied in to the line about a foot up. No bobber is used. Toss out the rig, let the sinker take

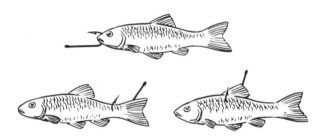

Three ways of putting minnows on the hook: hooking through both lips, through the tail, or under or ahead of the dorsal fin.

Occasionally large minnows are hooked with a double-hook rig.

A good method of hooking dead minnows for casting: pass hook and line through mouth and out gill; make loop around body; embed hook in side near tail.

156

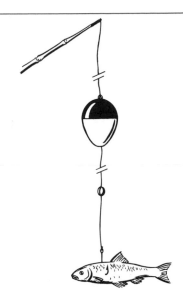

Casting the dipsey dropper rig and retrieving slowly along smooth bottoms or near weed beds is a telling method. All illustrations by Charles Dougherty.

A basic freshwater arrangement: bobber, sinker, baited hook.

the minnow to the bottom, then reel very slowly along cover edges. The sinker may drag weeds, but the minnow is free. It will keep trying to gain cover and thus attract notice of bass within range.

The dorsal-fin-hooking method is best, for it allows the minnow the most natural movement. Use hooks in proportion to bait size, and preferably a hook of thin wire to injure the baitfish as little as possible. The hook must not pass under the backbone or it will quickly kill the bait. That Florida guide who taught me about catching big bass on big minnows swore by gold hooks. He claimed the glitter was attractive. He caught his big golden shiners, incidentally, by tossing out a few slices of crumbled bread in shallow water,

waiting a few minutes, and using a small throw-net.

Minnows can also be hooked through both lips, or through the tail, or large ones by a two-hook rig, one in the lips, another on a short dropper through the side of the tail.

Fresh-dead baitfish cast or trolled will also catch bass. But rigging and fishing them is more complicated, and large bass are by no means as anxious to accept them. Their movement is not as natural as living bait, and big bass don't want to make a long pursuit. They prefer to lie in a favorite hideout and grab a large piece of forage in one lunge.

Nightcrawlers

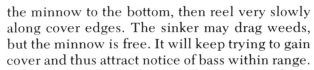

The nightcrawler, which the renowned plastic worm set out originally to imitate, is used today infrequently and only in scattered locations. Yet it is an awesomely lethal bass bait, far superior to, even though messier to use, than its modern plastic imitation. A good many of those huge southern California bass—the record is an ounce shy of twenty-one-pounds, the second over eighteen—have been caught on nightcrawlers.

The nightcrawler is a killer. It has its own distinctive smell, it is soft and wriggly, and bass can and commonly do nip off a tasty tail of one, which must taste great because they just as commonly

come back for the second bite, something not common with the imitation.

In places where nightcrawlers are still in vogue, bait stands handle them. But beware of ripoffs. Many southern bait dealers sell what they call nightcrawlers, but when you open the box you find just fair-sized angleworms. A nightcrawler is at least six or seven inches long stretched out, and the size of a lead pencil in diameter.

If you can't buy nightcrawlers, in most locales you can find your own. Some crawler gatherers shove electrodes into moist earth and drive the worms to the surface by light shock. The best

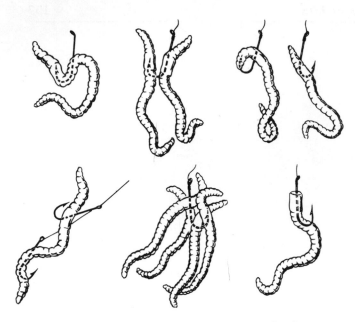

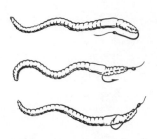

An excellent way to hook a night crawler is the famous Texas Rig that plastic worm anglers use.

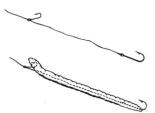

Some standard ways of putting worms on a hook.

Trick to nail short-striking fish: Crawler is threaded onto hook and up line, its head held by small hook tied onto line.

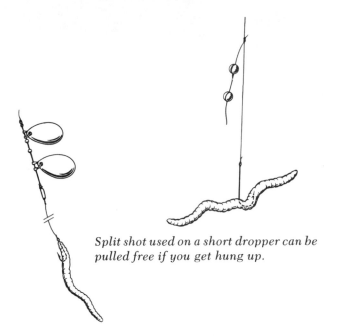

Split shot used on a short dropper can be pulled free if you get hung up.

Double or tandem-blade Indiana spinner with night crawler trailing on foot-long leader is great for bass and big bluegills.

method is to soak a lawn or patch of grassy loam with water, or visit it after rain has soaked it. Go out at night, with a red light—a flashlight with the lens painted or covered with transparent red plastic; walk very lightly so as not to spook them back into their burrows, and pick them up with quick grabs.

There are many ways of hooking crawlers. A pet method of mine, which catches tail-nipping bass the first nip, is to string the crawler on the hook, push it over the eye and on up the line so it is stretched clear out. A very small hook tied into the line here—about six inches up—holds the head. Hooked thus, a crawler is lethal when cast and retrieved with a slow creep along the bottom or around cover objects. Smallmouths in rocky shallows are unable to resist it.

Crawlers can also be effectively hooked with the so-called Texas rig used by most plastic-worm fishermen. For trolling or casting, a crawler can be threaded on a hook through about the first inch, and trailed a foot to eighteen inches behind a spinner. My favorite spinners are the old-fashioned June Bug and the twin-bladed and buoyant Indiana. If you get just a nip, drop back, letting the spinner and bait begin to fall, then set the hook immediately.

Crawlers can be fished any way you fish a plastic worm. One of the most productive ways to use them when bass are not eager is with a spinning outfit, either with no weight or with one or two modest-sized shot pinched on a brief dropper so they'll pull off if a hang-up occurs. Ease your boat quietly into the shallows, or within casting distance of a rock wall with underwater ledges, or near various objects or weed cover. Hook the crawler in the middle, threading enough on to hold well, or use a two-hook rig on monofilament. You can even hook two crawlers together in the middle of their bodies. Cast pinpoint to the best spots. Let the crawler waft down, using no motion from your rod whatever except if the bait drops on a ledge or log. Then pull it off. Keep a gently snug line and hit back at the slightest indication.

For stream bass, cast a crawler (hooked as above) up and across, keep your tip high, and let the crawler tumble downstream. Another favorite crawler rig and method that has proved extremely effective for me in smallmouth lakes and in others with short weeds on bottom is identical to the bell-sinker and dropper rig and slow-reel method described under "Minnows."

Frogs

Frogs, a natural bass food, are lethal, although not easy to catch, transport, and handle. They are used little nowadays, partly because few bait dealers keep them, and because some states regulate size and time of taking them. Meadow (leopard) frogs can be caught by stalking them with a long-handled fine-meshed net. Doing this at night with a flashlight is easiest.

Small frogs catch small bass galore and sometimes large ones. Frogs measuring three inches sitting are about right for large bass. The chief problem in using frogs for large bass is that fishing them on the surface is the most natural and productive method, yet trophy bass do not feed at the surface as much as smaller ones. A long rod—the old cane pole is still the ideal tool—plus a quiet approach, and the technique of reaching out to plop a live frog among lily pads or beside stumps is exceedingly productive. As a kid, I hooked a frog and tossed it out into a pool in a slow-moving river, with no sinker or bobber, and let it start to swim to bank. This works well in lakes, too.

Frogs can be hooked through both lips, or through a front or hind leg. Not many fishermen use the front-leg placement, but it does give the frog the most freedom and easy swimming. Old-fashioned frog harnesses can be found in some sporting goods stores. They are a nuisance to use, but do make it possible to cast frogs without undue injury, and also allow them freedom to swim.

Casting, or swinging a frog out to toss and plop it into likely pockets is the basic technique. Casts should not be long. The bait is easily killed by rough usage. No sinker should be used. Bass strike surface frogs explosively and you must instantly hit back to set the hook. Some bait anglers fish frogs on or near the bottom. A frog cannot live long underwater. The usual method is to hook the bait through the upper part of a hind leg, place a sinker a foot up the line, heavy enough to keep the frog down. It will try to swim upward of course, and its motion just above bottom mightily intrigues bass. It must be brought up every couple of minutes to breath, or a fresh bait used. Dead frogs are seldom effective.

Frogs can be hooked through lips or through hind or front leg. The latter, not often used, allows the frog more freedom of action.

Here's a deadly method of fishing a frog just off the bottom. Fairly heavy sinker keeps the frog from returning to the surface; but it keeps trying, thus attracting fish.

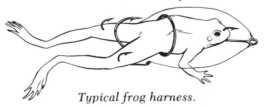

Typical frog harness.

Crayfish

The crayfish is one of the best baits for both largemouth and smallmouth bass. It may have an edge for smallmouths simply because rocky waters where they often live usually produce a husky crayfish crop. Some bait dealers handle them. In most instances you must gather your own, by hunting them in shallow rocky pools or streams and along lake edges, or raking out aquatic vegetation from ponds where they abound, such as farm ponds. They can be kept and transported in a minnow bucket with cool water and some aquatic weeds for them to hide in. Some of those huge southern California bass, incidentally, were caught on crayfish.

Best way to hook a live crayfish is through the tail from beneath.

Unpeeled tails of small crayfish make prime bait for bass.

Some "crawdad" enthusiasts break off the big claws before hooking one. This is not important one way or the other. Bass are used to eating them whole, claws and all. Crayfish shed their shells as they grow, just like other crustaceans. Turn-of-the-century bass fishermen swore that "soft craws"—right after shedding—far outcaught the hard ones. Those are difficult to find. A shell-softening method that is probably at least a hundred years old is to place a layer of aquatic weeds in a crock, a layer of crawdads, a heavy sprinkling of cornmeal over them, more weeds, then barely cover them with water. In twenty-four to thirty-six hours the shells soften. However, the crayfish don't always live. In my experience, though soft craws may be better, a live hard one can be plenty good enough.

Two popular hooking methods are through the tail, or under a couple of segments atop the tail. In either case, the hook point should be up, so it does not hang up on the bottom. The crayfish is a bottom-dwelling creature and is most effectively fished there. However, many users like to suspend the bait below a bobber and barely off bottom, so the creature can't keep trying to hide under a rock or in weeds. When fished more naturally, on bottom, it should be tugged every few seconds to keep it in the open. An utterly deadly technique is to use a long rod, move silently, and drop, toss, or flip the living crayfish down beside stumps or weed patches, submerged tree boles, or rocks. Leave it a few seconds to "work," move it a bit, then withdraw and repeat elsewhere.

Casting a crayfish is effective because it is a fairly tough bait. Keep the casts short. Add as little weight as possible, or none, and cast like a lure into bassy spots; then retrieve very slowly, well down on or near bottom and crawled over debris. Simply still fishing with live crayfish, using a free-line (slip-sinker) rig is deadly, particularly for large smallmouths. The bait is on bottom, but can move, and a skittish big bass that picks it up can move away without undue pressure on the line, yet the angler can feel it. The bait should be tugged every couple of minutes to keep it in the open. When a bass picks it up and moves away, pause a few seconds and then strike.

Some anglers break off the large claws before baiting with crayfish.

Large peeled crayfish tails are deadly on bass.

Crayfish tails, peeled or unpeeled, and threaded from the foreward end onto a hook are sensational bass catchers. However, most bass caught thus are from one to a maximum of three or four pounds. Most large bass like a substantial mouthful. Craws four inches long are none too large for them. In a few places—like Louisiana, where a crayfish species is a commercially important food item—there may be a season and limit. Be sure to check.

Hellgrammites

The hellgrammite is the aquatic, or nymph, stage of a large flying insect called the horned corydalus. The nymphal stage lasts nearly three years, during which time the rather ugly creature, with nippers on its head that can give you a painful snip, becomes at maturity at least two inches long. They live under stones or among vegetation along lake, pond, and stream shores. During the summer when metamorphosis occurs, they crawl ashore and under such debris as old boards or rocks, where they form small hollows in which they stay until "hatching" time. Few if any bait dealers have hellgrammites today. You gather your own by seeking them in their homes. They can be kept in cool, damp grass for some time.

This bait, eagerly snapped up by all bass, was once considered indispensable for the bass angler who doted on bait. Today it is seldom used or even known or recognized, except among a few old hands or specialists. I used to decimate smallmouths with hellgrammites in Michigan. Recently I read a reference to their use on the Delaware River in New Jersey.

The hellgrammite is a tough little critter. The hook should be run under the collar behind the head, the point entering at the head side. Care should be taken not to puncture the body cavity and kill the bait. A good trick is to snip off the two hooks or prongs at the rear end of the body. The nymph uses these to grab and hold on bottom.

Hellgrammites can be fished under a bobber, or by flipping or casting and a slow deep retrieve. The best place and method, however, is to use them for stream bass, casting up and across and letting one tumble down, with slight tugs to keep it from attempting to cling. Curiously, even though this is by no means an outsized bait, large bass, especially smallmouths, are always eager to grab it.

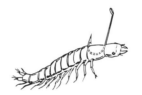

Hellgrammites hooked under the collar stay active a long time.

Salamanders

There are scores of salamander species ranging throughout the United States. Some are aquatic, some terrestrial, some live two-stage lives, partly aquatic and partly on land. Although all are good bass catchers, the larval or aquatic stage of the big tiger salamander, a sturdy creature four to six inches long with external gills and four partially developed legs and feet, has become famous over the past few years as a largemouth bass killer par excellence in the West.

This larval salamander is called by fishermen a "waterdog." The species range over much of the mountain West and the interior of the country. It is most abundant in shallow ponds in the Rockies, from which bait dealers glean tens of thousands, trucking them to the West Coast and many of the large inland western impoundments. In the southern California big-bass lakes, in renowned lakes Mohave, Powell, Mead in the southwest, in several of Oregon's and Washington's best bass lakes, in New Mexico and elsewhere, the live waterdog has become synonymous with big catches and trophy fish.

Not many bassmen have the opportunity to

Small terrestrial salamanders are sensational bait for bass, trout, and other gamefish.

A few southeastern bass anglers have discovered the fantastic bass-catching properties of an aquatic salamander called the siren.

Adult tiger salamander (top) and larval stages with external gills (below). The aquatic young, called "waterdogs," have become extremely popular in a number of large western bass lakes.

gather waterdogs on their own. But more and more bait dealers over a broader range are beginning to offer them. Demand might bring them to your area.

Waterdogs, which are tough, are cast exactly like a lure. They should be hooked from below upward through both lips. As little weight as possible should be used. You want just enough to take the bait down to bottom. Sometimes bass strike as the wriggling bait sinks. Once its on bottom, you have to keep it moving, a few inches pull every few seconds with the rod tip. This keeps it active and from hiding, which it will try to do.

Several large aquatic salamanders are found throughout the eastern states. They are seldom if ever used, a situation which sharp bass fishermen should look into. In Florida and along part of the southeastern Gulf Coast, another aquatic salamander, the long, snakelike siren, also with external gills but with only two (fore) legs developed, is a secret weapon used by a few bass anglers after bragging fish. Most catch their own, using a box with screen bottom, wading out among hyacinth patches, scooping up several plants and shaking the salamanders out from the roots upon the screen. Some sirens are twelve inches long. This lean, slinky salamander is tail hooked and allowed to swim free, usually with no sinker, although it can be fished beneath a bobber. It will attempt to burrow in mud so should be "worked" to keep it in view and swimming.

In the North and East knowledgeable anglers hunt terrestrial salamanders of several varieties under moist rotted logs or deep, moist leaves in woodlands along streams or lakes. Most varieties of these are much smaller than waterdogs, but all are bass killers.

Admittedly, using any of the baits covered here is more bother than fishing with lures. However, if you put aside purist ideas and try the *original* kind of bass fishing, you'll find not only a new and intriguing facet of the sport, but you may also surprise yourself with mounting-size bass from places where you've never before caught such busters.

15

Bassing with a Thermometer

ANTHONY A. CIUFFA

Largemouth bass are responsive to water temperatures. Increases in temperature from a colder state will usually raise their metabolic rate—provided that the starting colder condition is below the temperature that would establish their maximum metabolism. Once the temperature is reached that would produce maximum metabolic processes, any increase above that temperature will cause bass to seek a deeper and cooler level within their tolerance range. Decreases in water temperature will lower their metabolic rate—provided it is a drop in temperature from a level that would maintain proper body processes. For example: a decrease in water temperature from very warm surface water (which was in excess of that required for maximum metabolic rates) would actually support bass comfortably and permit them to feed regularly—provided the drop in temperature is not rapid, and that the new, lower temperature is not below that required for proper food assimilation and maintenance of proper metabolism.

A solid knowledge of how temperature affects bass can improve your bass fishing immensely.

The comfort range of the bass is not always a given water temperature but, rather, a relative reading. Bass that have moved into gradually warming surface waters in the early spring would find 60° a rather comfortable temperature because their metabolic rate at that time is not very high but just right for 60°. Having only recently been exposed to 40° water during the winter months, the gradual rise toward 60° would provide comfort. But if you tossed this bass into 80° water, it would become deranged and probably die. Yet if the surface water was, say, 85°, that same fish might be compelled to seek 80° or even 70° water as its preferred comfort range.

Of course, oxygen, clarity, photosynthesis, forage, and other factors ultimately control where bass will acclimate themselves during hot weather. Fishermen should not expect a bass population on a certain lake to be in a given cooler level that would be below the fish's tolerance range *at that time;* the tolerance range is somewhat controlled by the bass's ability to feed and breathe enough oxygen as well as by its metabolic condition at a given time.

The temperature of surface and near-surface waters must at all times be considered together with the type of forage the lake contains—the major source of the largemouth's diet. If bass must feed on gizzard shad as a primary source of food, the surface habits of these fish would cause bass to acclimate to higher average temperatures than bass for which crawfish and other bottom-

163

As temperatures rise in early spring, the metabolism or life processes of bass also perk up. Erwin Bauer

dwellers provide the bulk of their diet. As far as fishermen are concerned, preferred temperature ranges are thus relative to the forage and other lake conditions. Certainly bass that must forage closer to the surface, whether in daylight or at night, could not tolerate temperatures more than 10° or so cooler for very long, and even when they attempt to reach those levels they would probably go through a certain period of gradually exposing themselves to lower temperatures rather than merely diving from 85° to 75° water in one fast move. I'm certain that this is one of the reasons, among others, why bass *suspend* at times.

Another misconception is that bass have a constant preferred temperature and comfort range like some warm-blooded animals and humans have. Some warm-blooded animals, as well as all human beings, have a consistent comfort range of about 68° to 72°, depending upon the relative humidity. The only other variables that humans and some warm-blooded animals may have are age and health; in any case, they have a given body heat all year round, except for hibernating animals. Bass assume the temperature of the water and are at its mercy; therefore their comfort range is only relative to previous exposure and its difference from the temperature they find themselves in.

As temperatures rise in early spring, the metabolism or life processes of bass also perk up.

Water temperature changes have a tremendous effect upon bass behavior and vary by region.   Erwin Bauer

They now need food to keep up with their increasing activities and because they have not yet shaken off their winter stupor, lunkers are more easily fooled in the early spring than in late summer.

When early-spring winds start moving a lake surface, carrying the increasing heat in the air, surface water piles up at the shoreline toward which the wind is blowing. This forces deeper water to flow toward the side from which the wind is blowing. In this manner, the denser and colder bottom water is gradually circulated to the surface, where winds warm and aerate it. As this process continues, the entire lake, unless it is quite deep, temporarily reaches a stage where the surface and the bottom waters are about the same. When the wind does not blow enough to maintain circulation, and the sun becomes increasingly warmer, the surface temperature climbs and the water there becomes more buoyant. Then circulation will only continue in the upper layer, and stratification takes place.

With the first signs of the warming undercurrents, bass, which congregate in the deeper areas of a lake in winter, where maximum-density water exists at about 39° (where cold-air temperatures are the rule in winter) now move toward the more buoyant, upper mass of warming waters. They also move nearer to the warming shorelines, where prevailing winds are piling up surface water. At first, though they have bothered to stir out of the depths, they have little interest in prowling around the lake. They will move to the nearest shoreline. They will sun there, and absorb the warming condition.

If disturbed while in the warming layer, they will swim horizontally rather than back to the depths; they will want to remain within that depth which contains the warmer temperatures. Even before stratification begins, bass will begin to feel the life processes urging them to feed. The first to respect this signal will be the females, now laden with eggs that had their development in the previous fall. Egg development now will dictate some disrespect for mild temperature drops, a sort of delayed response limited to the females. This is indeed a ripe time to catch big bass, before they

As bass venture into shallow areas for spawning, they become vulnerable in springtime. This lunker was released, as are all bass on the author's catch-and-release waters in Missouri. A. A. Ciuffa

scatter to spawn. But it is also a ripe time to *ruin* a small pond or lake, to spoil all future bass fishing, if you keep those big females. Only a sick ego would knowingly do that.

As the heat-gain continues, bass will venture into various areas of the lake, preparing to build up their bodies for the spawning period. Should a cold front set in, the males and the immature females will respond negatively to the fisherman's efforts; but this negative response is belatedly followed by egg-bearing females, especially the jumbo sizes. At such times, fast-moving lures should replace the easy-gaited single-spin baits that are probably your best bet during the first awakening. Fish both types at this time.

Once the water temperature has circulated throughout most of the upper strata, the epilimnion is formed. At first its depth or thickness is relatively shallow, sometimes only five or six feet thick. This depends upon the water clarity, which controls the rate of heat absorption by the colder water just below the early epilimnion. Now the bass are prowling and hiding, following their prey into cover, stickups, flat areas of steep dropoffs, fallen trees, and wherever the habits of their prime forage species lead them.

This is the period I call post-spring and pre-summer, the in-between period for bass. This is the time when they're unpredictable, demanding several fishing methods, lures, and a frequent change of pace. Now the water temperature at the surface ranges from 70° to 75°. At this temperature, when the fish are close to the surface, light, wind, and other conditions near the outside air, bass are very choosy; the combination of all these factors puts most bass in a preferred comfort range. This is entirely different from the 70° to 75° temperature they might seek in deeper, darker depths, remotely located from a warmer 80° surface.

Following the in-between period, there is a period of renewed bass vulnerability: the early summer, postspawn period. This occurs after spawning, when surface temperatures push into the 76° to 80° range and forage species become more predictable; the bass settle down where they can find their food. Their vulnerability increases because the increase in water temperature, combined with the still relatively shallow epilimnion, puts hungry bass close to the fisherman. They prowl after schools of shad or lurk near nesting bluegills, and this makes them susceptible to running baits that dive from a resting position or run with an even, not-too-fast gait. Bass

now extend their feeding periods, overlapping with the feeding sprees of their various sizes, and while they more than likely would not now bother to run far for a fast Sonar, they'd take well to Bayou Boogies, Deep R's, Wiggle Warts, some topwater plugs, and probably a Zara II or a big Zara Spook in the early morning.

Finally summer makes its entrance and water temperatures rise into the eighties, where they'll usually stay for a while. The epilimnion continues to deepen. Now it carries its bottom surface like a stretched sheet of rubber several more feet downward, increasing water clarity and depressing suspended matter away from it, pushing it into the thermocline (if the lake is big and deep enough). But in general the deepened upper layer now contains a fresh amount of oxygen and bass are likely to be on deeper structures than they were during the early summer when the epilimnion was relatively thin. It is mid-summer now, a time when they are required to build up their bodies and make ready for probable periods of low oxygen that late summer will bring, especially if the rains don't come.

This mid-summer vulnerability occurs usually in late June through the third week in July in my parts. It is the ripe time for medium and deep bass fishing in the daylight hours, a time for shallow-water fishing during a good rain (when warm air warms the rain and fills it with new oxygen to supplement the additional photosynthesis and its oxygen-producing qualities). This is also a prime period for night fishing for tackle-busting lunkers. Water temperatures now range from about 84° to 88° at the surface and will not cool much below 74° at thirteen or fourteen feet down in most reasonably clear waters. Extremely clear water at this time would reduce day fishing success and increase night fishing, with or without a moon. Lakes that show water temperatures colder than 74° at thirteen or fourteen feet during this time would have suspended murky or cloudy water somewhere above those depths, or have a relatively small surface area in ratio to their depth—thus limiting the extent of circulation within the upper layer.

In contrast to the predictability of mid-summer fishing comes the highly unpredictable next period, late summer. This is a time when the surface water may even cool a bit, which appears to invite bass to work once again in the shallows. But big bass have taken a large amount of food during the first weeks of mid-summer, and have settled

As summer temperatures come on, hungry bass can be taken closer to the surface. Erwin Bauer

down where they no longer care to concentrate even if many are present. Above all, this is a time when most bass have built up their body condition to such a level that they can now afford to rest, take it easy, be plain choosy.

Night fishing or day fishing during this late-summer period requires several types of lures, but all in the slow-moving category. Smaller baits are more likely to succeed than larger lures, though you'll find that some medium-size lures are successful.

Early fall and falling water temperatures carry their own share of unpredictability. Good bassing will depend upon how fast the temperatures fall at

night and how well the heat of the day rejuvenates a lake. A fast-cooling trend will definitely lower the metabolic processes, at least temporarily, until enough body chemicals are used up during the period of abstinence.

If cooling turns out to be a rather slow, gradual process, without cold nights, topwater bass fishing might work well—in the middle of the day and then again about an hour or so before dark. Temperatures of both water and air must be monitored carefully at this time. You can capitalize on a return of a warming trend after water temperatures have made their first downward plunge, coinciding with the 70° to 75° of the

Lunker bass creates high-flying antics in one of the author's catch-and-release lakes. Mid-summer bass can be taken when conditions are right. A. A. Ciuffa

Big, coldweather bass are usually females. These fish were taken in early-spring fishing. A. A. Ciuffa

in-between period. But there's now a disadvantage that didn't exist during most of the in-between period: most bass are already well built-up, and the temperature levels are reversing. Bass were merely coasting during the in-between period, living on only a percentage of the chemicals they had begun to store, awaiting the demands of the high metabolism rates to come in mid-summer.

Depending where you live, late fall brings more cold nights, and the water temperature near the surface may now reach only 55° to 60°. Late fall brings on renewed vigor in the bigger bass, especially the big, fertile females. They now go through the process of initial egg development, which will continue until next spring, when the warming waters will again hasten their development and need to spawn. Even if a cold front takes over, the big females will carry with them that certain delay of negative response that will make them vulnerable while other bass—small and medium-size females, and small and large males—have gotten a deep case of lockjaw that only the first awakening next spring will cure.

The following chart has been prepared to distill my studies on water temperature and how it affects bass fishing. The figures and comments are based upon reasonable water clarity and normal oxygen content to support fish. Success rates are optimum when the bass population exists in at least fair numbers. Overharvested lakes prove their condition during the better periods by providing minimal success for even the most proficient bassmen. Be advised: without understanding the instructions and explanations in the foregoing text, this chart cannot provide enough information, by itself, to make you a successful fisherman under the many conditions that you will encounter while bass fishing. The indicator surface temperatures should be taken at twelve to eighteen inches below the surface.

NEAR-SURFACE WATER TEMPERATURES THAT ARE PRIME INDICATORS OF THE SEVEN PERIODS OF THE LARGEMOUTH BASS FISHING SEASON

PERIOD	GROSS TEMPERATURE	OPTIMUM TEMPERATURES	PROBABILITY OF SUCCESS WITHIN OPTIMUM TEMPERATURE RANGE
Spring: First awakening Development	50°–58° 59°–69°	55°–58° 58°–68°	Good to excellent: water temperature rising. Poor: falling or after temperature has fallen a few degrees. Egg-bearing females still vulnerable with an initial 5° drop. Sunny days better than cloudy. Midday best. Best time is when more heat gained in day than lost at night. Poor time when less heat gained in day than lost at night. Worse time: temperatures falling rapidly.
Shallow fishing: 2 to 4 feet, has the best average			
In-between	70°–75°	74°–75°	Fair to good when water temperature is rising or stable. Good when more heat is gained in the day than lost at night. Poor when temperatures fall or when more heat is lost at night than gained in day. Cold nights indicate slow fishing the following day. Warm nights herald probable good fishing the following day.
Shallow fishing: 1 to 3 feet, in cover mostly			

PERIOD	GROSS TEMPERATURE	OPTIMUM TEMPERATURES	PROBABILITY OF SUCCESS WITHIN OPTIMUM TEMPERATURE RANGE
Early summer	76°–82°	78°–82°	Excellent on cloudy days or in rain if temperatures are stable or rising. Good on sunny days if temperature is stable or rising slowly. Fair to good on sunny days when temperature is rising rapidly. Poor when temperatures fall, until they rewarm. Cold nights forecast poor morning fishing, with improvement at midday if warming.
Shallow fishing: 2 to 5 feet, near and in cover			
Mid-Summer Shallow: 2 to 4 feet; medium, 5 to 8 feet; deep, 8 to twelve feet	83°–90-plus°	83°–88°	Good to excellent when temperatures are generally stable. Excellent on cloudy or rainy days if the water temperatures are not cooled below the minimum optimum temperature. Fair if cooled slowly below 83°. Poor if rapidly cooling below 83°. Shallow fishing on rainy days. Medium depths on cloudy days: 5 to 8 feet in any of the optimum temperatures. Medium to deep fishing on sunny days when the temperature is above 85°.
Late summer Shallow: 2 to 4 feet; medium, 5 to 8 feet	80°–90-plus°	80°–84°	Good when temperatures are stable below 84°. Fair if temperature is rising, not beyond 85°. Poor if above 85°, especially if there has been no rain. Fair if cooling rapidly. Good if cooling slowly. Very poor when water temperatures are above 90°, especially if there has been no rain for three days and the lake is low. Night fishing dependent upon optimum temperatures and the presence of some recent moisture. Night fishing erratic—good to very poor.

PERIOD	GROSS TEMPERATURE	OPTIMUM TEMPERATURES	PROBABILITY OF SUCCESS WITHIN OPTIMUM TEMPERATURE RANGE
Early fall Shallow fishing, in general: 1 to 3 feet	80°–70°	80°–70°	Good when stable or rising, without colder nights. Even topwater action if heat restored during the day is a few degrees more than lost during night. Fair late-day and before-dark fishing on spinnerbaits if heat restored by sun is less than lost at night. Poor if cooling or no heat return from previously cold days or nights. Fair to good on cloudy days if there has been no heat loss the previous night or days, and if temperature is at least stable.
Late fall Shallow fishing: 2 to 4 feet, in general	69°–50°	69°–58°	Fair when water temperatures rise within optimum. Poor when temperatures fall. Fair if heat that surface lost on previous night is restored on sunny days. Good if heat into water exceeds that lost during night or previously cold days. Warming trends must be longer than cooling nights for fishing success to improve or last. Cold fronts at this time extract more heat than is usually recovered, causing slower fishing.

16

The Big Sky's Neglected Bass

NORMAN STRUNG

The Northern Rockies could hardly be called a bass-oriented place. As a matter of fact, if trout had wings, they'd be made the State Bird in Idaho, Wyoming, and Montana. Consequently, bass are hardly recognized as a gamefish. Their existence is unheralded and usually unknown, and only a small circle of bass addicts fish for them. This condition creates a fisherman's paradise, but one with some surprising twists.

My introduction to the sometimes weird wonders of Big Sky bass came a few years ago, at the hands of Bill Browning. Bill was living in Helena, but he originally hailed from Ohio, a state that's long loved the largemouth. Knowing of his background I was doubly impressed with his invitation to fish one of the best bass lakes he'd ever seen.

"Sure," I said, more than surprised that the fish were anywhere to be found. "I'd love to go. Hell, I haven't tied into a bull bass in over twelve years!"

That night I packed what I remembered to be bass essentials: a corncob pipe, topwater plugs, short-sleeve shirts, and wading shoes. The next morning, we were on the road.

Our general destination was Montana's Flathead Valley, a long finger of mountain-rimmed low country that lies west of the Continental Divide. This area boasts much of the state's bass water. Relatively mild winters and lots of

shallow lakes are the main reasons. We were heading for Ninepipe Reservoir, near Ronan. The impoundment was built some thirty years ago as a means to flood-irrigate nearby ranches and farms. Ninepipe amounts to about four square miles of water. It's a scant fifteen feet deep at the dam, and vegetation-bristling shallows reach out along every shore. It was one of the bassiest pieces of water I'd ever seen—a visual impression that undoubtedly prompted the introduction of that first pair of fish long ago. Although bass now thrive in Montana, they're not native.

"Man," I said to Bill, "this place has bass written all over it!"

"You're not alone in that opinion," Bill agreed. "It's probably the most popular pond in the whole state."

As we drove down the access road, he nodded toward a pickup parked next to a stile, then pointed to two cars on the wide dam. "See what I mean? And this isn't even a weekend."

He wheeled off the road and into one of the many empty parking areas around the government-owned reservoir.

I surveyed our chosen spot from the shore. It was a wide peninsula that jutted a good one hundred yards into the water. Offshore stands of reeds created little channels and runs. The water was dead calm, then I saw a swirl.

It had been twelve years since my last cast, but bass fever was back. Everything was just like it used to be, I thought.

"You're not wading in those, are you?" Bill asked as I began tying my tennis shoes.

"Sure. What's wrong? Bottom paved with nails or something?"

"No," he said. "But I've got an extra pair of waders and some wool socks in the camper—just in case you might want them."

"Okay, I'll keep that in mind," I said, puzzled. Then I grabbed my rod and hot-footed it down to the water. I cold-footed back immediately.

"Jumpin J-J-Judas, that water's chilly! Is this January or July?"

Bill, smiling, produced the waders. "Well, a little bit of both. The snow that fell in January is still up in those mountains." Bill nodded toward the snow-cap peaks of the Mission Range. "And it doesn't get much of a chance to warm up before it leaks down here."

I was immediately doubtful of our prospects and pointed out to Bill that no bass in its right mind would so much as think of biting until the water reached the 60° level.

"That's a pretty reliable rule down South," he said, "but our summers are so short that the largemouth seem to have adapted to the cold." These high-country bass, he explained, pay only minimal attention to temperatures in relation to their feeding schedule. While it's true that the level and frequency of feeding increases as the water gets warmer, they've been known to grab a bait just about anytime.

"And how's this for clinchers?" he offered by way of proof. "Anglers often catch bigmouths fishing through the ice. A few years back, a ten-pounder came out of a hole in the ice on this very lake."

Bill is the kind of guy who never stretches the truth, not even in fish stories, but I couldn't help but play the part of Doubting Thomas as we shoved off to wade the shoreline in warm boots and wool shirts.

My choice of terminal tackle was a froglike popper, a selection that made Bill frown after a few casts.

"Now you're gonna tell me that top stuff won't work because the fish keep thinking it's an ice floe or something?"

"No." Bill laughed. "In midsummer, top gear works great, but now I'd use a plastic worm. I've

got a hunch the bass are still bedding."

"On July first?"

"Yep, that's one facet of a bass's life that does work by temperature around here. Don't forget that we have a pretty late spring, so the fish usually don't start to spawn until mid-June. If you don't believe me, look around. There's some proof right in front of you." Bill pointed his rod at a sandy-white circle on the lake's bottom. Sure enough, there wasn't a speck of silt on it. A fish had been finning there. "And here's some more proof coming right up."

I watched his rod tip dip, then line funnel through the guides as Bill opened his bail and let the bass run. He snapped the bail back in place when the line stopped, then took up the slack and struck. A foot-long largemouth came rocketing out of the water, the black worm whipping back and forth as he tried to disgorge a meal that bit back. Before Bill had him landed, I'd tied on a hook and worm of my own.

It didn't take long for this Doubting Thomas to become a true believer. Not five minutes after Bill hooked his first, I tied into a scrappy two-pounder. The shoreline at Ninepipe was a delight to work. Reeds reached out to a point roughly waist-deep, then stopped dead. I scored most often by casting up along the reeds' edge, then slowly retrieving the worm. Occasionally there would be a cut in the vegetation—a channellike run that reached back into the reeds. These were natural bedding areas and practically a sure bet for fish. Another hot-spot proved to be the isolated islands of growth in the lake itself.

The fish we took that day weren't big by southern standards. They ran from ten inches to three pounds. But numbers count with me, and there were more than enough bigmouths to keep me not just interested but absorbed. I was so absorbed that one of the strangest sights I've ever seen on any fishing trip completely escaped my notice until I practically ran into the guy.

"Bill," I croaked. "Do you see what I think I see?"

Bill looked in the direction of my wide-eyed stare. "That guy fishing in a wet suit? What's unusual about that?"

The reeds, weeds and shallows that make Ninepipe a bass hotspot also make the area extremely attractive to waterfowl. Birds use it both for a resting spot during their fall migrations and a nesting spot in the spring. Since so few Montanans are interested in bass, the place is

Much great bass fishing goes untapped in the trout-rich West. Erwin Bauer

managed as a wildlife refuge first and a fishing hole second. To prevent the waterfowl from being disturbed, boats are prohibited on the lake.

Obviously this limits anglers to shore fishing only—that is, unless you have a skin-diver's wet-suit to keep you warm.

"The few guys who fish hard for bass claim that those islets are where the lunkers like to lay," Bill explained.

Since that first trip with Bill, I've done quite a bit of exploring on my own. And "exploring" is the right word. There's a lot more bass in the Northwest than you might imagine, but it's up to you to find them. Most people don't know or care what a bass looks like, so you bump into bass in odd places. Like when you're hunting antelope.

The prairies that lie around the town of Rawlins, Wyoming, could hardly be called bassy. They're dry as alum in the fall; trees are so rare they count as landmarks; and streams only run after a good rain—which is rare anyway. But that country is tops for antelope, and they were the main reason for a trip three friends and I took down there last fall.

In a tackle shop nearby, on a wild hunch that somewhere, someplace, I might be able to catch a fish, I questioned the clerk.

"Fishing?" he said. "Sure we got good fishing. But not in the river. Gets too silty down here for anything but catfish. There's some great places right around where you're hunting, though. Stock ponds."

Because of the lack of natural water over the high plains, ranchers dam up gulches to catch spring rains and provide a source of drinking water for their cattle during the dry summer and fall months. Most of these stock ponds are dinky, shallow affairs, less than an acre or two in size. But, according to the clerk, ranchers occasionally get ambitious and build some impressive impoundments. If they're big enough and deep enough to support fish life, the state stocks them initially with the species most likely to survive. The clerk pointed out on a map the general location of our mobile camp. Sure enough, there was a reservoir less than five miles from us, and it was stocked with bass.

My partners were understandably puzzled when I started rigging up a rod after lunch. "What you gonna catch—cactus?" one asked.

It took me a while to run down the reservoir in the look-alike flat landscape. When I finally found the place, it was a most unlikely bass pond. Gnarled sagebrush dotted the shoreline, but except for that western weed, not another tree or shrub could be seen for miles. Any form of aquatic vegetation, except for thick duckweed, was absent, and the only sign of life along the muddy shore was in the form of cattle tracks.

My doubtful offer was a #2 Mepps silver spinner. The water in the reservoir fell a little short of crystal clear, so the flashy attraction of silver seemed like it might work.

I was flabbergasted when a largemouth that looked a little over four pounds picked up my offering on the first cast. He took it not five feet into the retrieve, and came cartwheeling out of the water to throw the hook. The second cast brought nearly the same results, except that I landed that fish and a dozen more, which I filleted out for supper. They were delicious, but like the fishing I'd found, different. Eating fresh bass fries in the middle of the Great American Desert just didn't seem normal.

A trout isn't quite as strange a bedfellow to bass as an antelope, but the two species are seldom found together. Another bass-fishing discovery revealed a bass-trout relationship, and again, it was a matter of largemouth bass finding room in the back seat.

My wife Sil and I were easing down Montana's Jefferson River in our johnboat. The lower Jefferson flows by the town of Three Forks, so named because three rivers—the Gallatin, Jefferson, and Madison—meet there to form the Missouri.

Geologically, that area looks a little like a delta. The rivers' gradients smooth out, and the flowing waters meander around lazy curves. Occasionally these curves become so acute that the river takes a new course. It flows straight, cutting off the flow to the long bend and isolating it. Eventually that curve becomes a small lake with no connection to the river. Geologists call them oxbow lakes. There are at least six such lakes along the lower Jefferson, and we happened to stop for lunch on a bar that had formed one. As we ate, I couldn't help notice frequent swirls in the lily-covered water thirty yards back from the river. They caught Sil's eye too.

"Trout?" she asked.

I shook my head. "Too shallow and warm. Probably carp."

But by the time we finished eating, curiosity got the best of me. I rigged up a floating muddler minnow on my fly rod, and waded out. There was an umbrella-size circle of open water far to my left, and it looked awfully interesting. A foot or so beyond the circle, I could make out the barely perceptible twitches of a lily pad. Obviously something was under there making the thing move. Carp? Sunfish? A frog?

My line shot out. I feathered the cast, and the muddler drifted down onto a rimming lily, barely making a dimple in the flat, calm water. I eased the muddler off the pad and popped it once. Suddenly a dull flash rolled sideways. I saw it long before I felt the hit. Then, just as fast, the fish was on top, tail-dancing in a flurry of spray. His greenish sides and flared red gills were a giveaway.

"I'll be doggoned." I laughed. "We've found us another bass pond."

It was all the invitation we needed. We portaged the johnboat over to the oxbow and spent the rest of the afternoon happily bugging bass. Our discovery that day amounted to a whole new source of bass water. Since then we've found largemouth quietly abiding in three other oxbows in the Three Forks area, and along two other Montana "trout streams," the Flathead and Clark Fork rivers.

The Clark Fork held a second surprise. I was fishing with John Barsness, a friend and fellow writer who lives in Missoula, and we'd taken a stringer of ten to twelve-inch bass on a small, floating Rapala. I was surprised at the scrap those smallish fish had put up; they were on top of the water more than they were under it, dancing

Nice bass goes airborne in a western reservoir ignored by the region's trout addicts. Erwin Bauer

around in a frenzy of scales and spray.

"These are the scrappiest little largemouths I've ever seen," I said to John.

"Largemouths? Look again, my friend," he called back.

His meaning didn't register at first; the lateral line, the black spotting that feathered out along the side—they were bass, for sure. But they did have a funny tint to them and the mouth didn't look quite right. The *mouth!*

"Smallmouth . . . well I'll be damned!"

The possibility that decent smallmouth fishing existed in the Northwest had never occurred to me, but according to John, who was a bronzeback afficionado, it was as good as anywhere in the country. Like largemouth fishing, it was scattered, unpublicized, and known only to a handful of anglers, but it was there.

He put me on to two of the finest smallmouth rivers I've ever had the pleasure to fish—Idaho's Salmon, and the Tongue River in Montana. These places also paralleled the largemouth fishing in other ways. The salmon, steelhead, and trout in the Salmon River were all that anglers were interested in, or talked about. Smallmouth came off as one cut above a squawfish, just a little better than trash.

Most of the anglers in Miles City, where the Tongue joins the Yellowstone, had no idea there were bronzebacks in their backyard, or any notion of their scrappy nature. Gamefish to them meant catfish, sauger, and paddlefish, or trout in the mountains three hundred miles to the west. In both places, these attitudes led to what amounted to an untapped fishing resource, and ten to fourteen-inch bass that couldn't leave a lure alone.

There is no special secret to catching bass in the northern Rockies. Largemouth will strike at plastic worms, spinnerbaits, minnow plugs, and poppers, but you will have to delay what has come to be common timing. In the southern and central states bedding time runs from mid-March to mid-May. In the West, however, I've never found them fanning until mid-June. Plastic worms and big minnows work best at that time.

When it comes to topwater stuff, the fish only seem interested during mid-summer—mid-July to late August. In the early spring and fall, spinners, spoons, and underwater plugs produce the best.

Smallmouth strike a spinner, spoon, small minnow-plug, or a large nymph like the Woolly Worm or Montana Nymph, just about any time except during spring runoff, or when heavy rains cloud the water. The fishing is at its wildest in the late summer and fall, September through October.

If there is one trick to hooking a bass under the Big Sky, it is finding them in the first place, and the only rule-of-thumb I can provide is that you seldom find them within one hundred miles of the Continental Divide—elevations there are apparently too high, and winters too long and severe for these fish. But once you locate their lair, you'll learn, as I did, that some of the best bass fishing in the nation is hiding in the shadow of the Rocky Mountains.

17

Backcountry Bass

VAL LANDI

The chill autumn breeze slowly guided my canoe along the golden-red and evergreen-fringed shore of the cove toward the distant headlands of the Canadian Shield. I drifted, dreaming of the voyageurs who had paddled their trade through this country with their brigades of fur-laden freighter canoes, colorful caps and sashes, pipes and wood smoke, risqué songs and vermilion-tipped paddles as I quietly cast my bass bug hard up against a tangle of partially submerged cedar. I was slowly twitching the furry critter when the bronze flash of a big bass zoomed out and up from under the boom, torpedolike.

The fury of the explosion vanished, suddenly, with the jarring ring of the phone in the rustic garret I call my office, with its snow-flecked tudor windows, smack in the middle of Manhattan's Upper East Side, rudely ending another of my patent "Mid-Winter Day's Dreams."

It's one of my better inherited characteristics—or vices, if you will—to spend otherwise drab winter days planning and dreaming of potential trips for the coming season. Three of the most frequently recurring of my snowbound reveries focus on the great, unspoiled wilderness bass and canoe country of Minnesota's Boundary Waters area, Ontario's Quetico Provincial Park, and Maine's magnificent St. Croix watershed.

These fabled north-country bass areas form a primitive land of big lakes, eroded rolling hills, and mixed hardwood and coniferous forests, dotted here and there by several long-established sporting camps and outpost cabins, reached by forest road, charter fly-in, boat, and canoe-outfitting services. In addition to the northern sporting lodge operation, there are several types of trips to choose from: (1) the wilderness base-camp trip, where you are flown to a predesignated campsite or cabin location and are flown out on a pre-arranged date; (2) the wild river-lake chain fly-in trip, where you are flown in to a predesignated location, canoe and fish the system for the duration of the trip, and are picked up from an agreed-upon location that may be anywhere from fifty to one hundred miles downstream from your starting point; (3) canoe in and fly out from a predesignated location, or fly in and canoe out.

I prefer the wilderness base camp or outpost cabin trip. It allows you to set up a comfortable, safe, protected camp and provides the three essential elements for a productive backcountry bass trip: the time, comfort, and freedom to explore thoroughly and intensively a carefully selected area of a remote wilderness lake system. The key to planning a successful trip is a careful study of available topo and lake survey maps,

The camp is set, the fire is blazing, supper is on and all is well on this wilderness bass river. Grumman Canoe

which illustrate a wealth of useful manmade and natural features, including rapids, falls, hidden coves and feeder lakes, lake depth, shoals, reefs, islands, points, and portages. When planning a tent-camp bass-fishing trip to one of these north-country areas, I look for a campsite on the maps that gives me quick and easy access to both a lake and river, and practically guarantees success. If the bronzebacks should prove stubborn (as they often do), I have the option of fishing the river for walleye, salmon, or trout.

If you were to spread out maps of these three areas, you would find that they share characteristics common to great northern bass country: seemingly endless chains of jagged, irregularly-shaped glacial lakes, connecting streams, and wild rivers, with secluded, shallow, weed-fringed coves, bays, points, evergreen-clad islands, shoals, and cliff-lined rocky shores gouged out of the land during the Wisconsin Ice Age.

Quetico Provincial Park—believed to be named after the French *"la quête de la côte"* (the search for the shore)—stretches north from the jagged necklace of blue lakes known as the Boundary Waters along the Ontario–Minnesota border. This vast wilderness reserve covers an area of 1,750 square miles and, in the southernmost region, takes in some of the best wilderness bass country in North America along the great lakes chain where it adjoins the Boundary Waters Canoe Area and Superior National Forest to the south. The great Boundary Lakes chain stretches for almost three hundred miles following the Laurentian Divide along the historic Pigeon River voyageurs' route from Lake Superior west through Saganaga, Cypress, Knife, Birch, Basswood, Crooked, Iron, and huge, sprawling Lac la Croix to the Rainy Lake headwaters of Lake of the Woods. These big, wind-swept lakes are connected by a series of wild rivers—the Namakan, Bottle, Basswood, and Knife—characterized by numerous rapids, falls, chutes, and portages. The hundreds upon hundreds of hidden coves, bays, and the smaller, portage-linked feeder lakes form a smallmouth paradise. If you hit it right during late May and early June when the bass are on their spawning beds, it's not uncommon to catch up to a hundred fish a day in the two to four-pound class.

Access to Quetico and the Boundary Waters from Minnesota is by road to Ely, Crane Lake, or Saganaga Lake, via Grand Marais. You must clear Canadian Customs and Immigration at Saganaga Lake, Ottawa Island, or Prairie Portage on Basswood Lake, or at Sandpoint Lake for entry into Quetico at Beaverhouse Lake or Lac la Croix. Seaplane bases in the Boundary Lakes areas are situated at the Beaverhouse Lake Cabin, Lac la Croix Cabin, Ottawa Island on Basswood Lake, and Cache Bay at Saganaga Lake. Forest travel permits must be obtained at all entry points. A beautiful, full-color *Quetico Provincial Park* map and a *Quetico Canoe Routes* booklet are available free, along with detailed wilderness travel information, from the Park Superintendent, Quetico Provincial Park, Atikokan, Ontario. A full-color map of the Boundary Waters canoe area and Superior National Forest may be obtained for 50¢ along with travel and entry regulations from the Forest Supervisor, Superior National Forest, Duluth, MN 55801. A catalog of Boundary Waters–Quetico maps and charts may be obtained free upon request from W. A. Fisher Co., Box 1107, Virginia, MN 55792.

One of the finest camps with canoe-outfitting and charter fly-in operations serving both the Quetico and Boundary Waters areas is Bill Zups' Lac la Croix Fishing Camp and Outfitters, based at Crane Lake, Minnesota. Zups' main camp is a rustic lodge and guest-cabin affair on Lac la Croix, with wilderness outpost camps situated at several smallmouth hotspots including Iron, Crooked, and McAree lakes on the Boundary-Waters chain. Complete canoe outfit-

Numerous lakes and rivers offer backcountry fishing-camping opportunities. Erwin Bauer

Outboard latched onto square-sterned canoe makes expeditions from base camp easier for these bassers.
Grumman Canoe

ting and wilderness fly-in service is available, with quick access to the customs offices at Beaverhouse Ranger Station and Lac la Croix Ranger Station from pickup points at Crane Lake and Ely.

Equal to the Quetico-Boundary Waters bass country is eastern Maine's historic Washington County, a three-hundred-square-mile backcountry of pine and spruce forests, blueberry barrens, beaver meadows, and wild rivers, dominated by the big, jagged tributary lakes of the St. Croix River system. This legendary region, with its cool climate and sprawling, shallow lakes—such as island-dotted Baskahegan, Musquash, Sysladobsis, Grand Falls Flowage, Machias, Spednic, West Grand, Big Meddybemps, and the Cheputneticook lakes—is renowned for prolific surface fishing, particularly in the ghostly areas of flooded, dead timber, and log jams. As in the Quetico-Superior Country, June and fall are your best bets for fast action.

This sparsely populated region is served by several outstanding, long-established sporting camps and wilderness canoe outfitters. Sunrise County Canoe Expeditions at Cathance Lake (Grove, 04638) in the heart of Washington County, provides complete canoe-outfitting services and guided trips on the St. Croix and Grand Lake Chain. Canoe outfitting services are also provided by Maine Wilderness Canoe Basin (Springfield, 04487), located on the northern shore of Pleasant Lake, a major gateway to the Grand Lake Chain and forty miles of wilderness bass country. Playstead Lodge (Princeton, 04668) on Lewey's Lake offers rustic accommodations and some of the top bass fishing in the East, as does Leen's Lodge (Grand Lake Stream, 04637) on the Grand Lake Flowage, offering float-plane service. Grand Lake Lodge (Grand Lake Stream, 04637), located on the shore of West Grand Lake, offers housekeeping cottages, canoe and boat rentals, and guide service. Pocomoonshine Lake Lodges (Alexander, 04610) provide fully equipped cabins and guides. Weatherby's—The Fisherman's Resort (Grand Lake Stream, 04637) offers deluxe accommodations and services in a rustic setting. Chet's Camps on Big Lake (Princeton, 04668) offers cabins, boats, and guides. Spruce Lodge and Cabins (Springfield, 04487) is located on Sysladobsis Lake near famous Scraggly Lake and West Grand Lake in the St. Croix River chain.

Maine lake survey maps are available for all major lakes in the Washington County region. These useful maps show lake depth and major features, and contain detailed descriptions of each lake along with lake bottom composition and fish species present. The maps cost 15¢ each and may be ordered from the Maine Lakes Index, available free from Inland Fisheries & Wildlife, 284 State Street, Augusta, ME 04333.

The legendary wilderness bass fishing and canoeing areas of Canada are shown on the full-color *Canadian National Topographic Map Indexes*, available free upon request from the Canada Map Office, Surveys & Mapping Branch, Ottawa, Ontario K1A 0E9. The Canadian topographic maps show most manmade and natural features, including contours, forests, lakes and streams, mountain ranges, roads, settlements, trails, bogs, portages, rapids and falls, wilderness cabins, and magnetic declination of the compass.

Anyone planning a trip to the big north country should send for the *Canada Maps & Wilderness Canoeing Guide* (MCR-107), available free upon request from the Canada Map Office (address above). This valuable publication includes detailed information on planning your trip, making a trip profile, preparing a schedule, map symbols, barren land maps, navigating in the far north, types of map scales, and use of compass on a canoe trip. This full-color, illustrated guide also contains a "Canada 1:250,000 Scale Map Index."

Topographic maps of the United States may be ordered using *State Topographic Map Indexes* available free upon request from the U.S. Geological Survey Branch Distribution Offices at the following addresses: (for Western United States and Alaska) Federal Center, Denver, CO 80225 or (for Eastern United States) 1200 South Eads Street, Arlington, VA 22202. The indexes serve as a guide

Fishing solo, he seeks the peace, solitude, and action available on the waters you have to work hard to reach. Erwin Bauer

to ordering specific maps, which are available for a small fee.

It pays to get into top physical condition before you depart (be sure to get a thorough checkup from both your physician and dentist—request a prescription for antibiotics and pain-killers in case of an accident). Watch out for bad sunburns from the bright reflecting surfaces of the big lakes and rivers. To avoid exposure, wear a wide-brimmed hat and a pair of quality sunglasses, along with an effective sunscreen. A supply of salt tablets will restore sodium lost through perspiration. Be sure to pack a good supply of bug dope and head net and cotton gloves for travel during the black fly and mosquito season.

Backcountry bassing in Florida, where the airboat takes this lucky angler to waters seldom fished. Erwin Bauer

18

Hook and Line

A. D. LIVINGSTON

The complete bass angler of today streaks up and down the hottest new impoundment in a red-carpeted boat with a motor large enough to propel a small yacht. It is rigged with pedestal easy seats, a foot-controlled fishing motor, and enough electronic devices to intrigue even James Bond. The bassman's several free-spooling, ball-bearing, star-drag reels permit him to cast light lures and play large fish without backlashing and knuckle-busting. All his many-colored plastic worms and plugs and spoons and spinner baits and pork rinds fill a footlocker. It's not unusual these days for a bass angler to invest $5,000 in fishing equipment of one sort or another. With all this gear, the ordinary angler is apt to forget that only two things are essential to catching fish, and while attending to all his accessories he is likely to ignore his hook and abuse his line.

Most bass fishermen use monofilament line, and I have no doubt that monofilament will sometimes catch more fish than braided line will. But it will also lose more if it is not handled properly. Monofilament is tricky stuff, and the fisherman who uses it had better be very, very careful lest a big bass break loose from time to time. A knot or loop in the line, a nick from one cause or another, or a microscopic abrasion caused by rough rod guides will weaken monofilament consider-ably—sometimes drastically. At times monofilament will break for no apparent reason, leaving the angler wondering what happened.

Just the other day, for example, I was fishing near some lily pads about one hundred yards behind my house on an island in Florida's Lake Weir. I had previously taken a dozen lunkers from around the pads, and on that day I had put on a large golden shiner, hoping to interest the grandpa of the bunch. After a while the shiner started cutting up. It jumped completely out of the water. Then the float popped under, and the line zipped off fast. When I reared back to set the hook, the line popped. But it didn't break at the hook, where about 95 percent of all breaks occur. It broke about a foot or so from the end of my rod tip. I don't know why the line failed, but inspection led me to believe that I may have touched it, or come too close to it, with the end of my cigarette. Anyhow, I had connected with something solid on the other end.

Before I had rigged up again, I saw my float surface about 60 feet from the boat. I decided to up anchor and retrieve it. As I putted toward the float with my electric motor, under it went. I still had the fish hooked! I doubted that I could get it, but of course I watched all around for the float to surface again. Before too long it came up about fifty feet to

185

the left of the boat. Using my foot control, I started the motor and eased toward it. Down it went.

I must have played hide-and-seek for fifteen minutes before I got close enough to grab the line. I won't attempt to describe my hand-over-hand battle with the fish, but it turned out to be an eight- or nine-pound largemouth! It wasn't the grandpa that I had rigged up for, but it was a pretty big one that didn't get away.

Most fishermen aren't so lucky, and I have in fact caught several lunker bass that had hooks and plastic worms inside them. The black bass isn't as acrobatic as the tarpon, and it is better compared to a line-bucking fullback (who will take to the air if he has to) than to a scatback broken-field runner. Its initial surge of brute strength, together with its preference for hanging out in or near logs and limbs and other cover, makes the bass hard to stop. Many of the big ones do get away—and some that aren't so big get away too.

Monofilament line is almost always used for spinning and spin casting. In fact, the development of monofilament was really the big breakthrough in the development of spinning gear. But a good braided line works better on bait-casting outfits, and there have been some noteworthy improvements in braided lines during the past several years. Cortland's Micron, for example, has a very favorable strength-to-diameter ratio, and a number of other lines have been improved in this respect. Casting a modern twenty-pound-test line is as easy as casting a fifteen-pound line made a few years ago. I've recently tested a new Teflon-coated braided line, and it is very, very smooth to cast. I've also tested a "braided monofilament" marketed by Pflueger, and it also casts very well.

For bait-casting ease, the main advantage of braided line over monofilament is that it is more limp. Another advantage is that braided line has less stretch. And dacron braided lines have less stretch than nylon. Tests made by Gudebrod indicate that a twenty-pound weight will stretch certain monofilament line 20 percent, a braided nylon 15 percent, and a braided dacron line 10 percent.

Since braided line definitely spools better on bait-casting reels, why don't more bassmen use it? The main reason is that it is (or we believe it to be) more visible than monofilament. Even so, I believe that many bait casters are missing a good thing by not using braided line at times. I like it for casting fast-moving lures—but I hasten to add that I much prefer monofilament for fishing plastic worms and other slow-moving baits.

While an awful lot of bass are lost because the line breaks, a good many more are lost because the knot slips. Before discussing these problems in more detail, however, I would like to emphasize that not all monofilament is alike. One brand may be much better than another in one respect but much worse in another. It is difficult to improve one characteristic of a line without altering another, and the best the manufacturers can do is come up with a line of balanced properties. Anyhow, here are some of the things to consider when choosing a line:

Strength-to-diameter ratio. The strength of a line is expressed in the number of pounds required to break it; a twenty-pound-test line will support at least twenty pounds of weight without breaking. But the pound test published on a line's label isn't the whole story. Most line makers rate their lines a bit lower than the actual laboratory tests indicate. Another point to remember is that a line is stronger when dry than when wet. A line will slowly absorb a good deal of moisture from the air or from the water, and a fully saturated line loses about 10 to 15 percent of its strength.

Other characteristics being equal, a twenty-pound line with a diameter of .019 inch is obviously better than one with a diameter of .023 inch. The line with the smaller diameter will usually cast better, will be less visible to the fish, and will permit some lures with built-in action to do their thing better. But the strength-to-diameter ratio certainly isn't the only criterion for selecting a monofilament fishing line.

Stretch. The more a line stretches when one jerks on the rod, the less energy or pull available to set the hook. In other words, a line can act rather like a shock absorber. A degree of stretch is highly desirable to cushion the sudden jolt of a large fish, but most monofilament lines have too much stretch instead of not enough. Anyone who doesn't take monofilament stretch seriously should tie the end of a cheap line to a tree, back off about forty yards, and pull on it just to see how elastic it is.

Softness. Some monofilament lines are more limp or more flexible than others. Generally, softness is a highly desirable quality in a line. A soft line is easier to cast and results in better action on some types of lure. A wiry line inhibits lure action and tends to coil excessively after it has been put on a spool, causing bird's nests during the cast. On the other hand, a line can be too soft for use on spinning and spincast reels; if a line is too limp, it will not spring off the spool correctly and may ball

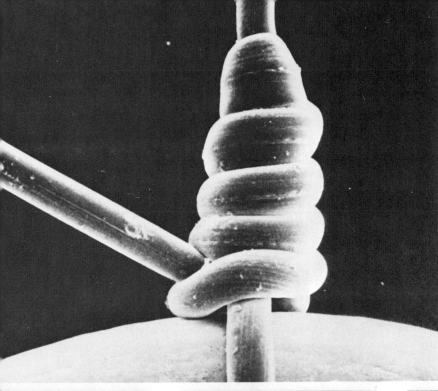

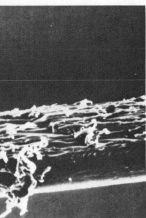
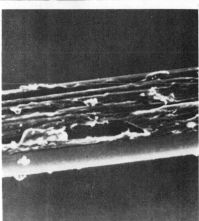
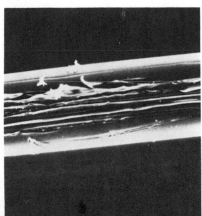

Here's an Improved Clinch Knot, photographed at 60 times natural size through a scanning electron microscope, used to examine line and knots at Du Pont's Experimental Station. The knot is tied with 2-pound test Mod II "Stren" fluorescent monofilament fishing line, into the eye of a No. 12 hook. This shows how the prescribed five turns cushion the line and protect against breakage in the knot.

Variations in durability shown in enlargements of three line brands after same number of cycles over an abrasive emery cloth in Du Pont test. After five cycles, line on left shows deep cutting action which resulted in failure after one more pass. Line in center shows flattening. Line on right is new "Stren" fluorescent monofilament which tests showed to be significantly more resistant to abrasion than same pound test of other leading monofilaments currently on the market. The photo shows lines magnifed 100 times, using scanning electron microscope.

Here's why an overhand is the most destructive knot a fisherman can tie in monofilament line. This photo, taken through a scanning electron microscope at Du Pont's Experimental Station, shows what happens when stress of only about 60 percent of the pound-test rating is placed on an overhand knot tied in 2-pound-test line. Arrow shows fracture of the line extending above the knot where cutting action occurs, causing it to break. The magnification is 200 times actual line size.

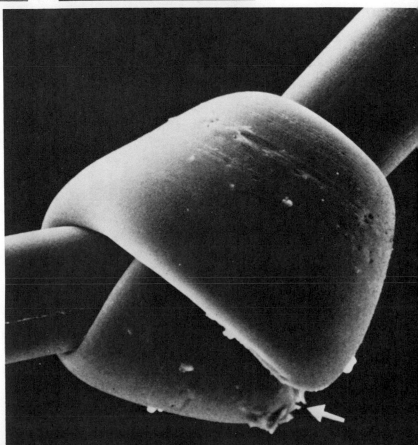

up under closed-face reels. A limp line also tends to slap the rod, which reduces an angler's casting distance because of friction. Generally, a very soft monofilament will also have too much stretch.

One obvious way to reduce or increase softness is to put on a lighter or a heavier line. A ten-pound line will be more limp than a twenty-pound line. But there is also quite a lot of difference in softness between various brands of monofilament of the same test strength.

Knot strength. When tying monofilament line to a hook or plug eyelet, or to another line, it is most important that you use the proper knot and tie it correctly. But some monofilament lines do have better knot properties than others. A very soft, highly elastic line, for example, compresses under pressure and tends to slip or fail. It is also difficult to draw a knot down properly with limp monofilament.

Visibility. Monofilament line is probably not entirely invisible to bass, but it is less visible than braided line. Some monofilament line is clear, while others are tinted with one color or another. I've never been able to determine whether or not bass can tell any difference between clear or tinted line, and frankly, I place more importance on diameter. Even so, I don't believe that visibility is as important in bass fishing as in trout fishing. Yet, I wouldn't want to go bass fishing with a plowline, and visibility is certainly a consideration when choosing a fishing line, especially when fishing plastic worms and other slow-moving lures.

For some kinds of fishing, I like to use a line that *I* can see (and which, hopefully, the bass can't see). I often use a line as a visual indicator because any twitch or change in line movement can mean that a bass has taken the lure. (Instead of striking a lure as is commonly believed, the bass usually engulfs it by opening its gills and sucking water and bait into its huge mouth, so that many strikes on still or free-falling baits are very gentle.) I can see a line twitch better when I use good polarized sunglasses, but some lines are more visible to me than others.

In addition to being very careful about selecting a monofilament fishing line and being very fussy about tying it to a hook or lure, the angler also had better be cautious when fishing with the stuff. Any number of accidents—such as pinching it in the hinge of a tackle box—can cause a line to break at far below its rated pound test. To list every conceivable way of line failure would be impossible,

but here are some of the more common causes, along with some conditions that alter a line's casting properties:

Abrasion. Figure 1 shows a frayed ten-pound monofilament line magnified sixty times. Believe it or not, this line would look smooth to the naked eye, although it would feel rough if run between one's fingers. Normal fishing will cause abrasion to one degree or another. Pulling the line through rod tips and guides, over brush in the water, or bumping it along the bottom all cause abrasion. During the casting process, the last few inches of line really catch hell, what with the lure being stopped and snapped forward at the end of the back cast. Catching a bass will often abrade the last few inches of line drastically. It always pays to cut off a few inches of line after catching a fish or when changing lures.

Although some degree of abrasion cannot be avoided if one fishes, it can be held to a minimum by careful inspection of the line and tackle. Grooves worn in rod tips and guides may cause a line to fray and can easily weaken it by 40 or 50 percent. On spinning reels, a worn pickup bail roller or line guide can cause severe abrasion. Although the bearing surface can be smoothed down, shoeshine fashion, with tiny strips of emory paper and polished with jeweler's compounds, it is best to install a new one. Replacing them isn't a major repair job on most spinning reels, and most reputable reel manufacturers will provide spare parts at small costs.

At best, abrasion is microscopic; at worst, it falls into the category of nicks and gouges. Nicks cause stress concentration, which means that the line's strength is drastically reduced. Incidentally, it is easier to nick or abrade stiff monofilament than soft. The reason is that soft monofilament is more flexible and elastic.

Rusty eyelets. A rusty or otherwise rough hook eye or lure eyelet can cause a line to fail at far below its test strength.

Impact. One cause of the line failure occurs when an angler sets the hook very hard into a large bass. Although impact failure sometimes occurs close to the boat, a more common cause is slack line, so that the full force of the angler's jerk hits suddenly. Plastic-worm fishermen using low-stretch line and stiff "worm rods" should be especially conscious of impact and should not set the hook until all the slack is out of the line.

Note carefully that a line's impact strength is lower than its tensile strength. Generally, the lines with high stretch are less likely to break from impact. And the more line that is out, the less the danger of impact failure.

Accidental knots. Every angler will occasionally get an overhand knot into his fishing line or leader. When he does, he had better get it out or cut the line above the knot. An overhand knot causes a severe stress concentration on the outer edge of the line. Such a knot reduces a line's strength by as much as 50 percent.

Sunlight. Prolonged exposure to sunlight (or fluorescent light) makes a monofilament line brittle and difficult to cast. It also weakens it. Even though some exposure is necessary in normal fishing, an angler should avoid leaving the rod and reel in the boat or on the patio or under the rear window of a car for long periods.

Heat. Temperatures below 120° have no permanent effect on monofilament line. Warm line, however, tends to be more flexible than cold line, so that temperature can have a bearing on a line's casting properties. Temperatures above 120° will have a detrimental effect on monofilament, but this is usually not severe until 200° is reached. Nylon monofilament melts at about 500°.

Water. Neither freshwater nor salt water has any *permanent* effect on the *nylon* in monofilament line. (But, as stated earlier, a line's wet strength is lower than its dry strength.) Most lines have additives to make them soft, and water will in time leach them out. Loss of the additives does not weaken the line, but it does make the line wiry and difficult to cast.

Line twist. An improperly balanced or tangled lure can cause severe line twist, especially when trolling. Another very common cause of twist among novice anglers is cranking a reel handle without taking in line, as when a large fish is making the drag slip. Twist can occur quite fast; reels having a 5-to-1 retrieve ratio will create five twists in the line every time the handle is turned.

A badly twisted line tends to bird's nest and is difficult to cast. Some twist can be eliminated by first removing all terminal tackle and then trolling the line behind the boat at high speeds. But a severely twisted line is hopeless and should be thrown away.

Improper spooling. For best casting results, the reel spool should be almost full of line—but not too full. On spinning reels, for example, a line will not cast properly if it only half fills the spool because too much friction will be created when the line goes over the top edge of the spool. On the other hand, if the spool is too full, the line tends to come off in coils, causing bird's nests. Most spinning reels should be filled to ⅛ inch from the top—but follow the manufacturer's instructions.

For best casting results with spinning reels, one should more or less match the line to the reel spool. Heavy line will not work properly on a small-diameter spool, and very light line will not spring properly from large-diameter spools. In other words, don't put twenty-pound line on an ultralight rig or four-pound line on a surfing reel.

Putting a new line on improperly can cause a degree of twist. This can be avoided by winding the line onto the reel the same way it comes off the spool.

Knots That Work

I use one knot for 95 percent of all my bass fishing with monofilament line. It is the clinch knot, which, if properly tied, retains from 90 to 100 percent of the line's strength. Some other knots, by comparison, reduce a line's strength by as much as 50 percent. But the basic clinch knot tends to slip with some lines, so I use the improved clinch knot. To tie this knot, run a couple of inches of line through the eyelet. Then bend the end over and wrap it five times around the rest of the line. Next, run the end back through the loop formed at the eyelet. Finally, run the end back through the loop that was formed by com-

pleting the previous step. When drawing the knot down, I hold the line in my left hand and the lure (or hook) in my right. While applying pressure slowly and steadily from both directions, I hold the loose end between my teeth and keep it tight. After the knot is drawn down, I test it for strength and slippage. If it seems all right, I trim the loose end close with nail clippers.

When tying this knot, some anglers make a double loop through the eyelet, and others use a double strand of line. Either method complicates the tying of the knot without adding appreciable strength. Personally, I prefer to have a perfect

Improved Clinch Knot

An old standby. Pass line through eye of hook, swivel or lure. Double back and make five turns around the standing line. Hold coils in place; thread end of line through first loop above the eye, then through big loop, as shown.

1

2

Hold tag end and standing line while coils are pulled up. Take care that coils are in spiral, not lapping over each other. Slide tight against eye. Clip tag end.

Surgeon's Knot

Lay line and leader parallel, lapping 6″ to 8″ of the two strands.

1

Treating the two like a single line, tie an overhand knot, pulling the entire leader through the loop.

2

Leaving loop of the overhand open, pull both tag end of line and leader through again.

3

Hold both lines and both ends to pull the knot tight. Clip ends close to avoid foul-up in rod guides.

4

Blood Knot

Lay ends of lines alongside each other, lapping about 6″ of line. Hold lines at midpoint. Take five turns around standing line with tag end and bring end back between the two strands, where they are being held.

1

Hold this part of the knot in position while the other tag end is wound around the standing line in the opposite direction and also brought back between the strands. The two tag ends should protrude from the knot in opposite directions.

2

Pull up slowly on the two standing lines, taking care that the two ends do not back out of their positions. Turns will gather into loops as they come together.

3

Pull turns up as tightly as possible and clip ends close to the knot.

4
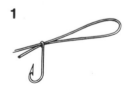

Palomar Knot

Easier to tie right, and consistently the strongest knot known to hold terminal tackle. Double about 4″ of line and pass loop through eye.

1
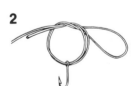

Let hook hang loose and tie overhand knot in doubled line. Avoid twisting the lines and don't tighten knot.

2

Pull loop of line far enough to pass it over hook, swivel or lure. Make sure loop passes completely over this attachment.

3

Pull both tag end and standing line to tighten. Clip about ⅛″ from knot.

4

Jansik Special

A strong knot. Popular with muskie fishermen. Run about five inches of line through eye of hook on lure; bring it around in a circle and run it through again.

Make a second circle, parallel with the first and pass end of line through eye a third time.

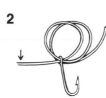

Bend standing part of line around the two circles. Bring tag end around in a third circle and wrap it three times around the three parallel lines.

Hold hook, swivel or lure with pliers. Hold standing line with other hand and tag end in teeth. Pull all three to tighten (arrows identify standing line).

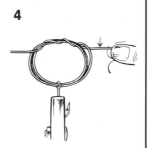

Surgeon's End Loop

Double end of line to form loop and tie Overhand Knot at base of double line.

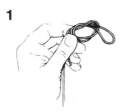

Leave loop open in knot and bring doubled line through once more.

Hold standing line and tag end and pull loop to tighten knot. Size of loop can be determined by pulling loose knot to desired point and holding it while knot is tightened. Clip end 1/8" from knot.

Spider Hitch

This is a faster, easier knot to create a double-line leader. Under steady pressure it is equally strong but does not have the resilience of the Bimini Twist under sharp impact. Not practical with lines above 30-lb. test

Form a loop of the leader length desired. Near the point where it meets the standing line, twist a section into a small reverse loop.

Hold small loop between thumb and forefinger with thumb extended well above finger and loop standing out beyond end of thumb.

Wind double line around both thumb and loop, taking five turns. Pass remainder of large loop through the smaller one and pull to make five turns unwind off the thumb.

Pull turns around the base of the loop up tight and snip off tag end.

Du Pont

knot than to have a double loop or a double strand.

It is very important when tying the clinch knot to wrap the line five times. Using only four turns can reduce the knot's strength by as much as 20 percent, and using more than five turns makes it difficult to draw the knot down properly.

The improved clinch knot has been around for some time and is still widely used on monofilament. The newer Palomar knot, which is said to be just as strong as the clinch and easier to tie on hooks and small lures, is gaining in popularity. Personally, I haven't used this knot extensively simply because I get along fine with the improved clinch knot.

The improved clinch and the Palomar are the only two knots that I recommend for tying monofilament line onto hooks, lures, and such tackle as split rings and swivels.

Hooks

The main requirement for a hook is that it be sharp. I always check the hooks on a lure—especially on a new one—before tying it onto my line, and a small Arkansas sharpening stone is a standard item in my tackle box. I also carry along a miniature file.

I prefer single-barb hooks to treble because I think they stick a fish better and hold it longer. They are also easier to sharpen. But a lot of artificial baits come with treble hooks, and I use them. I keep threatening to change them to single-barb hooks, but tampering with the hooks can upset the action and the balance of some lures. So, I usually fish with whatever hooks the manufacturer puts on the lures, but I'm not at all pleased with some of them. One of my favorite plugs comes with small wire treble hooks that are just too flimsy for some types of bass fishing. To be sure, they will hold the largest bass in open water if you have a dependable drag on the reel, but they are not always strong enough to horse a fourteen-pounder out of a submerged treetop.

I prefer the larger hooks for bass, but they are more difficult to set properly. The larger the hook, the farther it must penetrate to cover the barb; and the larger the bass, the tougher its mouth. So, if you're after a lunker bass with a large hook, the point had better be very, very sharp and had better be set with authority.

19

Playing and Landing Bass

HOMER CIRCLE

Catching the biggest bass of a lifetime is a thrill all anglers look forward to, and never forget. Many blow it because they commit some error at a crucial moment. They never forget that either!

So many things can happen to an inexperienced bass fisherman it's well to review them; so let's do it. Any one could save you that bass of your lifetime.

First off, we're going to assume your line is adequate in strength, that you've cut off a couple feet at the terminal end to ensure maximum security there, that your knot is a 90-plus-percenter you have confidence in, your reel is in top working order, and the guts of your rod adequate to the struggle. If you aren't sure, check them all.

The final thing you should attend to is the setting of the drag on your reel. This should be done with the line through the guides, tied to something immovable. With a full bend in your rod, tighten the drag to where the line would break if you kept pulling. Now, back it off to the point where it yields line smoothly as you move away, rod still under full bend.

Okay, you're ready. You're on the water at crack of dawn, eager, all senses alert. You know where you've seen a monster move, so you ease your boat into casting position.

Because your approach has been cautious, Mister Big doesn't know you're around and takes your

first offering. Your line pulsates, you slam home the hooks, and from the load on your rod you know this is it!

Did you set hard enough? Every bass fisherman with much seasoning gets this afterthought. And most set the hooks again, for security. But, hold it. This is okay on ordinary bass, but be careful with Mister Big.

If he just happens to ram in the opposite direction at the moment you double-set those hooks, it could pop a new twenty-pound-test-line. Instead, wait until that fish begins a steady pull, then dig those hooks home again.

Hold it out of heavy cover. If that bass is near cattails, lily pads, brush, hyacinth, fallen timber, a dock, or similar objects, do everything possible to keep on a steady pressure and get him headed away from trouble. You've got to give that bass all your tackle will take to keep it out of snaggy cover during this initial moment of combat. Once in tough cover, a big bass can foul your line and quickly break free.

Keep your rod bowed. Pressure that fish every moment from now on, and you can't do that with an unbowed rod. Never, and I mean *never*, point your rod toward Mister Big because this takes off the pressure and gives that bass freedom to make sudden moves against only your drag.

With a bowed rod and taut line, guide the fish

Many nice bass are lost during the final stages of the fight. Erwin Bauer

battle, nets have lost a heap of big bass. You might think that bass is pooped because it leads easily. But sticking a net into the water can spook a bass into a spurt that can tear loose a marginally hooked lure. Or the fish can dash past the net and inadvertantly snag the hooks of your lure in the outside mesh. This can give the bass the leverage, or resistance, it needs to pull free. So use the net only when you're certain the bass can be led into it easily.

Wait until it shows the white of its belly. When you have played the bass into submission, it will roll over and reveal a loss of equilibrium. Now you should be able to land it with a net.

One final word about playing bass properly. All the foregoing is the proper procedure if you know you have on a trophy bass and want to keep it. Smaller bass can be muscled in quickly and released as expeditiously as possible. If you don't intend to keep bass, the less you exhaust them the greater their chance for survival. This way these smaller bass can grow into lunkers, which can become an unforgettable catch to fellow bassin' men.

away from snaggy cover into open water. Once you have it in the clear, check your boat for any obstacles that can break a line should the bass suddenly come to you.

Clear the decks for action. Raise your outboard and the anchor. If you have a stringer overboard, bring it into the boat. Move your boat toward open water, using your electric motor, oars, or sculling paddle . . . all the time maintaining pressure on that bass.

Keep your cool. Now it's you and that bass; it's cunning and strength pitted against your tackle and intelligence. The moment you feel any yielding of pressure, or slackening in the line, reel until you again have a bowed rod and taut line.

Attempt to keep the fish moving in a big circle, around your boat, fighting against tension that slowly but surely tires it, lowering its ability to dash into cover.

Bring it to you. Slowly but surely lead the bass to you so that you can see just how large it is. Keep it moving in circles. If it dashes under your boat, let it go against the drag of your reel. Pass your line under the bow, or under the raised outboard, wherever you happen to be.

Don't reach for a net, yet. At this stage of a

Setting the hook properly takes more than muscle. Tom Gresham

Landing That Whopper

Landing a bass can be dramatic or traumatic, depending on whether you or the fish wins. More big fish are lost at this moment than at any other period of the battle between you and the fish. So let's do something about it. Let's analyze the various ways of landing fish and choose the one with optimum certainty. Or, as one of my Arkansas fishing buddies was wont to say: "There are so many ways to land a fish, you're bound to like one of them."

If the method you've been using has been satisfactory, stay with it. If not, stay with Uncle Homer while we run the gamut of the popular ways fish are landed; then you can decide which is best for you.

Landing net. It looks so simple to watch an experienced fisherman scoop up a fish in a landing net. And it is, usually. But in the hands of an inexperienced fisherman a net can be one of the surest ways to lose a trophy fish.

I said trophy fish. A whopper. The sight of one causes the adrenalin to flow, the heart to beat faster, and a sudden urge to "get it in the boat!" At this moment some fishermen suddenly grow eight more thumbs, the landing net becomes a swiper instead of a scooper, and they go beserk. They make a frantic swipe at the fish at it nears them and one of two things usually happens.

One: the net misses the fish but hangs on the hooks of the lure. This is all the leverage a big fish needs to jerk against the snagged lure and go free. And, two: the swiper misses both fish and lure, but spooks the fish so badly it exerts a super effort and shucks the lure.

Now let's examine the proper way to use a landing net as done by a fisherman with eight fingers, two thumbs, and cool.

He plays the fish until it is tired enough to allow itself to be led, or pulled, in a straight line. Only then does he reach for that net. He eases the net

Decision time: let the fish run, and it probably will break the line in the nearby cover. Apply too much pressure, and you may cause the line to break anyway. Prayer, anybody? Erwin Bauer

Netting a bass looks so simple. But many, many things can spoil the play, such as knocking the fish off with the net, tangling the net with exposed hooks of the lure, and just plain frightening the fish into a super burst of speed that pops the line. Erwin Bauer

Favorite bare-handed landing tactic, the jaw-grab. Watch those hooks, though. Glen Lau

into the water and leads the fish into it. Simple, when done methodically.

So, a landing net can save or lose fish. If you decide to go for this method, just be sure to get a net big enough to do the job.

The snatch method. Just like it sounds. You just snatch the fish out of the water, using your rod as a hoist. All it takes is a stout rod, a strong line, a sense of timing, and luck.

Sounds crude, hey? Well, it really isn't. Virtually all bass tournament fishermen, many skilled anglers and guides, put the snatch on all but trophy fish. When properly done, it is an effective maneuver. These fishermen use from fourteen to twenty-pound line on a gutty rod. This will easily snatch fish up to five pounds. The trick is in the timing.

With smaller fish you simply let the bend in your rod lever the fish into the boat. This works well on fish up to two pounds, maybe three, depending on the actions of the individual fish. With larger fish, up to five pounds, you play the fish

Don't laugh! The bellylift method really works! Glen Lau

until you can get its head above water and can drag it over the surface. Then you shorten your line, convert the drag into lift, and hoist the fish into your boat.

Tournament fishermen use this method because it saves time. And time to them means money. They aren't there to play a fish, or play *period*. Each fish can mean thousands of dollars in prize money. If there were a more efficient method of landing fish they'd be using it. Evidently there isn't.

But there are risks, too. A lightly hooked fish can tear loose. A docile fish when taken from the water can turn on the energy and shake free before you get it into the boat, just as you would if someone suddenly shoved you under water. As you learn the snatch method you will lose some fish until you develop a feel for it.

Gaffing. For freshwater fish I find this method so contemptible I mention it only because it exists. The gaff is a large hook on a handle. The hook is used to impale a fish through the jaw, gill, or body. That's all I can say for it except—it's a lousy way to terminate a sporting encounter.

Bare-hand landing. This is the method I have used most of my fishing years, for all species of fish. I find it more certain, more sporting, and more demanding of individual skill than other methods. Naturally, there are risks involved even when you know what you're doing. Let's look at how to bare-hand land fish without teeth, which include bluegills, catfish, crappie, perch, and bass. Lacking dentition these fish have jaws that are rimmed with rasplike borders for holding whatever they grab to eat. These are not sharp enough to puncture your flesh, so the jaw is a safe place to grab onto. Which brings us to:

The jaw grip. This is the safest, surest, most humane way to land a fish, especially if you plan to release a fish and want it to survive. To handle a fish elsewhere, especially around the gills and body, is to inflict it with hand acid which can

Gill-lift should not be used on fish you intend to release. Glen Lau

cause fungal or bacterial infection, and death.

Glen Lau, the nation's leading fish-action photographer, recently told me: "We've been studying carefully the best ways to handle bass without bringing on fungus. Unquestionably, grasping them by the lower jaw is the best way. We rarely get an infection now."

Here's why the jaw grip is so effective. After you subdue the fish, reach down and lay your thumb over the lower jawbone. At the same time, curl your forefinger directly under the fish's lower jawbone. Pinch with both fingers and lift the fish so that it hangs suspended.

The fish is paralyzed because suspending it over your forefinger causes the tongue to pull upward on the internal organs. This puts pressure against the central nervous system and immobilizes the fish. It will not flop and is safe to handle while you extract the hooks.

Gill-compression grip. Use this method when the hooks of a lure are exposed outside the fish's mouth. This is dangerous because if the fish thrashes as you reach for its jaw, you could wind up with you on one hook and the fish on the other.

The safest way to handle this situation is to subdue the fish, reach down and grasp the fish over its head with your thumb on one gill cover and your four fingers on the other. Squeeze firmly and lift the fish into the boat. Again, it is paralyzed because you are exerting pressure on its central nervous system. This gives you freedom to safely remove the hooks with the other hand. Or, you can now grasp the fish by the lower jaw by placing your thumb and forefinger in a safe spot away from the protruding hooks.

Exercise care with the gill-compression grip because too much pressure can mortally injure a fish. Use a firm grip, not a crusher.

But suppose you latch onto Old Goliath and the

A futile gesture, this. The fish is too green, the distance too great. Wait, friend! A. A. Ciuffa

fish's head is too large to span with your hand for the gill compression. Then you use the . . .

Belly lift. This works on all soft-belly fish I've tried it on, especially bass. Subdue the fish and bring it close to the boat. Run your hand over the fish's belly and cradle its body in your fingers. Slowly raise your middle finger and exert upward pressure on the fish's soft belly. Balance the fish with the other fingers and lift. Again, the pressure of your middle finger against the fish's innards paralyzes it. Now ease it into your boat and it will hang there, immobile, until you can grab its lower jaw in a safe place for hook removal.

I tried this on a big bowfin in early experiments with the belly lift. It laid there for about thirty seconds and I was beginning to grow a grin when that monster exploded. It busted me in the face, knocked off my hat and glasses, almost jerked rod and reel overboard, popped the line, and was gone. Man, did I feel dumber than a dogfish!

Let's wind up this chat with Uncle Homer revealing his best method for releasing fish with the greatest certainty for survival. I rarely keep fish and use this 90 percent of the time. I call it . . .

The jolt release. It works on any fish where you can reach the hook with a pair of longnose pliers, and when the hook is imbedded anywhere except in the gills. Your hands never touch the fish.

Play the fish until it's docile. Hold the line in one hand and the pliers in the other, with the fish still in the water. Raise the fish's head above water and firmly grip the shank of the hook that holds the fish. Lift the fish a few inches above the gunnel, outside of and close to the boat. Lower the fish suddenly, letting the pliers strike the gunnel with a sharp impact. The pliers and hook stop, but the fish keeps on going, untouched and unharmed.

Thought you had him, eh? Then, near the boat he pulls the trigger and bolts into another good run. Don't panic now by applying too much pressure. Let him go a bit, then start the fight all over again. Erwin Bauer

20

Trophy Bass
The Challenge and Prize

DAVE HARBOUR

The water explodes with the largest blur of headshaking fury you've ever seen. Your rod is bent from tip to handle, and your tight drag is screaming like a banshee. Sweat pours from your brow, and your heart feels as though it's coming through your chest. You keep repeating, "This moment can't be real! This monster is just too big to be a bass!"

But maybe you get lucky. At last, you're actually slipping a shaking thumb and fingers around a sandpapered lower lip as thick as your anchor rope. Finally you're admiring the biggest bass of your life, saluting her awesome splendor with exuberant thanksgiving still tinged with disbelief.

Most bass men are continually dreaming of the starring role in this drama, and plotting day and night to achieve it. This includes those of us who have caught real lunkers before, for there's always that *bigger* monster out there—*somewhere, some place*—that can be caught with the *right* bait or lure at the *right* time. Yes, the compelling drive to catch that lifetime monster bass is an incurable disease that few anglers have escaped from—or want to.

Discriminating guide services and fishing consultants, tackle manufacturers and dealers, editors and writers all capitalize on this wide-spread monster-bass disease—primarily because they're inflicted with it, too. I'm no exception.

It's Possible to Catch Your Dream Bass Anywhere!

The surging new interest in bass fishing during the past ten years has resulted in millions of printed words devoted to help you pinpoint the world's most promising and glamorous big-bass hotspots. Thanks primarily to the Bass Anglers Sportsman Society (B.A.S.S.), and the outdoor magazines, the finest big bass lakes and streams in Florida, California, Georgia, Texas, Louisiana, Mexico, and even Cuba and Honduras, are now household names in bass-fishing circles everywhere. But you *could* catch the biggest bass of your life anywhere—even in your own back-yard.

Chart 1 lists the weight of the official state-record largemouth caught in each bass state, plus the date and place each record fish was caught. This chart shows that bass weighing better than fourteen pounds have been taken in eleven states.

More and more monster bass are being taken from simple farm ponds. And it's a lucky youngster who can fight down a lunker like this.

CHART 1

ALL-TIME STATE LARGEMOUTH BASS RECORDS

(Courtesy Bass Anglers Sportsmans Society)

	State	*Weight*	*Year*	*Lake*
1.	Georgia	22–4	1932	Montgomery Lake
2.	California	20–15	1972	Miramar Lake
3.	Florida	19–0	1961	Lake Tarpon
4.	Arkansas	16–4	1976	Lake Mallard
5.	South Carolina	16–2	1949	Lake Marion
6.	Massachusetts	15–8	1975	Sampson Pond
7.	North Carolina	14–15	1963	Santeetlah Reservoir
8.	Tennessee	14–8	1954	Sugar Creek
9.	Alabama	14–4	1976	Mobile County Farm Pond
10.	Arizona	14–2	1956	Roosevelt Lake
	Virginia	14–2	1975	Gaston Lake
11.	Missouri	13–14	1961	Bull Shoals Lake
12.	Kentucky	13–8	1966	Greenbo Lake
	Mississippi	13–8	1974	farm pond
	Texas	13–8	1943	Medina Lake
13.	Ohio	13–2	1976	farm pond
14.	Illinois	13–1	1976	Stone Quarry Lake
15.	Connecticut	12–14	1961	Moshapaugh Lake
16.	Louisiana	12–0	1975	farm pond
17.	Michigan	11–15	1934	Bamfield Backwaters/ Big Pine Island Lake
	Oklahoma	11–15	1941	Kiamichi River
18.	Kansas	11–12	1977	farm pond
19.	Indiana	11–11	1968	Ferdinand Reservoir
20.	Maine	11–10	1968	Moose Pond
21.	Washington	11–9¼	1977	Banks Lake
22.	Wisconsin	11–3	1940	Lake Ripley
23.	New Mexico	11–0	1975	Ute Lake
	Nevada	11–0	1972	Lake Mohave
24.	Idaho	10–15	unknown	Anderson Lake
	Iowa	10–15	1970	farm pond
25.	New Jersey	10–12	1960	Mt. Kimble Lake
	New York	10–12	1975	Chadwick Lake
26.	Nebraska	10–11	1965	gravel pit
27.	Oregon	10–8	1915	Columbia Slough
28.	New Hampshire	10–6	1967	Lake Potanipo
29.	Maryland	10–4	1974	Prettyboy Reservoir
30.	Minnesota	10–2	1961	Prairie Lake
	Utah	10–2	1974	Lake Powell
31.	West Virginia	10–0	1968	Coal River
32.	Delaware	9–15½	1977	Noxen Town Pond
33.	Rhode Island	9–12	1936	Barber Pond
	Rhode Island	9–12	1963	Johnson's Pond
34.	Colorado	9–6	1970	Cherry Creek Reservoir
35.	South Dakota	8–12	1957	Fraiser Lake
	South Dakota	8–12	1974	Hayes Lake
36.	Pennsylvania	8–8	1936	Stillwater Lake
37.	Vermont	8–0	1937	Connecticut River
38.	North Dakota	7–12	1953	Welk Dam
39.	Montana	7–6	1973	Ninepipe Reservoir
40.	Wyoming	7–2	1942	Stove Lake

Twenty-eight other states have produced bass weighing ten pounds or better; and the remaining bass states have all produced largemouths topping the seven-pound mark. And these bass were taken from all types of waters, ranging from large lakes and reservoirs to small streams and ponds.

Few bass men have taken a largemouth that weighed better than six pounds; and the vast majority have never hauled in an honest ten-pounder. If you fall into these categories, don't fret because you can't afford regular trips to those faraway glamorous spots where your big-bass odds are bound to soar. A special combination of genes and the right habitat may have *already* produced your next dream bass in some lake, stream, or pond a short run from your own driveway. Your only problem may be to work hard and long enough to locate and catch that old monster. If you can't get her, be sensible and reduce your expenditures for nonessentials like food and clothing, and start saving for a trip to a "high-odds" monster hotspot like those to be discussed next.

Wall-Hanging Bass: Your Real Odds

Let's sample the world's current best big-bass waters: those widely accepted as providing any angler able to fish them with the highest possible odds for catching a monster bass. The first column in Chart 2 reflects the average number of angler days required to catch a ten-pound-or-better bass—and the second, a six-pound-or-better bass.[1]

When you study Chart 2, you'll probably be amazed at the small number of days required by the average guided angler to catch a six-pound or better bass in *all* top waters listed. Examples: less than *one day* in four Florida lakes and streams—and less than five days in each of the nine other top waters listed in Florida, Georgia, Texas, Louisiana, Mexico, Cuba, and Honduras. You'll probably be even more surprised at the small number of days required for the average guided angler to catch a ten-pound-or-better bass in Florida. Examples: *less than 4 days* for Florida's Rodman Reservoir, Oklawaha River, Lake Tohopekaliga, Lake George, and the St. Johns River. On the other hand, the chart indicates that in order to catch a ten-pounder, you would probably have to spend at least a month fishing fabulous Treasure Lake in Cuba or Yojoa in Honduras.

The evidence of how easy it *can* be to catch a monster bass, particularly in Florida, will be especially mindboggling to most bass men residing in the North, West, and Midwest. Monster Florida bass are comparatively easy to catch because of two factors. First, these waters harbor a strain of bass that grows larger than others; they probably contain more trophy-size bass per acre of water than anywhere else in the world. According to a recent report by B.A.S.S., quoting a Florida Game and Freshwater Fish Commission biologist, at least one of these lakes, Florida's Tohopekaliga, probably houses about one ten-pound-or-better bass per five acres of water. And in the Chart 2 summary, Toho ranks just *behind* Rodman Reservoir and the Oklawaha River, and *barely ahead* of Lake Kissimmee, Lake George, and the St. Johns River in terms of the small average number of angling days required to boat a wall-hanger! In other words, your odds for catching a monster bass are bound to skyrocket when you fish these waters because of their exceptionally high density of very large bass.

It is also important to note that the *impressive monster bass catch records reflected in Chart 2 are based on catches by anglers guided by skilled professional guides.* These guides know the waters they fish intimately; therefore, they can put their clients in the best lunker holes without delay, and advise them on the exact tackle and tactics most likely to produce a wall-hanger in that precise spot at the precise time of day and year they're fishing. This proves once again how ridiculous it is to spend the time and money required to travel to any distant monster bass hotspot, then to try to

---

The data in this chart, and those that follow, was summarized from catch data records maintained by Bass Champions, a unique cooperative of thirty-four professional guides specializing in trophy-bass angling in both the United States and international waters. These records are based primarily on catches by clients of Bass Champions, but also include other catches verified and recorded by the same agency. This record source was used because the author could find no other single record file as up-to-date, as complete, or as standard for all the waters analyzed. The valuable assistance of the Florida Game and Freshwater Fish Commission is also gratefully acknowledged.

◀

get your dream bass without the help of a good guide. *The importance of fishing with a good guide sinks home when one realizes that the average angler fishing Florida waters without a guide catches only one or two bass of any size per day*—a fact documented by creel counts of the Florida Game and Freshwater Fish Commission.

Yes, catching a wall-hanging bass usually isn't all that tough—if you fish in the best big-bass waters, and with a skilled professional guide. But the best guide cannot produce a wall-hanging bass for every client on every trip. The impressive catch data in Chart 2 reflects *average* catches by *average* guided clients. Unfavorable weather and numerous other factors can and do account for many "strike-outs" by clients of the best guides fishing in the best big-bass hotspots. Remember also that the proficiency of the individual client is also bound to influence the degree of success or failure achieved.

Author Dave Harbour, veteran angler and noted outdoor writer, lives in Florida but has sampled big-bass action in almost every state.

CHART 2			
ANGLER-DAYS REQUIRED TO CATCH A MONSTER BASS			
AVERAGE NUMBER OF GUIDED ANGLER DAYS REQUIRED TO CATCH A TEN-POUND-OR-BETTER BASS		AVERAGE NUMBER OF GUIDED ANGLER DAYS REQUIRED TO CATCH A SIX-POUND-OR-BETTER BASS	
Rodman Reservoir/Oklawaha River (Florida)	2.28	Rodman Reservoir/Oklawaha River (Florida)	.75
Lake Tohopekaliga (Florida)	3.15	Lake Tohopekaliga (Florida)	.77
Lake George/St. Johns River (Florida)	3.99	Lake Kissimmee (Florida)	.82
Lake Kissimmee (Florida)	6.70	Lake George/St. Johns River (Florida)	.96
Lake Okeechobee (Florida)	11.45	Lake Okeechobee (Florida)	1.03
Georgia Lakes: Seminole, Sydney Lanier, Banks, Blackshear, Hartwell, Sinclair	23.28	Georgia Lakes: Seminole, Sydney Lanier, Banks, Blackshear, Hartwell, Sinclair	1.32
Treasure Lake (Cuba)★	26.28	Lake Livingston (Texas)	1.69
Lake Yojoa (Honduras)	39.01	Treasure Lake (Cuba)★	2.37
Lake Livingston (Texas)	none recorded	Lake Martin (Mexico)★	2.56
Falcon Reservoir (Texas)	none recorded	Falcon Reservoir (Texas)	3.04
Toledo Bend Reservoir (Texas–Louisiana)	not recorded	Lake Yojoa (Honduras)	3.50
Lake Guerrero (Mexico)	none recorded	Toledo Bend Reservoir (Texas–Louisiana)	4.23
Lake Martin (Mexico)★	none recorded	Lake Guerrero (Mexico)	4.50

Note: ★indicates records for January through April 1978 only. Data not available for other months.

Where Should You Go for a Wall-Hanging Bass?

Chart 3 indicates the average weight of the largest bass caught each month from the top bass waters sampled. It also includes the weight of the largest single bass caught in each of the waters listed. This information combined with that in Chart 2 constitutes a reliable indicator for selecting "best bet" waters for your next monster bass hunt.

Florida's Rodman Reservoir, Oklawaha River, St. Johns River, Lake George, Lake Tohopekaliga, and Lake Kissimmee produced bass each month of the heaviest average weight (11.6 to 12.45 pounds). These waters were followed closely by Florida's Lake Okeechobee, Cuba's Treasure Lake, and Honduras's Lake Yojoa, all producing bass averaging better than ten pounds. All these lakes, except Okeechobee and Treasure, also gave up at least one wall-hanger, which weighed better than thirteen pounds, during this period. Okeechobee's largest bass in this period weighed eleven pounds three ounces, and Treasure's largest twelve pounds five ounces.

The remaining waters sampled, noted primarily for large numbers of bass, also produced occasional lunkers in a surprisingly high weight range. Georgia's lakes, Mexico's Guerrero and Martin, Livingston and Toledo Bend in Texas and Louisiana, all produced bass each month that averaged better than eight pounds, and at least one lunker weighing from over eight to over eleven pounds.

CHART 3		
MONSTER BASS PRODUCTION		
Average weight of largest bass caught each month by guided Anglers from January 1977 through April 1978		
	Largest Bass	**Average**
Rodman/Oklawaha (Florida)	14-14	12.45
St. Johns/Lake George (Florida)	13–9	12.16
Lake Kissimmee (Florida)	13–6	11.9
Lake Kissimmee (Florida)	13–1	11.6
Treasure Lake (Cuba)★	12–5	11.25
Lake Okeechobee (Florida)	11–3	10.16
Lake Yojoa (Honduras)	13–2	10.16
Georgia Lakes	11–10	9.41
Toledo Bend (Texas–Louisiana)	10–1	8.6
Lake Guerrero (Mexico)	9–3	8.41
Lake Martin (Mexico)★	8–10	8.25
Lake Livingston (Texas)	9–6	8.16

★ Based on largest bass recorded for January through April 1978 only. Data not available for other months.

Dave Harbour beams over a thirteen-pounder from Florida's Lake Griffin.

206

When Should You Go for a Wall-Hanging Bass?

Chart 4 summarizes the months that produced the largest bass in all top waters sampled. *Every* month produced bass weighing from ten to better than fourteen pounds in the Florida waters sampled. This indicates that the waters of central and southern Florida are never too cold—or too hot—to diminish your chances for a real wall-hanger.

All big bass, of course, weigh considerably more just before spawning than later. Therefore, it would appear that the largest fish should be taken during the spawning months and those just pre-ceeding, which in most Florida waters are January, February, and March. During much of this period, the real monsters are on or near beds and are easiest to locate and catch. However, the data in this article is based primarily on catches by Bass Champions guides—and they are *not* allowed to bed fish. Thus January, February, and March are *not* reflected as the best big bass months in Chart 4.

I applaud this "no-bed-fishing" policy, as I do their policy of encouraging each client to release all big bass except one earnestly desired for mounting. After all, it is the old heavyweight females that lay the most eggs and that pass on the genes which are most likely to perpetuate future trophy bass populations. Chart 4 also lists the specific months that produced the largest bass in all other domestic and foreign waters sampled.

CHART 4
BEST MONTHS FOR MONSTER BASS

Florida Waters:	(Especially those listed in preceeding charts.) All months produced ten to fifteen-pound bass. Largest bass caught in May, June, August, and December.
Georgia Lakes:	(Especially those listed in preceeding charts.) All months, except December, produced bass in the eight to twelve-pound range. May, June, and October produced the largest bass.
Toledo Bend:	All months produced occasional bass in the seven to ten-pound range. July, September, October, and November produced the largest bass.
Lake Livingston:	All months produced occasional bass in the seven to nine-pound range. Largest bass caught in April, July, and October.
Lake Yojoa:	All months produced occasional bass in the eight to thirteen-pound range. Largest bass caught in June, July, and November.
Lake Guerrero:	All months produced occasional bass in the seven to ten-pound range. Largest bass taken in January, March, and May.
Lake Martin:	Data available for January through April of 1978 only. All these months produced occasional bass in the eight to nine-pound range.
Treasure Lake:	Data available for January through April of 1978 only. All these months produced occasional bass in the ten to twelve-pound range.

The Best Is Getting Better

Currently, there is a determined effort by many respected groups to have Rodman Reservoir (also called Lake Oklawaha) drained in order to return the terrain it covers to its natural state and to discourage further decisions to resume construction of the controversial Cross Florida Barge Canal, of which Rodman is an integral and completed part. This position also is supported on the basis that Rodman is fast becoming overenriched, that the weed problem is becoming acute, and that fish production is diminishing.

Is Rodman's trophy-bass production actually declining? My research indicates that Rodman probably leads the world in year-around trophy-bass production and in the low number of days required for the average guided angler to catch a ten-pound-or-better bass. I compared the catch records of a four-month period in 1978 with the same four-month periods in 1976 and 1977.

The figures strongly indicate that lunker-bass fishing in Rodman was better in 1978 than in 1977 and far better than in 1976! This convinces me that although Rodman is getting older and weedier, it is also improving its trophy-bass production.

It now appears that we should delay the draining of Rodman until big-bass fishing actually declines seriously—if this ever occurs. This position is also supported by the fact that if Rodman is drained, it will take decades for the land it covers to revert to anything resembling its former natural state. It seems must prudent to spend available funds on weed control and weed-control research, which will benefit the lake for at least the next several years—then to make a decision, based on all new facts available at that time, whether or not the lake should be drained.

Other Monster Bass Hotspots

Most knowledgeable bassmen would agree that the waters just discussed are among the world's best for lunker bass. But many other waters have the potential to produce wall-hangers, too. These include almost every lake, stream, and small pond in Florida. For example, during the past ten years, I have taken over fifty bass from the Homosassa and Crystal rivers, and from lakes Harris and Griffin, near Leesburg, that weighed from ten to twelve-and-one-half pounds. And John McClanahan's Trophy Bass Guide Service has taken over four-hundred better-than-ten-pounders, including one over sixteen pounds in 1976, most of them from small Ocala National Forest lakes since 1975.

Many lakes, not previously discussed, in Georgia, Alabama, and South Carolina will probably continue to produce their share of wall-hangers, too. These include Alabama's Eufaula and Miller's Ferry; South Carolina's Santee-Cooper; Georgia's Lake Jackson; and Georgia's amazing $5-a-day lunker producer, Patrick's Paradise. Patrick's scores of lakes and ponds are now giving up around eighty bass a year exceeding the ten-pound mark, and they produced a seventeen-and-a-half-pounder in 1974. There, the minimum size limit is three pounds!

Many bassmen believe that California's San Diego County lakes (Otay, Murray, and Miramar) are almost sure to produce the next world's record largemouth. All are stocked with Florida bass, and Miramar has already given up the second largest recorded bass in history, a twenty pound fifteen-ouncer in 1973. However, drastic water fluctuations are causing problems in these lakes, and fishing regulations are very stringent. Striking out there *could* be easy, too!

A new Texas lake stocked with Florida bass in 1974 may also become a monster-producer soon. Texas Parks and Wildlife biologists believe that Calaveras Lake near San Antonio now has a far better chance than Toledo Bend, Falcon, or Livingston to produce a largemouth that will break the thirty-five-year-old state record of thirteen pounds eight ounces. This optimism is based on facts hard to argue with: this nine-year-old lake appears to be approaching its peak bass production with an optimum balance of nutrients, cover, and forage fish; being a power-plant-discharge lake, it remains comparatively warm the year around, a situation ideal for both forage fish and the fast growth of Florida bass; and finally, last February Calaveras gave up a whopping

Wading Florida's Lake Griffin, Dave Harbour enjoys the acrobatics of a bragging-size bigmouth.

eleven-and-a-half-pound Florida bass that couldn't have been more than *four years old.* However, if you hit Calaveras this spring, be aware that the northwest arm is closed to benefit spawning bass.

Yes, any of these waters, could give you the biggest bass of your life. But if you want the highest odds for accomplishing this goal, don't fail to make arrangements to fish with a reputable big-bass guide service—and to take their advice on where and when to fish. Addresses of several top guide services serving the waters discussed in this article are listed below. (Prices subject to change.)

Bass Champions, Route 3 Box 3200, Ft. McCoy, Florida 32637. 904/685-3177. Bill Martin, President. Dave Sturdivant is president of the Florida office. Principal guides assisting in research for this chapter: Holley Britt, Bob McRae, Hank Parr. Main headquarters located at Salt Springs Village near Rodman Reservoir, the Oklawaha River, Lake George, the St. Johns River and hundreds of lakes and ponds in the Ocala National Forest. New, fully equipped cottages from $25 per day. Guide fee for one or two anglers from $85 per day; "Tag-along" fee for additional boats is $25 per day. Excellent campground and restaurant in Salt

Springs. Family guide service to Silver Springs, Disney World, and other Florida attractions. Subsidiary offices in other states and the International Office (address same as above) also furnish fishing and hunting guide services, travel arrangements, and accommodations in all other domestic and international areas previously discussed. Complete package prices quoted on request. Bass Champions aircraft will meet guest groups at any city, fly them to the desired destination where all services are arranged in advance, then return them to the city of origin with no loss in travel time. An authorized group representative can sign one delivery ticket for all services rendered and a single itemized statement will be provided for the entire trip.

The Bait Shack, 1408 East Main Street, Leesburg, Florida 32748. 904/787-2314. Provides guides for lakes Harris, Griffin, Dora, and Apopka at $85 per day. Will make motel reservations on request.

Cuba Tours USA, Inc., P. O. Box 60394, Houston, Texas 77205. 713/443-6575. Eight-Day package trips from Tampa, Florida, to Cuba's Treasure Lake from $695—and from Houston to Mexico's Lake Guerrero from $595. (Treasure Lake trips contingent upon continuation of travel agreement between Cuba and the United States.)

Walker's Bass Tours, 3306 East Jefferson, Grand Prairie, Texas 75051. 214/264-2277. "Leave Wednesday—back Sunday" trips to Lake Yojoa, Honduras. From $595. Treasure Lake trips also available.

S & W Fishing and Hunting, Inc., Box 999, Forney, Texas 75126. Five-day charter flight packages from Dallas ($595) or Houston ($585) to Lake Guerrero include all required services. Similar charter flight trips to Lake Martin or Lake Palmito from about $650.

Victoria Bass, Inc., 315 Bastrop, Houston, Texas 77003. 713/222-2534. Five-day deluxe air-charter trip to Lake Guerrero from Houston from $565. Trip includes three full days of fishing or hunting, four nights of air-conditioned lodging, all meals, boats, guides, fishing licenses, and fish and birds packed and frozen for return flight. Weekend bass trips from $400.

Patrick's Fishing Paradise, Tifton, Georgia 31794. 912/382-1881. Fishing $5 per day. Camping $1 per person per day. Motels and restaurants available in Tifton from $10 to $25 per day.

Best Baits and Lures for Wall-Hanging Bass

The vast majority of monster bass caught from the Florida waters sampled were taken on native shiners from eight to fourteen inches long and weighing from a quarter pound to over a pound. Bass Champions has pioneered a new system for fishing these big live baits, which constitute the principal diet of Florida lunkers. This system is designed primarily to minimize the risk of wounding bass, and it does indeed accomplish this purpose.

The trick involves the use of a light 2/0 to 6/0 hook behind a leader and heavy line. The shiner is hooked in the back, *well toward the tail*. Since the bass swallows the giant shiner head first, the hook is rarely far down in the lunker's gullet. Thus, when the hook is set, it usually grabs the bass in the lip.

No weight or float is used. The shiner is merely let down into the water and given slack line until it decides to head for the kind of protective cover it is used to: usually a deep, dark cave under a ceiling of floating weeds or moss. Such lairs are also where most real Florida monster bass lurk. The shiner is allowed to swim freely and often for very long distances in those dark lairs where no artificial offering could be presented.

A monster bass charge is a hair-raising experience! Both shiner and bass in hot pursuit may burst through the floating cover and into the sky—often several times before the bass is able to grab his prey. Because of the long line out, the hook must be set with all the might you can muster. Your tight-set drag begins to scream, and whole lily pads or masses of weeds are blasted high into the air. It's then that you understand why your guide suggested using that twenty-five or thirty-pound-test line!

This brand of Florida shiner fishing is not a dull sport, or one likely to wound more bass than artificials. However, if you prefer angling with artificials, any guide, including those of Bass Champions, will oblige. The following list tells which

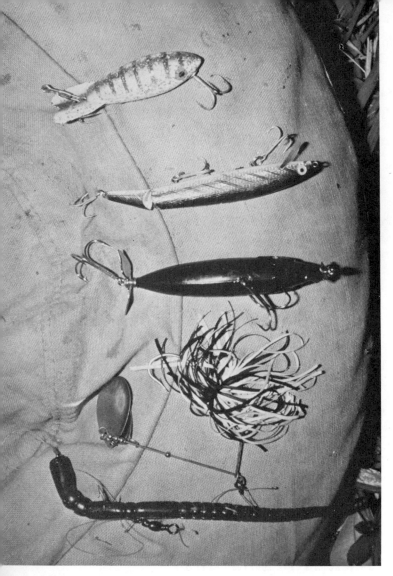

Dave Harbour's favorite baits for wall-hanging bass include worms, spinners, top-water plugs, and deep running plugs.

artificials most guide services recommend for big bass in the domestic and international waters just discussed.

This list of lures should be used as a guide only. Seasonal conditions and specific waters to be fished will determine the most effective lures for any single trip—and flight weight restrictions usually prevent bringing along a heavy tackle box. Most guide services can furnish all required tackle, including lures, at the destination. So, unless you intend to fish "on your own," discuss specific tackle requirements with a big-bass guide service before you pack.

1. *Spinnerbaits* (white or yellow skirts plus pork chunk or frog)
   Mr. Twister Lunker Buzz
   Mepps Musky Killer and Comet Mino
   Hildebrandt's Snagless Sally
   Bass Buster's Spider and Scorpion
   Bomber Bushwhacker
   Scamp's Bank Robber
   Strike King
   Vibra Queen
   Little George
   largest Gay Blade

2. *Plastic worms and lizards* (in black, purple, dark grape and brown)
   seventeen-inch Delong Snake fished on 6/0 lead-shank weed-guard hook
   twelve-inch worms fished Texas-style:
   Jake's Producer
   Mr. Twister
   Rebel Ring Worms
   Mann's Jelly Worm
   Sweet Willie Worms
   Bagley's Hardhead Worms
   Burke's Hookworm
   Creme's Scoundrel
   lizards: Mr. Twister's Lizard and Fliptail Lizard

3. *Crankbaits* (in silver, gold, or natural finish)
   Rapala Magnum and Fat Rap
   seven-inch Rebel and Big Rainbow Rebel
   Bagley's Killer B or Bang-O-Lure
   all Bomber models in large sizes
   Mann's Razorback Pig
   Norman's Big N
   Hotspot in large sizes
   Frantic Shad in large sizes
   Roger's Big R
   Cordell's Big O and Deep Big O
   Blakemore's Trouble Shooter
   Lindy Shade Lure

4. *Topwaters* (in frog, black, or natural finish)
   Big Hellraiser
   Big Florida Shiner
   Heddon Zara Spook
   Barracuda Dalton Special
   Big Diamond Rattler
   Musky Jitterbug (tops for night fishing)

5. *Spoons* (in silver or gold with pork rind or rubber worm)
   Johnson Silver Minnow
   Mepps Reflecto
   Hawaiian Wiggler

PART THREE

BOATS AND POWER

Every time I ease my more-than-ample backside into the plush seat of a modern bass boat, a twinge of memory makes me appreciate how far technology has advanced into fishing. The roominess and comfort, compared to the johnboats that I grew up with on Georgia's Ogeechee River, are but one aspect of that change. A glance that takes in the glistening array of dials, gauges and switches brings an almost overwhelming feeling of guilt. My angling roots contained none of these things: depth recorder, aerated livewell, electric motor, electronic thermometer, oxygen monitor, temperature probe, CB radio, power tilt, power trim, compass, speedometer, tachometer, electric bilge pump, and—why not?—beer holders. Are we going fishing or to the moon?

I must confess that my enjoyment of my bass-fishing toys quickly exiles my guilt to the fog of memory. I like tinkering with my bass-boat goodies, and I use them in a sensible way—not to put any kind of hurt on Mr. Bass but to gain extra dimensions in my understanding of the day and its occurences. The bass populations have not suffered.

I do playfully admonish some of my friends for making excessive use of the powerful engines available today. Antsy isn't the word for some of these guys. After five casts at a given spot, it's:

"They're not here! Let's race on!" And they're off, with a 35-knot roar and wake to check out another supposed "honey hole."

Actually, I am not completely addicted to bass-boat fishing. I still enjoy float fishing from a johnboat, plus using an assortment of crafts for pond fishing. Every year I make one long canoe trip for bass in some wilderness area.

But for a really full day on the big water, give me a modern rig and all its trinkets.

One thing we have to worry about, though, even when we can afford the finest rig, is keeping it powered up. All those little baubles we've added on board won't run on air, I can tell you, having personally invested enough in batteries and power systems to pay the national debt.

And when you're stuck dockside at dawn, or way up the lake at sunset, when there's no juice or gremlins have gotten into the machinery, you'll recall that sometimes, more is less.

21

Bass Boats
The Ultimate Fishing Platforms

TOM GRESHAM

It's not necessary to have a bass boat in order to catch bass. Bass are caught by fishermen in canoes, johnboats, innertubes, rubber rafts, while wading, and while standing on the bank. Some situations, like very shallow water, thick timber, small ponds, are fished better without the aid of a bass boat. But a great many fishermen have found that they can spend more time on the water and that they catch more bass when fishing from one of the superefficient fishing platforms that we call bass boats.

All the advantages of a bass boat fall into three categories. The many labor-saving features free the fisherman from chores like paddling, bailing, and lowering and raising anchors, allowing him to keep his lure in the water more hours each day. Some features and accessories are designed to help the angler fish more effectively. The basic design and many of the features of bass boats also enable us to fish large bodies of water and recklessly scramble around the boat in greatly increased safety.

Many things that evolved into being, rather than being invented outright, have an unclear history, and that is somewhat the case of the bass boat. Its immediate ancestor appears to be a narrow, flat-bottomed, wooden craft made in Shreveport, Louisiana. The Skeeter Boat was great for getting through flooded timber on the many new reservoirs being built twenty years ago. It achieved a degree of stability by having a top deck/gunwale that protruded into the cargo area in kayak fashion. This kept fishermen and cargo away from the splashes and spray at the sides of the boat.

In the early 1960s, as even larger reservoirs were built in the South and much of the standing timber, rotted and fell, anglers were confronted with large stretches of open water that had to be crossed. The need for a more stable, larger, swifter fishing boat was obvious, and the fiberglass bass boat was the answer.

The first models, and in fact some models today, had flat bottoms. Most were twelve or fourteen feet long, and almost all used stick steering.

The most sophisticated bass boats of today are as far ahead of the early bass boats as those pioneers were ahead of the wooden boats they succeeded.

How to Choose the Boat You Need

The fisherman in the market for a bass boat today is confronted with a bewildering array of hull designs, floor plans, features, and accessories. He may be quite satisfied with a simple rig

The comfort and great range of the modern bass boat enables anglers to fish longer, cover more water. Evinrude

with the barest of accessories, or he may legitimately need the largest boat-and-motor combination topped with an instrument/accessory package that looks like a jet cockpit. The enjoyment a fisherman gets from his new bass boat will depend largely on how well he matches his floater to his type of fishing.

There are three basic hull configurations to choose from. The flat-bottom fiberglass hull does a good job in most situations but it has a few disadvantages. In rough water it pounds its passengers and rides very "wet." It also isn't as fast or fuel-efficient as the modified V hull. The modified V, an outgrowth of racing-boat designs, is faster, drier, smoother, and gets better gasoline mileage than the older flat-bottom boats. The third design is really a fancy aluminum johnboat that provides many of the advantages of a bass boat at a lower cost than the high-powered fiberglass rigs.

Select your boat with your type of fishing in mind. If you stick to small waters or fish thick timber a lot, a smaller, fourteen-foot or shorter flat-bottom fiberglass or aluminum boat may be best for you. On the other hand, if you plan a steady diet of large reservoirs where you will do a lot of motoring and may get caught in rough weather, the modified V hull in a larger boat, sixteen feet or longer, is probably what you need.

Keep in mind that a larger boat is more expensive, not only in initial cost, but in the cost of a larger outboard, more powerful electric motor, larger trailer, and larger engine and reduced gasoline mileage in your towing vehicle. This is probably the biggest reason for the popularity of the aluminum bass boat.

One other consideration you may have when choosing a bass boat is the possibility of using it for family outings and skiing. Some models come in a "fish and ski" configuration, but they give up something in both areas. A pure bass boat is suited only for fishing.

Once you have decided on the length and hull design you want, you can begin evaluating the

Though lacking the comforts and frills of today's bass boats, the common johnboat is still the favorite of many bassers, particularly for river fishing. Erwin Bauer

features different models offer. One of the big differences is in the method of steering.

Stick steering allows the driver to sit in the front of the boat and steer by moving a lever forward and backward with one hand and operating the throttle with the other hand. This convenient setup gives the driver good visibility over the bow and makes it unnecessary for him to move to the forward fishing position after every run down the lake. However, stick steering should be limited to boats equipped with 35 hp motors or smaller. The torque developed by larger outboards is capable of jerking the stick out of the operator's hand during a tight turn. Larger motors call for a console with a steering wheel.

Console steering puts the driver in the middle or the back of the boat where he won't be thrown out the front should he hit something. It also gives him something substantial to hold on to in rough weather and a wheel has a better mechanical advantage than the stick, making it easier to overcome torque. Larger bass boats are also frequently equipped with a number of instruments and accessories than can be mounted on the console.

Rowboats have not left the bassing scene, despite the bass-boat invasion. They still are perfect on ponds and smaller waters. Erwin Bauer

Sorting Out the Options

There are a number of options available when choosing the layout of a bass boat, and they can distinctly change the character of your fishing craft. A majority of the boats now built have the "pro" configuration of raised casting decks fore and aft. Padded swivel seats on the decks are usually removable so that passengers don't have to use them in a raised position when running the large motor. Riding on raised pedestal seats is not only very dangerous, but it is illegal in many states. Moving the forward seat to the floor of the boat also gives the driver better visibility. Although some seats are available with arm rests, fishermen usually find that accessory hinders casting.

Built-in storage compartments should be designed to keep out water. The compartment should have a lip about one inch high that the lid

The flat-bottom Skeeter Boat was the forerunner of the modern bass boat. The pointed bow and narrow beam suited it for moving through timber. This boat is equipped with stick steering.

rests on. This will keep water from running into the compartment and possibly ruining expensive electronic gear and fishing tackle.

Rod holders mounted inside the dry-storage compartments can take up a lot of room, but they do keep your rods organized. A number of fishermen put rod racks on the outside of the compartments so they can have several rods handy while fishing. Others keep rods handy by placing them on top of the compartment without the benefit of racks.

A lot of bass boats now have built-in live wells with aeration systems for keeping bass alive. Some national bass tournaments require that boats used in competition be equipped with a live well to keep the bass alive. An alternative to a built-in unit is to use a forty-eight-quart or larger plastic ice chest with a separate aerator available at tackle stores. That saves room when you don't want to use a live well.

One item that should definitely be included on all bass boats is carpet of some kind. This provides sure footing for occupants and deadens sounds that might spook bass.

One small, inexpensive item cannot be considered an optional feature or an accessory; the kill switch is as important as the motor you hang on the rear. Attached to the driver by a short lanyard, the kill switch cuts off the motor should the operator leave his seat, as in the case of being thrown overboard. There is no room for debate on this item. Buy a kill switch. Have it installed correctly. Hook it up every time you run the motor. Period.

Sterndrive or Outboard?

After you've chosen the hull design, length, and layout, you're not quite half way finished with decisions and expenses. In a bass boat the power plant and the accessories make the boat.

The decision of whether to go with outboard or sterndrive power has traditionally been decided in favor of outboards by most bass fishermen. However, improvements made in sterndrives in recent years has made the decision more difficult. Arguments in favor of outboards are: they weigh less, are faster than the same horsepower sterndrives, and don't take up room inside the boat. The sterndrive presents a lower center of gravity, which can help stabilize the boat in rough water, it gets better gasoline mileage, it doesn't require oil and gasoline to be mixed, and sterndrives are available with more horsepower than outboards (a dubious advantage). Sterndrives are a bit heavier than outboards, although the difference in the amount of water a sterndrive boat draws is small. Sterndrives do take up a bit of room inside the craft, but with a rear fishing chair mounted atop the motor housing, that space isn't wasted.

It's really a tossup. Look around and find out what other fishermen in your area use. Ask them why they chose what they did and if they are satisfied with it. In fact, that's a good idea for checking out a lot of the options you are looking at. Utilize the experience of those who already own a bass boat.

Any outboard larger than 50 hp needs to be equipped with a power tilt—a motor that lifts the lower unit clear of the water. This can save the driver a strained back. High-performance boats, those with a modified V hull, should have a power tilt and trim unit that will also vary the angle of the lower unit while the boat is under way. Careful use of this control will get maximum speed and fuel efficiency from a motor. The power tilt is also useful for slow running in shallow or log-infested water.

Underwater Eyes

Following immediately on the heels of the motor, and some fishermen would give it equal importance, is the depth-finder. No single piece of equipment, including the bass boat itself, is more useful than the instrument that functions as the fisherman's eyes to let him "see" the bottom and everything suspended between it and the boat. The depth-finder is a small sonar unit that bounces sound waves off the bottom of a lake and indicates the depth. Knowing the depth of the water and being able to locate depth changes and other types of cover, many fishermen now concentrate on "structure" fishing. This has freed them from the dependency on shorelines and paved the way to catching suspended bass—a major revolution in bass fishing.

Depth-finders are divided into two categories: flashers and recorders. The first units available were flashers and they remain the most popular and least expensive. A tiny light bulb rotates rapidly around a circular dial, flashing at a point that indicates the depth of the bottom and any obstructions between the boat and the bottom. The flashes are so rapid that they appear as a solid light opposite the foot markings on the scale. The recorder prints a chart that can be studied at leisure and is easier for a novice to interpret correctly. With a bit of practice, however, the flasher is easily understood.

Both units use a transducer mounted either outside the boat on the transom or in the bilge area, sending sound waves through the fiberglass. If mounted inside the boat, it must be located so that it reads through only a single layer of fiberglass. It won't work through the foam flotation found in all of the floor but the bilge area. Depth-finders also can't read through wood or metal.

A flasher unit has the disadvantage of requiring the fisherman to look at it at all times, or he will miss something important. The chart is a record of the bottom, freeing the angler to look elsewhere until he wants to check the bottom. The common practice of leaving a flasher running the entire day is impractical with a recorder, however, because the chart paper would fill the boat, and chart paper is expensive. The compromise many fishermen have reached is to have both a flasher and a recorder, or a combination flasher/recorder unit and use the recorder only when they want to check something of particular interest.

It is fairly common for bass boats to be outfitted with one depth-finder on the steering console and one on the forward casting deck. With this arrangement, the transducer for the forward unit can be mounted on the shaft of the bow-mounted electric motor and will read directly under the fisherman. This can be helpful when trying to hold the boat over a small piece of structure. Boats with only one depth-finder should have a swivel mount so the console-mounted unit can be read from the bow while fishing.

Sitting on the padded pedestal seat, today's bass fisherman can silently glide down a shoreline, casting constantly, without ever touching a paddle. The bow-mounted electric motor pulls even the heaviest of bass boats in any direction the angler wants to go. Personal preference dictates the choice between a foot-controlled or a hand-controlled model.

More Electronic Goodies: Do You Need Them?

Electronic instruments give the bass angler knowledge of where bass should be and where bass can't be, thus narrowing considerably the water he needs to concentrate his fishing efforts on.

The electronic thermometer, either in a console-mounted surface-measuring design or a hand-held model with a probe that can be lowered to a specific depth, tells the fisherman what parts of a lake are best suited for bass at a given

Proper use of power trim lifts the bow of this modified V-hull bass boat out of the water, increasing speed and fuel efficiency.

Sonar depthfinders are the most important fishing tool, besides tackle, a fisherman can have. At least that's what a lot of fishermen think. Many bass anglers use both a flasher like the unit on the left and a recorder (on the right) to locate structure and even to see fish.

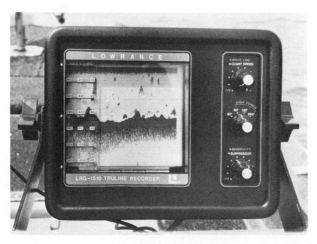

This recording depthfinder prints a permanent chart of the bottom and anything suspended above it.

time of the year. In early spring the fisherman may be looking for warmer areas where bass are moving into the shallows to spawn and his thermometer will indicate coves that are warmer than the rest of the lake.

The instrument that tells where bass can't be is the oxygen meter. By measuring the dissolved oxygen in the water and comparing the reading with the levels that bass need to survive, the fisherman can avoid fishing areas with oxygen content too low for survival or so low that bass there would be sluggish. A lot of tournament fishermen rely on the oxygen meter to eliminate much "dead" water.

The jury is still out on the value of the Ph meter. This meter measures the acidity of the water. A relatively new development, the Ph meter is not being used by the number of fishermen that the thermometer and oxygen meter are.

Instruments necessary or helpful to the safe and efficient running of a bass boat include tachometer, speedometer, compass, bilge pump, running lights, and a CB radio.

The transducer is the sensing device of a depthfinder that sends sound waves out and receives echoes from objects the sound waves hit.

The tachometer and speedometer provide information necessary to determine if the engine is running correctly and if it is equipped with the correct prop. A compass is a godsend when running at night or in a fog. Of course, running lights are necessary for running at night and should be included on all boats. Even if you don't intend to fish at night, you may get into a school of bass right at dusk and end up running back to the landing in the dark.

An electric bilge pump is necessary since the built-in gas tank and batteries in the stern of a bass boat prevent manual bailing.

While some bass fishermen like to talk on the CB radio to their buddies on the lake, swapping information, many others install a CB for safety alone. If your motor conks out ten miles downwind from the marina, that radio can summon help in a hurry. Maximum range over water is about fifteen miles, sometimes a lot less.

Electric anchors take care of a big chore, especially when anchored over a worm hole in thirty feet of water.

One important necessity, frequently bought as an afterthought, is the trailer. Spend a couple of hundred collars more to get a really good one. You'll be glad you did. A cheap trailer that doesn't support your boat correctly can ruin the hull. Then what happens to the money you saved on the cheap trailer?

Your trailer should have automobile-size wheels—thirteen, fourteen, or fifteen-inch—and you should carry a spare. Your car's bumper jack won't work on a trailer, so get a trailer jack. Guide bars on the side of the trailer with tail-lights mounted on top are worth the extra money also.

The one decision that may well be more important than any other you make concerning your bass boat is the dealer you buy it from. A good one will skillfully guide you, making sure you get what you need, but no more. He will rig the accessories correctly (very important) and will stand behind his work. He'll also be there when you have a problem with your new rig, and you *will* have a problem or two. An outfitted bass boat is a complicated machine that is bound to have a bug or two in it, but a good dealer will quickly correct the problem and have you back on the water in no time.

Shop for a dealer by asking fishermen in your area which one they use and how they like his service. Be prepared to pay a little more for your boat to get the service that is so important.

Choose your boat and accessories carefully, and take care of them and you will get years of pleasure from your bass boat.

Electric anchor reels are yet another labor-saving accessory many bass fishermen find helpful.

An electronic thermometer mounted on the console tells the fisherman the surface temperature of the water.

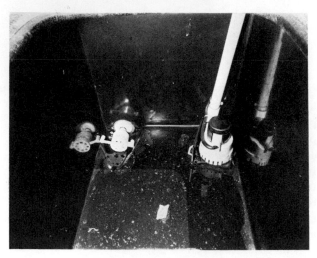

A live well is nothing more than a fiberglass box with a drain and an aeration system.

This instrument panel on the steering console contains a fuel gauge, cigarette lighter/map light, and switches controlling navigation lights, aerator for the live well, bilge pump, and an additional accessory.

With the power trim control on the throttle/shift lever, the driver can change the angle of the motor without losing control of the boat. The small cord in the lower right part of the photo is connected to the kill switch which cuts the motor off should the driver be thrown out of his seat.

The Ph meter measures the acidity of the water. Although not used as much as thermometers and oxygen meters, it is gaining some advocates.

A tachometer, engine temperature gauge, and speedometer keep the boat operator informed on how his motor is running. The tach and speedometer are also necessary for matching the right prop to boat.

Padded pedestal seats and electric trolling motors allow fishermen to fish more comfortably, thus they can spend more time on the water.

This panel on the forward casting deck contains the switch that allows the batteries for the electric motor to be charged without being removed from the boat. It also has a motor tilt switch, allowing the fisherman to raise the motor without having to return to the console.

The oxygen meter is a hand-held unit with a probe that is lowered into the water. It measures the amount of dissolved oxygen in the water in parts per million. Angler is Grits Gresham, the author's dad.

Don't try to save money by buying a cheap trailer that could end up ruining the hull of your bass boat. The extra money spent on a good trailer is worth it in worry-free operation.

The bowmounted trolling motor pulls the boat in any direction the fisherman wants to go.

A depthfinder mounted on the forward deck with its transducer on the electric motor helps this fisherman keep his boat positioned over a dropoff he wants to fish.

Bass Boats Options

EQUIPMENT	IMPORTANCE	DISADVANTAGE
Console Steering	A safety requisite for large outboards and I/Os. Less tiring, especially on long runs. Good spot for instruments and electronics.	Utilizes more room in the boat. Slower response.
Stick Steering	Requires less room in the boat. Very quick response. Permits bow seat operation, which gives better visibility and places operator in best position to fish.	More dangerous. Suitable only for smaller outboards—up to 40 hp. More tiring on long runs.
Raised Casting Platform	Standard on all "pro" model boats. Places angler in better position to see and fish. Gives more leverage for setting hook, important when fishing deep with plastic worms.	Angler more visible to bass, a minus when fish are shallow or when fishing shallow water. Raises center of gravity.
Swivel Seats with Backs	More comfortable, permit extended fishing with greater efficiency. Padded seats especially comfortable. Adjustable pedestals allow seat to be lowered while running; raised for fishing.	Not as safe. Raises center of gravity when on high pedestal. May swing violently during sudden maneuvers. Greater windage.
Armrests for Swivel Seats	Greater safety. Gives angler something to grab. Eases strain on arms.	They bother some anglers by getting in the way.
Alternate Seat Positions	Highly recommended in pro-style boats with raised bow and stern casting platforms. Permits bow seat to be moved to lower, rearward position for running. Gives a safer, more comfortable running position for the passenger and gives better forward visibility for the operator.	None except modest additional cost.
Storage Compartments	Permits permanent or semipermanent storage in the boat for fishing gear under lock. Usually standard.	Takes up room in the boat.
Rod Holders	Keep spare rod and reel rigs neatly in place.	Take up room on top of storage compartment or on the side of the boat.
Carpet	Quiet, comfortable, nonskid, colorful.	Can be more difficult to keep clean.
Live Well	Keeps fish alive for culling or releasing as desired. (Well must be aerated to be effective.) Required on boats at major bass tournaments.	Takes up room in boat. Can be difficult to keep clean. Make sure it can be completely drained and flushed with fresh water after using.
Built-in Gasoline Tanks	Larger fuel supply. Neater installation. More difficult to mix oil and gasoline.	Must take entire boat to service station for refill.
Outboard Power	Greater horsepower choice. Easier installation. Less susceptible to damage. Requires less room in boat. Easier service. Better performance.	Greater fuel consumption.

EQUIPMENT	IMPORTANCE	DISADVANTAGE
Inboard-Outboard Power	Offers greater fuel economy. Mixing oil and gasoline not necessary. Quieter than outboards.	Requires more room inside boat. Poorer performance. More prone to explosion. Are 400 to 500 pounds heavier.
Tachometer	Very valuable in determining performance of engine.	None.
Speedometer	Another aid to determining operating efficiency. Useful to operator in selecting speeds appropriate to conditions.	None.
Compass	Essential for operating on large lakes, especially at night or in fog. Useful in relocating good fishing spots by taking shore bearings.	None.
Searchlight	Helpful for operating at night. Excellent in emergency.	Permanent mount units can get in the way while fishing if location isn't selected with care.
Running Lights	Required by law for night operation. Standard on most bass boats. All boats should have them.	None.
Bilge Pump—Electric	Essential for ridding boat of water quickly. Automatic bilge pump operates automatically when water in boat reaches a certain depth, a great advantage if boat takes on water (from rain or leak) while unattended.	None if properly maintained. Debris can clog intake and can render automatic feature inoperative.
Bilge Pump—Manual	Desirable on larger boats as backup in event electric pump fails.	Requires full time of one man to operate.
Remote Anchors	No bass boat is complete without bow and stern anchors. Remote electric anchor winches permit angler to lower them much more quickly and quietly than can be done with just an anchor attached to a rope.	Require permanent mounting on bow and stern. Extra wiring. Should have safety lock for running.
Spring-Loaded Mooring Reel	Convenient for quickly mooring boat with spare line coiled out of sight on reel beneath gunnel.	None, except for occupying space beneath gunnel or deck.
Electric Motor	Transforms a bass boat into a fishing machine. Angler can maneuver boat without effort and without touching a paddle. Most important bass boat accessory. Permits fishing in wind which would make angling impossible for the paddle-wielder. Bow mount most popular and is most efficient position, pulling boat rather than pushing it. Some guides prefer stern mount to put their bow-positioned client in the best fishing spot first. Foot-controlled bow mounts most popular, giving total control along with freedom of both hands for fishing.	Must carry one or two 12-volt batteries and recharge them frequently. Larger, heavier bass boats need power of a 24-volt electric motor.

EQUIPMENT	IMPORTANCE	DISADVANTAGE
Sonar Depth-Finder	The eyes of a bass fisherman, telling him more about his lake in days than he could learn in years without one. Quality units will indicate fish below, but prime value is to tell depths and bottom structure. Locates habitat which bass prefer.	None. Deserves protection any sophisticated electronic unit should have. Proper installation and mounting of transducer is easy, but is critical to proper operation.
Recording Depth-Finder	Gives permanent graph record of bottom (and fish). Two "runs" across each honey hole, at right angles to each other, give fisherman a permanent file record of that hot spot for future reference. Frequently locates possible hot spots (drop-offs, creek beds, submerged islands, brushtops) when moving rapidly from one part of lake to another, hot spots which would be missed by the boat operator who must watch where he's going rather than watch the flashing light continuously. Best when used in addition to, rather than instead of, the typical fish "flasher."	Rolls of tape must be replaced at intervals (about every 12 hours of operation). Since unit isn't operated continuously this figures out to one or two chart rolls per year for the average angler.
Combination Flasher-Recorder Depth-Finders	Gives both capabilities in one unit.	Bigger size. If one unit needs repair, both are out of operation. Recorders on these units are not the "straight line" type, which are the most accurate.
Oxygen Monitor	Reveals areas of high oxygen content which attract fish. Eliminates water with insufficient oxygen to support fish life.	None.
Electronic Thermometer	Reveals water temperatures at all depths. Angler can then fish in zone bass prefer, coordinating it with other requirements of the species.	None.
Combination Oxygen Monitor Temperature Probe	Gives both capabilities in one instrument.	More complicated. If one half is out of order, then both are out of operation when sent away for repair.
Kill Switch	Immediately stops outboard if operator is thrown from his seat. Prevents boat from continuing to run in circles if operator is thrown overboard.	Operator must remember to attach lanyard to his belt.
CB Radio	Adds to pleasure and efficiency in communicating from boat to boat. Valuable in emergency to get help in case of a breakdown in remote area of the lake.	None, except that range is usually limited to 3–15 miles.
Power Tilt	Permits outboard to be tilted from operator's position with a flick of a switch. Raises lower unit above underwater obstructions, and permits slow speed, shallow-water operation.	None.
Power Trim	Performs all functions of power tilt, but also permits angle adjustment of lower unit at all speeds. Essential for getting maximum performance from larger rigs.	None.

22

Power to the Bassing People

BOB STEARNS

If you are like most anglers, you're not getting enough fishing hours out of your electric motor. After an early-morning start, the electric begins to lose power by the middle of the afternoon, and usually within an hour or so it lacks the punch to position the boat properly under even ideal conditions.

Don't blame the electric, however. It's probably not using too much juice—as you might think—so that your battery runs down too quickly. And it's likely that you do not need a bigger or stronger battery. Instead, it's almost certain that you're using the wrong battery, and perhaps the wrong battery charger, too.

If you browse through battery catalogs you'll find a bewildering array of battery types, styles, and sizes. It is easy to select the wrong battery for the job.

The lead/acid storage battery is the type usually used to start automobiles, outboard and inboard engines, push golf carts and loading vehicles, and even provide power for your electric trolling motor. Other batteries you'll find sometimes are "automotive," "marine," "maintenance free," and "deep cycle."

It's the *deep-cycle* battery you really need for your electric motor. Though many dealers will tell you that any marine battery—or any automotive

battery—will perform satisfactorily with your trolling electric, it's not true.

All automotive and marine batteries belong to a group called "SLI," for (starting, lighting, ignition). The only real difference between automotive and most marine batteries is that the case used for marine batteries is ruggedly constructed to take on-the-water punishment. The internal plates of marine batteries are stiffer for that same reason, and the terminals are usually designed for eye-clamp hookup.

The SLI battery is a sprinter. It's designed to deliver a huge amount of current in short bursts. From 300 to 600 amps are required to crank most automobile, inboard, or stern-drive marine engines of six cylinders or more. The rule of thumb is you need a minimum of "one cranking amp" per cubic inch of engine displacement at normal temperatures, and double that in extreme cold. Thus, a 300 c.i.d. V-8 would require 300 amps on a warm day, and possibly 500 to 600 on a very cold morning.

Except for that brief burst of energy, the SLI battery loafs. It is quickly recharged by the generator/alternator, which also provides enough current to keep air-conditioning, headlights, radio, and ignition systems going without any battery drain. The SLI battery is designed to "live" in a state of full charge at all times.

A SLI battery is made up of many "plates" or layers. The more plates used to build the battery, the greater the burst of electrical current it is capable of delivering for short periods. A SLI battery has poor endurance, and can't take a long-term steady drain at 5 to 50 amp levels. If it is heavily discharged by constant or frequent intermittent use, such as the typical 10 to 20 amps per hour required by most electric outboards, the battery suffers irreversible internal damage.

Any battery is considered deeply discharged when its voltage drops below 10, and for all practical purposes dead when the 9 volt mark is passed. Each time that battery is depleted to a state of near total discharge, it is referred to as having been "deep-cycled." If you deep-cycle any SLI battery—either automotive or marine—a dozen or more times, its capacity is severely diminished.

If you start out with a SLI battery rated at 100 amp/hours (the twenty-hour rate is most commonly used), after twelve or fifteen days of heavy use on the water with your electric outboard, its capacity will drop to 50 or 60 amp/hours (or less). And this is regardless of how much and how long you recharge that battery, and the type of charger you use. To make matters worse, using the wrong type of charger can damage that battery (or any battery) even more.

Even new 100 amp/hour SLI batteries won't deliver as many hours of use with an electric outboard as a deep-cycle battery designed for that type of application. An electric drawing 20 amps with a 100 amp/hour SLI battery is good for three to three and one-half hours of hard use. The same capacity deep-cycle battery is good for four to five hours.

This difference is caused by plate design. The number of plates in a true deep-cycle battery are fewer, and of heavier construction. In a SLI battery the chemical ingredients must react together as quickly as possible. SLI plate construction utilizes a special channel-type separator to keep the plates apart and still allow rapid liquid circulation. The internal components of this battery are built for speed, and therefore large power surges.

Frequent long-discharge cycles, followed by long slow-recharging cycles, quickly wear out the open high-speed plates in a SLI battery. These discharge/recharge cycles wash the active material off the plates, and it falls to the bottom of the container. The process is called shedding, and the more active material shed by the SLI's plates, the lower its capactiy.

Deep-cycle battery plates are designed so that discharge/recharge cycles cannot remove any of the active plate material. They can be deeply cycled two hundred to three hundred times without significant loss of capacity, provided they are properly maintained. In fact, most D/C batteries seem to develop *increased* capacity for the first twenty or thirty discharge/recharge cycles—they actually improve with use—while SLI batteries are usually shot after twenty-five deep cycles.

Deep-cycle batteries have been around for many years, but only during the last few years have they been available in sizes that would fit the standard long marine battery box, and with voltages suitable for electric outboard use. Golf carts, for example, use D/C batteries, but they are 6-volt models that usually weigh seventy to one hundred pounds each. Imagine carrying four hundred pounds of batteries in your average bass boat just so you can have enough capacity to run that 24-volt electric all day!

Modern bass boats need plenty of battery power and recharging capacity to keep their accessories working.

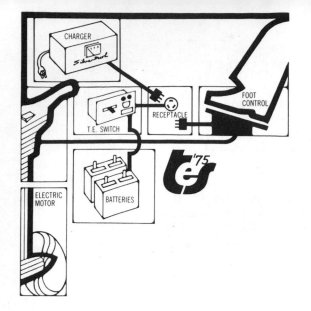

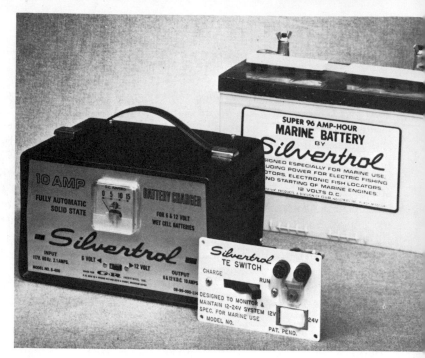

Silvertrol's (G&R Ind.) deep cycle battery and Total Electric charging system.

Deep-cycle batteries are now available from manufacturers and suppliers in 12-volt sizes. The most common capacity sizes are 95 to 105 amp/hours, but at least one company (Gould) also offers smaller sizes (80 and 34 amp/hours) too. The 95 to 105 amp/hour batteries are slightly larger than most marine SLI batteries, but will fit in the standard thirteen-and-one-half-inch long marine battery box. They weigh the same as a SLI battery of equivalent capacity.

Don't confuse deep-cycle batteries with "maintenance-free" batteries. The only maintenance-free battery currently available is the SLI type, and they are designed for automotive use. At least one company (Gould) will be introducing a maintenance-free marine battery shortly, but it is not a D/C type. If you use a maintenance-free battery for your electric, it will go downhill just as fast as any other SLI type.

Another real advantage of the D/C battery is that it can be used to crank your gasoline engine under normal conditions without damage to the battery. The only difference here is that the D/C battery cannot deliver that continuous burst of amps for as long as a SLI battery, and a balky motor might be tough to start. An engine in good condition can be easily started with any D/C battery of more than 80 amp/hour capacity that is at least 40 to 50 percent charged.

I once cranked a cold V-4 85 hp Johnson outboard (without choking it) on a cool morning with a 105 amp D/C battery until it started. By my

To reduce the probability of damage to the battery when navigating a rough chop, the battery box should be anchored securely in place. This is especially important when the batteries are carried in the bow of the boat.

watch the cranking process took almost twenty continuous seconds, and the starter motor never slowed down until the outboard caught. I also ran my 20 amp electric quite a bit that day with that same battery, even though I frequently cranked the outboard with it too. Since that time I've ceased carrying one battery for starting and another for the electric—a weight saving of fifty-two pounds.

Anyone using a 12 or 24-volt electric motor on a bass boat or other craft of similar size will need a 95 to 105 amp/hour battery (two for a 24-volt system). Most of the electrics used with boats of that size draw 20 to 25 amps at full thrust. In a typical day's fishing, it's not uncommon to pile up a total of three-and-one-half to four hours full thrust (or its equivalent) time on the electric through frequent intermittent use. The D/C battery will still be going strong by the end of the day, but a SLI would be deeply discharged and probably damaged.

A D/C battery (like any other battery) is much like the fuel tank for your main engine. It stores

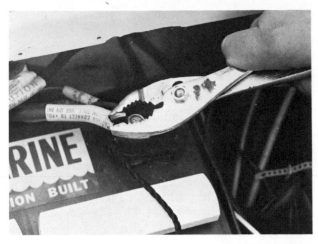

Use pliers or wrench to tighten terminal connections at battery. Loose connections steal power, and finger tightening isn't reliable. Vibration can loosen terminals.

Special battery cleaners (Tempo Prod.) help remove corrosion from terminals.

amps the way your tank stores gallons of gasoline. The more current you draw, the faster it will become depleted. It's important to select a battery of sufficient capacity for any D/C application, just as you would make sure you had enough gas on board for the trip you are planning to take. If you wish to troll steadily for six to seven hours with an electric that draws 10 amps, then the minimum size you need would be an 80 amp/hour (95 would be better) battery. Intermittent use, such as positioning, drains the battery less and also allows some partial recovery. A good estimate is that intermittent use would allow at least twice as much operating time as continuous use.

Equally important for proper battery selection is your choice of battery chargers. It should be able to provide enough charging current to recharge the battery *fully* overnight, but not so much that it charges too rapidly. Excessive charging rates will generate a lot of heat. This causes the plates to buckle, and therefore the battery loses capacity. Most D/C battery manufacturers suggest a 10 to 20 amp charger, but definitely *not over* 30 amps.

Using a "quick" charger in a service station to recharge the battery in a half hour will ruin a D/C battery. (It's not really good for a SLI battery either.) On the other hand, chargers of less than six to eight amps minimum won't charge that battery rapidly enough, and chargers under six amps (i.e. "trickle" chargers) are not capable of fully charging a battery anyway. The low charge rate cannot overcome the internal resistance of a battery once it becomes 75 percent charged.

If your charger does not have an automatic cutoff, check your battery's charge level with a hydrometer and allow the charger to run only long enough to charge the battery completely. Overcharging is like charging too fast: too much heat is generated, causing internal damage.

You can reliably estimate the battery's state of charge with a simple floating-ball hydrometer. They're inexpensive (usually less than $2), and they're small enough to be stowed easily in any tackle box. You can use them to check the battery several times during the day's fishing to determine just how fast you are depleting its charge.

When you check the battery at the end of the trip, and you find that, for example, only 25 percent of the charge in your 100 amp/hour battery remains, then you know you must "put back" approximately 75 amps. For your 10-amp charger, that would theoretically mean seven-and-one-half hours. But because the charge rate tapers off as the battery becomes progressively charged, more time is needed. A good thumb rule is one-and-one-third times the theoretical time required, which would be ten hours in this case instead of the theoretical seven-and-one-half.

If your charger doesn't have a fully automatic cutoff, unplug it at the end of the charging period or use one of those plug-in appliance timers to turn it off for you. Those chargers billed as automatic only because their charging rates taper off really aren't going to prevent possible overcharging, and they should be treated as nonautomatic.

Proper maintenance will significantly affect your battery's performance. There really isn't any such thing as a maintenance-free battery. The term just means that the battery is sealed, and you don't have to add water. To obtain maximum performance, there are other maintenance factors that must be recognized.

All connections at the terminals must be se-

Corrosion doesn't have to be this visible to steal battery power.

curely fastened. Loose connections can drastically affect the total power output, and thereby reduce the amount of time the battery will deliver energy at a high rate of use. Use pliers or a wrench.

Dirty or corroded terminals will rob your battery of more energy than you might think. A 100-amp battery can become less efficient than a 60-amp battery if the terminals are really dirty. Don't assume the terminals are clean just because they don't look corroded. Dirt or other nonconductive films between the terminals and the connectors might not be visible. Disconnect the terminals every few months, clean them gently with steel wool or a wire brush, and spray them with a moisture displacing lubricant such as WD-40, CRC, SS-1, or P-38. After refastening the connectors, coat them with a light layer of vaseline or silicone grease to protect them from corrosion.

To protect the battery from physical damage, it should be placed in a battery box and that box should be anchored securely to prevent it from being battered around. Severe shock can loosen plates and end that battery's effectiveness. If the battery doesn't fit snugly within the box, use small pieces of plywood or board to wedge it in securely.

Check the liquid levels in the battery at least monthly. Fill according to the manufacturer's instructions when needed. Even though most manufacturers will state that tap water is fine, I've found that distilled water is usually better. A gallon of distilled water will last a year or two, and in many cases will double the effective life of the battery.

Proper off-season storage is important. Remove the batteries from the boat, charge them fully, check the liquid levels and fill if needed, then store in a dry location (preferably away from freezing temperatures). Check them at least every month or two with a hydrometer, and if the charge drops below 75 percent, recharge. If you use the batteries all year but trips become infrequent during winter, disconnect them between trips and recharge. Check with a hydrometer every month or two.

It's important to start each fishing trip with batteries that are fully charged. This is especially true if you use one of the D/C batteries as a cranking battery, too.

If your system utilizes a 24-volt trolling motor, you'll need to charge both 12-volt batteries at once if you are going to have them both fully charged overnight. There are several ways you can go about it. One is to use two battery chargers, and charge them separately. Or, use one 15 to 30-amp charger and charge them both in parallel. Charging in parallel is fine if both batteries have been depleted to exactly the same extent. But if one has a higher charge than the other, it will try to charge the weaker battery just as if you were trying to jump-start a dead battery. If the connecting cables aren't very thick, i.e., approximately the same thickness as starting cables, they can easily become overheated and possibly start a fire.

Charging in parallel can be made perfectly safe by the use of a battery isolator (Sure Power Products) in the circuit. Various models start at less than $20, and make the job completely safe by isolating two or more batteries from each other. Also, by the very nature of an isolator, it will direct the greatest charge to the weakest batteries, thus bringing all to a full charge at exactly the same time. It's possible to charge two batteries together, even when one is hooked up to the engine as a starting battery, if the system is connected correctly.

At least two manufacturers (Silvertrol and Sure Power Products) offer a built-in switching system that can be installed permanently in your boat. All you need do at the end of the day is plug in the charger at the dock or on your trailer. All batteries will be fully charged by morning. The heart of the system is a console switch that you flip to the charge position before plugging in the charger, and back to run position to use the electric the next day. There are no wires to unhook or reconnect.

One note of caution, however. If your battery charger doesn't have a built-in isolation transformer (to keep stray AC current from leaking over into the DC output), you should disconnect the

1 CHARGING WITH AUTO (NEGATIVE GROUND ALTERNATOR)

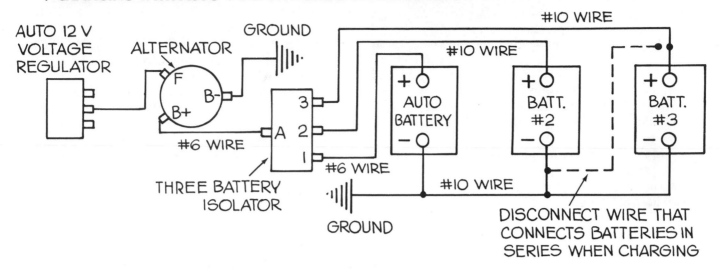

AUTO 12 V VOLTAGE REGULATOR
ALTERNATOR
GROUND
#10 WIRE
#10 WIRE
F
B−
B+
#6 WIRE
A
3
2
1
THREE BATTERY ISOLATOR
#6 WIRE
GROUND
#10 WIRE
AUTO BATTERY
BATT. #2
BATT. #3
#10 WIRE
DISCONNECT WIRE THAT CONNECTS BATTERIES IN SERIES WHEN CHARGING

2 CHARGING TWO UNCONNECTED BATTERIES

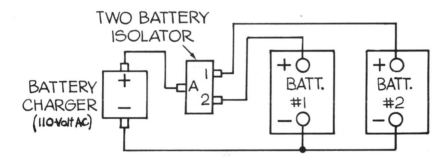

TWO BATTERY ISOLATOR
BATTERY CHARGER (110-Volt AC)
A 1 2
BATT. #1
BATT. #2

3 CHARGING TWO BATTERIES, CONNECTED IN SERIES, TO OUTBOARD AND ELECTRIC MOTORS

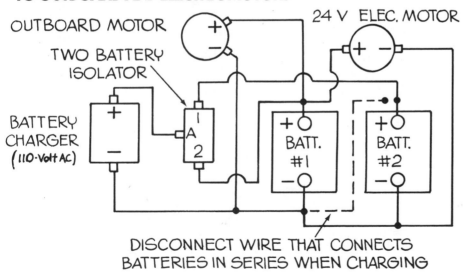

OUTBOARD MOTOR
TWO BATTERY ISOLATOR
BATTERY CHARGER (110-Volt AC)
24 V ELEC. MOTOR
A 1 2
BATT. #1
BATT. #2
DISCONNECT WIRE THAT CONNECTS BATTERIES IN SERIES WHEN CHARGING

The diagrams show how to use battery isolators. Note the following points: In Diagram 3, disconnect cable from (−) terminal of Battery 1 to (+) terminal of Battery 2 when charging, to avoid a short circuit. Do same for Diagram 1 (Batteries 2 and 3). In Diagram 2, the method is same even without outboard. In Diagram 3, use two-battery isolator if charging only one battery in car trunk or boat. A shorter wire to batteries improves charging rate.

batteries being charged whenever you recharge at dockside. Only the purest fresh water conducts no electricity, and stray electrical currents in the water can damage seriously your lower unit, out-drive, or any other submerged metallic fittings. This situation becomes worse in salty, brackish, or even chemically polluted water.

Most automotive alternators recharge your car's SLI battery at a rate of 35 to 50 amps per hour, while most outboard alternators only put out 6 to 10 amps. That's why you cannot keep the battery used to power an electric motor suitably re-charged just by running the gas engine. Besides, the gas engine needs some electric power, too. Eventually, you will put more hours draining the battery with the electric than you put in running hours with the gas engine to recharge it, and the battery dies.

You can utilize part of your tow car's high alternator output to charge one battery while en route to a fishing spot if the drive is long enough (an hour or more). By installing the correct isolator between your auto's alternator and battery, you can shunt charging current not needed to keep the car's SLI battery charged into your D/C batteries in the boat or trunk of your car.

There's no reason why you shouldn't have all the power you need for a hard day's fishing if you follow the steps outlined below:

1. Use only deep-cycle batteries for the electric. Make sure they are of sufficient capacity, and fully charged. You can possibly get by using one battery as a cranking and trolling motor battery (12-volt system) if your daily electric use isn't excessive. Use two for 24-volt applications. Not all D/C batteries are labeled "deep cycle." Make sure what you are buying is actually a deep-cycle battery by sticking with reliable manufacturers and suppliers. Deep-cycle batteries cost about the same as a premium SLI battery, but they last so much longer they are actually *far* cheaper to use.

2. Use the correct battery charger, and be sure you do not overcharge the battery. Never allow a deeply discharged (25 percent or less charge remaining) battery to go more than ten or twelve hours without recharging; even the best battery will lose some of its capacity. Three or four such occurrences can reduce a 100-amp battery to 50 or 60 amps capacity. Even allowing a "dead" battery to go three or four days before recharging can have this same effect.

3. Maintain the batteries properly, including the liquid levels. A few minutes here and there at the right time will add many hours of life to the battery.

The following table compares discharge rate (amps used) with the number of hours available for continuous use (nonstop) for deep-cycle batteries of various capacities. Intermittent use, especially when using the electric for positioning purposes under normal conditions, will usually more than double the available times.

DISCHARGE RATE, amps	RATED CAPACITY, Amp/hours			
	34	80	95	105
2.5	5.9 hours	32 hours	37 hours	41 hours
5	3.2	14.5	17	19
10	1.7	6.3	7.7	8.5
15	1.2	3.9	4.8	5.3
20	54 minutes	2.8	3.4	3.8
25	45 minutes	2.2	2.7	3.0

PART FOUR

AFTER THE CATCH

My favorite bass receipe works like this:
Find a smallmouth lake on the Minnesota-Ontario border that has
little creeks flowing in and out and other lakes a short portage over
the ridge. Pour in an afternoon with an easy breeze in the tops of the
white pines and owls calling from the little hills that are dark against
the setting sun down the lake. Add a blazing camp fire and its circle
of light and warmth. Shake the smallmouth fillets you just brought
up from the edge of the lake—they seemed still to be quivering as you
washed them in the numbing water—in a sack of white corn meal.
Mix in salt and pepper and put 'em in the pan. Add a buddy named
Pat Smith, whom you admonish to stop acting like a damned New
York bartender and to pour a proper slug of whisky into your tin cup.
Thank Pat. Taste the whisky. Taste the smallmouth fillets.
Thank God.

23

Care of the Catch

VIN T. SPARANO

Keeping and Cleaning

If you sit down at the dinner table and bite into a poor-tasting bass fillet from a fish that you caught, there's a good chance the reason for the second-rate taste is your own fault. In all probability, the fish was not handled properly from the moment it came out of the water. Fish spoil rapidly unless they are kept alive or quickly killed and put on ice.

Here are the necessary steps involved in getting a fresh-caught fish from the water to the table, so that it will retain its original flavor.

First, the decision to keep a bass dead or alive depends on existing conditions. If you're out on a lake and have no ice in your boat, for example, you'll want to keep all fish alive until you head home. Under no circumstances should you toss the fish in the bottom of the boat, let them lie there in the sun, then gather them up at the end of the day. Try that stunt and the fillets will reach your table with the consistency of mush and a flavor to match. Put your fish on a stringer as quickly as possible and get them back in the water, where they can begin to recover from the shock of being caught.

Use the safety-pin-type stringer and run the wire up through the thin almost-transparent membrane just behind the bass's lower lip. This will enable the fish to swim freely and it will not be injured in any way should you decide to release the fish at the end of the day.

Do *not* shove the stringer wire under the gill cover and out of the mouth. This damages gills and kills fish fast. Also avoid cord stringers, where all fish are bunched in a clump at the end of the cord. This may be acceptable on short trips for small panfish, but if you're after bass and want to keep them alive and fresh, either for the table or release at the end of the day, use the safety-pin stringer.

If you're rowing or trolling slowly, you can probably keep the stringer in the water. If you have a big boat and motor, however, it's a good idea to take the stringer into the boat for those fast runs to other spots. If the run is fairly long, wet down the fish occasionally. But don't tow a fish in the water at high speed—you'll drown it.

On a recent trip to Quebec, where the best fishing spot was a three or four-mile run from camp, I used another technique to get fish back alive. Whenever returning to camp with a stringer of fish, I'd stop my boat every half a mile or so and ease them over the side. I'd let the fish swim around for five minutes or so before hauling them back in the boat and continuing the trip to camp. During the course of a week, I made such trips several times and always reached camp with lively fish to be put in our shoreline fish box. Keeping fish alive is especially important on extended trips to remote areas, where ice in sufficient quantity isn't generally available.

If you're in a remote area where ice is not available, how can you keep fish alive for a week or more? I use a homemade collapsible fishbox, which can be weighted with a rock in a foot of water on shore or floated in deep water. Either way, the fish will stay until the end of the trip. Keeping fish alive for lengthy periods on in remote areas is impossible without such a box. Keeping fish on a stringer at dockside will *not* work for long periods. With some wood and wire mesh, a fish box is easy to build. The box in these photos will give you a rough idea of size and construction.

We're assuming, of course, that a fish has been unhooked and is placed in the fish box in good condition. If it has been deeply hooked and appears to be dying slowly, it's best to kill the fish immediately, gut it, and keep it on ice.

Here's how to put a fish on a stringer. Wire is run through transparentlike membrane in lower jaw. Don't run stringer through both lips or through gills. Get the fish back into the water with a minimum of handling and it will stay alive.

Here's my collapsible fish box for use on long trips where ice is not available. Floated in deep water, the box will keep a good number of fish alive during an extended trip. Note size and construction of the fish box.

Fish box need not be floated in deep water. It can be weighted with a rock along shoreline, so fish can be conveniently dropped in without hauling box out of the water.

Carry a couple of plastic bags in your tackle box. They work out fine when an ice chest is not available. Put ice in one bag and your fish in the other. Then place the bagged fish in the bag with the ice. Your catch will be iced but NOT in direct contact with ice, where it will get soggy in water from melting ice.

Killing a fish quickly is simple. Holding the fish upright, impale it between the eyes with the point of your knife or rap it on the head with a heavy stick. Kill the fish quickly, since the more slowly it dies the more rapidly its flesh will deteriorate.

If you're a stream fisherman, it's wise to carry your catch in a canvas or wicker creel. The canvas creel works fine, so long as it is occasionally immersed in water. The traditional wicker creel will work just as well, but it should be lined with ferns, leaves, or wet newspaper. The important factor is to keep the fish cool and out of the sun.

Regardless of the various ways to keep fish cool, they should first be cleaned properly. With a bit of practice and a sharp knife, the job can be done in less than a minute. First, insert your knife, blade outward, in the anal opening of the fish and slit the skin forward and up to the gills. With the fish opened, cut and pull out the gills and entrails. Next, with the fish on its back, run your fingernail against the backbone and remove the blood sac along this area. Now wash the fish out. Try to avoid washing the inside of a fish more than once,

since water directly on the flesh tends to make it soft and cuts down on flavor. Some veteran anglers simply wipe out their fish and cook it, with no washing at all.

Getting your fish home in good shape is as important as cleaning it properly. Placing gutted fish on ice is not good enough. The ice will melt and the fish will soon be underwater. The flesh will absorb water and become mushy and tasteless. There is a really only one way to handle the problem and that is to pack the fish in plastic bags and place the bags on ice in an ice chest.

If you don't have an ice chest, you can still work out a solution. Place the fish in one plastic bag, then place that bag in another bag full of ice. Your fish will be iced down, but not in direct contact with the ice—and you won't even need an ice chest. You can plan ahead for such situations by carrying plastic bags in your car or tackle box.

Now that you know how to get your catch home in good condition, chances are that most of your attempts at putting together a fish dinner will turn out all right.

Filleting Fish

Last summer, three friends and I loaded our two boats for the return trip from an Ontario outpost cabin to the main lodge. We had just wrapped up a week of good fishing for smallmouth bass and walleyes in the province. In addition to a lot of gear, we were taking our possession limits of fish home to our families, and we were doing it with one medium-size cooler and some ice. How were we able to get nearly fifty bass and walleyes, plus ice, in one ice chest? The answer is "filleting." We were hauling only fillets, leaving heads, fins, and innards behind for the 'coons.

Making it easier to haul fish out of the backwoods is only one reason for filleting. There are others. When putting together a shore lunch, for example, a fillet is a lot easier and faster to cook up in a skillet than a fish that is only field dressed.

Then there are the guys with fish-bone phobias, and I'm one of them. There are no bones in a fish fillet, so I fillet whenever possible. I also have small children who enjoy fish and who literally take on more than they can chew. I rest a lot easier knowing they are eating fillets that are free of sharp bones.

Also, since entrails are left intact when filleting, it is not necessary to field dress the fish. Neither is it necessary to scale the fish, since the final step of the filleting procedure is skinning and the skin is discarded, scales and all.

The accompanying photographs show, step-by-step, how to fillet a fish. While it looks like a complicated job, the five-pound largemouth bass in the photographs was actually filleted and skinned in about four minutes. Note that the bass was filleted with very little mess to clean up, since gutting and scaling was not necessary. This method can be used with just about all species of fish, from big salt-water striped bass to small panfish. Even the bony pike and pickerel can be filleted with some practice.

A word of caution. In some regions, such as Ontario, the skin must be left on the fillet so that identification of the species can be determined by fish and game officers. If you're unsure of the law where you're fishing, check it out with local authorities or leave the skin on the fillet until you get home. Skinning a fillet literally takes only a few

HOW TO FILLET YOUR BASS

With a sharp fillet knife, make two cuts, one on each side [of] the dorsal fin and as close as possible to the dorsal fin. [The] cuts should go as deep as the backbone and run length[wise] from behind the head to the tail.

Slipping the knife into one of the initial cuts made alongside the dorsal fin, begin to work the blade around the backbone and rib cage, cutting the fillet away from the body. Use the flexible blade to help you carve off a complete fillet without any waste.

Keeping the blade flat, continue to cut around rib cage a[nd] down to the belly skin.

Using a slight sawing motion and keeping the blade flat and against the skin, work forward and separate the meat from the skin. A slightly dull knife works better for skinning than a sharp fillet knife.

Here are the two finished fillets—completely free of bones a[nd] for the pan. Remember that gutting and scaling is not neces[sary].

Another view of cuts.

Now make a diagonal cut, as shown, just behind the head and down to the backbone. Take care not to cut into or puncture the stomach and entrails.

When the meat is freed from the carcass, cut through the belly skin and separate the fillet completely from the fish. Now turn the fish over and cut away the fillet on the other side exactly the same way.

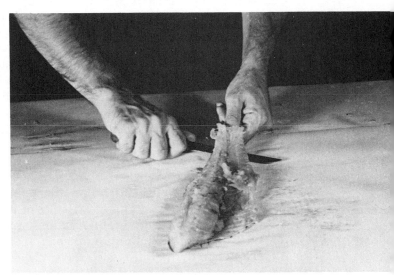

To skin the fillet, place it flesh side up as shown here. Hold the fillet down with fingers or the tines of a fork if it is too slippery. Work the flat of the blade between meat and skin.

Another view of what you should have after completing the job: The skeletonlike carcass with entrails intact, two skins, and two boneless fillets.

seconds and you'll make almost no mess in the kitchen.

Obviously, the best time to cook and eat fish is immediately after your catch is filleted, when original flavor is at its peak. This is all right for a shore lunch or with a small catch when you reach home, but some problems do arise when fillets cannot be eaten this soon. I use a few rough rules-of-thumb that work for me. If I've caught small fish that I have not filleted, I see nothing wrong with wrapping the field-dressed fish in clear plastic wrap and placing them on a platter in a refrigerator—so long as you plan to eat them within *twenty-four hours*. Some flavor will be lost, but not enough to be concerned about. Fillets, however, whose meat is completely devoid of skin and scales, should be eaten within *twelve hours*. Ideally, they should be eaten the day you catch them. Unfortunately, eating fresh fish fillets this quickly is not always possible and they must be frozen. Some flavor will always be lost when freezing fish, but it's a matter of degree. Do the job right and you may never notice the difference. Don't drop fillets in a plastic bag and toss them in a freezer. There will be air pockets in the bag and you're well on your way to producing a fillet loaded with freezer burn.

The ideal way to freeze fillets, or fish in any form, is in a block of ice. Any container can be pressed into service, such as milk cartons, pie plates, trays made from aluminum foil, and so on. Don't let any part of the fillet touch the surface of the container. The fillet should be completely encased in ice. Though this is the ideal way to freeze fish, it is not always practical, especially with small freezers. An alternative is to wrap the fillets carefully and tightly in one of the various brands of freezer paper. I prefer the clear plastic

wrap because I can get nearly all the air out and prevent freezer burn. I can also see what's in the package if the label should fall off. So long as the fillets are wrapped properly and frozen quickly, it's safe to say that lean fish, such as bass, can be kept in a freezer up to six months before it begins to lose quality. If the fish is frozen in a block of ice, however, it can just about be stored indefinitely.

Many people also claim that you cannot safely refreeze a fish. These people are only half right. If you take a couple of fillets out of the freezer and later change your mind about having fish for dinner, the fillets *can* be refrozen *but only if there are still ice crystals on the flesh*. The fillets will lose some flavor and texture, but as long as they are not completely thawed, they can be refrozen for another day.

What about fish knives? Some anglers may be able to fillet a fish with the same sturdy sheath knife they used to dress out their buck last season, but they'd be much better off with a filleting knife with a flexible blade about four to six inches long. It's also wise to carry a sharpening stone. Since you will be making initial cuts through fish scales, your blade will lose its edge rather quickly. A few strokes on a stone between cuts will make the job a lot easier. The only time a sharp knife is not necessary is during the final skinning stage. Actually, a dull knife works better, since it will not accidentally slice into the fillet.

The less a fisherman tampers with fresh fish, the better it will taste. The largemouth bass fillets in the photographs were floured, dipped in egg, and rolled in bread crumbs. All they required was a light browning on both sides in a frying pan with hot oil. It's pretty tough to come up with a simpler recipe that will make fish taste as good.

The proof is in the eating. It would be tough for even a confirmed meat eater to walk away from these golden-brown bass fillets with all the trimmings.

Many youngsters, and some adults, can't cope with fish bones. For these persons, learning how to fillet a fish is especially important. Using the method shown here, the fillets will be free of bones. The boy is Matt Sparano, author's son.

On camping trips, where cooking facilities are frequently limited, it would be tough to get a five-pound bass in this frying pan. It's no problem however, if the fish is filleted and tossed in the skillet.

24

Cooking Your Bass–Basics and Beyond

JOAN CONE

We're all for conservation. Everyone wants to return fish to the water. Yet releasing every fish can be a mistake. Those that are badly hooked, or dragged about on a stringer all day, will probably die anyway. They'll wobble off and expire, providing food for turtles and other scavengers.

Besides, bass are very good to eat. Largemouth, smallmouth, Kentucky and spotted bass all taste much the same—delicious. Part of the fun of bass fishing comes with the wonderful meals that follow, made possible by your angling skill.

With the price of fish in supermarkets today, it makes sense to get some good fresh bass as a bonus on your time outdoors. What many people don't realize is that a good bass dinner starts long before you return to the dock.

If you're going to eat bass, the first step is to kill them and put them on ice immediately. Dragging them about on a stringer in warm water means they'll eventually die and start to decompose almost at once. You keep your beer cold, so why not keep your fish cold too. Take a cooler and plenty of ice, and get those fish iced down at once. It makes a tremendous difference, believe me.

Superchilling

What if you're far away from home, or come home too tired to clean fish or prepare them for the freezer? The best idea then is to superchill your fish according to the method developed by the Food Science Department of North Carolina State University. Superchilling guarantees your fish will stay fresh for a week, and all you need is a cooler, plenty of crushed ice and salt (rock salt or table salt are both fine). You need one pound of salt for every 20 pounds of ice.

All you do is put about four inches of crushed ice in the bottom of your cooler or ice chest, place your fish on this layer of unsalted ice, and cover them with the mixture of ice and salt. If you've been very lucky, you can add layers of fish and salted ice until your chest is completely full. Then close the lid, and keep it closed. All you have to do is drain excess water from the bottom of your cooler.

This superchilling method lets you get fresh fish home without cleaning them first. If you do clean them, wrap them in plastic to keep them away from the ice and salt solution which won't hurt anything, but may take some flavor from your catch.

The fantastic bass fishing of the Louisiana bayou country led Joan Cone to her super-delicious Bass Creole recipe.

When you finally get down to cleaning bass, both largemouths and smallmouths, and such related species as Kentucky bass, skin them right away. The muddy flavor most folks dislike comes from the skin, and it's about as fast to skin a fish as scale it anyway.

Maybe you won't eat your bass right away. You can freeze them for long periods of time. Some people freeze fish in milk cartons of water which is fine but takes up too much space in a small freezer. Something that works as well and takes up little room is a protective dip also developed by North Carolina State University for the local seafood industry. Use it, and then wrap, and your bass will stay fresh for a year. Here it is:

PROTECTIVE DIP FOR FREEZING FISH

2 envelopes or 2 tablespoons unflavored gelatin
½ cup lemon juice (either fresh or reconstituted)
3½ cups water

Stir gelatin into cold water-lemon juice mixture. Heat slowly over low setting, stirring constantly until gelatin dissolves and mixture is almost clear. Cool to room temperature. Dip your fish into liquid and drain. Wrap your fish in plastic film using a drugstore fold down center of package. Fold ends several times over. Don't use foil alone to wrap bass for freezing. It punctures easily and a tiny hole can result in freezer burn.

Why does this protective dip work? The gelatin is an airtight film holding the lemon juice in contact with the fish. The lemon juice serves as an antioxidant, odor inhibitor and color stabilizer. That's why this easy step lets you freeze bass for a year, and maybe even longer.

Let's get down to cooking. Of course you can cook a bass whole, and larger bass are sometimes even better if poached, boned and used in many different ways. There's an important rule for cooking your bass and other fish . . . *don't overcook them.* Overcooking dries out bass and makes them tasteless. Here's a whole-bass recipe to use with those smaller fish:

PAN-FRIED BASS

Wipe your fish dry with paper towels. For several small bass, use ½ cup flour, fine cracker crumbs, cracker meal, or cornmeal and mix with 1 teaspoon salt. (One-fourth cup flour mixed with ¼ cup of cornmeal is excellent too.) Roll your fish in this mixture. Meanwhile, in a shallow frying pan or electric skillet, heat four tablespoons of butter, or two tablespoons butter plus two tablespoons of vegetable oil or margarine. Place your fish in the pan and cook slowly until brown on one side. Turn carefully with a pancake turner and brown the other side. Test with a fork and when fish flakes easily, it is ready.

Squeeze some lemon juice into your hot butter drippings and stir well. Then pour this sauce over your fried bass and sprinkle them with chopped parsley.

If you really want to dress up your fried bass, try this wonderful gourmet sauce.

AMANDINE SAUCE
½ cup butter
½ cup slivered almonds
1 tablespoon lemon juice
2 tablespoons dry white wine
salt and pepper to taste

Melt butter in a small pan. Add almonds and sauté over low heat to a delicate golden color. Then add

Before freezing, the fish is dipped into a protective liquid. Longer freezer time results.

Frying bass fillets on a camp stove. Lining the skillet with aluminum foil keeps it clean and serving is easy.

remaining ingredients and shake pan over heat for two minutes. Pour contents over cooked fish. Make this sauce at the last moment, otherwise your almonds will become soggy from absorbing liquid.

Now here's a great recipe for average-sized bass of from twelve to eighteen inches. That's probably about 80 percent of the bass caught these days, isn't it?

BAKED BASS IN WINE

Start this excellent recipe by placing your fish in the center of a sheet of heavy-duty aluminum foil. Cup the foil around your bass, and sprinkle the fish with salt and pepper before topping with 1 tablespoon of butter or margarine and two thin slices of lemon. A dash of dill or rosemary can be added for an extra delightful flavor. Then pour two tablespoons of white wine over your fish, pull foil edges together, and seal to make a tight package, leaving a small air space inside. Bake in a moderately hot oven of 400°F. for thirty minutes or until ready.

Are you in a hurry to get your bass on the table? Here's a great dish you cook in a skillet. It takes less than twenty minutes for everything.

LEMON DILL FISH WITH NOODLES

¼ cup water
2 tablespoons lemon juice
1 tablespoon grated lemon peel
2 teaspoons salt
¼ teaspoon black pepper
1 teaspoon sugar
1 pound bass fillets (thaw if frozen)
6 ounces medium noodles
2 teaspoons dried dill
1 cup (8 oz. carton) plain yogurt

Bring water, lemon juice, peel, salt, pepper and sugar to a boil in your ten-inch skillet. Then add fish. Again bring liquid to a boil, and reduce heat to low. Simmer covered for ten to fifteen minutes or until fish is cooked. Meanwhile, cook noodles in boiling salted water according to package directions. Drain noodles. Stir dill and yogurt into fish dish and heat thoroughly and serve immediately over drained noodles.

Lemon Dill Fish with Noodles tastes as delicious as it is attractive, maybe more so.

Louisiana's bayou country is the home of so many large bass this recipe could be almost dedicated to them.

BASS CREOLE

2 tablespoons butter or margarine
¼ cup chopped onion
¼ cup chopped green pepper
¼ pound sliced mushrooms
1 can (1 lb.) tomatoes, drained
2 tablespoons lemon juice
¼ teaspoon dried tarragon leaves
1 bay leaf
¼ teaspoon Tabasco sauce
½ teaspoon salt
1 pound bass fillets

Melt your butter in a large skillet adding onion and green pepper. Cook until tender and add mushrooms. Cook another three minutes. Now put in your drained tomatoes, lemon juice, tarragon, bay leaf, Tabasco and salt. Cover and simmer for twenty minutes. Then add bass fillets; cover skillet and simmer five to ten minutes, or until fish flakes easily when tested with a fork. Serve this dish with cooked rice. It's a great meal. Serves two to four.

Bass have been around for millions of years, and microwave ovens are new. Yet it's a great combination because microwave cooking doesn't dry out fish. If you own a microwave oven, be sure to use it for fish casseroles and also for poaching. The following two microwave recipes are superb for bass fillets and add a little zip to their rather mild flavor:

MICROWAVE BASS FILLETS WITH TOMATOES

1 to 1½ pounds bass fillets, skinned and boned
onion powder
salt
1 large tomato, cut into small pieces
2 tablespoons of butter or margarine
½ cup shredded Swiss or Cheddar cheese

Thaw fillets if frozen. Arrange them in four portions, and place within a 13×9×2-inch Pyrex baking dish with thicker pieces of fish toward the outside. Sprinkle fillets with onion powder and salt. Cover with tomato pieces and dot butter over tomatoes. Sprinkle with cheese. Then cover and cook on high for eight to ten minutes or until fish flakes easily when tested with a fork. Turn baking dish once during the cooking process.

A Pyrex baking dish is often used to poach fish. It takes four cups of poached, flaked bass to equal one pound of fresh fish.

POTATO CHIP BASS FILLETS

1 to 1½ pounds bass fillets, skinned and boned
½ cup Caesar salad dressing
1 cup crushed potato chips
¼ cup shredded sharp Cheddar cheese

Thaw fillets if frozen and cut into serving portions. Then dip each piece of fish into the salad dressing. Place them in a 13×9×2-inch Pyrex baking dish with thicker pieces of fish along sides of baking dish. Combine chips and cheese and sprinkle mixture over fillets. Cover and cook on *high*, for eight to ten minutes or until fish flakes easily when tested with a fork. Turn your baking dish around twice during the cooking process.

Looking for an easy bass recipe to use for a wonderful water's edge dinner? Here's one you'll enjoy and there's nothing quite so wonderful as the aroma and taste of fresh fish cooking beside a lake or stream. Bass have long been known to be wonderful in chowder. Here's a favorite chowder recipe you can easily prepare on an open fire or with any type of camp cooking stove:

DOWN HOME BASS CHOWDER

1 pound, more or less, of skinned, boned, fresh bass chunks
½ cup chopped onion
2 tablespoons of melted shortening
2 cups cubed potatoes
1 cup boiling water
¾ teaspoon salt
pepper to taste
2 cups milk
1 (8¾ oz.) can cream-style corn

Cut your fillets into inch-square chunks. Then sauté onion in your melted shortening until soft, before adding potatoes, water, salt, pepper and fish. Cover and simmer for fifteen minutes or until potatoes are tender. Then add milk and corn, heat thoroughly, and serve piping hot.

Whether you're old enough to remember President Eisenhower doesn't matter. What does, is that the following was one of his favorite bass recipes and is a great way for fixing bass on any outdoor grill at a fishing camp, or in your yard at home:

GRILLED BASS A LA EISENHOWER

butter or margarine
1 medium onion, thinly sliced
1 whole bass, (1 to 3 pounds) cleaned, skinned,
    head and tail off
salt and pepper
fresh parsley, dill, thyme or any favorite seasoning

First tear off a large enough piece of heavy duty
aluminum foil to wrap your bass completely. Then
spread out foil, and spread butter or margarine in
center, placing half your onion slices on top. Put
fish directly on onion slices and sprinkle body
cavity with salt and pepper. Arrange remaining
onion slices and herbs over fish. Sprinkle with salt
and pepper, then dot generously with butter.
Bring foil up over fish and seal to make a tight
package. Place on grill. A medium fire will cook a
pound-fish in about fifteen minutes, a two-
pounder in twenty-five minutes, and an honest
three-pound bass in thirty-five minutes. Enjoy.

So far we've been talking about fillets and entire
bass. Now we're getting into many delicious ways
to prepare dishes from bass, usually larger ones,
which have been cooked and flaked. The first
step, in all these recipes, is to poach the fish by any
of several methods in order that you can easily
remove all the bones.

An easy way to poach without smelling up your
kitchen is by using an oven cooking bag. Use any
size that fits the quantity of bass you'll be cooking.
Just make sure that the fish, whether whole, or
already filleted, is only one layer deep. Begin by
heating your oven to 350°F. Place your oven bag in
a two-inch-deep roasting pan large enough to let
the bag lie flat. Put fish inside bag and arrange in
single layer. Add *no* liquid. Close bag with twist
tie, make six half-inch slits on top and cook for
twenty to thirty minutes, until you can easily flake
fish with a fork through the bag. You'll find fillets
cook much faster than a whole fish. *Do Not Overcook.* Then remove bones, and skin if not already
skinned, and flake what's left. You can, if you
wish, freeze this steamed fish for later use. It takes
four cups of flaked, boned, skinned, poached fish
to equal one pounds of fresh bass.

If you have a microwave oven, poaching fish is
even easier. All you do is place your fish or fillets
(thawed of course) in a single layer in your Pyrex
baking dish. Cover with plastic wrap and cook
from five to seven minutes per pound of fish, or

*To poach fish without smelling up your kitchen, use an
oven-cooking bag. Just make sure the fish, whole or
filleted, is only one layer deep.*

*Poaching is simple with a microwave oven, and only
takes five to seven minutes per pound of fish.*

until it flakes easily when tested with a fork.
Drain, and reserve liquid to use as stock. Remove
bones and any skin, and flake fish as before.

The following wonderful dishes are made with
cooked, flaked bass. You'll find them delicious.
Besides, if you cook more than you can eat, freeze
the leftovers and use them later.

To begin with, you've probably never thought of making canapes from your bass. Here's a terrific recipe that uses cooked, flaked fish:

BASS TOASTIES

1 cup fish flakes
2 tablespoons mayonnaise
3 egg whites, stiffly beaten
⅛ teaspoon salt
2 teaspoons paprika
2 tablespoons onion juice

Blend all these ingredients, spread the mixture on small, lightly salted crackers, and place under broiler until lightly browned and puffy.

Ever heard of bass sausage? Well, fish is a great source of protein and makes a good cost-cutting filler. The following sausage doesn't taste like fish. Everyone likes it.

JOAN'S SPECIAL BASS SAUSAGE

1 cup flaked poached bass
1 cup pork sausage meat
1 teaspoon salt
½ teaspoon black pepper
¼ teaspoon red pepper
½ teaspoon sage

Mix all ingredients thoroughly, using your hands. Form into small patties and place these in a cold frying pan. Add two or three tablespoons of water, cover your pan and cook over low or medium heat until water is evaporated. Then remove lid and continue cooking until patties are cooked through and brown on both sides. Depending on how fatty your sausage meat is, you may decide to add a little butter or margarine during the browning process. Serve your sausages hot! This recipe makes fifteen to twenty of them.

Most of us like meatloaf. Fish loaf, especially when made with bass, is absolutely wonderful. Even people who claim they don't care much for fish, will go for this:

BLUE RIBBON BASS LOAF

1 egg, beaten
¼ cup light cream

2 cups, poached, flaked bass
¾ cup bread crumbs
½ teaspoon salt
¼ teaspoon paprika
2 teaspoons lemon juice
1 tablespoon melted butter
2 tablespoons minced parsley
1 small minced onion or
1 teaspoon dehydrated minced onion

Combine the egg and cream and add to your flaked bass. Then add all remaining ingredients and mix thoroughly. Place the loaf in a greased baking dish. Bake in a hot oven (400°F.) for thirty minutes and serve piping hot.

Now here's one for the children, especially those who stick to a dreary chant about not liking fish. All kids love pizza, and this one's made with bass. Although it's really a microwave recipe, you can use your regular oven just as well by adjusting cooking time. About twenty minutes at 350°F.

BASS PIZZA ITALIANO

2 cups cooked, flaked bass
1 cup catsup
½ teaspoon instant onion powder
1½ teaspoons oregano leaves
4 hamburger buns cut in half or
8 individual small pizza crusts
1½ cups grated cheese

Combine catsup, onion powder and oregano. Add fish and mix well with fork. Place pizza crusts or hamburger bun halves in baking dish and heat for one minute in microwave oven. Place several tablespoons of fish mixture on each half bun or pizza crust. Sprinkle about two tablespoons of cheese on each small pizza. Then heat uncovered for five to seven minutes in microwave oven until fish mixture is hot and cheese melts. Turn dish once during cooking.

Try some of these recipes and you'll experience a new appreciation of your favorite gamefish. Remember, traditionally part of the fun of fishing is in the eating. As the trout fishermen urge, "Limit your kill," but keeping a few bass for your own use won't hurt the population, and will help your food budget.

PART FIVE

TOURNAMENTS AND CONSERVATION

No paragon of virtue I, but in a certain amount of time spent knocking about in the outdoors I've tried to stick to a couple of principles of sportsmanship that were drummed into my towhead brain long before I could even spell "ethic." Among the practices my elders frowned upon were such misdemeanors as ground-sluicing quail, criticising another man's dog, hogging the shots, claiming all the birds, avoiding my turn at the paddle, and offering unsolicited advice.

Avoidance of these don'ts, I was told, would leave my companions afield generally thinking of me as a nice fellow worth inviting back. Recently, though, I found myself reflecting on the significance of one other aspect of my personal code—that competitiveness in the field distorts the true outdoor ethic. This infrequent spot of deep thinking was brought on by Peter Miller's article for this section on the growing popularity of bass tournaments throughout the nation.

I'm convinced that Ray Scott and his B.A.S.S. organization are doing a heck of a job in sparking new interest in bass fishing and fighting to save our bass waters. Whether or not the tournament bug has bitten you, you can't help being impressed by the skills and dedication of most of the play-for-pay bassers.

One cast beyond the issue of competitiveness we face the most important issue of bass conservation: Are we taking too many fish? It's a complex, emotional question that varies from one body of water to another. But with technology providing more and better equipment, and with no end in sight to the growing number of people who want bass fishing, we need all the research and discipline we can muster. We may have to rethink completely the tradition of "bringing home the big one." Put the little fish in the pan, let the big ones go on giving our waters the wild hardy strain of toughness that made them big to begin with.

As my friend Lee Wulff says, "Some fish are just too valuable to be caught only once."

25

Bassing's Tournament Trail
An Inside Look

PETER MILLER

North Head, North Carolina, 3:00 P.M., *an October Monday in the mid-1970s.* A spit of land between the Atlantic Ocean and the brackish water of Currituck Sound. As three chartered buses wheeled into the drive of the mustard-yellow Carolina Hotel, the Manteo High School Marching Band, in orange and black uniforms topped with white and black helmets, struck up a brisk tune. Nubile cheerleaders did flips on the grass. In front of them, neatly dressed as an honor guard, were nineteen Ranger bass boats, fully equipped with depth-gauges, trolling engines, 115-horsepower engines, hydraulic seats, electronically hoisted anchors, aerated reservoirs, carpeting and a green-flecked finish. Retail value—$7,880.

The buses slowly disgorged their contents—journalists from all regions of the country, manufacturers' reps, executives, officials and technicians, and thirty bass anglers and their wives.

Judging from the record, the bass anglers are the best in the world. Some of them make $50,000 a year from bass competitions and from endorsements of rods, reels, lines, bait, outboard motors, electronic equipment, and from radio, TV, newspaper and magazine columns. True, some of them have a bank account as thin as monofilament and went in hock to raise the money to compete on

the bass-fishing circuit. But what the hell?—This is the B.A.S.S. Masters Classic, the most prestigious bass-catching contest in the world. In three days of competition, these thirty anglers spent 765 hours casting some 225,000 times from the Ranger boats into Currituck Sound.

Bass they caught—402 of them weighing in at over 700 pounds—which they put in aerated reservoirs. The live bass were transported back to the Carolina Hotel, placed in plastic bags, weighed in before the photographers and a crowd that clapped for the big catches. The bass were then dropped into a large aerated tank, which eventually was emptied back in Currituck Sound, where all the bass had been caught.

Jack Hains, a twenty-five-year-old Louisiana coon-ass cropduster, beat out the big names by catching more poundage—forty-five pounds, four ounces—than any other angler, so he took home a check for $15,000, just under $20.72 an ounce. It was a fun, hectic contest that cost the sponsor, Bass Anglers Sportman Society (B.A.S.S.) $140,000. And it was only one of eight contests B.A.S.S. sponsors. A competitive organization, the American Bass Federation, also sponsors eight contests. This year the two organizations will pay out an estimated million dollars in prize money. There are innumerable other

Anglers like Jack Hains (left) will be receiving even bigger checks from Ray Scott and B.A.S.S.

contests—regional, local, even some strictly for females (a feminist counterploy, as many bass contests have the taint of male-chauvinist-pig outings).

Two old friends chuggin' 'cross a Florida lake in a johnboat with a 6½ horse. The sun is orange big, heating the sky and water. The boat creaks as the water churns astern into neat angles. The air smells fresh. A light wind ripples the surface. It's a good day for bassin', oozing away from the work week, worries squirreled away, beer in the cooler, a good friend up front to sass and a new bunch of jelly worms to try out on that hawg missed last week.

Along comes a fast-moving bass rig, powered by a young competitor out to catch more bass than anyone else and win a big cash prize. His wake rocks the johnboat.

"You cotton-pickin' sumbitch!" yelled one of the old timers in the johnboat.

The competitor circles back in his bass rig, cuts the motor, lets the boat settle into the hole and drifts up to the old man.

"You callin' me a sumbitch?"

"You heard me," said the old man in the johnboat.

"Old man," yelled the competitor, "I'm tired and I'm hot and besides that," and he started to flail the old man with his rod, "I *need twenty pounds of bass!*"

The old man and the young competitor were both out on the lake, having fun. Both love to fish for bass. But they are fishing poles apart. One likes solitude and simplicity. The other goes for technology and competition.

Which is really fishing?

Bass contests—fishing for money—leaped to the surface in the late 1960s when Ray Scott, an Alabama salesman who at one time sold burial insurance ("a nickel cheaper, a foot deeper"), sponsored the first All-American B.A.S.S. Tournament with a prize fund of $5,000. Scott is now a millionaire. His B.A.S.S. club has over 270,000 members and the manufacturers have reaped in profits as that old American know-how was applied to the production of bass-catching technology—oxygen meters, depth-locators, underwater temperature gauges and high-performance jock boats that plane along with ease at 50 mph. Modern bass fishing is a scientific, sophisticated methodology of patterning a lake to catch more bass. Less and less is left to that lucky jingle:

Fishy, fishy bite
For your mother says you might
On this Sunday, Sunday afternoon.

Historically, freshwater fishing has been more to the tastes of the meditative and philosophical than to the competitive. In fact, the history of fishing, from that famous carp-ball angler, Isaak Walton, up to the effete Eastern trout and salmon purists, who lunch regularly in their club in downtown New York, has been that of a sport participated alone and in the splendor of nature. Competition always began far from the fact, with whopping lies told over drinks and dinner.

The surge of bass contests has polarized freshwater fishing. Many anglers are horrified at the concept of fishing contests run like a pro-football league. Others abhor the lack of reverence bass competitions have toward the traditions of angling. Some anglers, needless to say, look askance at the bass competitions through their social and personal prejudices. They not only dislike bass competitions, they dislike bass fishing.

Trout and salmon anglers are traditionalists who believe in the purity of the sport, the aesthetics of quiet, pristine streams, the delicacy of presentation, the fine wispy lightness and beauty of their rods and flies. They consider themselves the elite on the fishing ladder.

"How can you compete on a stream or lake?" demanded a trout-angler friend of mine, who fishes in the northeast and in Montana. "You can't.

Fish are kept alive in aerated wells, weighed in plastic bags, and released.

It's impossible. It's . . . it's unprincipled. Besides," he muttered, "bass are garbage fish." Trout purists hate the sight of a stranger casting into their favorite pools. They are, for the most part, loners. Their opinion of bass anglers is about the same as their opinion of bass.

"A bass has a brain of his own," affirmed John Powell, an old-time bass angler and a persistent competitor on the bass-contest circuit. "Competing with him is like competing with a turkey or a deer. A bass is smarter than a trout. I say that to a mountain boy and . . . *wooooo* . . . I got a fight. The bass is the smartest fish that swims." Trout and bass anglers are just like the fish they catch. The former is secretive and selective, the latter is sassy and competitive.

Charles Fox is a Pennsylvania angling author who enjoys equally trout, bass, and muskellunge fishing. He has no prejudices against the fish or the angler, but he is against contests. "I don't like getting into a boat with another fellow and competing. I don't like to be restricted. I don't want someone else calling the shots. I like to take turns rowing with another fellow. The reward is personal satisfaction, not monetary.

"I've met some of the big names in bass fishing, such as Bill Dance and Tom Mann. They are nothing but good as individuals. I'm impressed by them. I won't ever compete with them, but I would like to go fishing with them."

"Ain't that funny!" laughed an old-time swamp rat who grew up near the Everglades. "They get all fancied out in those jumpsuits and life vests and scurry up the water, roaring about. Hell, all you need is some old boat, some old pole, and a bucket of bait. Why, we catch bigger 'uns than they ever do. They're too much in a godawful hurry to wait out the grand daddies."

Still others, anglers and nonanglers, are against the contests for ecological reasons. There are the bleeding hearts, of course, who have turned their "Guns of Autumn" tirade onto the contests and consider it vastly cruel to catch a bass, subject it to a watery jail, weigh it on land, then throw it back. Some believe fish and animals should have an equal rights amendment before the women do.

"The bass contests are good as far as we can see," said Dick Kronin, fish biologist and Information and Education Officer for The Massachusetts Fish and Game Department. "We've had no complaints from other anglers. Our bass are relatively unharvested and the contests stimulate bass fishing. It's a good way of teaching and getting experience in fishing.

"If two hundred bass are caught, maybe only two get killed. But if they took fish and kept them—there would be some fervor. The biggest complaints are with the nature lovers who believe animals and fish should be treated better than their neighbors. They're preaching antibass contests right down to the school level."

Some conservationists, including fish biologists, are worried about the trauma a bass goes through in catch, hold, weigh and release contests. Verified statistics show that 16 percent of the bass caught in contests die before being released in the water. (At the B.A.S.S. Masters Classic, six out of seven-hundred died before release.)

California recently allowed bass contests. "There were no adverse effects of taking the fish out of the water, weighing them, and putting them back," said George McKinnon of the California Fish and Game Department. "In one study we tagged the fish that were released in the general area where they were caught and offered a $5.00 reward for the return of the tag. We received 70 percent of the tags. Our observation is that there is less than 5 percent mortality if the fish are handled carefully. But we are studying what happens when the fish are released at the docks and what happens during the spawning season when the male is guarding the nest." Of all states, California has the most stringent laws pertaining to bass contests and requires a state observer (at $100 per day) to oversee the event. If the water temperature is over 70°, the observer can require more than one weigh-in per day. So far there has been no reaction to bass fishing contests in California.

Some eastern bass fishermen are against keeping the fish for any length of time and advocate a catch-and-release program where prize money is awarded on the length as reported by the bass angler and verified by an on-the-boat observer-angler.

"Many New Jersey clubs have elected in their tournaments that all bass be released immediately after a simple length measurement, which is later computed into pounds," said Mark Canter, a bassin' dentist who in a political move led a picket line of anglers against another bass association. In justification of the picket line, he did bring up the ecological point of some eastern bass anglers. "It is our contention that small lakes such as we have in New Jersey cannot sustain the same pressures as can the sprawling southern impoundments. There is a vast difference between a 2,000-acre lake in New Jersey, with its shorter growing season, as compared with Santee-Cooper

Day's competition began on Currituck with three starting heats of ten boats each.

in South Carolina, with 171,000 acres."

Some western bass anglers, concerned about the catch-transport-weigh-release vs. the catch-measure-release method, have suggested an official on-the-water weigh-in boat. There are a few problems. The sponsors of large tournaments would receive little publicity from the weigh-in, and, in the case of Santee-Cooper, the weigh-in boat might get lost.

What many anglers and conservationists forget is that in all bass-angling contests, the fish are returned alive to the water. Most run-of-the-mill bass anglers, out for a day of fishing, do keep their catch. Texas biologists have come up with the figure that the bass contestant, fishing on an unfamiliar lake, will average .05 fish per hour against .07 for the local angler. If there is a concern about bass population, perhaps it should be directed at the angler who keeps every fish he ever catches.

Perhaps this mini-furor is not caused by the catch and release of bass, but by the fear that the organized competitor is invading what many consider their territorial rights—their favorite fishing holes and the fish in them.

The Pro Bassman

Who is the bass competitor? Some consider the bass competitor to be the type who drives a pickup, keeps a backyard full of coon hounds, chews Redman, and is a frustrated stock-car racer.

That is a long stretch from the truth. Although bass angling and bass competition are most popular in the south and southwest, bass are America's favorite sport fish. Bass competitions have been held in thirty-three states. The modern bass pro is probably the most technically competent of all anglers. He knows how to read the structure of a lake and how oxygen, water temperature and depth can affect the fishing. He knows what color bait to use on a bright or dull day, down deep or on the surface. Last year these anglers donated $200,000 to the Bass Research Foundation, which is dedicated to upgrading bass management.

A good bass fisherman can crawl a plastic worm on the bottom and feel the instant a bass mouths it (and sometimes spits it out). He knows when to fish a worm on the surface, or swim it over the weeds. His accuracy in casting is phenomenal. He has perfected his form for long casts, short casts, underhanded pitches. He knows how to cast side-armed and skip the lure deep under a hanging pier or tree. He has the knowledge to jury-rig a bait when the weeds are thick and the bass are striking short.

"Well, I established my pattern on the first day," said Hains, who won the B.A.S.S. Masters Classic. "Fishing off pilings and duck blinds, I mostly used a Fleck Weed-Wader with a purple-yellow tail, but I also went to worms and a Johnson Spoon. But on the last day the water temperature had dropped 10° to 55° and the fish were hitting short so I put a trailer hook on the Fleck spinner-bait, then I put another trailer hook on that. Heck, I put a trailer hook on everything." During the last two days of the contest, Hains caught four of the six biggest bass. He used his head.

Hains is a typical young bass competitor. He has an easy smile, a soft way of talking; he is modest, relaxed, extremely polite. He does have one thing in common with stock-car racers and football players—he loves to compete. During the summer he lives near Zolle, Louisiana, and likes nothing better than bass fillets. "Dinner or breakfast, it doesn't matter."

Roland Martin is the number-one bass competitor in America who has won a total of $47,823.80 in bass contests. He is an Oklahoman with blond hair, piercing eyes, and an aquiline face. His mind is quick, and he's competitive. He'll make three battle plans to attack a contest, each plan dependent upon the wind, weather, or other factors that can affect his catch. In one contest he found some good structure where a stream was coming in. He also knew there was a dam upstream and called to find out when they drew off water. He knew the current would make the fishing good and pulled out twenty pounds of bass when the dammed water swirled into the impoundment. He also uses psychology. "You know, people answer a negative better than a positive question. If I say, 'I just can't catch a fish on a worm and I bet you didn't catch a fish on a worm,' chances are he'll say, if he did, 'Oh, I did.' Watch

the inflection. Put enough negatives together and find out if they want to lie. Sometimes I'll say, 'Bill, I saw you fishing the bridge today.' I never saw him all day, but he'll say, 'Oh, no. I wasn't at the bridge.' Then I know he was on some other pattern."

Bill Dance is the number-two bass angler of America, with over $35,000 in cash prizes, endorsements and radio and TV commitments to afford an agent and leave him an income around $50,000 a year. He is bespectacled, quiet-spoken, affable, and friendly to everyone. He is also aggressive as hell. "The mind is the strongest thing in the world," he says. "If you believe hard enough, you will do it. I think of the present contest and forget all. If you fuss with your wife, or the house needs paint, or the grass needs mowing, or you argue with the boss, then you might as well pull the boat out of the water and head for home. You can't fish with your worries. I sell myself on catching them, then I go find them. Eighty percent believe you find and then catch them and that is not true. "In these contests you push, push, push. It's competitive but fun. You release bass all the time. They spawn, you catch them again. It's not as final as deer hunting. You can't pull a .308 out of a buck, pat him on the head and send him off to catch him again next year. Say 8,000 bass are born; four reach maturity. They have so much pressure. I'm a firm believer in releasing bass. If I want to eat fish, I like to catch a mess of bluegills and crappies. You know, I fish up to 280 days a year. I love a day when I get up in the morning and go fishing by myself."

John Powell is the old-timer on the circuit, tenth largest money winner ($14,052.10), a retired Air Force sergeant who is now competing against anglers he originally taught how to fish. He is an affable, smiling, bespectacled gentleman who likes a stiff drink and straight talk. "Look at the dudes in this room," Powell said, glancing at the competitors and manufacturers' reps during one of the nightly cocktail parties during the Masters Classic. "Only twenty of them make money. The way to make money fishing is to catch catfish or snapper. You don't fish for bass—not for money. Why, bass must cost me $20.00 a pound.

"Eight years ago we all fished with a 6 ½ horse-power. Now look what we got—the 175 horse-power Black Max. Now a bass boat costs you $4,000 stripped. Eight years ago, it was a $160 for a johnboat.

"You know, this sport has millionaires and then

there are some who have their shotgun hocked to enter the tournament. The influence now is in the bass boats and tackle, line and technique. When you buy a rod and reel, the influence comes from this room.

"Lot of these guys here have the killer instinct. Me, I ain't got it in me anymore. You know, Roland Martin calls me a dimestore fisherman because I work with carp. I fish with kids—deadheads, some from industrial schools, blacks. I'm not on any kind of ego trip."

Powell had another drink, his face red, his eyes gleaming, yet snaking around the room as if searching for a hole in the lily pads to cast to. "See that guy over there? That's Bob Cobb (public relations man and vice president of B.A.S.S.). See him look at us? See those guys over there? They're Stren. See them looking over here? Know what they're saying? They're saying, 'Shut your mouth!' But I'll tell you anyway. You know what you're really competing against? Not those guys," and Powell gestured with his drink at the other competitors. "You're competing against the cotton-pickin' fish. That's it!"

Bass-fishing contests have much broader appeal than competition. It's those depth-finders and fish-locators and a bassin' rig in the hole. Rev it up and the bow thrusts up like an erection. The boat is on the pad, the stomach sucks in and the tri-hull rises out of the hole, over the hump and on the plane, moving out at 50 mph. At the end of the day there might be a big check. Between that time, there's a battle plan to work out against those bass. It's a social jamboree. It's a bass happening. And with all due respect to the traditional angler, it's where the psyche of the young bass angler feels at home.

Witness this example:

Tom Mann is a tall, good looking and easy smiling Cherokee-blooded bass angler who fifteen years ago invested $500 into designing and manufacturing bass lures. Now the Mann Bait Company of Eufala, Alabama, grosses over $2 million a year. Mann also happens to be one of the top bass competitors in the country. This is a diary of his first day during the Masters Classic on Currituck Sound, North Carolina.

6:30 A.M., 28 October. Ten bass boats cluster three-hundred yards off shore on Currituck Sound, their motors idling. B.A.S.S. president Ray Scott gives the start signal. Tom Mann holds his hat in one hand and revs the boat up to 40 mph. The water is still, flat, the sun a cool disk just rising over the trees. Tom motors about half a mile into Kitty Hawk Bay to a small cove.

6:36. Tom makes his first cast with a Johnson Silver Spoon with a six-inch black jelly worm for a trailer. He manufactures the jelly worm. (This one is grape flavored.) He casts twice, standing in the bow of the boat, working the electric motor.

6:38. Moves one hundred yards deeper into the cove. Tom knows the fish are here. In practice he caught and released over half a dozen. "Fish look out!" Mann says it as more of a prayer than a threat. There is no wind.

6:39. Mann is fishing where the milfoil, an underwater weed, is thick. "It's so slick I can't see the grass good enough to spot the holes."

6:41. Tom lands his first fish, a two-pounder. Time: ten seconds from being hooked to boated. He uses two Eagle Claw six-and-a-half-footers, which he helped design, and a Daiwa 2500C spinning reel with a 5 to 1 gear ratio, which he prefers to the normal 3.5 to 1. "I like a fast retrieve and it gives better control." His line is seventeen-pound Stren. Tom works from the bow, standing, casting to port, then starboard, then port. The quiet is only broken by the whisssh of the reel, the plop of the lure hitting the water, the lick, click-click of the retrieve. "It's just too quiet. I'd like to see just a little ripple of wind."

6:56. Misses a bass. Mann starts to work the lure on the surface—swimming it. Bass misses it twice. Mann changes to a spinnerbait. "Something noisy might get them stirred up a bit." He makes two casts. "It don't run right," he mutters, and changes back to the Johnson Silver Minnow, which happened to be one of the best lures for Currituck Sound during the contest.

6:57. Second bass is boated. It also is plopped in the aerated holding well. Competitors don't play with their fish—they don't want to waste time. Ten seconds is average play time.

7:00. Bass number 3. "I counted on four from this area."

7:03. Bass number 4.

7:09. Troll about fifty yards and Tom casts into a hole in milfoil. A bass rolls after the lure. Tom casts again. "Got him," he says. "Why, it's old Leroy's cousin!" The bass is the biggest he was to catch all day (six pounds ten ounces, only two ounces lighter than the largest bass caught during the three day tournament). Tom is all smiles as he boats the bass. "After he followed it, I respected that fish, so I slowed my retrieve and started twitching the lure. He picked it right off then."

I ask who Leroy is.

"I have an 18,000 gallon aquarium at home, twenty-four feet long, twelve feet wide and eight feet deep. I have it equipped for sound and with lights. I learned a lot about bass there. Leroy Brown is a five-pound, three-year-old bass. He's a teacher, nips other fish to keep them active, nudges a dying fish, is always moving, hustling, gets the others to strike. Lotta Mama is another bass; then there's Dolomite, Big Mo, a catfish and a number of others. Big Bertha was my favorite. She weighed in at eleven pounds and died when she was ninety years old in our age. (One bass year equals ten of ours.)

"Some bass just exist. Some are smarter, and I know one that's like a lion in a cage, another that's a roamer. Others pick a home and become as content as can be. Basically, bass are very social. But there're others that hate each other and fight a lot. The worse types are the half breeds, a cross between a largemouth and a redeye. They hate everybody.

"Bass learn quickly. They get wise. You have to change pattern and color often to make them strike. They prefer dim light. They are like quail. You find them in covers. Bass strike for hunger, but bump a lure a lot. They come up on the side. I found a lure needs a shine on it and that's why I use acrylic finish and nickel blades on my baits—the flash attracts the fish."

7:19. Bass number 6, using a Johnson spoon with a black jelly worm with yellow spots. Many perch are in the bay and are delicacies for the bass. Tom casts about thirty yards and fishes like a careful woodcock hunter going through every bit of cover.

7:31. Bass number 7. It's a small one, and he throws it back.

7:33. Bass number 8. Tom is still fishing the small cove. "There must be several limits in here." Mann fishes about three days a week, ten to twelve hours a day. He's been fishing since he was six.

7:36. Bass number 9, pulled out of a hole in the weeds. Tom casts with accuracy to fish the holes. He prefers to fish with a friend except when he's trying out a new crankbait and is trying to get the balance of it. He designs all of his company's baits. Mann made his first bait while he was a conservation officer. "I carved it on government time, so I called it Little George, after Governor Wallace. It's a fish-catching son of a gun. We've sold five million. Governor Wallace has one and writes me now and then."

7:41. Bass number 10, a small one. Tom throws him back.

7:42. Bass number 11. "I like to fish my own plugs, you know, it's like hunting your own dog. But I do use others, like the Johnson spoon."

7:45. Bass number 12. Tom checks the holding tank and picks out the smallest bass, then throws it back in the Sound.

7:46. Bass number 13. "My goal is to catch twenty pounds per day and I'd sure love to have twenty-two to twenty-four pounds. You can win or lose a lot of publicity on the first day. Tournaments really help my business. I love them. They help sell tackle and I learn something from every one. Besides, I'm just plain competitive."

8:10. Bass number 14, a four-pounder pulled out of a clear patch of water surrounded by milfoil. "You got to be in shape for a contest, or else you get tired and can't cast as much. If your arm is in shape, you have better accuracy. Being ready means a lot. You need split-second timing and accuracy."

8:35. Bass number 15. "That old Leroy, he hatched nine females one year. Fish are like men—some are better daddies than others. Some let bluegills into their home to steal eggs. Leroy always stayed with those fish he hatched. Males are important for they're willing to guard the home. Bluegills—they're like hyenas; they group around a bass nest and dart in."

8:40. Bass number 16. Tom culls the bass in the well to the biggest.

8:57. Tom's brother, Don, also a competitor, motors up. "Got three," he says. "Got my limit," answers Tom. "Been flooding the lure on top this morning." Tom moves out of the cover, revving up the Sound at 45 mph, and passes a dory fisherman. He's standing in his boat, hand in pocket, cigar in mouth, staring at us, as if to say, "What the hail?"

9:19. Arrive in small cove. "One pocket here on practice I caught six bass." He doesn't raise one.

9:25. Move several hundred yards and scatter up about five hundred bluebills. "I'll have to try and get my limit tomorrow the first thing. The light's getting brighter and it's getting tougher and tougher. The bass are going back under the grass."

9:40. Tom changes to a black worm with the yellow spots. "A guy can lose confidence in a meet and run with something he heard and do nothing. Confidence is the key. Don't fish too fast."

9:50. A competitor comes within shouting distance. "I got sixteen pounds," said Tom.

"Dance has 25 pounds," said the other angler. "Top walking."

"Yeah," muttered Tom, to himself. "That means Dance has found a hole and is fishing deep." He pulls in bass number 17.

9:51. Bass number 18.

9:53. Bass number 19.

10:21. Troll motors to an old duck blind, rust-colored with age. Tom pitches the worm in and misses a bass. "This is my pattern now. Those bass like to live right under the blind, where it's cool and dark." Moves four hundred yards to another duck blind.

10:24. Bass number 20, a small one.

10:45. Motors north to a channel. Most of the Sound is five feet or less, but in the channel, the depth meter reads up to fifteen feet. Tom does poorly.

11:18. Tom runs into his close friend and competitor, Bill Dance.

"No shit, how many pounds you got?" asks Dance.

"'Bout nineteen."

"I got about fourteen."

"I got one nine pounds, six pounds, five pounds. I got eighteen."

"No shit," says Dance. "I got sixteen."

"Boy," says Tom, "you better stop and fish next door."

"I think you're woffin' me."

"I got about twenty-two pounds," boasts Tom. "I got some hawgs, boy!"

"Oh, so do I," says Dance, a bit timidly.

Dance comes up and looks in Tom's well. "You got me," he says.

Tom looks in Dance's tank. Dance has not fared well. "Really," says Tom, "I only have about fourteen pounds."

11:40. We move south. Dance moves north. "Boy," says Tom, "he'll start humping now."

12:01 P.M. Bass number 21.

12:20. Move to a duck blind and Tom jigs a worm under the gunner's platform. He flips the worm about two feet with uncanny accuracy and pulls out bass number 22. "Spinning rod is good for the underhand throw. Duck blinds are the afternoon pattern."

12:43. Bass number 23.

1:10. Two duck blinds later, Tom latches on to bass number 24, a two-and-a-half pounder.

1:12. Bass number 25, a small one.

1:14. Bass number 26. The wind has come up

Tom Mann is happy here but still ended up in fifth place in this tournament.

and the fishing is more difficult.

1:22. Try a new blind. "Older the blind, the better, but it can't be too shallow. Most people just rim the blind with their casts. You got to get in there and pitch the worm right under the platform, right through the front door of their home."

1:32. Hit another blind and scare out a duck. "I get lots of letters from kids between the ages of eight and sixteen. 'I want to be a big tournament winner,' they say. 'I'm fourteen. Please send me some baits.' I often do."

1:33. Bass number 28. The average bass from Currituck Sound is two pounds.

1:37. Bass number 29.

1:41. Bass number 30. "You know, a bass is curious. He's got to come out and see what's going on."

1:50. Tries a skeleton blind, but it is only oc-cupied by two water turkeys and a seagull. They depart from the blind and Tom departs too, at 45 mph down the Sound to where he had started in the morning.

2:33. Bass number 31. "To win in these contests you have to be versatile. John Powell, for instance, is good in shallow water. I have a reputation with the worm, but I'm a switch hitter—good on the top and down deep."

2:55. Return to the dock, where the boat, with Tom in it, is lifted out of the water and driven back to the hotel.

At the weigh-in, Tom's keepers—eight bass— came out to twenty-two pounds, three ounces. Good enough for second place. His luck didn't stay with him and he ended in fifth place with a total catch of thirty-two pounds, fifteen ounces.

Bass Organizations

For more information on bass tournaments at the national or local level, write to one of the following bass organizations:

American Angler
P.O. Box 433
Lufkin, TX 75901

Bass Anglers Sportsman Society (B.A.S.S.)
P.O. Box 3044
Montgomery, AL 36109

Bass Caster's Association
P.O. Box 888
Mattoon, IL 61938

Bass 'N Gal Association
P.O. Box 1666
Grand Prairie, TX 75051

International Bass Association
P.O. Box 390
Prairie Grove, AR 72753

National Bass Association
  (combined with American Bass Fisherman)
215 South Burke Street
P.O. Drawer 2299
Lake City, FL 32055

Mid-America Bass Fishermen's Association
Box 14B
Osceola, MO 64776

Midwest Husband and Wife
P.O. Box 231
Hendersonville, TN 37075

Northern Bass Fisherman, Inc.
P.O. Box 2526
South Bend, IN 46680

Professional Bass Association
P.O. Box 15115
Nashville, TN 37215

Southern Bass Association
P.O. Box 281
Millington, TN 38053

United Bass Fishermen
P.O. Box 1405
Lake Alfred, FL 33850

Western Bass Fishing Association
P.O. Box 2027
Newport Beach, CA 92663

26

Catch and Release
The Salvation of Quality Angling

ANTHONY A. CIUFFA

To most bass anglers the fight of a high-quality bass is a thrilling episode that lives only in their fantasies. Unfortunately, if fishing philosophy continues as it has in the past, few fishermen will know what truly good bass fishing could be like. The false assumption made by most fishermen is that when a large bass is caught it must be killed and taken home, no matter how rare the presence of big bass in that lake.

This practice has plagued fishing from the day someone first picked up a fishing rod; it is a major factor in the overharvest of bass populations. In addition, old wives' tales are still embedded in many minds, like the belief that once a large bass has been caught it will "get smart" and likely never be caught again. Not so. If this were a fact, I would not have been able to gather the information my catch-and-release bass fishing has provided me. Many bass that my partners and I have hooked, marked, and released have been caught again and again, and many of them are still there to encounter us at least once more.

Of course there are fatalities to bass in this form of fishing, but with a few common-sense rules, most of these fish demonstrate the capacity to be tough, and if released immediately after capture will be caught again. In our experience, *several* fishermen, including guests who had never hooked a big bass in their lives, have enjoyed battle with real tackle-busters, instead of only *one* fisherman, as happens in "catch-and-keep" fishing.

Until the day arrives when bass fishermen realize the detrimental effects to the sport that lie in overharvest of this species, which will be sooner than we think, and until state regulations protect the various size-classes in proportion to their density in a lake, we will continue to see good bass fishing only on relatively new waters, and then have to watch it deteriorate into mediocrity.

Over twenty years of catch-and-release bass fishing in controlled waters, as well as on isolated structure on large public impoundments, have proven that bass fishing as practiced today by most fishermen, under most of the present state regulations, provides for only short-term quality. This is primarily the result of overharvest, where the supply of bass is decimated faster than nature can replace them in sizes the peak years of the lake had provided. At some point in the overharvest, even before bass are noticeably depleted, other species begin to fill the spaces and set in force the mechanism that destroys the environment for successful bass reproduction and survival.

Quality fishing like this is maintained consistently on Tony Ciuffa's catch-and-release lakes through sound management policies. All photographs by A. A. Ciuffa

Tagging: The Best Information Bank

In my catch-and-release fishing, most of the bass tagged were fish of two pounds and larger. The majority of these fish were identified with monel jaw tags, and some, in later years, with yellow plastic spiral bird legbands. Many facts were recorded for each fish, such as date, time of day (or night) caught, lure, approximate depth, water clarity, water temperature, thickness of the warmed layer in each period of the seasons, effectiveness of slow, medium, or fast retrieve, type of terrain surrounding the catch area, bottom structure, wind direction, rising, stationary, or falling air temperature, cloud condition, and much else. All this provided ever-varying rules for catching

bass. In addition, much information was compiled for better management of catch-and-release waters through experiments performed with chemical, electro-seine, and stocking operations.

I eventually came to realize that bass cannot maintain a sound population structure for good catches if they are protected by the usual number-per-day system. The need for regulations controlling the weight distribution relative to the ratio of abundance of each size-class became obvious. While bass cannot be stock-piled indefinitely without a need for some controlled harvest, it became clear that most lakes eventually contained far fewer bass than their potential carrying capacity for this species. Unfortunately, these dire conditions are brought on by the bass fishermen themselves, resulting in fun-for-all at the onset, and then years of spotty success.

Recently I have met with biologists working on the same subject. One of them, Dr. Richard O. Anderson of the University of Missouri, has provided invaluable information and assistance in the area of management techniques and in the study of the vulnerability of the largemouth bass in my catch-and-release test waters. His electro-seine census operations, stocking of forage fish for better bass, and compilation of data could help produce the best bass waters in the world. In Dr. Anderson's words, "The overharvest of this top predator in a fish community is a serious problem, not only because it can have an adverse effect on the harvest of bass and bluegills, but more importantly because it can lead to an inferior quality of fishing. From this standpoint, what is harvested in a recreational fishery is less important than what is left to provide the catch and harvest next week, next month, and next year."

A fish population normally contains more small individuals than large ones. There are exceptions, but under normal conditions, there would naturally be more eight to ten-inch bass than eleven to thirteen-inchers and larger. Obviously, natural mortality factors, in addition to those inflicted by

Monel band on upper jaw or lip of a bass. Erosion will eventually break jaw if this fish is not caught within one year. Tag would then be moved to opposite jaw if erosion is evident.

man, reduce the individual fish's odds of survival as time passes. With management techniques geared to developing more larger bass, there would be reduced harvest of larger fish and more harvest of smaller ones in order to permit the survivors of the smaller size-classes to grow into the more desirable sizes. This would provide a better proportioned harvest in ratio to the natural abundance of the various size-classes.

When Big Bass Are Vulnerable

As a rule of nature, bass are caught in a ratio to the abundance of individuals in each size-class. That is, fishermen are more likely to catch more bass of a size or sizes that are most abundant, given that the lures used are within the acceptable size for hooking these more abundant fish. Unfortunately, the preceding is not an infallible occurrence. There are times, especially in the spring, during a rapid warmup from colder water temperatures, and again in early and mid-summer, when bass concentrate on selective structures, that larger bass can become denser in a few areas of a lake than they would be at any other time of the year. At such times, there is also the probability that female bass—the real aggressors and larger fish of the species—would comprise the majority of the victims, thus permitting the harvest of a select group.

When these densities of larger bass coincide with heavier fishing pressures by expert bassmen, a substantial number of this select minority group are harvested within a period that would not permit that normal reaction time bass eventually develop in resisting capture due to increasing food availability as their numbers are reduced. This decimation of quality fish is possible because during these warming periods of the prespawn season the egg-bearing female has a delaying reaction to cold spells that intervene during the warm-up toward summer. While the smaller fish, as well as lunker males, respond negatively to the fisherman's offers following the first signs of some heat loss from the warm layer, the larger egg-bearing females remain aggressive for a day or more after the onset of the cold.

It follows, therefore, that a limit of ten bass, or

Dr. F. A. Paschek with legendary lunker bearing Tag No. 35 from one of Ciuffa's lakes. This fish, weighing six and one-half pounds in this picture, has been caught and released thirteen times!

any fixed number, may not be a sufficient protection for quality, size-class distribution; nor are such limits a decent method for rationing harvestable poundage in tune with nature's ability to replace the removed sizes. Replacement poundage is soon characterized by more small bass and progressively fewer larger fish.

An exemplary limit for an established bass population composed of a sound standing crop of small, medium, and large fish, would be one bass twenty inches or over, one within the lengths of eighteen to sixteen inches or over, one within the lengths of eighteen to sixteen inches, three within the fifteen to thirteen-inch range, and five fish from twelve inches and under. Total protection of the inbetween sizes would provide replacements for the legal lengths taken and would facilitate enforcement to some extent. If the above limits resulted in the increase of certain classes, fishing pressure could be focused on these. And if a shortage of a class or two developed, proper regulations

could be established to control the matter. With new lakes, where most of the bass first fall within one or two strong size-classes, regulations should provide for the culling of some, but never with most of the long-standing, easy-out methods used today.

A fixed length limit is a step forward but it is neither permanent nor enough. At some time within the duration of such regulation, bass under the legal size would be stock-piled; these would eventually consume most of the available food in their "bite size."

Meanwhile, fishermen would be following another part of this regulation: removing those fish that are within and larger than the legal length. The stock-piled smaller fish would not recruit into the legal sizes as fast as the legal lengths were removed. The end becomes inevitable: slow-growing small bass; other species, whose habits are detrimental to bass propagation, increasing; and finally a uniform, mediocre brand of bass fishing.

Most of the current practices permit the bass-population pyramid to end up with its top side, the quality side, cut off entirely. On the other hand, regulations that would protect and ration the quality sizes, permitting harvest in proportion to the density of size and age-classes, would be like evenly slicing off the sides of the pyramid; bigger fish, which exist in smaller numbers, would be harvested in smaller numbers, within a proportionately safe poundage per acre. The fishery managers can and must establish such quality regulations soon, and we must stand ready to help finance the added cost, if any.

In addition to control of size-class harvest, certain areas of large impoundments should be zoned off as catch-and-release waters. Large areas of this type would reduce the total area of the lake used for the harvest of bass, thus establishing rearing grounds to replenish the catch-and-take sections; at the same time, they would create a smaller man-hour harvest per acre for the total lake. Large catch-and-release areas would undoubtedly provide holding sections for some of the older, larger bass that I suspect prefer a rather small range if cover and food are available; we all know of large lunkers repeatedly hooked within very small spaces, even on large bodies of water, throughout the year.

I'm positive that once bass fishermen know what real lunker-catching could be like—mixed with an assortment and quantity of medium-size fish—a new fishing philosophy will take over the sport. This has already happened among our friends, cooperators, and even some former meat-fishermen who probably always loved the joy of *catching* bass more than anything else.

Hopefully, our new generations will grow up in a true bass-for-sport culture—like that in which my children and those of my fishing friends have been raised. Youngsters in our group shudder at the thought of keeping a lunker, yet understand when it is necessary to harvest the more abundant classes in order to maintain good fishing. And bass in our catch-and-release waters are providing excellent sport for the dedicated fishermen as well as for their youngsters. Where else can a five-year-old like my grandson, Matthew, hook into bass and learn the reflexes required for good fishing at such a tender age? When I proudly watch him reeling in a bass I can't help thinking of the many community lakes, and private ponds and lakes, throughout the country where other youngsters could also enjoy quality fishing—if these waters had not been ruined by the fathers and other relatives of these young, eager sport-fishermen.

Dr. Paschek scores on topwater plug in cold spring weather during a super-aggressive period of bass behavior.

Proper Techniques for Tagging and Releasing

Over twenty years of catching, tagging, and releasing has taught me how tough bass can be. Our catch-and-release fish have been hooked repeatedly by both treble and single-hooked lures. Though single-hook lures are better, it was surprising how often some fish would be taken and successfully released on both types over the years.

The one sour factor in fish-tagging is the fact that bass eventually break the upper-jawbone where the jaw tag has been affixed, or in time reject other kinds of tags. In placing monel bands on the upper jaw, care must be taken to leave some space between the flesh and the band, but the tag must not be so small that when such space is allowed, the butt-ends of the tag do not touch. It is better to use the correct size or a larger tag and to overlap the ends, taking care to keep them snugly against each other, and to establish the space between flesh and metal so that room for growth and water is provided. In recent years I've used yellow plastic legbands, normally used for bird banding, with reasonable success. Care must be taken to assure that the spiral band is rolled onto the lip without overstraining the plastic; then you should work it with your fingers into a snug roll before releasing the fish.

Regardless of how carefully these tags are placed, if the fish is not recaptured at least once a season—to permit examination for erosion at the tag site, so that the tag may be removed and placed on the opposite upper jaw, if necessary—the upper jaw will eventually erode and break. Some bass, however, carry a tag on the same side for several years without need of replacement to the other jaw.

Of all the tags I experimented with, I had the

Jim Saettele and evening lunker hooked on Jitterbug on a catch-and-release lake.

best returns with the plastic band and monel band jaw tags. In about two thousand taggings, both on catch-and-release and on public impoundments, I used the monel band, the plastic spiral bird leg band, the gill-plate tag, and the dorsal-type plastic-tube tag. Bass tagged with the gill-plate or tube insert were also tagged with a jaw tag. Most of the fish that were later brought to the boat still had the jaw tag, but most had rejected the tube type from between their dorsal bones, or the gill-plate

tag. All bass that carried a jaw tag at least two seasons had rejected both the dorsal tube tag and the gill-plate tag.

It is obvious that anything inserted into the flesh of fish, man, or beast will be rejected due to possible infection, festering, or other body processes. The best method is probably some form of tatooing, which fisheries biologists should work on.

The Swallowed-hook Myth

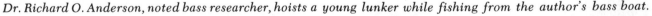

When a bass swallows a lure—as it may do when caught on a soft plastic worm—it will be gut-hooked. A healthy bass, sixteen inches or over, has better than a two-to-one chance of survival *if* the hook is removed. With gut-hooked fish, the mortality rate is about 95 percent if the hook is left in the stomach and the fish is then released. The old tale that a swallowed hook will dissolve, and the fish survive, is just that—an old tale.

I have compiled records of bass that had been gut-hooked, listing tag numbers of those that had the hook removed and those that had the hook left in them. Most of the larger fish that had the hook removed were caught again at a later date, full of fight and apparently healed. Most of those that had the hook left in the stomach were found dead and afloat. This experience has been repeated many times over the past twenty years; it leaves no doubt in my mind about the heavy mortality rate when a hook is left in the fish. I am shocked that some conservation departments still advise the public to cut the line and release the fish with the hook still in its stomach. I have witnessed caged bass purposely gut-hooked, then left with the hook either embedded or removed. *One hundred percent* of the bass left with the hook in them were dead within several days to two weeks. Sixty percent of those from which the hook had been removed survived. These bass were twelve to thir-teen inches; larger fish would have had a better chance of survival.

Gill-hooked bass also survive, but the percentage of survival is about 5 percent of the larger fish so injured and less than 1 percent of those under thirteen inches. The degree of damage was chiefly what determined whether they would survive or perish.

In catch-and-release fishing you must learn to remove a swallowed hook quickly, properly, carefully. The best method is to pull on the line with one hand, until the hook point is exposed, including the entire barb. Then, while still holding the line tight and the lower jaw with the same hand (this requires practice but it *can* be done), reach under the gill cover and between the gills with good, long-nosed pliers and press the barb tight to the shank. Then, still holding the line taut, reach into the mouth and grasp the hook eyelet and part of the shank with the long-nose pliers, and push in toward the stomach until the point leaves the entry hole. Continue to push gently further down the "throat," while holding the fish by the lower jaw, then turn 90° with the pliers (which are still holding the hook), move to one side, then lift out the hook. Two people can perform this feat better than one, but with some practice I managed to do it alone when needed.

Dr. Richard O. Anderson, noted bass researcher, hoists a young lunker while fishing from the author's bass boat.

Author Tony Ciuffa and a typical catch-and-release lunker on a rainy day.

Keeping Track of Old Friends

You can learn a lot about bass and their behavior by tagging and keeping the right records. The biggest problem is that one needs a well-guarded lake to prevent the loss of fine specimens to other fishermen; still, I have recaptured some tagged bass on public lakes near isolated, hard-to-fish structures. Many of my tagged lunkers revealed marvelous secrets. A few demonstrated that they had an uncanny preference for a particular lure, if presented in a certain fashion. Some of the largest

fish—one was ten and a half pounds on its last capture—preferred getting caught either in the early spring when the waters began warming or on a hot summer night. My fishing partners and I still talk about several of these, calling them by their number, like "Old 35," "A92," "A14360," and so forth.

Before it disappeared, "Old 35" fell prey thirteen times in several years, and left evidence each time of its preference for certain lures and cover.

Tony's son Robert shows a 16-incher to another bass-budding Ciuffa, Tony's grandson Matthew.

This lunker, like many others, may have been caught more than thirteen times on record, but due to the fact that several of the specimen lunkers were caught with a broken upper jaw, right at the location where the jaw bands are usually placed, the sequence of recorded captures for these was lost forever. It is obvious that those previously tagged fish, bearing only the marks where a tag had been placed, could have been "Old 35."

It would have been sad for fish like these to have been removed on their first capture. They contributed so much to the quality of the sport. I have learned a hundredfold by using them, then releasing them for another day. They have also taught me where their relatives on other lakes would most likely be under many subtle and otherwise obscure conditions.

When fishermen grow wise enough, there will be more of that—and more big bass for everyone, too. Catch-and-release is our best chance to build and preserve quality bass fishing.

PART SIX

FIRESIDE BASSING

Somewhere along the way I got into the habit of saving my best fishing books for winter reading. When the sleet is rattling in the bare branches, and fishing seems light years away, I really enjoy sinking into my favorite fireside chair with some old or new friend of a book and going fishing in my head.

But, darn it, I've had one complaint all along. Almost all hardcover books of fishing stories are about trout, saltwater, or big-game fishing. My bass has been confined to how-to books and magazine articles.

That's why putting this section together was such a pleasure. I've always wanted a great big chunk of just plain old bassing tales, with people who seem real and days on the water I can share through print.

I hope you enjoy these as much as I liked digging them up. They're among the very best I know.

27

Striped Bass and Southern Solitude

ELLINGTON WHITE

The best way to fish is alone. The best time to fish is the fall. Believing these simple truths to be self-evident, I set out alone each fall to fish the rivers and creeks that flow out of Virginia into the Chesapeake Bay. It is a good time of year all around. Everybody else in the world is watching a football game. Leaves cover the roadside beer cans, and the traffic is light. Whenever a car appears pulling a boat, I know it is bound for the city, not the sea, for the water skiers have beached their skis and skin divers have taken up bowling. Praise the fall.

In truth, fishermen should do as fish do in the summer—lie low. We should give the beaches to the sunbathers and admit that during this idle season, when the great fiber-glass fleet rules the waterways, the thing to do is haul in our lines and run for cover. Of course, we will never do this. We aren't as smart as fish. We persist in thinking that the summer is big enough for all of us— fishermen, skin divers, water skiers, the whole shebang. What a delusion.

But now it is the fall, and I am driving east on Route 33. Pine trees crowd the shoulders, and the morning sun is hot. In the Tidewater, summer and fall merge with each other so quietly that for a few weeks you need a calendar to tell where you are. Straddling two seasons, one foot in each, you feel both seasons at once.

At West Point, under a cloud of pulpmill smoke, I cross the Pamunkey and Mattaponi rivers, tributaries of the York River, which enters the bay just north of the James. All of these rivers belong to the fall in my mind, the James especially, where I once saw the fall arrive.

I had taken a boat up the river to fish for bass in the mouth of a small creek near Presque Isle Swamp, about twelve miles below Richmond. Here the James takes its time, dawdling along between odorous mud flats, mesmerizing fish and fishermen alike. It just about put me to sleep that day, I recall. After several hours I had had enough, and started back, half paddling, half drifting down the river on the outgoing tide, drowsing among the slumberous sounds of wallowing carp and turtles dropping off logs.

If was a warm day in early October. Most of the clothing I had started out in lay heaped in the bottom of the boat. I was glad the tide and I were going the same way. Farther down the river a handful of gulls was circling a row of stakes that had once supported fish-nets. The shoreline slid past, marshy and still. I drifted by a small bay and across a gravel bar. By this time the gulls were wheeling overhead. The fog lifted just enough for me to catch the glimmerings of an idea, something about gulls following stripers. . . . Oh, nonsense, I thought. Nevertheless, there was the rod resting against the middle seat. All I had to do was pick it up. Why not? I cast into the shore. It was an idle cast and went farther than I had intended it to, landing among a drift of leaves and pine needles. The surface plug bobbed a few times. The leaves bulged and then blew open. It was an astonishing moment. I had often driven hundreds of miles chasing stripers up and down the eastern seaboard, and here I had *drifted* into a school of them. Later I visualized our paths as two crooked lines, wobbling all over the river, and somehow miraculously bisecting under a flock of gulls. In ten minutes it was all over. We had drifted apart, and without a motor I had no way of following them. It didn't matter, though. I had four of them, all about six pounds, flopping on top of my clothes.

I don't know of any fish that gives as much pleasure to as many fishermen as the ubiquitous striper. He may not be as dazzling as a bonefish or as much a roughneck as a snook, but he covers more ground than these fish do and so comes into contact with more people. There is nothing provincial about him, either. He can get along in fresh water just as well as he can in salt water, river water as well as ocean water, shallow water or deep water—it's all the same to him. People fish for him in boats, on banks, in the surf or by wading. They use trolling rods, boat rods, casting rods, spinning rods, fly rods and every kind of bait made—wood, plastic, feathered and live. And he survives them all. Praise the striper, I thought, looking at my four, the most democratic fish that swims.

By the time I reached the landing, the temperature had dropped sharply. A chill wind swept across the river. I climbed back into my clothes and walked home smelling of fish. That was six years ago. The sweater is still with me, as is the scent. Maybe nobody else can smell it, after tons of mothballs and innumerable dry cleanings, but I was putting the sweater in the car this morning, prior to setting off down Route 33, and caught a whiff of it again, every bit as strong as that day I passed through a school of stripers.

Stutts Creek, my destination, is one of many tidal creeks found along the Virginia side of the Chesapeake Bay. Itself a branch of the bay, it sprouts still other branches and ends up looking on a map like a tree that has fallen into the bay's marshy fringes. Once a waterway for crabbers and oystermen, it has become in recent years something of a playground as well, conveying many more svelte Chris-Crafts than lumbering work-

boats. But like playgrounds everywhere, it is crowded in the summer and all but empty during the winter.

When I fish Stutts Creek I always stay with a man who was raised on it, Norris Richardson, who runs Pine Hall, an inn for fishermen and exhausted city dwellers who drive down on the weekends from Richmond. Pine Hall is a large white house overlooking the creek from a summit of green grass. Norris runs the place as though he were not really trying to, and as a result it is one of the best-run places I know of. You have the comfortable feeling that everyone is there to relax, even the help. Norris is a small, distracted man with an inexhaustible supply of country stories, little pastoral romances about coons and possums and what happened to old Uncle So-and-so when a pail of crabs turned over in his kitchen. Listen to enough of these tales and you forget all about Vietnam and overpopulation. I always like to hear one or two before setting off up the creek. They are like steppingstones to another world.

Stutts Creek enters the bay between two islands lying off the mainland. One of these, Gwynn Island, is a well-known vacation spot, but the other, Rigby Island, is little more than an exposed sandbar. There is a channel between the islands, but elsewhere the water is shallow and marshy.

Stripers seem to regard the bay as a school they have to complete before graduating into the Atlantic Ocean. The school lasts four years. A few dropouts may tackle the ocean sooner than that, but the majority are content to wait until graduation day. Then they are ready to join the big ocean community on the outside. At least, this is what a tagging program instigated by the Atlantic States Marine Fisheries Commission indicates. The young striper just out of school tends to stay pretty close to home for the first year or so, but as his size increases so does his boldness, and off he goes to prowl the New England coast 700 miles away. In the fall he frequently returns, packing weights of twenty and thirty pounds. It is a curious fact that stripers reach the bay about the same time that alumni are arriving in Charlottesville, Virginia, to watch Mr. Jefferson's eleven take another licking, but if you think *that* homecoming is worth watching you ought to see what happens when the Old Boys get together in the bay. It's an alumni secretary's dream. Gulls throw up tents all over the place, covering the big feeds, and the campus becomes one huge thrashing contest. Before long the racket reaches the shore, and here comes a fleet of fishermen pounding out to join in the fun.

It's great sport if you like that sort of thing, and most striper fishermen do, but not caring for homecomings myself, in Charlottesville or the bay, I cut the motor and drift into the shallows behind Rigby Island. It's quieter there. You can hear the tide running through the grass. I toss out the anchor, rig up a rod, stuff my pockets with flies, climb into a pair of boots and wade off in search of a few first-graders.

Cold nights have distilled the water. Croakers, spot, crabs, nettles—all of summer's impedimenta—have been frozen out, and the once-green marsh is now the color of bronze. A line of pine trees stand on the far shore; nearer, dead limbs mark an oyster bed. Where the bay has breached Rigby Island slightly left of center, the tide crosses a sandbar and then spreads out over the marsh, dividing it into a number of small grassy clumps. The water is a hard, glinty, blue.

I have never yet caught a fish on a first cast, nor have I ever made a first cast without thinking I would catch a fish. My heart pounds, my hands shake. I tie on a white streamer, wet it with saliva so that it will sink fast, and drop it at the edge of the marsh. It crosses the tide on a series of swift jerks and returns to my feet untouched. I pick it up and cast again. By the fifteenth cast my hands are steady and my heart has resumed its normal tempo. Now begins the long haul.

Stripers like moving water, and when the tide is slack so are they. I walk along casting. Hours pass. I switch to a popping bug and try that until the marsh is brimful of water and a gold chain leads across it to where the sun is settling into a thicket of trees. Lights appear on shore. Gulls are coming in to roost on the channel markers. Soon it will be dark. I want a fish to whack the popper right out of the water, and I hold onto this hope as long as there is light. Then, when there is no more light, I return to Pine Hall.

So begins the first of many fall weekends on Stutts Creek. As the days shorten, my clothes increase. Sweaters pile up. By December I look like a woolen balloon with legs. Norris Richardson's dogs jump aside when they see me coming. Some mornings dawn fair, others overcast and wet. The best mornings are those when frost covers the ground and a brittle stillness films the creek. Coming up, the sun looks like a forest fire. The worst mornings come out of Canada on a northwest wind that wants to shred you alive, and you need more than sweaters to keep warm. Some fishermen use insulated underwear, some carry bottles, some turn on the furnace words of the English language. I resort to fantasy myself. As soon as numbness reaches the top of my waders, I wrap myself in the vision of a big striper who has gotten tired of homecoming and returned to the shallows of his youth. I see him passing through the inlet just as I am rounding the marsh directly in front of him. There was a time when he would not enter the shallows without company, but now that he has grown up the rewards of fellowship have diminished and he finds that the marsh is something of a relief after the tumult of the bay. So here he is enjoying the freedom of being alone, and here I am doing the same—smothered in wool, walking toward him. I see him nudge the grass. His tail lifts a cloud of sand, then carries him into the mouth of a small feeder creek. (In actual fact, there is such a creek, though it lies closer to Pine Hall than it does in my fantasy. I never pass it without thinking what a wonderful place it would be to catch a striper—smooth sandy bottom, tufts of grass choking the mouth, a line of pine trees to break the wind.) Once he is in the creek, however, the striper finds that the water is not as deep as it appeared to be on the outside and he starts back, cruising like a porpoise. By then I have planted a popper squarely in the middle of the opening, and when he is within sight of it I twitch the line and the popper jumps forward. You can guess the rest.

It is astonishing how much heat a scene like that can generate.

For a moment last Thanksgiving Day I thought I had caught this fish. I went out early in the morning and fished straight through until dusk. It was a cold, blustery day. The wind piled up big waves and hurled them at the shore. Casting a heavy saltwater fly rod is hard work in itself, but casting it in the wind for seven or eight hours is pure torture. In the middle of the afternoon I found three small fish, two- and three-pounders, huddled up in a pocket of deep water, but catching them had rekindled no fires, and by evening I was numb and sore all over.

Even my fantasy had quit working. The tide had just about run itself out, and so had I. I switched to a spinning rod, a less taxing instrument than a fly rod, and waded out along a point of land for a few final casts. I tossed the lure, a weighted jig, into a trench the tide had dug between two sandbars. It was an ordinary sort of place, a place you fish because you know you should rather than because it appeals to you. I had fished the place many times before, ever since Brook Jones, a fine fisherman from Richmond, had pointed it out to me. Brook takes fish out of it all the time, but I had never had much luck with it. Today was different. The lure bounced down one wall of the trench, disappeared in deep water, then climbed up the other wall. It had just reached the top when a shadow rose off the bottom and pulled it back down. I knew it was a big fish by the size of the shadow. He lunged around in the depths for a while, then plowed off across the shallows with a second fish right behind him. Why the second fish, I don't know. Perhaps the two of them had been lying in the trench getting fat together. In any case, the follower soon veered off in the direction of the channel while my fish bore straight ahead. There is nothing spectacular about the way stripers behave after they are hooked. A heavy fish simply lays into a line and bulls his way along. He's a plodder. I could have let this striper run a mile before he reached anything to break off on, but it had been a long cold day and I was taking no chances. I could plod, too. So I set a hard drag and in time wore him down the way you break horses—with sheer force.

One thing he had done was thaw me out. I could feel again. He would go eight or nine pounds, I supposed. Holding him up against the horizon, I found there was more light left in him than was left in all the sky—no fantasy fish, but a good solid striper, all the same.

Bass Convert

NICK LYONS

Though I have been publicly judged a "trout junkie," I recently acquired an addiction that may prove harder to kick: bass madness, of the smallmouth variety.

Now one can do a thing for a long time without becoming an addict; and I did not begin to fish for smallmouths last night. But some time during my misspent teens I lost my heart to those "rose moles all a-stipple upon trout that swim," and bass, perch, pickerel, pike, bluegills, crappie, and carp and every other fish I'd caught in freshwater has played a slow second to them ever since. Until last year—when the accumulation of twenty years of random bass fishing, whenever there were no trout, suddenly came to a fever pitch.

The first smallmouths I caught were in a feeder creek that emptied into a reservoir I fished for trout in early April. I was thirteen, and had come up from the city by train, alone, and had fished ten hours without so much as a tap. Then, in rapid succession, on night crawlers, I caught three hard-battling fish, about fourteen or fifteen inches apiece, in the creek. I'd never seen such fish before and, in my city-bred ignorance, called them "green trout"—though they fought harder for their size than any trout I've ever taken. A rather gruff warden advised me what they were, and became much more genial when the fish, released from my stringer, miraculously managed to swim feebly away. The bass season started in three months.

I also caught good smallmouths in the Ten Mile River, near Wingdale, New York, in the late summer and early fall, again while fishing for trout. Mort Seaman and I would cast the lethal little C. P. Swing across and slightly upstream, let it swing down with the current, jerk and jiggle it a few times, letting it flutter there, fall back, dart up again, and then retrieve. There'd be a sharp twitch—usually while the spinner fluttered—and then a tug, and the line would quickly angle to the surface and the fish was up and out and shaking.

"Got one?"

"Bass"—with a certain disgruntled, sinking of the voice. "Only a bass."

Though they fought hard, they were always a disappointment: I was fishing, I figured, not for bigger or stronger game but for fairer. Imperceptibly, I was becoming not only a trout addict but, worse, a trout snob.

The only times I deliberately fished for smallmouths were on trips to the Thousand Islands near Alexandria Bay with Mort and his father. We usually went in October, when the trout season was over. For anyone, like me, glued to the grey city but loving woods and particularly waters passionately, those trips were a special joy. We'd fish with a well-weathered, knowledgeable old guide, and I can still see him standing at the prow, with baseball cap, grey chino pants and shirt, his hand on the steering rod, squinting into the spray as the long grey boat swept across the choppy waters of the St. Lawrence, its prow dipping and rising as he steered a sure course toward a passage between two islands. Sometimes we'd fish our largest shiners for northern pike in the thin green weeds along some island's shore. It was wild to see those four-inch shiners come back with four or five teeth gashes along their sides, but even the six-pounders seemed sluggish: the guide didn't like pike and, though they were larger, neither did we. Nor, particularly, did we like drifting certain channels for largemouths, which also ran larger. We'd come for smallmouths and that's what we wanted most.

There was a special hole—called, as I remember, Dick's Dock—and every time we approached it during the years we went to the St. Lawrence, my heart would begin to pound and flutter. The spot had gotten its name from an abandoned wooden dock that served as the principal marker for a dropoff thirty yards from shore. The guide would bring the boat in close to shore and then, working the anchor along the bottom, he would move us out on a line with a lighthouse on the opposite hill until the anchor suddenly fell free and dropped twenty-five feet. In October, when the winds blew chill and the trees had turned flaming orange and red, the smallmouths would school up just below the ledge off Dick's Dock. We always had good luck there, every time we tried it—even, years later, when Mort and I went back alone.

We'd take a live shiner from the bait well, hook it firmly through the lips, and cast it over, using two or three heavy split shot for weight. You didn't have to do much more than wait, and now and then lift up lightly to make sure you weren't hooked on the bottom. Sometimes the bass would take when you lifted.

Thump. Thump. Thump. You could feel the bass taking with steady tugs, deep in forty-five feet of water, and then you counted six or seven, gave the fish several feet of line, and struck hard. You didn't have to do much to induce the bite, but hooking them was something of a problem. You either had the touch or you didn't. You couldn't explain it to someone else. Mort's father got plenty of strikes but he caught far fewer fish than Mort or myself: we'd been born to it.

If it was a good fish, you could not turn it, did not dare to, but heard the line pull out against the drag on your spinning reel even as you reeled. Then the fish would begin to angle up toward the surface, thirty, maybe forty feet from the boat, and the guide would say, "He's a big 'un, all right. Don' try'n turn him now. Let him jump four, maybe five times. Keep that line taut!"

And up the fish would go—bright green and leaping fiercely, with sky hooks, hanging and twisting and then falling back with a crash. Two more jumps. Then another. And then you'd settle into the happy work of edging him always closer, closer to the boat and the guide's ridiculously large—but helpful—boat net.

Sometimes the fish would run to four or five pounds. Mostly they'd be two or three—but never weak-willed.

Mort and I even had a special handshake that represented that special *thump, thump, thump*; we'd use it when we met, even, eventually, in mixed company, and we still use it today, twenty-five years later. It is an emblem.

We enjoyed those long brisk days on the St. Lawrence, those memorable meals at a Canadian farmhouse—·with endless platters of chicken and steak followed by homemade blueberry pie topped with fresh strawberry ice-cream. And we enjoyed and later often talked about the fine fishing we'd had. But after a trip or two by ourselves, we never went back. Not in all those years. Mort found the lure of the salt and the size and gameness of stripers, bluefish, bonefish, and tarpon too alluring. Who could blame him? And I lost my heart to the long rod, a box of feathers, and the elusive trout. Who, I thought, could blame *me*? I was having more fun than ever—and isn't that what we all go out for, anyway?

Then, last August, I visited some close friends in Maine—not particularly to fish, though, as always, I had a fly rod tucked in with my luggage, just in case. They arranged for me to spend three days at Ed Musson's deer camp on a little island in

Great Pond, near Aurora, and for three days all thought of trout vanished. To be sure, I asked about trout first, but Ricky, Ed's young son, said the lake got too warm and you could only catch trout in the spring; but he'd caught a four-pound smallmouth on a frog just the other day and I might possibly get some on my fly rod in the evenings or early mornings when they came in near the lily pads. If I had a mind to.

I did.

I'd never caught a smallmouth on a popper, though I'd taken bluegills that way. It was worth a try.

I'd never been to Maine and I looked long before I began to fish. This was a different world. The water was auburn with tannic acid seepage from the woods. Somewhere across the flat little lake, a loon cried long and shrill. From the back of the island, you could see neither house nor telephone pole, only a broad marsh and pine and hemlock and oak. The place was lousy with black flies. Were you to take those away, I'd as well be on Great Pond for a week as any hallowed trout stream. It was still and magical and wild.

I discovered that first afternoon that there is a different, slower rhythm required for bass-bugging than for dry-fly fishing; the added weight of the bug jerked the line and leader awkwardly. The first adjustment I made proved a sound one: I reduced the length and also the tippet size of my leader, from over ten feet and 4X to eight feet and 1X. The difference immediately changed the zig-zag verticles I'd been throwing; it also proved no deterent to the bass. I've since gone to seven feet and 0X, which gives me even better control. The bass don't seem to mind.

I also cut two feet from the end of my double-taper, which further improved my casting. Now, using the 5-weight glass rod I'd brought along, I began to cast comfortably, waiting that extra second for the slower bug to straighten the line behind me, then pushing the line forward with more deliberation.

One's first bass on a popping bug is a memorable shock.

I'd begun my serious fishing on Great Pond about seven o'clock, after spending the afternoon on shore, fussing with my equipment. I kept the rowboat casting distance from the edge of the lily pads and let it drift slowly down their length, casting in and retrieving with short upward jerks of the rod that made the bug ploop enticingly. Sometimes I dipped the oar to turn the boat

slightly but the lake was placid and my movement never more than a touch. I knew I was too early. Ricky had said the fish didn't come in until the sun went down, and he looked like a young man who knew what-of he spoke. I didn't get my first strike, a short, until after eight o'clock. Suddenly the water boiled behind the bug, I struck back ferociously, and nearly put the #2 hook in my right eye.

The size of the swirl set my heart to thumping. This was a brand of surface fishing for larger stakes than I'd realized. I cast another twenty, thirty times, probing the open pockets in the pads, twitching the bug, letting it rest, jiggling it, popping it loudly—trying to find the proper recipe. I was not there at the right season, but with some hard work I hoped to pick up a fish or two.

Ploop. Ploop. Rest.

Slam. The water exploded.

The fish took in an awesome swirl, jumped once, twice, then sounded. With my heavy leader I turned it before it reached the pads, then followed it with the rod as it angled past the bow of the boat and out into deep water. In a few more minutes I had it in the net, my first smallmouth on a fly: a chunky, hemlock-green hellion that, pound for pound, as Henshall insisted, outfought any other fish I'd ever had on.

For all the fight it had put up, and its dramatic rise, I was surprised the fish wasn't larger. Well, larger ones would come someday when I was better at this new game, and if they acted like this one had . . . well, this thing might be worth pursuing.

When I left Great Pond three days later, I wondered precisely what had produced such a memorable experience for me. Surely the surroundings were part of it all; smallmouths, like trout, thrive best, and are best fished for, in wild, unpolluted water. This lake was ideal. Though it was too shallow in the summer for trout and land-locks, it was ideal bass-bugging water—and no more than a handful of people fished it. When I fished in against the pads, I could see only the pines and hemlocks along the shore, the slate-grey boulders, the lighter shades of green as the water grew shallow over weed and rock—and I heard only the tuba-croaks of bullfrogs and that shrill, haunting call of loons. Except for the nasty black flies, which I forgot once I started to fish, and the fact that this was not moving water, one could want nothing fairer. The world of the lake was as mysterious and charged with life as a stream. And I enjoyed the curious mixture of lazy, languid, intensely quiet floating and casting, and the bold drum of expectation. I was all eye and ear. I watched the little bug grow alive on the surface, heard it gurgle and ploop—watched and felt and heard those chunky smallmouths explode upon it.

I took several more—not many, not every time, morning and evening, I went out: but enough. None was over two-and-a-half pounds, but each filled me.

I was hooked.

Then all that winter I readied my gear—buying hair-bugs, cork poppers, large balsa-wood poppers; bass-bug-tapered lines and leaders; even another rod, a #6 weight, to give me a bit more leverage. Though many oldtime bass fishermen recommend a 7 or 8 I managed everything I wanted to do with the 6, and enjoyed its lightness more.

Every year does not bring a trip to Maine, but I happily settled for an extended stay in the Catskills. There were trout streams—old friends—I wanted to revisit, creeks I wanted to explore. "Was there any smallmouth fishing?" I asked a number of fellow trout addicts. Several didn't know and didn't care. "Bass? Are you sinking *that* low, Lyons?" One said the lower Schoharie was worth exploring, another that the lower Esopus had some good bass. The Ashokan might be worth a try.

I tried—and it was a delight. Slowly, as the summer wore on, I found myself preferring the reservoir more and more. There were not many, but I enjoyed wading the shores, casting a long line, waiting expectantly. Each night, as I wended my way back through the skeletal trees in the dark, I carried home new lessons and new respect for this great game fish.

Where had I been?

How had I missed them all these years?

And would the passion flag or hold?

In September, a voluble doctor I knew invited me out on the reservoir in his new boat. I leaped at the chance. I'd never fished the Ashokan except from the shore; perhaps I'd take one like the monster I'd seen leaping, too far out, several nights in a row.

The day was windy and sharply chill; grey-black clouds rushed unpleasantly across the sky. We set out, me rowing, the good doctor ensconced in the back seat comfortably, trolling a Rapala the size of most trout I catch.

"That way. Toward the island!" he shouted against the wind.

The wind and the choppy waves kept carrying me further off course—right, then left. The sky grew darker.

"*That* way! Over *there*!"

"I'm trying."

"Don't you know how to row?"

I leaned forward, then pulled back with all due muscle. "I know how to row."

"It's no good out here at all," he said, shaking his head vigorously. He'd fished the lake precisely once before with his new spinning rod and his new aluminum boat. He'd always summered at the shore and fished for blues.

A fat red welt began to form on my left palm. Working against the heavy waves, my shoulders ached.

"No. No-no-no. Where are you going? *Oooops.* Had one then. I'm sure of it. They'll hit like that and let go, won' they? You're the expert. Maybe you should circle around." I began to circle. "No. Better head over to the island. The island is where they are. That way. That's where they are."

I settled into my work. I was glad to be out, as I always am, and my hour—the witching hour—would come.

"There's one. Ah-ha! Got him. I got one! See?"

I saw. A rock bass smaller than the Rapala.

Ten minutes later: "There's a good one. See!"

I saw. A thirteen-incher—ill-fated. It came straight in. Right to the top guide. Then it found itself on the bottom of the boat, with me disengaging the fifty-seven hooks. It was no use. It couldn't be turned back: that rapid trip it had just taken, the perfect plethora of hooks would, as the sage Mr. Woody Allen says, have caused "cardiac arrest in a yak."

"Ha. See how good this Rapala is? Great little lure, isn't it? Fifty times as good as that little thing you've got on. Why aren't you catching any? Ha. You're the expert."

I rowed some more. Rain began and swelled and pelted the hell out of us. The bottom of the boat filled with bilge. The doctor kept talking. "That's three, right? Three already. Some little lure, this Rapala. Why haven't you caught any?"

I dropped the oars and made two hasty casts into the heavy wind, my first of the day. I hadn't been aware that I was in the Bassin' Man's Olympics. The casts went about ten feet.

"Not much you can do with that rod, is there?"

I put the long rod down carefully and took up my oars again. I was soaked and freezing and the rain came in with greater and greater rushes.

Suddenly the doctor bellowed like a moose: "WHERE ARE YOU GOING? YOU'LL BREAK MY LINE!"

Behind the boat, his line stretched out high and far.

"You've hooked me onto something," he protested, shaking his head. "Back up. Back up. BACK UP QUICK!"

I obediently backed a few feet. "You sure it's hung up?"

"DAMMIT. What *else*?" He was livid. He did not want to lose his Rapala.

What else was soon apparent. A gigantic—I mean, absurdly huge, fat, and bronze-green—smallmouth, on what must have been atomic power, raised itself a foot up out of the water, sloshed and fumbled, felt the fifty-seven hooks, thrashed with a swirl larger than a garbage can thrown in, and took the Rapala away with it to munch for dinner.

The doctor sat stone silent for a moment.

Then he slammed his rod down on the water.

Then he shook his head.

An hour later and the rains had stopped and it was dark and we were drifting close to the spot where he beached the boat. The water was glassy below the swirling mist. I could barely make out the bug chugging, plooping along the surface. But I could hear it. The doctor had not said a word in an hour. He had not hooked another fish. I had

taken one two-pounder and released it. In a moment another swirled at my bug, took it, lurched away, and soon found itself—in the faint reflection of the moon—having a single hook extracted from its jaw.

"Got one!" shouted the doctor.

"Great!" I said, genuinely pleased.

"Feels big!"

"Be careful with it. Don't pull too hard."

"Something's wrong."

As he reeled, the boat edged slowly toward the shore, on which the gigantic Rapala was safely hooked.

It is a new spring and the lure is still there, quite untroubled by my last day out last fall. Trout remain a delight to me, and always will. But I'll never unhook my brain from the abrupt, electric crash when a solid two-pound smallmouth takes my popper at dusk, bending my rod—and heart. I doubt, really, whether I'll fish with the good doctor again—bass snob that I am—but I'll see that reservoir this year. And instead of mooching some dry flies from Dave Whitlock this winter, I commissioned him to make me up some sinking hair-frogs, to expand my day a bit beyond dawn and dusk. I have this dream, see, about taking big ones during the day, on Hi-D line and frogs, fished very, very deep.

Perhaps there's a message in that.

Black Bass and Dark Nights
FRANK WOOLNER

In this enlightened age accomplished black bass fishermen wear jump-suits adorned with colorful tournament patches, con boats big enough to challenge salt water, and enthuse about "hawgs" hooked away down in structure. Undoubtedly a scientific angler catches more fish, and I could get all fevered and twitchy on a contest circuit. Trouble is, some of the magic would be missing.

Sportfishing is never easy to describe—indeed

it is seldom well documented because most of us are afraid to let our emotional hair down and admit to things that have nothing to do with the heft of a catch, but somehow evoke innocent romance and a mystique necessary to the psyche of man.

Few are soft-headed enough to admit this, fearing the censure of hard-hearted fellow creatures, yet I note that a lot of hair-chested outdoorsmen—carefully peering right or left to see that nobody bears witness—sigh with relief when they escape a man-swarm to commune with simple fishes and quiet waters far from the clatter of traffic and the know-all of sophisticated technology.

That's pretty hard to do today, since there are few secret places where the highway ends beyond a mountain thataway, and the little bush planes do not swing into the wind to land on lakes still doggedly tenanted by Indians—who need air-freighted petrol to feed the outboard motors on their aluminum birchbarks.

There is a way, though, and perhaps I betray a scattering of colleagues by advising a nighttime expedition. After sunset the old and relatively silent wilderness returns to marginal ponds lying almost in the flare path of metropolitan neon light and the amplified uproar of that which is now solemnly referred to as music. You too, as the come-on ads declare, can be a loner.

I offer a case history, mine—and it began because I was fretful and vaguely discontented on a humid night when moths were vainly assaulting an office window. Gradually, or maybe it was just an accumulation of memories, I realized that June was phasing out—so I called my brother, Jack, who is now some sort of a satrap in ecological public relations for the State of Massachusetts, and I said unto him: "Let's go fishing!"

He thought that was a fine idea, undoubtedly figuring stripers or blues—maybe white marlin on a coming weekend. "Sure," he said. "When?"

"If my watch is right," I told him, "the season on black bass gets under way two hours from now, at midnight, I'll pick you up and we'll start at the Boston Ice House."

Jack humors me, undoubtedly sure that I am as "tharn" (crazy) as the Rabbits in Richard Adams' lovely novel, *Watership Down*. After a moment of silence he said, quietly: "The Massachusetts' season on black bass began in mid-April."

About then I heard a little intake of breath and knew that he'd remembered. "Okay, swing by. I can stand another opening day, even if it's in the middle of the night!"

Right here I'd better explain two things. There was a time, in Massachusetts, when the bass fishing season actually began on July 1st, a time of year when sunset brought no chill and a man could "wade wet," soft mud seeping through tennis shoes, almost alone and world-forgotten in warm darkness if he could dismiss the distant wail of a train's whistle and adjust to heat lightning

over black jungle foliage. Now bronzebacks become legal in mid-April, just before dawn, and it's cold and the fish are sluggish and everyone seeks trout that are quite as numbed by an omnipresent northeast wind and frigid temperatures.

Second, the "Boston Ice House" is—and has been for about forty years—just a location at the southern extremity of Lake Quinsigamond in the township of Shrewsbury, Massachusetts. There *was* an icehouse, prior to refrigeration in every household, and the brave, bronzed boys of the 30's used to dive off its deteriorating roof before a lightning bolt turned the thing into an inferno and tumbled its charred timbers into Quinsigamond. A few cement pilings remained, and they are still there, and still the questing bronzebacks prowl on summer nights.

In our latitude, July 1st was a logical zero-hour for bass. We synchronized our watches and made no cast until the witching hour of midnight, and then it was every man (and fish) for himself. This was almost a holy rite.

My four-wheel drive Blazer found a few of the pot-holes that had jarred an ancient Model-A, yet there was little change—if you could forget the lights of an industrial complex southward and the steady rumble of traffic on a main artery across our direct front, a mile away. Water still lapped at a weedy gravel beach and the pilings jutted dimly, like latter-day facsimiles of a druid shrine called Stonehenge.

Kipling wrote: "Smells are surer than sights or sounds to make the heartstrings crack," and here it was! Shoreside vegetation breathes during long night hours. Gasses bubble out of pad beds, a scent just bordering the good side of revulsion—saved by streams of perfume from burgeoning sweet flag. Only one thing was missing: we should have carried citronella as an insect repellent. It smells lots better than the modern concoctions.

Our rods on this safari were tubular fiberglass and graphite, hardly a major advantage over the maple shafts, split bamboo, solid steel and tubular steel of yesterday. The reels were better, of course, still quadruple multipliers, descendants of the classic Meeks that came out of Kentucky, but fitted with freespool, smooth star drags and anti-reverse locks. Prior to World War Two the winches would have been Shakespeare Criterions or Pflueger Nobbys with red glass end bearings. Those of us who fancied our talents removed level-wind worn gears to ensure greater distance in casting. After all, a man's thumb could be trained to level-wind almost instinctively. Knowing better, I still find that left thumb moving back and forth like a metronome.

Cowardly at middle age, we wore waders instead of tennis shoes—perhaps proof of herd-thinking since this water shelved very gradually. The old floating island was gone, but a night heron quawked in passage overhead. Stars glittered in a blue-black zenith. We didn't talk much, almost as though conversation might profane a brooding silence. It was sweet music to hear the long, expiring sigh of a reel and the distant plop of a surface plug dropping in.

They were the old plugs, incidentally, chosen for the same reason that this trip was swiftly planned as a return. In those somnolent years prior to Hitler's war we swore by such nonpareils as the Heddon Blue-Nose, the Woodpecker, the Shakespeare Mouse, later the Jitterbug. All were surface swimmers or commotion types: sometimes we went to Creek Chub's immortal Pikie Minnow, but not often because it was a sub-surface job, thought better by day than by night.

Good plugs in that time slot sold for something less than a dollar, and dollars weren't easy to attain. We often whittled our own copies and I remembered a midnight when I shucked off all clothes and swam to retrieve a home-made version of the Mouse ineptly snagged on a stump. None of my colleagues thought *that* very unusual, although they urged me to wait until they'd worked the area.

Nothing happened and by the time luminous watch hands had crept around to 1 A.M., I suppose both of us wondered whether "Boston Ice" was a lost cause. Then, comfortably casting and retrieving, I saw Jack's plug drop an inch from a cement piling—just a little splat and widening ripples, right on target. At least he hadn't forgotten accuracy. As teen-agers we practiced in the back yard, unhappy unless a five-eighth ounce weight went into a felt hat at fifty feet.

Now the widening ripples disappeared and I knew he was waiting for a few seconds before twitching the lure and starting it back. Jack grunted just before spray flew and a dark, writhing shape shattered the mirror. In spite of dim starlight, the white belly of this largemouth was clearly seen as it wallowed and swapped ends.

After a while there was more splashing close to shore, and I crunched down to bear witness. Jack has caught a lot of big seagoing fish, and just as many fresh water trophies, but for some strange reason his voice broke a little.

"It'll go three pounds, anyway! Boy, did he ever take that Blue-Nose!"

A penlight's thin beam caressed the gasping trophy, and there was the well remembered scent again—a clean smell, musky and a little fishy, but *clean* fishy. My brother removed a large, neatly folded bandana from a trousers pocket, used it in his left hand to hold the bass rigid, and carefully removed the plug from its face. Just as gently he slid the fish back into the water and watched it swim away.

"Got your handkerchief all slimey," I commented.

"Yeah, got a fish too," he grinned.

They came hard that night, but there were times in the golden era when you couldn't buy one, so it was nothing new. Finally I nailed a two pounder on a Jitterbug, and lost one that must have weighed five. When I lose a fish it's always a lunker.

Sounds prosaic, I know, since most fishing tales are punctuated by screaming reels, leaping monsters and big strings—but it was pleasant to mooch along, casting rhythmically, picking out the odd backlash. I think I missed the big one because I was recalling other nights, other places.

For example, a rice paddy reservoir near Alexandria, Louisiana, where the folks in Cajun parishes still speak Evangeline's tongue. It was saucer-eyed adventure to go in well before dawn, sliding along in a pirogue while the hooty-owls quavered and Spanish moss trailed gray lace. There were cows feeding brisket-deep in a fragrant backwater, and each loomed up like some prehistoric monster in the gloom.

Bass were there too, largemouths running four to five pounds, with a few heavier. They came charging out of little openings in the jungle brush to pounce on surface plugs, creaming the dark water and thrashing wildly. Unfortunately the eastern sky paled too soon and dawn was born, and it was all sub-surface work with a variety of lures. Grand sport, but not the same since the magic of a shrouded world had disappeared. Daylight curbs racing imaginations.

Or maybe I was thinking of Florida, up in the citrus country where a trusting magazine editor had sent me to report the amazing productivity of those tropical ponds that are more jungle than water. For a week we'd pushed through beds of hyacinth, tall grass and channels kept open by questing bass boats. Every hole had its complement of largemouths, but none were very heroic and a majority of outdoor publications want photos of pot-bellied monsters to prove a chronicler honest. Maybe I came close to qualifying for a Seminole stake-out in the Everglades by mentioning that I could catch fish in the shadow of Boston.

Howard "Charley" Anderson, now an honest resident of Marathon in the Keys, was then a public relations slave for the Florida Game and Fish Commission. One evening, over glasses of something tinkly, Charley said, "we might catch a few after dark" and I hit that lure as avidly as the tiddlers we'd been tonguing.

So ol' Chas—we were both young guys at the time—"got holt" of a local expert who was crazy enough to cruise the 'gator holes after sunset. Friends should not assume that this operation entailed any danger, simply that there were plenty of bass under the sun—so it took a Rebel with imagination to brave the bugs of the dark hours with a damn-Yankee in tow.

We all piled into an asthmatic pick-up truck with the Confederate guts to haul itself through fords that kept our feet elevated over the floorboards, and we went in to prospect a half-dozen cricks and deadwaters lit only by stars burning overhead. Once again, with the added delight of listening to my companions' voices—soft and drawley and laced with the idiom of the Deep South—it was homecoming.

There were mosquitoes galore, a thing Sunshine State flacks hate to admit, but you'll make their acquaintance any time a journey into the back country is necessary. There was one little alligator that came off a sloping bank like a scrambling jet fighter to hit the water spread-eagled. A wild 'gator can run like hell, a thing rarely appreciated by fearful northerners, but they are no menace to mankind.

That wonderful night we swatted mosquitoes and caught a lot of bass, in that order. Insects stridulated and birds unknown to me serenaded the darkness. A Glove Plug, one of the oldest good ones in existence, seemed a secret weapon—and the fire-eyed largemouths walloped it. There were none of the storied record-breakers, yet most weighed more than daylight conquests. They fought well. I have never seen much difference in the fury of a southern largemouth and a Yankee specimen. Maybe we make comparisons based on the nonsense of provincialism.

This operation ended at dawn when the anhingas had begun to dry their wings. The local guide insisted that we go back to his digs for a breakfast of fresh mullet, hush-puppies and cabbage palm. It was better than ham and eggs—better even than the southern grits I love. And maybe I'm truly out of my cotton-pickin', but I am one bluebelly who enjoys the life style of the South and come back to New England drawling "How y'all" to astonished neighbors.

In this adventure I hadn't toted a strobe-lighted camera and I never wrote about the sidebar. My editor didn't want that sort of stuff, because people are afraid of the dark, and snakes, and alligators, and all that baloney. He knew that night was best, but his readers wanted daytime heroics. You'd be surprised how much good reporting is choked off because it is not current faddism. People are afraid of things that go bump in the night: they ought to learn better. Night, as a Pennsylvania Dutchman might say, is nice.

It doesn't have to be tropical either. Away up at Maine's Big Lake, head of the St. Croix Flowage, four of us outboarded into the vicinity of White Island at sunset. We'd spent a day on West Grand, a landlocked salmon haven in that state's Washington County, and we were sort of sunburned. A local's words were enough: he said that smallmouth bass were plentiful, so we gulped our supper and climbed into a pair of tin boats.

Mosquitoes were there in clouds, particularly close to the island where they must have bent shoreside brush with body-weight, but we had spray cans of repellent and wore light foul-weather parkas. It wouldn't be fair to say that each cast brought a determined stroke, but I guess there'd be no harm in saying—every other cast. The barred warriors were plentiful and each had a yen for aerobatics. They ran to an average two pounds, with a few in excess of four, and we kept not one.

After a while visibility improved and we took time to admire a lopsided moon, not quite full, but slowly shedding the shadow of earth. At least the mosquitoes seemed to think that brilliance threatening, and so did the bass: they became selective and there were periods of doldrums.

Back at camp, a log cabin complex nestled close to the Big Lake end of Grand Lake Stream, owner Walter Elliott was still up and moseying around the premises. He asked how we'd done and we admitted to catching a few, and he looked in the boat and declared, "See you didn't keep none."

One of us said "nope," laconically because nobody'd understand you in Maine if you got talky, and we all went to our respective beds bemused by the humid night and the furious bass and a slice of life hard to forget.

Arnold Laine, then a rod and line commercial

striped bass fisherman on Cape Cod (thoroughly enjoying a sabattical in Maine) said sleepily, apropos of nothing: "It's about half-tide now; you can tell by the moon."

I don't think he was yearning for great stripers in the clashing rips, because he was full of little smallmouths shattering the ebony surface of a Down-East lake, shaking their heads, making a case for levitation. I figure Arnold drifted off to sleep with a smile on his Finnish kisser, perhaps counting the times a brown bird on a river bank whipped poor Will.

You will not hold it against me if I admit something private? I prefer night bass when they are stalked in marginal ponds close to metropolis, the places too often referred to as "fished-out." After the bathers and water-ski athletes repair to their walled cocoons, a blessed peace descends and the bronzebacks go hunting in shoreside shallows. An angler has it all to himself. Well, nearly all.

There are occasional lads and lasses, dreaming along in the warm darkness, hand in hand and fishing for other game. Music, wafted across a still water and muted by distance, is curiously soporific. There is much more visibility than a daytime angler would believe, starshine and reflection from cumulous cloud, or maybe a sickle moon, horns up to catch a star.

Man alone in the deep night feels ancient emotions and there is nobody around to make snide remarks. Somehow a muskrat etching a vee of silver across a surface film is precisely right, as are the stertorous voices of bullfrogs and maybe a contented chuckling of black ducks back in the pickerel weed. Up north a loon is sure to wail, the mad, exultant laughter of the far places—and if you are a far-out nut like me you will always answer, and the loon will trade scream for scream.

Black bass are creatures of the night, owl-eyed aquatic tigers. Now an angler must cast almost instinctively, although that's a bad word since you know where a stump is positioned and must place a plug in its darker-than-dark shadow. It is possible to do this on a very black night, having prospected the ground, and often it will be just as

profitable to work a bathing beach or a dockline where the cruising predators prowl.

This sport is far from a journey into the unknown, and yet there is something of mystery involved. We may protest, thee and me, but we are all a little afraid of the dark. For man to be all alone is adventure in itself. The night is all-enfolding and the stars peer down. Far-away commerce and music is somehow disembodied, a voice from a world remote.

I say that a black bass in the night is something very special: he takes a surface lure in a bombburst of spray—and that is easily seen unless you have destroyed night vision with too much artificial light. He thrashes on the surface and makes reel-protesting runs. At the last he comes to you, to hand or net on the beach—and his eyes will glow under a flashlight's beam. He is completely wild and untamed and beautiful, too good to kill, so you slip the hooks free and let him scull back into the dim corridors of night.

Is this better than structure fishing for tournament acclaim? I don't know, and I am not about to castigate competitors. Yet I hold that there are things beyond perfection, methods that may not be most productive, but a way of life for those of us who count memories better than the concrete evidence of success. What's better than a nice fish going free after a stirring battle?

Give me the scent of sweet flag and citronella, the chance of encountering a frightened little alligator in Florida, owls hooting over a Cajun marsh, the mosquitoes and no-see-ums on a northern lake populated by crazy loons.

Nowhere is that feeling of communion with an aboriginal past so strong: night itself, deep and luminous, peopled by forgotten ghosts: the *feel* of it, casting and retrieving, dreaming a lure along in a wash of black and silver—the close-quarter combat under old stars.

Where black bass are concerned, I favor a midnight opening—the hands of a wrist watch clasped, praying to Red Gods—and then the long, expiring sigh of a reel's spool and the little, liquid chunk of a plug going in.

Bottoms Up

GENE HILL

I have read that John Woods, chief of the Fisheries Division of Florida, had discovered that bourbon obscures fish-frightening human odor. I don't know Mr. Woods personally, but I do know several fairly well-thought-of scientists, and while they might admire this "discovery" they would assuredly question his methods. His laboratory technique and the consequences are what capture my imagination.

Why bourbon? Or why only bourbon? Did Mr. Woods similarly try blended scotch whiskey, rye, wine, beer, brandy and gin? What about that old bass-fishing standby, corn liquor? How about applejack? Hard cider? And now, what kind of bourbon? Sour mash? Straight whiskies, blended bourbon, Kentucky bourbon, Tennessee bourbon, or Virginia bourbon?

I further must assume that Mr. Woods, though he may know Florida bass fishing down to its common fractions, does not know Florida bass fishermen. I am fortunate enough to know several—and telling them that bourbon makes bass feel secure in their presence, is like telling them that you just caught two 15-pound fish on a plug. Whereupon fishermen would endanger your life if you didn't tell them what make plug, what size, what retrieve, what color and so on.

Every Florida bass fisherman (let's just say every bass fisherman and not single out Florida) has several hundred lures—that's just types, I'm not counting color and size variations. Nor am I adding plastic worms, pork rinds, flies, popping bugs, jigs and live bait rigs. I want to be conservative and believable. You go on and tell a bass fisherman that using bourbon will help him catch more bass, and you'd better either complete the sentence you started or stand back.

I'm afraid, that in the short piece I read, Mr. Woods further neglected to say how this bourbon was to be used by the bass fisherman. I can guess how most bass fishermen would interpret this, but I don't think that's how Mr. Woods meant it to be taken; although I see no harm in it, used judiciously.

Using the same logic he used in plowing his daughter's dowry into bass boats, motors (gas and electric) fish-finders, electronic thermometers, Lord knows how many spinning rods, casting rods, worm rods, fly rods and matching reels along with 24,000 miles of various kinds of lines, leaders and not counting swivels, snaps, sinkers and so on, what drastic steps is the average bass fisherman going to take regarding bourbon? The mind reels, if you will permit.

Did Mr. Wood try his secret bourbon method on trout or catfish? These fishermen have a constitutional right to know. Or is the work in progress? If that's so, then perhaps we should all pitch in and shorten the research time. I, for one, am perfectly willing to carry a small flagon of scotch whiskey in my trout waders, and I'm reasonably sure that if I asked similarly scientific-minded fishermen that I know to do likewise, they would, like little soldiers, to a man, *do* likewise.

I personally find drinking bourbon or scotch or whatever, less tiring to my eyes than tying No. 18 bivisibles in various shades, and would substitute one for the other occupation like a shot. (Should the type of whiskey turn out to be a greater factor in successful fishing than patterns and sizes and presentations, I would invest in a fishing tackle company or a distillery or both.)

I think we'd all like to know more about this. What about smallmouth bass? Bream? Yellow perch, walleyes and shad. Are we close to needing less than a thousand casts per muskie if we dip a Dardevle in Wild Turkey? Will gin be outlawed for Atlantic salmon along with the weighted fly? Will fish become "lure shy" if a lake is bombarded with bourboned plugs and refuse all but the rarest blends? Will white wine work better on clear days and red on cloudy days?

If this is the long-sought secret what will happen to fishing writers like our Homer Circle and Tom Paugh who, by now, are unable to do an honest days work? Will they devote their lives to research in this new field? Will tackle-box manufacturers start building portable bars. Will the hollow glass rod now serve a new function? Will plugs be made in 86-proof and 100- proof sizes?

We'll have to revise all the old jokes like "we planned to fish for a week but we ran out of whiskey and had to come home in three days." Will this create another era of bootleg stuff? Will all the guys who write on new patterns of flies and new lures and so on start experimenting with yeast, sugar and grain? Will the whiskey sour replace the Muddler Minnow? I don't really know how fish react to bourbon, personally, but I do know how a lot of fishermen react to it. And if fishermen and fish are as alike as a lot of people think—I know a lot of lakes I'm not going to fish on a summer Saturday night.

There's an old saying that goes "when the fisherman feels good—so do the fish." I once believed this had its basis on barometric pressures. Now I'm not sure. Maybe someone stumbled over the whole fish and whiskey idea some time ago.

Sometimes man's brightest ideas are out of phase with the essential character of man as a whole. Alfred Nobel invented dynamite as an aid to society and never dreamed it would be used in heavy weapons and bombs. Men first split the atom to find a source of cheap power to replace oil and coal. When Dom Perignon discovered champagne he said "I am drinking stars." He had no idea it would be used at weddings.

What will be the ultimate outcome of Mr. Woods' discovery? I don't know, I'm a bit too cynical to scoff right yet. Some men take new ideas with a grain of salt. I'll take this one with a dash of bitters.

Three Short Ones

RED SMITH

Bass from the Homosassa

Dave Newell, who operates the tourist attraction called "Nature's Giant Fish Bowl" down here in the Dazzy Vance country and encourages piscicide on the Homosassa River, reported that the black bass were massing for attack. It was midafternoon and sunny when he put two visitors in a launch and clambered in after them with his assistant, Elmo Reed, whom he had drafted as guide.

At the boat landing, needlefish raced along the surface of the water and bream swam lazily near the bottom. All over the river, which was wrinkled by a brisk wind, mullet were practicing broad jumps. The sputter of the boat's motor startled two blue heron into flight. An osprey made wide circles in the sky, a cormorant dived steeply and settled on the water.

The boat plowed down the river and Elmo gestured toward a bed of water hyacinth along the shore. "Caught me a mess of lunkers there yesterday," he said.

"You were working in the office all day yesterday," Dave protested.

"I know," Elmo admitted, "but I'm a guide today. And that's standard guide-talk, isn't it?"

The boat pulled in at a landing and an old pappy guy came out of a shack and was asked whether he had some live bait. He went to a minnow trap and, using a dip net, scooped out half a dozen struggling fish which he called "shiners." They were deep-chested roach, running from a half to three-quarters of a pound.

"Are those for bait?" a visitor demanded. "I'll be satisfied to catch a bass that size."

A quarter-mile farther down the river Elmo shut off the motor and let the wind push the boat slowly upstream. The water was shallow and weedy, with "grass" thick on the bottom and patches of vegetation on the surface. Dave Newell rigged a casting rod and chose a floating bass plug; one of the visitors tried another lure called "Slim Jim," a slender plug with a propeller fore and aft and two gang hooks. The other visitor sat in the stern and sunned himself like a lizard.

The two fishermen cast and retrieved, cast and reeled, cast and cursed. That is, the visitor cursed. No master of the casting rod, he got a backlash on four casts out of five. Every time he had to stop and untangle the bird's nest on his reel, "Slim Jim" sank into the weeds and got snarled in a great gob of greenery.

A bass hit Dave's lure and got off. The inept tourist got a strike, remembered too late to set the hook, and lost his fish. Dave brought in a bass, maybe a foot long. Dave and Elmo jeered at the catch, a minnow in their eyes, although it seemed a substantial fish to a Yankee.

Another bass, same size as Dave's, hit "Slim Jim" and hooked himself. The tourist brought him in, gloating. The boat was drifting now over some especially weedy flats, and on his next four casts the visitor got three strikes. He brought one bass up to the boat but there the fish dived, took the line under the keel, and got loose. Another lunged for the lure at the end of a retrieve, not ten feet from the boat, and the cretin handling the rod struck frantically, snatching the plug away from the bass. Still another missed the plug entirely, and only a swirl of water behind the lure indicated his presence.

Dave got rises fairly often too, but the bass were striking short, not really trying to eat the plugs. Elmo, alternately running the boat and combing marine flora off "Slim Jim," took the boat across the flats again and again, but action was slow and no more fish were hooked.

"We'll soak some bait," Elmo said, and he ran upstream a little way, nosing the boat into a jungle thicket on the shore, at the lower point of a small scrummy cove. Elmo removed "Slim Jim" from the visitor's line, tied on a hook the size of the Queen Mary's anchor, and baited it with a half-pound roach, which he hooked just behind the dorsal fin. He flung this monster across the cove and it landed with a tremendous splash alongside a tangle of hyacinth, weeds, roots, vines and assorted jungle growth.

As he handed the rod to the energetic tourist, there was a monstrous splash as of a hippo at play. "Give 'im line," Elmo said. "Let 'im take it right off the reel." His pupil obeyed, making no effort to set the hook. The line lay slack on the water for an interminable time.

"Let's see if he's still on," Elmo said. He took hold of the slack line ever so cautiously. He tightened it until he could feel a faint movement.

"He's still there," he said. "Leave him alone. He'll need time to swallow that bait and get the hook in his mouth. If he feels any resistance, he'll get suspicious and spit it out."

There was a long, terrifying silence. Then the line began a leisurely movement. When it drew tight, Elmo yelled, "Hit him hard." The tourist yanked on the rod, and water boiled beside the hyacinths.

"He's hooked," Dave shouted. "Let him have all the run he wants. The line isn't strong and he's a nice bass." All of a sudden the reel handle jerked out of the angler's grasp. The line burned against his thumb, coming off the spool. The bass ran into deep water, surfaced once with a swirl, then dived.

There was no action, just a great, straining weight. The bass had dug his heels into the muddy bottom and was leaning backward like a rebellious child, sulking against the pull of the rod. The fisherman just hung on, trying to hear and obey a dozen shouted instructions not to fight too hard. The fingers of the left hand ached, gripping the rod. Painfully, a quarter-turn of the reel at a time, the beast was dragged in.

When he came alongside the boat Elmo leaned over and said, "Open your mouth." The bass complied, Elmo thrust his arm in to the elbow, and hauled the critter over the side. A basketball player could have shot a field goal into that mouth from forty feet. What come into the boat was built like Sophie Tucker with face wide open to hit a high note. A solid ten pounds of aggravated muscle.

When the boat pulled into the dock, an aged colored boy named Andrew saw the fish and his eyes grew wide. "That's all fish," he breathed. You could read his mind easily. He was picturing the brute on a platter, baked, with a watermelon in its mouth.

Evil Old Fish

Micropterus dolomieu, the smallmouth black bass, is an evil old fish. There are few recorded cases of the bass intentionally picking a fight with a man in a boat, but he has never been known to retreat. He's a fish with scales on his chest.

For the last month a war of extermination has been conducted against smallmouth claiming riparian rights to the wooded bays and craggy coves and shoals of Lake Michigan and Green Bay. When the contest was called today on account of August, the score was tied.

Casualties had been heavy among the piscine population. On the other hand, losses to the attacking force included one broken fly-rod tip, unmeasured yards of six-pound-test nylon leader, a wide assortment of artificial lures, hooks and lead shot, one landing net kicked overboard in the heat of battle and a vast quantity of selected delicatessen—night crawlers, crawfish, minnows and false hellgrammites.

Now, the enterprising angler works these waters in the early morning and in the evening, for bass operate on the American plan, breakfasting and dining at those hours along the shoreline. At such times they will rise to almost any surface lure smaller than a birch-bark canoe, but as sun and temperature climb they retire into cool submarine rathskellers, where they lunch chiefly on cold cuts. Once in a while, though, the slugabed can get action at midday without dragging live bait across the bottom.

One day while the Seahorse was being clamped on to a boat, a frantic minnow came racing in toward the beach with a bass snapping at his tail. They were less than a foot from dry sand, and clearly visible in the shallow water, when the bass made a final pass, engulfed his prey and departed, smacking his gills.

This should have been the tip-off that the smallmouth were on the prowl outside regular business hours, but the signs weren't read correctly until the boat had anchored at the wreck of an old lumber schooner.

The water was glassy. Live bait dropped near the old wreck's shadows was seized upon avidly, but meanwhile bass were breaking water all around the boat, wolfing minnows which skittered over the surface ahead of them. Here was a chance to deceive the enemy with a simulated minnow. A ridiculous item was chosen from the tackle box, a feather fly of orange and green with a silver spinner.

Apparently it looked pretty ridiculous to the small bass that responded to the first cast. He followed the silly thing at a respectful distance, like a small boy tagging behind the elephants in a circus parade, curious, delighted and pacific. On the second cast, three or four newcomers joined the retinue, trailing the lure but leaving it untouched.

When you're arousing that much interest, you're reluctant to change lures, even though the fish aren't hitting the one offered. One of these casts, you tell yourself, there'll be an adventurer more reckless than the rest—oops!

Out of the dark depths beneath a sunken spar came a pale torpedo shape, moving with speed and purpose. He moved at right angles to the path of the fly, and he wasn't a sightseer, he was after lunch.

He grabbed himself a mouthful of feathers and barbed steel, turned swiftly for home, and was halted by a jolt from the rod tip. He did what bass invariably do in this circumstance. He leaped straight up like a child in a tantrum.

He was a good bass. He came in reluctantly, seething with rage and embarrassment. The hook in his bony mouth was nothing to him, a minor inconvenience.

It was the sneaky deception that infuriated him, the realization that he'd been had by a counterfeit. *Micropterus dolomieu* has his pride.

That's how it went for hours. A dozen casts, each followed by a platoon of rubberneckers. Then an attack by a chief of the riot squad. If there is a peacetime occupation more exciting than an encounter with a surface-feeding black bass, it has never been experienced here.

When the water is as clear as it was that day, you see the boss fish coming. There is a flash as he rolls sidewise for the strike, you see him turn, and you drive the barb home. He leaps, using vile language, and you laugh.

Harrowing Day

All that excitement about the *Queen Elizabeth* getting a hole punched through her hull seemed kind of amusing after two weeks of fishing from Jim Dietman's boats, because Jim builds holes into his. He bores through the bottom near the stern so that rainwater and waves shipped over the side in lumpy weather can drain right out into the bay.

This might strike some people as odd, but it saves an awful lot of bailing. Jim affixes a little brass pimple to the lower side of the bottom just forward of the hole, and makes a brass plug which screws into the hole. When the boat is in motion you unscrew the plug, the brass wrinkle creates a vacuum that keeps the bay water in the bay, the thrust of the outboard lifts the bow sending all casual water into the stern, and it's just like pulling the bathtub plug. When the boat stops, of course, the hole becomes a two-way street.

At the end of a trip when the boat has been hauled up on the ramp at his Wanawalk cottages, Jim usually removes the plug and sloshes a few buckets of water into the boat to wash it out. Now and then a plug gets mislaid this way.

There was this day when a fisherman was going out to pick a fight with some smallmouth bass. A guest named Art helped him shove off, and because there was a stiff sea rolling in from the southwest he rowed out maybe fifty feet so's not to get smashed on the rocks while starting the motor.

"Got the plug in?" Art called from the dock.

"Sure," the guy said and just then he saw the geyser in the stern. "Oops, sorry."

He scrambled back and pressed a palm over the hole while searching frantically. No plug in its usual place near the hole, no plug under the thwarts, no plug in the tackle box or between the floorboards. No plug. The guy rowed back hastily, beaching the boat stern foremost on the rocks. Water in the bottom was about three inches deep.

Jim came along while Art was getting a plug from another boat. Meanwhile the fisherman checked the gas gauge. It read zero, but when the tank was joggled it made sloshing sounds. The guy didn't figure on going far, anyway. With the hole plugged, he set off again. On the first pull, the motor sputtered and died.

"Got the gas line connected?" Jim called.

"Sure."

"No, you haven't," Jim said, "it's dangling over the stern." He went away shaking his head. He looked a trifle pale.

The boat drifted fast while the guy hooked up the gas feed, tightened up the tank cap, pumped pressure into the line, choked the motor and yanked at the starting cord. Again the motor sputtered and died. Nothing for it but to row back.

The guy was inching laboriously upwind when Mike Dietman, Jim's son, rowed down in a lighter boat. "Anchor so I can come aboard," he said. Somebody had lost the regular anchor, a common occurrence in these waters. You go fishing off Quarry Point or Buoy 26 or Cabot Point or the Flat Rock, and when you go to haul up the hook it's jammed between great limestone boulders on the bottom or under the timbers of an old wreck, and you have to cut the lines free. For a new anchor, Jim had put a chain through a big cement building block and attached it to the severed line.

Mike got aboard and started the motor. There was gas in the tank after all; the carburetor had been flooded. Towing his boat, Mike ran in big circles with the plug out, draining away about half the casual water. Then he replaced the plug, got back in the small boat and departed cheerily. The guy started fishing but he had missed the reef he was aiming for. The boat dragged anchor into deep water.

He hoisted anchor, got it balanced precariously on the bow deck, started the motor and removed the plug to bail. He steered with his right hand and held the plug firmly in his left, taking no chances on losing this one.

A gust of wind snatched at his cap. It's a peachy cap, cost a cool half-dollar in Bohn's Drug Store in town. He grabbed with his left hand and saved the cap. Something went splotch away out off the stern. The plug.

Chances are he let go of the tiller for an instant, for just then the boat yawed, flinging the concrete anchor overboard. Now he was anchored out there on the tossing deep with a hole in the bottom of the boat. He sprang for the bow, sat down again when he saw the anchor line dragging loose; it had parted as the big stone straightened it out.

At least the boat was still moving, and as long as that was so the water would keep running out, not in. The gas gauge still read zero.

He swung around for home, opened the throttle. The boat leaped downwind, dry as Kansas. The helmsman missed the landing but charged on fearlessly, running the bow up on the rocky shore.

As he cut the motor and tilted the prop out of water, a geyser shot up his pants leg. Home was the sailor, home from the sea.

Bass are Bass

ARTHUR R. MACDOUGAL, Jr.

"How about some bass fishing?" I asked Dud, one suggestive morning in June.

Dud Dean simply shook his head.

"Why not?"

"Jist ain't interested. Never see a bass, as I rec'lect."

"But it is said, that pound for pound—"

"Aya, I've heard that one, an' it don't sound reasonable to me. Thar ain't no pound of nothin' that can put up a bigger an' better show'n a white-water salmon."

"Get your rod," I challenged, "and I'll show you that the black bass need not dip his colors to anything that swims."

But Dud simply leaned back against one of the shade trees along our main street, and began to fill his antique pipe.

"Look here," he said, squinting at the sky. "I can see that ye're itchin' to go fishin', Mak, an' I know where thar's some prime salmon jist waitin' to grab a Jock Scott. I mean *salmon*, mind yer!"

I countered with, "A fellow just told me about a pond where we can catch black bass—bass that will outstage any of your salmon." You see, I wanted to inveigle Dud. A day's bass fishing with the old veteran promised so much.

Dud stared at me. For a moment his sense of humor was paralyzed. I had blasphemed against his prince of fresh-water fishes.

"By crotch, Mak, yer can't mean that! What's chewin' in your head?" Then, recovering from his shock, he added with a grin, "Mak, I'm 'shamed of yer."

"But," I persisted, "you wouldn't deny a fact,

would you? I am offering to prove that pound for pound—"

"Crotch, Mak, a fish ain't a fact. It's a fish. A whole lot of foolishness c'ud be avoided in this world, if folks w'ud keep their facts an' fish separated."

Well, it looked as though I were trying to drive my logs against a head wind, as Dud would have put it. "Hang it all, Dud," I said, "I want to take you bass fishing. Try it once!"

"How many miles is it to this bass pond of yours?"

"It's over in the back part of Solon—say, ten miles."

"As near as that? Fust thing we know, somebudy'll be plantin' them warm-water fish up here. An' I've been given to understand that they're sunthin' desperate on trout. Which puts me in mind of what Hen Barnaby told the jedge when he fined Hen for contempt of court. Says Hen, 'Mister, thar ought to be a law ag'inst sich a blarsted outrage.'

" ' That'll cost yer five dollars more,' says the jedge, 'an' every time yer open your head ag'in, it'll cost yer five more'n that.'

" 'Kin I ask jist one question?' says Hen.

" 'It is irregular,' says the jedge, 'but I'll permit it.'

" 'What I want to know is,' says Hen, 'are you God Almighty, er jist a plain two-legged critter like me, only a darn-sight meaner?' What I was thinkin' of was that thar ought to be a law ag'inst puttin' them bass—"

"But what do you say?" I broke in. "Will you

give the bass a tryout?"

"Wel-el, ter tell the truth, I d'know but that I'd try most anythin' right now, becuz Nancy's gittin' worked up fer another house cleanin'. It's in the air. She's sniffin' out the corners, an' squintin' erbout fer imaginary cobwebs. D'know but I'd go cusk fishin' to escape that, although cusk fishin' is so low-down that it's ag'in the law in Hell Huddle, an' sh'ud be everywheres."

And so it came about. When Dud showed up, he was carrying his best rod. That was significant. But he persisted in maintaining his skepticism of bass.

"Yer know, Mak, I feel ornery," he said, "I feel as low-down as I did the day I skipped school, years ago, an' found out in the afternoon that it was a holiday anyway. Here we be, you an' me, goin' bass fishin'. The mighty has fallen flat, as Doc Brownin' useter say."

I passed that off with a grin. I could afford it. I had accomplished my objective that day. Once on the road, an expression of deep contentment settled over Dud's fine face. And as we rolled along the road, I fell to thinking about the many trips I had enjoyed in the company of this mellow, home-town philosopher. I have spent many days afield in such good company.

A chuckle interrupted my reveries. "I was jist thinkin'," Dud explained, "erbout the fust automobile Nancy an' me bought. Prob'ly yer ain't noticed it, but Nancy has got opinions of her own. One of 'em is that a woman can do anythin' a man ever done, an' do it better. So when automobiles came erlong in this country, it galled her awful to hear folks talk as if no woman c'ud ever learn to drive one. An' she got it inter her head that we'd got to have one. At fust, when she brought up the subject, I argued that I c'ud never learn to drive one of them things. But that jist made Nancy look scornful.

"Wel-el, bad news blows wherever it listeth. An' one day a feller come to our house, all dressed up like it was Sunday. He was sellin' automobiles, of course. The one he had was all trimmed up 'ith brass an' doodads. The bulb on the horn was 'most as big as a football. Nancy was taken 'ith the looks of the whole rig. She took lessons on it, till finally that slicker told her that she c'ud drive it as good as any man that ever come down the pike. That clinched the deal. I fergit what the whole thing cost, but we bought it.

"A few days after that, Nancy an' me started out. We got erlong slick as a beaver, at first, but everythin' we met had a devil of a time. For instance, we met old Ben Hall comin' erlong, leadin' a black-an'-white cow. I was scared, becuz it looked like Ben an' the cow warn't never goin' to turn out.

" 'Blow that horn,' I says. 'That's what a horn is fer.'

"Nancy musta been a little scared herself, becuz she did jist what I told her to do. I never saw a cow as quick as that one. She jerked Ben right off his feet, an' the goldarn idgit hung to the rope. The last I see of them, Ben was wrapped 'round an apple tree, but the cow was jist goin' over a fence in the next field.

"Nancy never said a word, an' we kept right on, like nothin' had happened. Bineby, I see that we was comin' to a bad turn in the road ahead. An' we was goin' so fast the tears was runnin' out of my eyes. Crotch, we must have been goin' twenty miles an hour!

" 'Here comes a turn,' I sings out. 'Look out fer that bad turn in the road! Slow down. D'yer hear?'

"If she slowed down a mite, I c'udn't see it. But I guess that she w'ud have made that corner, if she had changed the wheel after we got 'round it. But she didn't.

"Thar was a nice little white house on that turn. An' it had a white picket fence eround the front yard. We went through that fence like it was built of matchsticks. Thinks I, 'A fence like that is no protection at all.' An' the next second we hit the house sunthin' wicked. But it never budged a bit.

"It was a Sunday afternoon, an' the old couple that lived thar came runnin' out, 'ith their arms up in the air, like they was willin' ter surrender 'ithout an argument. But when the old feller see that it was us that had hit his house, instead of sunthin' supernatural, he begin to swear. He was a pitchur, 'ith his long hair awavin' in the breeze. An' his flow of language beat anythin' I ever heard, except Doc Brownin's. Thar was a while when I thought that the old codger had an edge on Doc, but he got to repeatin' hisself, 'long at the last. I guess he had the talent, but lacked Doc's eddication.

"Nancy's hat was down over her eyes, but she give it a poke, and when she see where we was, she acted like somebudy had played a dirty trick on her. 'Dudley,' she says, 'git down an' crank this machine.'

"So I climbed down, an' cranked. An' that automobile started like it had never stopped. I got in ag'in an' Nancy got all set ter back out. She tramped 'round on them pedals, like an organist gittin' ready ter play 'The Lost Chord.' An' we backed out of that yard as neat as a crab c'ud. Then we got stalled ag'in, afore Nancy had got straightened away. So I got down, an' cranked some more.

"By that time, a crowd had gathered from nowhere. Thar was a lot of loud talkin'—most of it from the old feller, who hadn't run down none. I s'pose it all made Nancy nervous. Anyhow, she stepped on a pedal, intendin' ter back up a little more. An' by crotch if we didn't shoot back inter the yard ag'in. An' if we was goin' twenty miles an hour, when we hit that house the fust trip, we was doin' thirty when we struck it the second time.

"The old lady of the house had been down on her knees, sort of moanin' over a bed of red geraniums we had run over on our first trip in. She never had no time to straighten up, but jist crawled out of our way by the skin of her teeth.

" 'Thar, by gad!' Yells the old man at her. 'Yer git inter the house, er they'll kill yer!'

"But I can't say that even the house seemed like a real safe place ter me, by that time. I warn't jist calm after we'd fetched up, an' I says ter Nancy, 'If ye're goin' to do that ag'in, I'm goin' to get out an' walk home.' Soon's I said it, I was sorry, becuz I see that Nancy was 'bout ready to bawl.

"Jist then, a young feller stepped up an' says, 'Havin' some trouble, er jist tryin' her out?'

"By crotch, that was jist erbout the last straw, as Dan Nye said, tellin' how bad his hay fever had been, an' I was jist agoin' to git out ter show that young squirt sunthin', when he added that he was an automobile mechanic, which was what we needed, as sure as a ship ever needed a sailor. Wel-el, he offered to back us out an' git us squared off fer home. Which he did. Then he offered to drive us home, but Nancy 'lowed that she was perfectly capable from thar on, thank yer. After we'd gone a few rods, I begin to git back a little confidence. An' by crotch if we didn't sail erlong nice, until we got to our house. Seemed like stoppin' was one of Nancy's troubles. So we rode inside the barn, 'ithout openin' the doors, An' the blarsted thing never stopped, until we fetched up ag'in a post."

We were going down Gilman Hill when Dud finished his story. One gets a partial view of Iron Bound Pond from that elevation.

Dud, who apparently had not noticed the road while he had been recalling his first automobile trip, sat up straight. "Why didn't yer say we was comin' over to this pond?" he demanded. "I've been told that thar's some good salmon in this water."

"Bass, too," I added.

We left our car at the foot of the hill, and then walked down to a black, weather-beaten house, where, I had been informed, we might hire a boat. The negotiation was simple. And at the landing we picked the most attractive craft. Dud took the stern seat, asking, with an oar poised paddlewise, "Where?"

I explained that I had been instructed to fish the lower end of the lake; that the bass were supposed to favor that section.

"They w'ud," grunted Dud.

But in spite of his show of indifference, I noticed that Dud toyed with his nice rod, as he put it together.

"A split bamboo," said my old friend, "is a great contraption. The other day I was readin' a list of great inventions. The feller that made it up claimed that each invention he listed had turned some tide of hist'ry, but the goldurn chump never mentioned the split bamboo."

I passed my fly book to Dud. "Here are some bass flies," I said, "which are also great inventions."

Dud looked at the bass flies dubiously. "They look like I expected," he said. "An' they ain't fit to put on the end of a light leader, let alone usin' on a good rod. Guess, if you don't mind, that I'll stick to my own. I'll jist fool 'round 'ith a Jock Scott. Maybe thar's some *real* fish somewheres erbout this pond."

I selected a bass fly with a silk body, bound with silver, and wearing regulation wings and hackles. Dud watched me, out of the corner of his eye, but continued his own beautiful casting without further comment.

The next two hours seemed to confirm my opinion that our coldwater bass would not take a fly, although I had been assured that they would. We moved about, but hung to the lower end of the lake. Finally Dud remarked, with evident disappointment, that the salmon must be few and far between in Iron Bound Pond.

"Maybe I had better try one of them frog-ketchin' rigs of yourn, Mak. I jist see a fish feedin' over by that bunch of grass, but most likely it's nothin' but a pickerel."

Again I offered my fly book.

"These ain't flies," Dud muttered, "but here goes, as Clum McGlouster said, time he fell off the barn roof. Is this thing s'posed to float, er sink?"

I turned to inspect the fly he had picked out. It was one that a friend had tied, and he had used the tip of a red squirrel's tail, with a bit of hackle from a white Leghorn rooster. All in all, I felt compelled to admit it the most unlikely fly in the book.

Without waiting for a reply to his question, Dud cast. "It's floatin' purty good," he commented.

"Let her float," I said.

Dud twitched the fly lightly. Something swirled up from the deep water. Spray broke, as though a miniature depth bomb had gone off, and a nice little bass smashed Dud's fly on the rise. For a moment the fish stood out against the afternoon light, vibrating from gills to tail. Then it hit the water, tossing the hook from its mouth.

An odd look of surprise appeared on Dud's lean face. "The lowdown tud," he muttered in an undertone.

Then he addressed me. "Turned that trick purty slick, didn't he? Guess I'll have another try at him, like Doc Brownin' said, time a three-year-old colt kicked him flat."

Dud dropped his next cast upon a small stool of grass. At a hint from his rod, the fly dropped into the water. Nothing happened, although the thing had been perfectly done, and Dud said with a ludicrous trace of anxiety in his voice, "Yer don't s'pose I gummed up the works, do yer?"

And at that moment I connected with a two-pound bass—not a big bass, but a bass. As Dud said, later, "A hooked salmon kinda scoots up inter the air, like it knew jist how it oughter be done, but a bass jist rears up an' lets her go, like it didn't care a dang how it's done."

When Dud had netted my fish, he examined it with interest. "By crotch," he muttered, but volunteered no more. I looked off to the east, grinned, and winked at nothing in particular. And then we continued our casting. Presently I hooked another bass, but fumbled it. And soon Dud took a bass that would weigh a pound and a half. As I netted it, I looked to Dud, supposing of course that he would direct me to turn it loose.

"Dang it, Mak, I know what ye're thinkin', it ain't big but I aim to keep that bass. Some of the fellers might want to look at him. Yer know, it's been a month of Sundays since a fish slipped me as neat as that fust big 'un did."

The fish that Dud referred to could not have weighed over two pounds, but I refrained from saying so. Dud was warming up to bass fishing! But the day was far spent.

It is superfluous to mention that spell which haunts the woods and inland lakes at twilight. Night and day are one for a moment. Day lingers. Night procrastinates. Lights become duns. Colors of sunset become diluted tints. Sounds assume a new resonance, with the harsh notes whittled down. The day balances its books, and turns over the accounts to the night and the stars. Twilight is the prelude before the deep rest from growing toils. It is the return of the eternal lull.

"Geehosaphat!" exclaimed Dud. "Did you see that?"

It was the swirl of a mighty fish in the dark water.

"Ain't that a sight! Right under our noses! It was a salmon, er maybe a trout. Acted ter me like one of them old bottom sinners that cruises up once in a blue moon ter see if the sky is still on top of the world."

As he talked, Dud pulled out his own immense fly book and searched through its pages.

"Ten to one," I said, "it was a black bass."

Dud did not look up, but said, "Guess yer didn't notice that fish, Mak. It was a fish that 'ud weigh five pounds er more. . . . Now here's a female Black Gnat—black wings, white edges. That's a nice fly, Mak. Bright colors fer salmon, sure, but don't fergit to try a Gnat, now an' then."

"For trout, maybe, for salmon, sure, but for—"

Dud interrupted me. "Aya, for salmon, sure!"

"It's a total loss," I said.

"Fer how much?"

"Any amount, if you want to gamble."

"Sish. Make it ten thousand, Mak."

Of course I couldn't stand a figure like that, even in fun, but before I could alter it a startling commotion occurred in the vicinity of Dud's fly. In fact a he-fish had smashed Dud's Gnat, as though it were a tiny ship riding at anchor with all her lights hung out. Fish like that do not come often, in these days, for the simple reason that it takes several years to raise one. When Dud set the little hook, the fish plunged away like a heavily loaded ferryboat. But please don't let that figure convey the impression of ungainliness!

"Whoa, thar!" said Dud. "You ain't goin' inter them bushes if I can help it. Doggone it, Mak, why don't I have more faith, er less confidence. I've gone an' put on a leader that's too light fer a fish like this."

The bass came out of the water, tossing itself into the air like a punted football. For a brief moment it stood out in the twilight.

"If that ain't a fat salmon, I'll eat him," drawled

Dud. "Them black salmon is always bottom feeders. He's loaded heavy, an' he fights deep. Seems like he's got a whole bagful of new tricks. Right now, I can feel him standin' still, an' shakin' his head, like a dog 'ith canker in both his ears. Acts like he was mad as a forked bull."

The fighting fish was beginning to rush circles about the boat. Dud was busy gathering in line that he must soon allow the fish to take again. But Dud was having a big time. Grin after grin chased across his face.

I waited for the remark I had heard so many times, under similar circumstances. At last it came:

"Crotch, Mak, this fish thinks it can git away from me! Hope that hook don't wear a hole in his mouth, an' fall out. Got to keep a tight line, if he ties me up in a hundred knots. Seems like I never see a salmon pull so. Yer can see it ain't no bass, becuz no bass 'ud last this long, even if I can't put all the strain on him that I w'ud if I had a fittin' leader. Nothin' in fins can match these salmon. Cousins, they are, to the kind that useter run up from the sea. Great fish they was, Mak. Grand fish, they be!"

I kept my peace. In the half-light, I could see the grin etched all over Dud's face. Now and then he blew great gulps of air through his lips, tilting his gray mustache askew.

"Mak, I ain't had so much fun, seems like, since the fat lady, over to Embden Fair, tipped back in her chair an' fell off the platform. Look at that cuss toss his head, when he comes up to swear at me."

I uttered an enthusiastic tribute. "It's a fine bass!"

Dud was as near to anger as I ever saw him.

"Holy Moses, Mak! That ain't no bass! Stop sayin' it, er I'll be mad at yer, fust thing yer know."

I watched the fish break and leap a half-dozen times thereafter, but each smashing plunge upward occurred in the shadows, and I could not be sure it was a bass. Still the tactics were reminiscent of bass. And I held, in silence, that it *was* a bass.

The battle began to lag. "I'm afraid that it's sunset an' evenin' star fer this fish," said Dud. "I hate to lick 'em, an' I hate to git licked. That's fishin'!"

There were a few more dogged plunges, and an abortive leap, and the old warrior rolled on his side at the surface.

Dud swung him into the boat, where I could easily reach him with the landing net.

"See," I said triumphantly, "it *is* a bass!"

Dud stepped to the middle of the boat, and we both looked down at the beaten fish. "Must be a salmon," he insisted.

"Look at it!" I exclaimed.

Dud got down on his knees, to see his fish the plainer, in the dim light. "Shucks," he grunted, "I thought it licked too easy fer a salmon."

I carelessly slid the net toward the fish.

"He's all done," said Dud, "but save him. I want to show him to the boys. Some of 'em never saw a bass."

Then a coiled spring seemed to let go in that bass. An astonishing explosion of energy occurred. Dud and I threw back our heads, but Dud's face got a liberal splashing of pond water. Getting to his feet hastily, he exclaimed, "By crotch! What swallowed that fish?"

But of course the spurt of life was short, and that game old bronzy had to come in at last. Again I slid the net under him—that time cautiously—and lifted him into the boat.

Dud sat down, wiping his face.

"Have you got that bass? Can't get away to save hisself, can he? Licked, ain't he?"

"Absolutely," I answered.

"Well, then, by crotch, is he dead?"

"No, but I'm going to hit him over the head with this paddle."

"No, sir! Don't yer do it! Goldurn him! Let him go! The old son of a gun."

Feebly moving his tail, his gills working gaspingly, the old bass sank out of our sight. The inky waters welcomed him home again.

"Thar!" said Dud. "That's over. But jist the same, I'd have liked to show him to Nancy. I don't s'pose she ever see a bass."

"Can a bass fight?" I asked.

"Well," began Dud, as he took down his rod, "that reminds me of Robby and Mike Fitzpatrick. They bet on a dogfight. The dog that Robby picked had some advantages.

" 'By the lovely, lovely,' says Robby, 'my dog licked yourn.'

" 'By the roarin' Jorus,' says Mike, 'not from where I was standin', he never!' "

"But," concluded Dud, "it's up to me to say that a bass is a bass. An' what d'yer say if we try 'em ag'in, someday?"

The Lord of Lackawaxen Creek

ZANE GREY

Winding among the Blue Hills of Pennsylvania there is a swift amber stream that the Indians named Lack-a-wax-en. The literal translation no one seems to know, but it must mean, in mystical and imaginative Delaware, "the brown water that turns and whispers and tumbles." It is a little river hidden away under gray cliffs and hills black with ragged pines. It is full of mossy stones and rapid ripples.

All its tributaries, dashing white-sheeted over ferny cliffs, wine-brown where the whirling pools suck the stain from the hemlock roots, harbor the speckled trout. Wise in their generation, the black and red-spotted little beauties keep to their brooks; for, farther down, below the rush and fall, a newcomer is lord of the stream. He is an arch-enemy, a scorner of beauty and blood, the wolf-jawed, red-eyed, bronze-backed black bass.

A mile or more from its mouth the Lackawaxen leaves the shelter of the hills and seeks the open sunlight and slows down to widen into long lanes that glide reluctantly over the few last restraining barriers to the Delaware. In a curve between two of these level lanes there is a place where barefoot boys wade and fish for chubs and bask on the big boulders like turtles. It is a famous hole for chubs and bright-sided shiners and sunfish. And, perhaps because it is so known, and so shallow, so open to the sky, few fishermen ever learned that in its secret stony caverns hid a great golden-bronze treasure of a bass.

In vain had many a flimsy feathered hook been flung over his lair by fly-casters and whisked gracefully across the gliding surface of his pool. In vain had many a shiny spoon and pearly minnow reflected sun glints through the watery windows of his home. In vain had many a hellgrammite and frog and grasshopper been dropped in front of his broad nose.

Chance plays the star part in a fisherman's luck.

One still, cloudy day, when the pool glanced dark under a leaden sky, I saw a wave that reminded me of the wake of a rolling tarpon; then followed an angry swirl, the skitter of a frantically leaping chub, and a splash that ended with a sound like the deep chung of water sharply turned by an oar.

Big bass choose strange hiding-places. They should be looked for in just such holes and rifts and shallows as will cover their backs. But to corral a six-pounder in the boys' swimming-hole was a circumstance to temper a fisherman's vanity with experience.

Thrillingly conscious of the possibilities of this pool, I studied it thoughtfully. It was a wide, shallow bend in the stream, with dark channels between submerged rocks, suggestive of underlying shelves. It had a current, too, not noticeable at first glance. And this pool looked at long and carefully, colored by the certainty of its guardian, took on an aspect most alluring to an angler's spirit. It had changed from a pond girt by stony banks, to a foam-flecked running stream, clear, yet hiding its secrets, shallow, yet full of labyrinthine water-courses. It presented problems which, difficult as they were, faded in a breath before a fisherman's optimism.

I tested my leader, changed the small hook for a large one, and selecting a white shiner fully six inches long, I lightly hooked it through the side of the upper lip. A sensation never outgrown since boyhood, a familiar mingling of strange fear and joyous anticipation, made me stoop low and tread the slippery stones as if I were a stalking Indian. I knew that a glimpse of me, or a faint jar vibrating under the water, or an unnatural ripple on its surface, would be fatal to my enterprise.

I swung the lively minnow and instinctively dropped it with a splash over a dark space between two yellow sunken stones. Out of the amber depths started a broad bar of bronze, rose and flashed into gold. A little dimpling eddying circle, most fascinating of all watery forms, appeared round where the minnow had sunk. The golden moving flash went down and vanished in the greenish gloom like a tiger stealing into a jungle. The line trembled, slowly swept out and straightened. How fraught that instant with a wild yet waiting suspense, with a thrill potent and blissful!

Did the fisherman ever live who could wait in such a moment? My arms twitched involuntarily. Then I struck hard, but not half hard enough. The bass leaped out of a flying splash, shook himself in a tussle plainly audible, and slung the hook back at me like a bullet.

In such moments one never sees the fish distinctly; excitement deranges the vision, and the picture, though impressive, is dim and dream-like. But a blind man would have known this bass to be enormous, for when he fell he cut the water as a heavy stone.

The best of fishing is that a mild philosophy attends even the greatest misfortunes. To be sure this philosophy is a delusion peculiar to fishermen. It is something that goes with the game and makes a fellow fancy he is a stoic, invulnerable to the slings and arrows of outrageous fortune.

So I went on my way upstream, cheerfully, as one who minded not at all an incident of angling practice; spiritedly as one who had seen many a big bass go by the board. The wind blew softly in my face; the purple clouds, marshaled aloft in fleets, sailed away into the gray distance; the stream murmured musically; a kingfisher poised marvelously over a pool, shot downward like a streak, to rise with his quivering prey; birds sang in the willows and daisies nodded in the fields; misty veils hung low in the hollows; all those attributes of nature, poetically ascribed by anglers to be the objects of their full content, were about me.

I found myself thinking about my two brothers, Cedar and Reddy for short, both anglers of long standing and some reputation. It was a sore point with me and a stock subject for endless disputes that they just never could appreciate my superiority as a fisherman. Brothers are singularly prone to such points of view. So when I thought of them I felt the incipient stirring of a mighty plot. It occurred to me that the iron-mouthed old bass, impregnable of jaw as well as of stronghold, might be made to serve a turn. And all the afternoon the thing grew and grew in my mind.

Luck favoring me, I took home a fair string of fish, and remarked to my brothers that the conditions for fishing the stream were favorable. Thereafter morning on morning my eyes sought the heavens, appealing for a cloudy day. At last one came, and I invited Reddy to go with me. With childish pleasure, that would have caused weakness in any but an unscrupulous villain, he eagerly accepted. He looked over a great assortment of tackle, and finally selected a five-ounce Leonard bait-rod carrying a light reel and fine line. When I thought of what would happen if Reddy hooked that powerful bass an unholy glee fastened upon my soul.

We never started out that way together, swinging rods and pails, but old associations were awakened. We called up the time when we had left the imprints of bare feet on the country roads; we lived over many a boyhood adventure by a running stream. And at last we wound upon the never threadbare question as to the merit and use of tackle.

"I always claimed," said Reddy, "that a fisherman should choose tackle for a day's work after the fashion of a hunter in choosing his gun. A hunter knows what kind of game he's after, and takes a small or large caliber accordingly. Of course a fisherman has more rods than there are calibers of guns, but the rule holds. Now today I have brought this light rod and thin line because I don't need weight. I don't see why you've brought that heavy rod. Even a two-pound bass would be a great surprise up this stream."

"You're right," I replied, "but I sort of lean to possibilities. Besides, I'm fond of this rod. You know I've caught a half-dozen bass of from five to six pounds with it. I wonder what you would do if you hooked a big one on the delicate thing."

"Do?" ejaculated my brother. "I'd have a fit! I might handle a big bass in deep water with this outfit, but here in this shallow stream with its rocks and holes I couldn't. And that is the reason so few big bass are taken from the Delaware. We know they are there, great lusty fellows! Every day in season we hear some tale of woe from some fisherman. 'Hooked a big one—broke this—broke that—got under a stone. That's why no five-or six-pound bass are taken from shallow, swift, rock-bedded streams on light tackle."

When we reached the pool I sat down and began to fumble with my leader. How generously I let Reddy have the first cast! My iniquity carried me to the extreme of bidding him steal softly and stoop low. I saw a fat chub swinging in the air; I saw it alight to disappear in a churning commotion of the water, and I heard Reddy's startled, "Gee!"

Hard upon his exclamation followed action of striking swiftness. A shrieking reel, willow wand of a rod wavering like a buggy-whip in the wind, curving splashes round a foam-lashed swell, a crack of dry wood, a sound as of a banjo string snapping, a sharp splash, then a heavy sullen souse; these, with Reddy standing voiceless, eyes glaring on a broken rod and limp trailing line, were the essentials of the tragedy.

Somehow the joke did not ring true when Reddy waded ashore calm and self-contained, with only his burning eyes to show how deeply he felt. What he said to me in a quiet voice must not, owing to family pride, go on record. It most assuredly would not be an addition to the fish literature of the day.

But he never mentioned the incident to Cedar, which omission laid the way open for my further machinations. I realized that I should have tried Cedar first. He was one of those white-duck-pants-on-a-dry-rock sort of a fisherman, anyway. And in due time I had him wading out toward the center of that pool.

I always experienced a painful sensation while watching Cedar cast. He must have gotten his style from a Delsartian school. One moment he resembled Ajax defying the lightning and the next he looked like the fellow who stood on a monument, smiling at grief. And not to mention pose, Cedar's execution was wonderful. I have seen him cast a frog a mile — but the frog had left the hook. It was remarkable to see him catch his hat, and terrifying to hear the language he used at such an ordinary angling event. It was not safe to be in his vicinity, but if this was unavoidable, the better course was to face him; because if you turned your back an instant, his flying hook would have a fiendish affinity for your trousers, and it was not beyond his powers to swing you kicking out over the stream. All of which, considering the frailties of human nature and of fishermen, could be forgiven; he had, however, one great fault impossible to overlook, and it was that he made more noise than a playful hippopotamus.

I hoped, despite all these things, that the big bass would rise to the occasion. He did rise. He must have recognized the situation of his life. He spread the waters of his shallow pool and accommodatingly hooked himself.

Cedar's next graceful move was to fall off the slippery stone on which he had been standing and to go out of sight. His hat floated downstream; the arched tip of his rod came up, then his arm, and his dripping shoulders and body. He yelled like a savage and pulled on the fish hard enough to turn a tuna in the air. The big bass leaped three times, made a long shoot with his black dorsal fin showing, and then, with a lunge, headed for some place remote from there. Cedar ploughed after him, sending the water in sheets, and then he slipped, wildly swung his arms, and fell again.

I was sinking to the ground, owing to unutterable and overpowering sensations of joy, when a yell and a commotion in the bushes heralded the appearance of Reddy.

"Hang on, Cedar! Hang on!" he cried, and began an Indian war-dance.

The few succeeding moments were somewhat blurred because of my excess of emotion. When I returned to consciousness Cedar was wading out with a hookless leader, a bloody shin, and a disposition utterly and irretrievably ruined.

"Put up a job on me!" he roared.

Thereafter during the summer each of us made solitary and sneaking expeditions, bent on the capture of the lord of the Lackawaxen. And somehow each would return to find the other two derisively speculative as to what caused his clouded brow. Leader on leader went to grace the rocks of the old bronze warrior's home. At length Cedar and Reddy gave up, leaving the pool to me. I fed more than one choice shiner to the bass and more than once he sprang into the air to return my hook.

Summer and autumn passed; winter came to lock the Lackawaxen in icy fetters; I fished under Southern skies where lagoons and moss-shaded waters teemed with great and gamy fish, but I never forgot him. I knew that when the season rolled around, when a June sun warmed the cold spring-fed Lackawaxen, he would be waiting for me.

Who was it spoke of the fleeting of time? Obviously he had never waited for the opening of the fishing season. But at last the tedious time was like the water that has passed. And then I found I had another long wait. Brilliant June days without a cloud were a joy to live, but worthless for fishing. Through all that beautiful month I plodded up to the pool, only to be unrewarded. Doubt began to assail me. Might not the ice, during the spring break-up, have scared him from the shallow hole? No. I felt that not even a rolling glacier could have moved him from his subterranean home.

Often as I reached the pool I saw fishermen wading down the stream, and on these occasions I sat on the bank and lazily waited for the intruding disturbers of my peace to pass on. Once, the first time I saw them, I had an agonizing fear that one of the yellow-helmeted, khaki-coated anglers would hook my bass. The fear, of course, was groundless, but I could not help human feelings. The idea of that grand fish rising to a feathery imitation of a bug or a lank dead bait had nothing in my experience to warrant its consideration. Small, lively bass, full of play, fond of chasing their golden shadows, and belligerent and hungry, were ready to fight and eat whatever swam into their ken. But a six-pound bass, slow to reach such weight in swift-running water, was old and wise and full of years. He did not feed often, and when he did he wanted a live fish big enough for a good mouthful. So, with these facts to soothe me I rested my fears, and got to look humorously at the invasions of the summer-hotel fishers.

They came wading, slipping, splashing downstream, blowing like porpoises, slapping at the water with all kinds of artificial and dead bait. And they called to me in a humor actuated by my fishing garb and the rustic environment:

"Hey, Rube! Ketchin' any?"

I said the suckers were bitin' right pert.

"What d'you call this stream?"

I replied, giving the Indian name.

"Lack-a-what? Can't you whistle it? Lack-awhacken? You mean Lack-afishin'."

"Lack-arotten," joined in another.

"Do you live here?" questioned a third.

I modestly said yes.

"Why don't you move?" Whereupon they all laughed and pursued the noisy tenor of their way downstream, pitching their baits around.

"Say, fellows," I shouted after them, "are you training for the casting tournament in Madison Square Garden or do you think you're playing lacrosse?"

The laugh that came back proved the joke on them, and that it would be remembered as part of the glorious time they were having.

July brought the misty, dark, lowering days. Not only did I find the old king at home on these days, but just as contemptuous of hooks and leaders as he had been the summer before. About the middle of the month he stopped giving me paralysis of the heart; that is to say, he quit rising to my tempting chubs and shiners. So I left him alone to rest, to rust out hooks and grow less suspicious.

By the time August came, the desire to call on him again was well-nigh irresistible. But I waited, and fished the Delaware, and still waited. I would get him when the harvest moon was full. Like all the old moss-backed denizens of the shady holes, he would come out then for a last range over the feeding shoals. At length a morning broke humid and warm, almost dark as twilight, with little gusts of fine rain. Of all days this was the day! I chose a stiff rod, a heavy silk line, a stout brown leader, and a large hook. From my bait box I took two five-inch red catfish, the little "stone-rollers" of the Delaware, and several long shiners. Thus equipped I sallied forth.

The walk up the towpath, along the canal with its rushes and sedges, across the meadows white with late-blooming daisies, lost nothing because of its familiarity. When I reached the pool I saw in the low water near shore several small bass scouting among the schools of minnows. I did not want these pugnacious fellows to kill my bait, so, procuring a hellgrammite from under a stone, I put it on my hook and promptly caught two of them, and gave the other a scare he would not soon forget.

I decided to try the bass with one of his favorite shiners. With this trailing in the water I silently waded out, making not so much as a ripple. The old familiar oppression weighed on my breast; the old throbbing boyish excitement tingled through my blood. I made a long cast and dropped the shiner lightly. He went under and then came up to swim about on the surface. This was a sign that made my heart leap. Then the water bulged, and a black bar shot across the middle of the long shiner. He went down out of sight, the last gleams of his divided brightness fading slowly. I did not need to see the little shower of silver scales floating up to know that the black bar had been the rounded nose of the old bass and that he had taken the shiner across the middle. I struck hard, and my hook came whistling at me. I had scored a clean miss.

I waded ashore very carefully, sat down on a stone by my bait pail, and meditated. Would he rise again? I had never known him to do so twice in one day. But then there had never been occasion. I bethought me of the "stone-rollers" and thrilled with certainty. Whatever he might resist, he could not resist one of those little red catfish. Long ago, when he was only a three- or four-pounder, roaming the deep eddies and swift rapids of the Delaware, before he had isolated himself to a peaceful old age in this quiet pool, he must have poked his nose under many a stone, with red eyes keen for one of those dainty morsels.

My excitation thrilled itself out to the calm assurance of the experienced fisherman. I firmly fastened on one of the catfish and stole out into the pool. I waded farther than ever before; I was careful but confident. Then I saw the two flat rocks dimly shining. The water was dark as it rippled by, gurgling softly; it gleamed with lengthening shadows and glints of amber.

I swung the catfish. A dull flash of sunshine seemed to come up to meet him. The water swirled and broke with a splash. The broad black head of the bass just skimmed the surface; his jaws opened wide to take in the bait; he turned and flapped a huge spread tail on the water.

Then I struck with all the power the tackle would stand. I felt the hook catch solidly as if in a sunken log. Swift as flashing light the bass leaped. The drops of water hissed and the leader whizzed. But the hook held. I let out one exultant yell. He did not leap again. He dashed to the right, then the left, in bursts of surprising speed. I had hardly warmed to the work when he settled down and made for the dark channel between the yellow rocks. My triumph was to be short-lived. Where was the beautiful spectacular surface fight I expected of him? Cunning old monarch! He laid his great weight dead on the line and lunged for his sunken throne. I held him with a grim surety of the impossibility of stopping him. How I longed for deep, open water! The rod bent, the line strained and stretched. I removed my thumb and the reel sang one short shrill song. Then the bass was as still as the rock under which he had gone.

I had never dislodged a big bass from under a stone, and I saw herein further defeat; but I persevered, wading to different angles, and working all the tricks of the trade. I could not drag the fish out, nor pull the hook loose. I sat down on a stone and patiently waited for a long time, hoping he would come out of his own accord.

As a final resort, precedent to utter failure, I waded out. The water rose to my waist, then to my shoulders, my chin, and all but covered my raised face. When I reached the stone under which he had planted himself I stood in water about four feet deep. I saw my leader, and tugged upon it, and kicked under the stone, all to no good.

Then I calculated I had a chance to dislodge him if I could get my arm under the shelf. So down I went, hat, rod, and all. The current was just swift enough to lift my feet, making my task most difficult. At the third trial I got my hand on a sharp corner of stone and held fast. I ran my right hand along the leader, under the projecting slab of rock, till I touched the bass. I tried to get hold of him, but had to rise for air.

I dove again. The space was narrow, so narrow that I wondered how so large a fish could have gotten there. He had gone under sidewise, turned, and wedged his dorsal fin, fixing himself as solidly as the rock itself. I pulled frantically till I feared I would break the leader.

When I floundered up to breathe again the thought occurred to me that I could rip him with my knife and, by taking the life out of him, loosen the powerful fin so he could be dragged out. Still, much as I wanted him I could not do that. I resolved to make one more fair attempt. In a quick determined plunge I secured a more favorable hold for my left hand and reached under with my right. I felt his whole long length and I could not force a finger behind him anywhere. The gill toward me was shut tight like a trap door. But I got a thumb and forefinger fastened to his lip. I tugged till a severe cramp numbed my hand; I saw red and my head whirled; a noise roared in my ears. I stayed until one more second would have made me a drowning man, then rose gasping and choking.

I broke off the leader close to the stone and waded ashore. I looked back at the pool, faintly circled by widening ripples. What a great hole and what a grand fish! I was glad I did not get him and knew I would never again disturb his peace.

So I took my rod and pail and the two little bass, and brushed the meadow daisies, and threaded the familiar green-lined towpath toward home.

When a Lady Undresses

HAVILAH BABCOCK

It was a dismal afternoon. It had been misting for two days, a warm October mist, and the earth was sodden and fogbound. The weather was preordained for grading themes, the poorest pastime the mind of mortal man ever conjured up. Our radio announced the humidity was 99. It could go on and attain perfection if it would be any happier, I perversely reflected. I was standing at the window, absently watching a bedraggled sparrow trying to lift a scrap of ribbon from the driveway, when the telephone rang.

"What are you doing, Doc?" It was the quiet voice of Tip Hazzard.

"Nothing in particular. Just moping around and contemplating self-destruction if this weather keeps up. I'd planned to go fishing, but of course—"

"Can you run with me out to the pond awhile? I left something out there that I need right bad."

"You surely picked a cheerful day to do your forgetting," I grumped.

"Didn't I. And bring your rod along. Just in case."

When we reached the pond it was still misting. The sky was overcast and lowering. Patches of fog lay low over the water, rising here and there in slow swirls.

"You sit in front," suggested Tip. "I'll paddle across to where I left it. And take your rod and that pink-bellied topwater. Just in case."

"What did you leave that's got to be recovered in such headlong haste? And when, pray, did you leave it?"

"Laros catch meddlers! Get in," he tersely ordered.

The boat seat was puddling wet, and there was no cushion. I plopped my reluctant rump down suddenly to get it over with—and felt sort of self-conscious and ashamed for several minutes thereafter. The boat tipped a small water-soaked gum. An overloaded branch disburdened itself and sent the cold water cascading down my backbone as I humped over my tackle box. Rather be at home

fussing over nouns and pronouns or squabbling with Alice, I dejectedly decided.

"Let it drop on that low cypress stump," Tip said, easing up on his paddle.

"Do what?"

"On that cypress stump, eighty feet to your left. And flip it gently into the water. If old Grampa can do it!" he grinned amiably.

"A grandpapa can do anything a papa can do. Especially out-of-doors," I countered.

I dropped the top-water soundlessly on the sodden stump, flipped it into the water, and let it execute a few trial didos. A patch of fog drifted between me and the capering plug. There was a resounding smack. No, not really a smack at all. I've just been reading too many books. That's not the way a really big bass strikes.

Your three- or four-pound sophomores smack resoundingly. But your real fish, your juggernauts, your deans and full professors sort of roll ponderously and engulf your lure. I sensed rather than saw a heavy swirl, and set the hook with a spirited yank. It became immediately apparent that something seventy feet out there in the fog, something massive and powerfully set in its ways, had no interest whatever in going with me home.

Now I would like to say that I played the quarry with great dexterity and skill, adroitly depressing and elevating the rod tip in anticipation of its every maneuver, artfully pitting brain against brawn, and that after a gallant battle of thirty-four minutes, during which I remained as composed as a horse opera cardsharp holding four aces, I boated a twelve-pounder and had it mounted for the delectation of posterity.

That's what I'd like to say. But it would be a masterpiece of prevarication. In fact, it would be a monumental lie. Now I am not saying what it would be if *you* told it. You are the custodian of your own conscience. I'm just saying it's a lie when I tell it.

I've never hung a ten-pounder yet without being scared to death until I had him in the boat, with my scrawny buttocks astraddle his floundering carcass. I might as well be honest about it. In my long and sinful life I have had many a 10- or 12-pounder *play me*, but I'll just be damned if I have ever intentionally played *him*! It is too late in life—and I am too well known—to start being a hero now.

Anyway, I vigorously addressed myself to the task of abridging the distance between the fish and me. A few minutes later—not many—Tip leaned over the gunwale, thrust a hand into a cavernous jaw, and hoisted our passenger aboard. It was a nice bass, not a belt-holder exactly, but a right considerable fish. About an associate professor, I'd rate him, who might have become a dean had he looked after his p's and q's and gone to church regularly.

"How much will he go?" I asked.

Tip hefted him a speculative heft or two. "In the discriminating phraseology of you outdoor writers, he is somewhere between a lunker, a behemoth and a leviathan. Which would put him in the neighborhood of eight pounds."

"Now you get up here and make a few passes at 'em," I offered.

"No. We've worn our welcome out for the present. After that fracas your bass raised, the customers in this corner will be a wee skittish. We'd better sashay down to the ledge and come back here later."

"By the way," I remembered, "what was it you left here and came back to get? Something you needed badly, you said."

"Could have been the one you just landed, but it felt more like his uncle. I'm always needing a fish like that."

"Do you mean that you were here fishing this morning in this soupy weather, and that you lost a big bass? Why, you double-dealing, two-timing—"

"In that brush pile," Tip nodded eloquently.

"But fish aren't supposed to bite in this weather. It's about the worst day in the year, and you know it," I complained.

"Ain't it though! I've been waiting weeks for it. Just about made to order," he rhapsodized.

"What do you mean?"

"Although this place is heavily fished, a respectable bass is seldom taken, and the pond is generally regarded as fishless. Yet you and I know that there are big bass here aplenty. They just don't bite on the beautiful sunny days that people fish for them. A fisherman is a self-centered sort of person anyway. When he says it's a beautiful day to go fishing, he means from *his* point of view, not from the fish's point of view. Now do you admit that a fish has a point of view?" he challenged.

"I'll admit anything if you'll just keep talking. And hand me the other paddle. It's a quarter of a mile to the ledge."

"This water is exceptionally clear," Tip resumed. "You can see a plug three of four feet deep. To the fish it must be something like a mirror, especially on sunny days when the surface is calm. They can see a moving boat a hundred yards away, can see the motion of your arm when you are casting, a plug arcing through the air. Haven't you ever seen the startled jump of a fish before your plug hit? Yes, these clear-water bass become boat-wise and man-wary."

"Keep preaching on that same text," I encouraged. "My attention is what you might call rapt. In the meanwhile, let's put more elbow grease into our paddles. That ledge—"

"Clear water, when sunlit and still, allows the customer too close an examination of your merchandise," he continued. "A cagey bass can detect phony offerings and synthetic glamour. But on a dark, foggy day like this, when the water is rain-splattered, Mr. Big's eyesight is not so good. He is off guard and unsuspicious. You can sell him a wooden nutmeg, if it has a ribbon around it."

"You mean he figures that nobody would be damned fool enough to be fishing in such abominable weather, and therefore lets his guard down? Well, there's an old codger on the Waccamaw who fishes only on Tuesdays. Says fish are less suspicious then. Gives them Monday to recover from their week-end disillusionment."

"Can't say I subscribe to the Tuesday theory," Tip smiled indulgently, "but the first rule of fishing is *not to let the fish know they are being fished for*. They are naturally somewhat off guard in weather like this because they don't figure anybody has designs on them. When a fine lady is undressing on a beautiful summer night, she is careful about pulling down her shades. But if the night is black and stormy—Get my point?"

"Get it, but don't like it. Your figure of speech is ungentlemanly. I reject any suggestion of similarity between a mickle-mouthed, pot-bellied bass and a lissome lady in her negligee on a moonlight night," I gallantly defended.

"Of course," continued Tip, unimpressed by my chivalry, "there might be another factor involved. Bass are of all fish the most scatterbrained and unpredictable. It may be that the unregenerate sons of Belial feed in weather like this just because they like to. Anyway, a fact is a fact, and it is a mistake to get too analytical about something that already suits you. Besides, there's the ledge ahead, and if you will pass the word on to your paddle—"

The black pool undercutting the base of the ledge was a favorite place for the old alumni to hold their class reunions. More than once we had seen the bay-windowed gents lolling in their arm-chairs, but we had never been able to sell them any nutmegs.

Tip dropped his top-water soundlessly on the wet rock, deftly flipped it into the water, and put Little Egypt through a few provocative gyrations. Tip could make the little strumpet show her panties as coyly as an ingénue. A four-pounder smacked lustily, came up to see how things looked on topside once or twice, and was added to our passenger list.

"Lunker class," commented Tip. "You know, there was a heavy-bodied swirl before that fish hit. Made by something else. Maybe Junior there beat his old man to the draw. We ought to play a return engagement here about dark. But it's your turn now, so hand me the paddle. I'll take you to the cypress log at the tip of the island."

"What about a few more passes around the ledge?" I suggested.

"Help yourself, but it's probably useless. They know they're being fished for."

It didn't take long to convince me his diagnosis was right, and we headed for the tiny island, our boat ghosting silently through the deepening fog. When Tip and I are fishing from a small boat, only one of us casts at a time. There are never two lures in the water. Tip has a theory that it's one of the things one man can do best, that one caster will take twice as many fish as two. It's a pretty sound theory, I suppose. Too many cooks spoil the broth. So we regularly take turn-about with rod and paddle.

At the tip of the island a bass *whooshed* at my top-water so hard the hooks jangled, and Little Egypt tightened up her garters. Two feet nearer he *whooshed* and missed again. Whew! I whewed. Would he hit a third time? If this sort of thing kept up long, the strongest characters would crumble. Little Egypt lay on her back and panted for a moment, then switched her hips seductively and started crawling toward me. *Whoosh!* And this time the pitcher had gone to the well too often. A three-pounder joined his disillusioned brethren in the boat.

"A spirited young cuss, wasn't he?" admired Tip. "Now if you'll give me another whack at that precious brush pile—"

Fifteen minutes later Tip humped motionless in the prow, idly balancing his rod and biding his time. The brush pile outlined itself in the fog ahead, and I eased off. With a flick of his wrist, Tip sent a long cast arcing through the air. Deftly pinching the line with his thumb, he feathered the plug down within a scant foot of the brush pile.

There it lay motionless and inert for a minute. For two minutes. For three—and then the battered old jade that Tip wouldn't swap for a horse and buggy impudently switched her hips, leered brazenly over her shoulder, and started down the street. There was a ponderous roll, a heavy *thwump,* and Tip stood up and addressed himself to the business at hand.

"Pretty fancy old rooster I got here," he said. "Seems to have notions of his own. Keep easing the boat away from that blessed brush pile."

A pretty fancy old rooster he was, around nine pounds I estimated as I lifted him into the boat. Maybe a shade better.

"Let me see that gent's mouth," said Tip.

Prying the jaws apart, he studied them minutely for a moment. "I'm not asking anybody to believe it, but just for the sake of science, this is the same fish I hooked and lost here this morning. I had him alongside the boat and noticed precisely how he was hooked."

"I've a notion that happens oftener than people think," I corroborated.

"Somehow I can't get that ledge off my mind. We've got time to make it by dark if we lean against the whiffletrees. Let's go," suggested Tip.

The mist had now become a steady drizzle, falling in a monotonous patter on the water. Apparently it had set in for the night. Darkness was settling like a visible cloak upon the water, and the blackest of black nights would soon envelop the pond. By the time we reached the ledge, the rock was almost indistinguishable in the gathering gloom.

My first cast overreached itself and had to be snatched free from debris alongside the rock. My second brushed lightly against the rock and pluffed precisely into the pool, and my fisherman's instinct told me that I had the old master of ceremonies himself on 90 feet of line. Have you ever had an argument with a big bass in the dark? If you have, you know the wave of helplessness that washes over you.

But Mr. Big and I were adjusting our differences pretty well. Stubbornly he headed for the log jam on my left, for the rocky ledge ahead, for the stump-studded shore line, but was effectually turned each time as Tip expertly maneuvered the boat. Then as if suddenly resigned and docile, he allowed himself to be brought alongside the boat. But as Tip carefully fingered for his mouth, he zoomed under the boat like a Missouri mule with the bit in its teeth.

"That line slackened so suddenly I almost toppled backward. I reeled in the limp line and fingered the break. He had absconded with fifteen feet of good nylon.

"That line hung something in the boat. I heard it *zing!*" thought Tip. From his tackle box he produced a pencil flashlight. "There it is—a jagged nail that some bream fisherman drove in the boat. There's a scrap of line still around it."

I wasn't happy about it, of course, but I wasn't altogether unhappy either. The fish I remember most vividly are those I didn't quite bring home. We had fish aplenty anyway. If a fellow killed every bird he shot at, or landed every fish that bit—

A hundred yards across the pond there was a mighty *suwash! suwash!* The abdominous old glutton didn't like that hot tamale he had bitten into and was trying to spit it out. In a day or so I'd likely find my beloved top-water floating.

"I wanted to see you land that golly-whopper," consoled Tip, then added cryptically, "but I can't imagine anything duller than getting what you want."

Back at the landing, we put the car lights on and admired our string in the drenching downpour—a nine-pounder, an eight, a four and a three, about all a man wanted to tote. With the rain sluicing over our faces, we grinned like pranking schoolboys in an attic.

"How is your corporosity sagaciating, Grandpa?" Tip asked. "And how do you like fishing in the rain?"

That corporosity business produced a wide grin. When I was a country boy in Virginia thirty-five years ago it was the way one dude greeted another. Ultra-slick stuff, we considered it.

"My corporosity is okay," I replied. "And as for the weather, it's been the worst of days, and the best of days. I am as wet as a pair of flannel drawers in a washtub. Water is running out my ears, squidging out my shoe tops, sluicing down my back and spouting off my tail bone. And I never felt better in my life."

"Will it give you a cold?" asked Tip.

"No, and that's an oddity that might interest the medical professional. I never catch cold from getting wet *if I have had a good time getting wet.* It's a gospel fact."

Since that initial experience, I have repeatedly verified the soundness of what might be called foul-weather fishing. And I have asked other bass fishermen about it. Billy Fisher, one of the most astute anglers of my acquaintance despite his total blindness, kept a minute record of the exact weather conditions under which he caught fish for fifteen years. This fifteen-year record furnished the raw material for several surmises, Billy says, and one scientific fact: that, especially in clear-water ponds, bass feed actively during a warm rain. The next best time, his log shows, is when a warm breeze is ruffling the surface of the water.

There are some rains that are uncongenial, however. I have never induced bass to strike *immediately* after a flooding downpour that sends the water roaring over spillways. A few days should be allowed for the water to become homogenized and return to normal temperature. I don't relish an electric storm either. It is unsafe, and I think profitless, to cast for bass when the earth is quaking and the skies are rent overhead. Fish go down and bide the passing of the storm.

A kind of rain I do like is the brisk, quick-passing storm in the spring—the April showers that bring May flowers. Right after such a rain, the fish will follow you home—almost. But the best fishing rain in the whole repertoire of the master showman, J. Pluvius, is the Devil-is-beating-his-wife variety. All of us have witnessed this phenomenon: the spirited shower that streams down through the bright sunshine. "The Lord is using his sprinkling pot," my lovely mother used to say.

There comes a time in every man's life when he is either going to go fishing or do something worse. It is a sort of safety valve that keeps him from exploding. So I often go regardless of weather or what the fish's point of view might be.

But sometimes on beautiful sunny days, when almost every other car that passes my house bears the indubitable stamp of *pisces*, I sit at home in strange contentment. I grade my papers, work on income tax returns, and sing Oh-do-you-know-the-muffin-man with my three-year-old granddaughter—and dream of the dismal, fog-bound days that Indian summer is sure to bring.

ACKNOWLEDGMENTS

For arrangements made with various authors, their representatives and publishers, where copyrighted material was permitted to be reprinted, and for the courtesy extended by them, the following acknowledgments are gratefully made: "Ole Iron Jaw" by Pat Smith originally appeared, under a different title, in *Rod and Reel* Magazine, Manchester, Vermont. "The Basses" by Grits Gresham, from *The Complete Book of Bass Fishing*, Outdoor Life Book Club and Harper & Row, New York. "Friendly Invader" and "Better Baitfishing" by Byron Dalrymple originally appeared in *Outdoor Life*, reprinted by permission of the author. "World Record Bass" by Vic Dunaway originally appeared in *South Carolina Wildlife*, reprinted by permission of the author. "How Light and Color Affect Bass" by Jerry Gibbs originally appeared in his book *Bass Myths Exploded*, David McKay Co., Inc., New York, reprinted by permission. "Reading the Water" by Mark Sosin and Bill Dance was taken from *Practical Black Bass Fishing* © 1974 by Mark Sosin and Bill Dance, used by permission of Crown Publishers Inc., New York. "Plastic Worm Fishing" by Jerry Gibbs is taken from separate articles in *Outdoor Life*, used by permission of the author. "Plugging" by Roland Martin, as told to Larry Mayer, appeared originally in the May, 1979, issue of *Outdoor Life*, used by permission of the authors. "Spinnerbaits" by David E. Morris originally appeared in *Outdoor Life*, used by permission of the author. "The Fly Rod on Bass Water" by Dave Whitlock was adapted from separate articles by Dave Whitlock appearing originally in *Sports Afield* magazine and *Angler* magazine and is used by permission of the author. "Smallmouth Specialties" by Jerry Gibbs originally appeared in *Outdoor Life*, reprinted by permission of the author. "The Big Sky's Neglected Bass" by Norman Strung originally appeared in *Sports Afield*, reprinted by permission of the author. "Hook and Line" by A. D. Livingston is adapted from the book *Fishing for Bass* © 1974 by A. D. Livingston, reprinted by permission of J. B. Lippincott Co.,

New York. "Playing and Landing Bass" by Homer Circle originally appeared in *Sports Afield* and is reprinted by permission of the author and the Hearst Corp., New York. "Trophy Bass" by Dave Harbour originally appeared in *Sports Afield*, reprinted by permission of the author. "Power to the Bassing People" by Bob Stearns originally appeared in *Outdoor Life*, reprinted by permission of the author. "Care of the Catch" by Vin Sparano originally appeared in *Outdoor Life* as two separate articles, reprinted by permission of the author. "Cooking Your Bass" by Joan Cone originally appeared in the *Sports Afield 1978 Bass Annual*, reprinted by permission of the author. "Bassing's Tournament Trail" by Peter Miller originally appeared in *Outdoor Life* in somewhat shortened form, reprinted by permission of the author. "Striped Bass and Southern Solitude" originally appeared in *Sports Illustrated* magazine, reprinted by permission of the author. "Bass Convert" by Nick Lyons originally appeared in *Gray's Sporting Journal*, reprinted by permission of the author. "Black Bass and Dark Nights" by Frank Woolner originally appeared in *Gray's Sporting Journal*, reprinted by permission of the author. "Bottoms Up" by Gene Hill originally appeared in *Sports Afield* and later was reprinted in Gene Hill's book *Hill Country*, published by E. P. Dutton Co., New York, and is used by permission. "Three Shorts Ones" by Red Smith originally appeared in the book *Red Smith on Fishing* published by Doubleday & Company Inc., Garden City, N.Y., 1963, and are used by permission of the author. "Bass Are Bass" by Arthur R. MacDougal Jr. originally appeared in *Dud Dean and His Country* © 1942 by Coward McCann, New York. "The Lord of Lackawaxen Creek" by Zane Grey, © 1979 by Zane Grey, Inc., used by permission of BP Singer Features, Inc. "When a Lady Undresses" by Havilah Babcock is taken from *Tales of Quail 'n Such* published by Greenberg Publishers, New York, and later republished by Holt, Rinehart and Winston, New York, reprinted here by permission.